CULTURE
of
CORRUPTION

CULTURE

—— of ——

CORRUPTION

OBAMA AND HIS TEAM OF
TAX CHEATS, CROOKS, AND CRONIES

MICHELLE MALKIN

Since 1947
REGNERY
PUBLISHING, INC.
An Eagle Publishing Company • Washington, DC

Cataloging-in-Publication data on file with the Library of Congress

ISBN 978-1-59698-109-6

Published in the United States by

Regnery Publishing, Inc.
One Massachusetts Avenue, NW
Washington, DC 20001
www.regnery.com

Manufactured in the United States of America

10 9 8 7 6 5 4

Books are available in quantity for promotional or premium use. Write to Director of Special Sales, Regnery Publishing, Inc., One Massachusetts Avenue NW, Washington, DC 20001, for information on discounts and terms or call (202) 216-0600.

Distributed to the trade by:

Perseus Distribution
387 Park Avenue South
New York, NY 10016

"Byrdes of on kynde and color flok and flye allwayes together."

"Associate with men of good quality if you esteem your own reputation; for it is better to be alone than in bad company."

"The accomplice to the crime of corruption is frequently our own indifference."

FOR THE WHISTLEBLOWERS

CONTENTS

ALL HAIL THE ACHIEVATRONS!

P hew. Janitors in newsrooms across America worked overtime in the halcyon days after Barack Obama won the presidency. It wasn't easy cleaning the drool off laptops and floors in the offices of journalists covering the Greatest Transition in World History.

New York Times columnist David Brooks laid claim to the most soaked keyboard and stained carpet in the business. He praised Team Obama's "open-minded individuals" and "admired professionals." He raved about their "postpartisan rhetoric" and "practical creativity." And—ooooh-la-la!—how about the brains of all those brainy brainiacs? So smokin' hot:

> This truly will be an administration that looks like America, or at least that slice of America that got double 800s on their SATs. Even more than past administrations, this will be a valedictoc-racy—rule by those who graduate first in their high school classes. If a foreign enemy attacks the United States during the

Harvard-Yale game any time over the next four years, we're screwed.

Already the culture of the Obama administration is coming into focus. Its members are twice as smart as the poor reporters who have to cover them, three times if you include the columnists. They typically served in the Clinton administration and then, like Cincinnatus, retreated to the comforts of private life—that is, if Cincinnatus had worked at Goldman Sachs, Williams & Connolly or the Brookings Institution. So many of them send their kids to Georgetown Day School, the posh leftish private school in D.C., that they'll be able to hold White House staff meetings in the carpool line.[1]

It had only been seventeen days since Election Day. But the president-elect (complete with his own "Office of the President-Elect" logo) and his team of valedictocrats (armed with their Ivy League degrees) had already bowled Brooks over with their organizational prowess:

And yet as much as I want to resent these overeducated Achievatrons (not to mention the incursion of a French-style government dominated by highly trained Enarchs), I find myself tremendously impressed by the Obama transition....

Most of all, they are picking Washington insiders. Or to be more precise, they are picking the best of the Washington insiders.

As a result, the team he has announced so far is more impressive than any other in recent memory....

...Believe me, I'm trying not to join in the vast, heaving O-phoria now sweeping the coastal haute bourgeoisie. But the personnel decisions have been superb. The events of the past two weeks should be reassuring to anybody who feared that Obama would veer to the left or would suffer self-inflicted wounds because of his inexperience. He's off to a start that nearly justifies the hype.

And Brooks's employer has profited mightily from the hype. Celebrating Obama's 100-day mark, *New York Times* reporter Jennifer 8. Lee exulted that the financially troubled Fishwrap of Record had sold $2 million worth of Obama-themed merchandise.[2] The *Times* has a vested financial interest in propping up the Obama administration.

At ABC News, former Democrat operative-turned-objective newsman George Stephanopoulos also exhibited the symptoms of the Obama transition's salivary gland stimulus. "We have not seen this kind of combination of star power and brain power and political muscle this early in a cabinet in our lifetimes," Stephanopoulos dribbled.[3] After blotting his chin a bit, he added: "[H]e's managed his transition with the same kind of precision and discipline that he managed to show during the campaign. . . . It's hard to imagine this transition going much better for the president-elect."[4]

The *Washington Post* and *Newsweek* both indulged in Transition-mania, launching websites featuring by-the-minute blogging of Barack Obama's "historic" and "unprecedented" ascension to power. The *New York Times* told the story of how the savvy Obama made a phone call thirteen days before the election to send a feeler out to General James Jones for the national security adviser post.[5] Thirteen whole days! As if no other incoming president over the last 232 years had come up with the genius concept of reaching out to potential nominees before inauguration day.

This used to be called planning ahead.

In the most "historic" and "unprecedented" incoming administration in our lifetimes, Obama's phone call was hailed as a visionary advance mobilization for the benefit of Western civilization.

An inconvenient aside: For all the hype about the Greatest Transition in World History, Obama failed to beat the pace of the Reagan White House. By Day 100, Obama had 65 officials confirmed. Reagan had 73—and the Evil Republicans did it without all the bungles and baggage that the Angels of Obama brought with them.[6] "Obama's a faster turtle, but he's still a turtle," transition analyst Paul Light observed—his voice of reason drowned out amid the media frenzy.[7]

Journalists and cable TV talking heads chattered endlessly about Obama's "record speed" on the one hand and his "exhaustive" vetting process on the other. Application forms ran on for 7 pages and 63 questions, the *New York Times* marveled.[8] (The Bush-Cheney vice presidential application form was 200 pages. But when Republicans require rigorous background checks, it's not "exhaustive," it's a paranoid invasion of privacy. But I digress.)

President-elect Obama next dispatched hundreds of meticulous "agency review team" members—"135 people divided into 10 groups, along with a list of other advisers"—into the bowels of the federal government. Their mission: To "rigorously examine programs and policies" and expedite the transfer of power.[9] The transition team leaders wore smart yellow badges on the job with "Yes, We Can"-do attitudes to match.

Awestruck *Good Morning America* anchor Robin Roberts of ABC News echoed the conventional wisdom: "Some would say it's a team of rivals, à la President Lincoln, or is a better comparison a team of geniuses as FDR did?"[10]

I wrote this book to give you the exhaustive answer that President Obama's gyrating media harem doesn't want you to read.

"Crony," William Safire tells us, comes from seventeenth-century college slang at Cambridge University in England. The word is rooted in the Greek *khronios* ("long-lasting") from *khronos* ("time"). Safire traced its etymological evolution in the United States:

> ...[C]rony took on a pejorative connotation as the sinister side of "friend"—more of a hanger-on, the recipient of favors for old times' sake. In 1946, when President Harry Truman's poker-playing friends brought disrepute on his Administration, the *New York Times* columnist Arthur Krock wrote that "New Dealers and Conservatives found themselves together in opposition to what a press gallery wit has called a 'government by crony.'"

Obama's team—the "best of the Washington insiders," as David Brooks called it—is a dysfunctional and dangerous conglomerate of business-as-usual cronies. They play basketball with the president now instead of poker, but they are every bit as disreputable and demanding as their 1940s counterparts. The administration is teeming with long-lasting favor-seekers in government, business, and the lucrative bridge in between. The corruption stretches from wealthy power brokers Rahm Emanuel and Valerie Jarrett, to pay-to-play-tainted Michelle Obama and Joe Biden, to ethically challenged, bailout-bungling money men Larry Summers and Tim Geithner at Treasury, crime-coddling corporate lawyer Eric Holder at DOJ, to the crooked Service Employees International Union, the shakedown artists at the Association of Community Organizations for Reform Now, and the ever-expanding swamp of Washington lobbyists.

This book pulls together the familiar and not-so-familiar pieces of the transition in crisis to force Obama hagiographers to confront an alternate narrative. A reality-based narrative. A narrative of incompetence, nepotism, influence-peddling, and self-dealing that defies the stubborn myth that Barack Obama is the One True Agent of Hope and Change.

While pundits cooed over Obama's "Achievatrons" and their unbridled "star power," nomination after nomination imploded. The White House and its allies dismissed each failure as a "hiccup," a "bump in the road," or a "goof." Meanwhile, the pace of withdrawals and botched appointments was "record-setting" and "unprecedented." Some of the names you'll recognize. Some you've never heard of because Obama's cheerleaders were too busy glorifying the Greatest Transition in World History. Among the fallen:

- Bill Richardson (corruption scandal)
- Tom Daschle (taxes, ethics)
- Nancy Killefer (taxes)
- Annette Nazareth (allegations of incompetence)
- Caroline Atkinson (taxes)
- H. Rodgin Cohen (conflicts of interest)
- Frank Brosens ("personal" reasons)
- Scott Polakoff (allegations of fraud)
- Jon Cannon (ties to embezzlement scam)
- Charles Freeman (foreign government cronyism)

And those were just some of the bodies thrown under the bus before the 100-day mark. Heckuva job, Obama vetters!

But getting through the confirmation process was no guarantee of ethical cleanliness or competence. Treasury Secretary Tim Geithner, of course, tops the list of Senate-confirmed Obama bombs. Mentored by Wall Street power brokers Robert Rubin and Larry Summers, he played key roles in bungling Indonesia's economy and engineering the Bear Stearns and AIG bailout fiascos. And that was before his prolonged failure to pay back taxes on illegal immigrant household help (along with his acceptance of reimbursement money for taxes he didn't pay) was discovered and before his sheepish admission that he had approved the AIG bonuses his boss decried as "shameful" and "outrageous."

After Bill Richardson and GOP Senator Judd Gregg bowed out of the Commerce Secretary position, President Obama settled on former Democrat Governor of Washington, Gary Locke. The national papers called him "strait-laced" and hailed his "clean reputation." Both liberals and conservatives in his home state called that a crock. As governor, he gave billions in tax breaks to Boeing while failing to disclose that he had retained a paid Boeing private consultant and auditor to advise him on the matter. In the governor's mansion, Locke had his own Billy Carter—a brother-in-law who mooched off the family name to secure tax breaks and job opportunities. And on top of all that, the corporate lawyer Locke (who specialized in trade issues with China) was involved in not one, not two, but three campaign finance scandals involving tainted Asian cash. Perhaps suffering from Commerce Secretary withdrawal fatigue, the Senate confirmed Locke by unanimous consent.

Hostility to transparency is a running thread through Obama's cabinet:

- The No. 2 official at the Department of Housing and Urban Development, former King County, Washington, Executive Ron Sims, has the distinction of being the most fined government official in his state's history for suppressing public records from taxpayers.
- Secretary of State Hillary Clinton for years fought disclosure of massive donations from foreign governments and corporations who filled her husband's library and foundation coffers.
- Top Obama advisor David Axelrod ran fear-mongering campaigns in Illinois in support of a huge utility rate

hike—and failed to disclose that his ads were funded by Commonwealth Edison in Chicago.

- Labor Secretary Hilda Solis failed to disclose that she was director and treasurer of a union-promoting lobbying group pushing legislation that she was co-sponsoring as a congresswoman.

- Attorney General Eric Holder overruled his own lawyers in the Justice Department over the issue of D.C. voting rights (which he and President Obama support) and refused to make public the staffers' opinion that a House bill on the matter was unconstitutional.

President Obama set the tone, breaking his transparency pledge with the very first bill he signed into law. On January 29, 2009, the White House announced that the Lily Ledbetter Fair Pay Act had been posted online for review. One problem: Obama had already signed it—in violation of his "sunlight before signing" pledge[12] to post legislation for public comment on the White House website five days before he sealed any deal.[13] "[W]hen there is a bill that ends up on my desk as a president, you the public will have five days to look online and find out what's in it before I sign it, so that you know what your government's doing," he had vowed.[14]

But Obama broke the pledge again with the mad rush to pass his trillion-dollar, pork-stuffed stimulus package full of earmarks he denied existed. Jim Harper of the Cato Institute reported in April 2009: "Of the eleven bills President Obama has signed, only six have been posted on Whitehouse.gov. None have been posted for a full five days after presentment from Congress. . . . The President has signed most bills within a day or two of their presentment from Congress, violating his campaign promise. He has signed two bills more than five days after presentment, but—ironically, because it preserves the broken promise—not posted them on Whitehouse.gov."[15]

It's this utter disregard for taxpayer accountability that prompted hundreds of thousands of citizens to take to the streets on Tax Day 2009 for Tea Party protests. The trampling of transparency in the stimulus debate inspired signs that read: "No legislation without deliberation" and "READ THE BILL FIRST." Obama's response was first to claim that he hadn't even heard of the Tea Party movement and then, on his 100-day celebration, to deride all those Americans he is supposed to represent of "playing games."[16] Projection, anyone?

Despite his crusading on disclosure of campaign bundlers, Obama refused to supply occupation and employer information for his top fundraisers (McCain provided the data). And he carried on the tradition of late-night document dumps to minimize scrutiny of his wealthiest Cabinet members. Moreover, in a grand end-run around the public confirmation process, President Obama created a "historic" and "unprecedented" number of "czar" appointments through executive orders—essentially creating a shadow cabinet of secretaries overseeing every aspect of domestic policy with unchecked powers beyond congressional reach.

Environmental czar Carol Browner, auto czar Steven Rattner, and health czar Nancy DeParle all have extensive financial ties to the industries they were assigned to oversee—ties that would have progressive supporters of Obama's "new politics" screaming bloody murder if they had been Republican nominees.

Urban czar Adolofo Carrión is in a class of his own. As Borough President of the Bronx, he specialized in cash-and-carry deals with developers seeking approval for projects in his district. He received tens of thousands of dollars in donations from the real estate firms just before and after the developers snagged lucrative deals or crucial zoning changes for their projects. In turn, he made millions in public tax dollars available to his cronies. In one case, he arranged for a developer to renovate his front porch and failed to pay him until after his czar appointment. The Hope and Change administration blew off Carrión's critics.

――――――――――

On the Obama-Biden Change.gov website, the ethics agenda page enshrines a famous quote:

> I am in this race to tell the corporate lobbyists that their days of setting the agenda in Washington are over. I have done more than any other candidate in this race to take on lobbyists—and won. They have not funded my campaign, they will not run my White House, and they will not drown out the voices of the American people when I am president.[17]

Obama made this bold promise in Des Moines, Iowa, in November 2007. A year later, he threw open his transition office and the Oval Office to the nation's leading lobbyists and influence peddlers:

- Tom Daschle was a lobbyist in everything but technical terms;
- Attorney General Eric Holder was registered as a lobbyist at Covington & Burling as recently as 2004;
- Tom Vilsack, the former Iowa governor who is Obama's Agriculture secretary, was a registered lobbyist for the National Education Association in 2007;
- Ron Klain, chief of staff to Vice President Biden, was a lobbyist at O'Melveny & Myers until 2004;
- Leon Panetta was a lobbyist-lite who raked in hundreds of thousands of dollars from corporations in consulting fees;

- Patrick Gaspard, former chief lobbyist for the Service Employees International Union's behemoth New York health care affiliate, Local 1199, served as Obama's campaign national political director and transition deputy director of personnel;
- David Hayes, deputy secretary of the Interior, was a lobbyist at Latham & Watkins through 2006;
- William Corr, executive director of the nonprofit Campaign for Tobacco-Free Kids and a registered lobbyist until September 2008, was Obama's choice for deputy Health and Human Services secretary;
- Former Goldman Sachs lobbyist Mark Patterson was tapped by Treasury Secretary Timothy Geithner for chief of staff.

In the first two weeks alone of his infant administration, no-lobbyist Obama had made seventeen exceptions to his no-lobbyist rule.[18] In the earliest days of the administration, *National Journal* reported, the White House "invoked a clause allowing the Office of Management and Budget director to waive restrictions to allow former Raytheon lobbyist William Lynn to become deputy Defense secretary. And in February, the administration issued two more waivers: one allowing Jocelyn Frye, former general counsel at the National Partnership for Women & Families, to serve as first lady Michelle Obama's director of policy and projects; and one clearing the way for Cecilia Muñoz, the former senior vice president for the National Council of La Raza, to become White House director of intergovernmental affairs."[19]

And that's not counting the spouses and relatives of many of Obama's top officials involved in the favor-trading trade (including Joe Biden's son Hunter Biden and environmental czar Carol Browner's husband) whom I document in this book.

In short: This is a government of the crony, by the lobbyist, and for all the well-heeled, well-connected people Barack Obama spent his entire campaign demonizing.

Obama's defenders will, of course, resort to moral equivalence games. But what about Jack Abramoff? But what about Bush's cronies? But what about Sarah Palin's clothes scandal? But what about John McCain's seven houses? But what about corrupt pay-for-play Republicans like Ted Stevens and former Connecticut Governor John Rowland?

Funny they should ask. Jack Abramoff is a slimeball serving five to ten at a graybar hotel in Maryland. George W. Bush and his cronies—many of whom I vigorously investigated[20] and criticized publicly[21] during the last eight years—are no longer in office. Taxpayers didn't foot the bill for Sarah Palin's wardrobe. Or John McCain's seven houses. And the same kind of arrangements involving home renovation freebies from corporate suitors that urban czar Adolfo Carrión got away with resulted in multiple criminal convictions for Stevens[22] and Rowland.

Fortunately, not everyone on the Left remains paralyzed in an irreversible state of Obama inebriation. This book would not have been possible without the contributions of some brave and lonely liberals—whistleblowers at the Association of Community Organizations for Reform Now (ACORN) and the Service Employees International Union (SEIU), independent journalists and government watchdogs—who rejected the excuse-making and whitewashing of Obama's culture of corruption. While Obama sycophants in the mainstream media celebrated his "hipness"[23] and his "swagga,"[24] a few principled progressives finally began to question the cult.

But they are still in the minority. And there will be more predictable excuses. As I document in this book, Obama's cronies of color (beginning with his own wife) reach for the race card when their dubious judgment is questioned. And when all else fails, there's always the "I inherited the problem" alibi.

To which I reply: Read the book. Barack Obama owns this cabinet of tax cheats, crooks, and cronies. It is his and his alone. In the era of "new politics," judge him as you would judge other mere mortals. Judge him not by the company that preceded him.

Judge him by the company he keeps.

CHAPTER 1

ONWS

OBAMA NOMINEE WITHDRAWAL SYNDROME

As America thrilled to the inauguration of its 44th president and a new First Lady, the West Wing was filling with a kaleidoscopic army of policy aces, whiz kids, and veteran advisers, all focused on the long-haul, no-drama work to which Barack has called them . . . [1]

The enchanted editors of *Vanity Fair* magazine could not contain their glee. In March 2009, they rolled out a "SPECIAL COMMEMORATIVE INAUGURATION ISSUE" replete with "HISTORIC PORTRAITS OF WASHINGTON'S NEW ESTABLISHMENT" snapped by celebrity photographer Annie Liebowitz. President Obama's fanboys and fangirls at the glossy publication hailed "the vibrant diversity of the New Guard." Beltway journalist Maureen Orth, who interviewed Obama's "kaleidoscopic army" for the issue, pronounced herself "amazed." She was dazzled "not only by the audacity of their ideas but also by their apparent belief that in this stratified and partisan town they will be able to effect a sea change in attitudes." [2]

Vanity Fair editorial associate Julian Sancton squealed: "Together, the images in this collection document the dawn of an era. Hold on to this issue. Posterity will thank you." [3]

Annie Liebowitz's first group photo showcased Obama's seven A-list cabinet members and nominees. Secretary-designate of

Labor Hilda Solis stood with arms akimbo in a hot tomato power suit. Secretary of Homeland Security Janet Napolitano donned a Garanimals's red turtleneck and beaming smile. Secretary of Transportation Ray LaHood and Secretary of Veteran Affairs Eric Shinseki both looked relaxed in solid ties and dark suits. Secretary of Agriculture Tom Vilsack struck an oddly pensive pose with downcast eyes amid his jubilant peers. Perhaps he has clairvoyant powers.

In the far-right corner of the class picture, Secretary-designate of the Treasury Timothy Geithner wore shirtsleeves and a furrowed expression of bewilderment (which would soon become his trademark image). And on the far-left end of the set, Secretary-designate of Health and Human Services Tom Daschle looked straight into the camera with the toothiest, most self-satisfied grin.

"This is our opportunity to change the health-care system in this country for the first time in a comprehensive way," *Vanity Fair* quoted Daschle in the lead caption on the power portrait. "Expectations are very high. We are ready to go." He wasn't kidding. On January 25, 2009, word had already leaked that Daschle had "scored a ground floor office in the West Wing."[4] Maureen Orth's accompanying piece (obsequiously titled "Can Obama's New Team Make Government Cool Again?") reiterated the ready-to-go theme: "Former Democratic leader in the Senate Tom Daschle, now secretary of health and human services, vowed to transform health care, the thorniest issue of all. 'There is a tremendous opportunity to launch this new era in a much more positive tone,' he said."[5]

Orth's anointing of Daschle, alas, was premature. The supermodel-style photo spread and drool-drenched Cabinet profiles were published on the *Vanity Fair* website at the beginning of February. Daschle was not yet secretary of health and human services. Nor would he, notwithstanding *Vanity Fair*'s unilateral coronation and official portraiture, ever be.

On February 3, 2009, Daschle withdrew from the HHS nomination as furious funnel clouds of ethical scandal, conflicts of interest, and tax avoidance darkened White House skies. "Old ways doomed new job for Daschle," the *Washington Post* intoned.[6] "Daschle Out as Health Nominee Due to Tax Problems," the Associated Press reported.[7] "Daschle ends bid for post; Obama concedes mistake," the *New York Times* announced.[8]

Public expectations may have been very high, to borrow Daschle's words. But the Obama vetters' standards were trapped in a ditch. The Daschle disaster came on the heels of former New Mexico Governor Bill Richardson's withdrawal from the Commerce Secretary nomination over a long-running pay-for-play probe in New Mexico—which was followed by disclosure of Treasury Secretary Geithner's "tax goofs" involving his failure to pay $43,000 in federal self-employment taxes for four separate years (until, that is, he was tapped for his Obama post).

And these were just the first three of a hapless series of botched nominations involving Obama's "policy aces, whiz kids and veteran advisers." By the end of his first 100 days, Obama had set a turnover record for an incoming cabinet with four major withdrawals (including Republican Senator Judd Gregg's withdrawal as Richardson's replacement at Commerce over fiscal policy disagreements) and a spate of lower posts (such as CNN medical journalist Sanjay Gupta's decision to forego the Surgeon General's post for family and timing reasons). By comparison, former President Bill Clinton had six major nominee dropouts during the course of his eight-year presidency; George W. Bush had two; George H. W. Bush, Ronald Reagan, and Jimmy Carter had one each, according to *National Journal*.[9] By the hallowed 100-day mark, Obama had announced fewer than half of the Senate-confirmed Cabinet department positions he needed to fill, and only 10 percent had been confirmed. Given the fact that Democrats had an overwhelming majority in the Senate, delayed confirmations couldn't be blamed on partisan opposition. Perhaps the new president figured that a disastrously bungled appointment process is the way to Make Government Cool Again.

The administration's handling of the U.S. ambassadorship to Iraq is in a category all by itself. After being told by Vice President Joe Biden, Secretary of State Hillary Clinton, and national security adviser James L. Jones that he had the job, four-star Marine General Anthony Zinni told the *Washington Times* in early February 2009 that the appointment had been withdrawn without explanation in favor of a veteran diplomat, Christopher Hill.[10] Hill was confirmed in April 2009. Zinni recounted the disastrous treatment of the situation to *Foreign Policy's* Laura Rozen:

> "To make a long story short, I kept getting blown off all week," Zinni said. "Meantime, I was rushing to put my personal things in order," to get ready to go.
>
> "Finally, nobody was telling me anything," Zinni said. "I called [national security adviser James L.] Jones Monday several times. I finally got through late in evening. I asked Jones, 'What's going on?' And Jones said, 'We decided on Chris Hill.'"
>
> "I said, 'Really,'" Zinni recalled. "That was news to me."
>
> Jones asked him if he would like to be ambassador to Saudi Arabia, Zinni said. "I said, 'You can stick that with whatever other offers,'" Zinni recalled, saying he had used more colorful language with Jones. Asked Jones's response and if he was apologetic, Zinni said, "Jones was not too concerned. He laughed about it."
>
> Zinni said particularly galling is that had he not managed to get through to Jones on Monday night after repeated calls, he would have found out about the Chris Hill appointment in the *Washington Post* the next day with everybody else.
>
> "You know, I would have appreciated if someone called me and said, 'Minds were changed,'" Zinni said. "But not even to get a call. That's what's really embarrassing."[11]

Zinni told the *New York Times* that he was offered the ambassadorship to Saudi Arabia as a consolation prize. "I told them to stick it where the sun don't shine."[12]

Two months into the Hope and Change presidency, a popular joke made its way around the Internet:

> *What is the difference between Obama and Jesus?*
> *Jesus could actually build a cabinet.*[13]

You never get a second chance to make a first post-inaugural impression. Less than three weeks into his first 100 days, Barack Obama left indelible marks on his nascent presidency: the marks of incompetence and hubris. Despite the administration's much-touted wealth of sharp minds and seasoned strategists, the transition was an abject disaster. The myth of "no-drama" Obama quickly gave way to constant-trauma Obama as nominee withdrawal syndrome bogged down what was allegedly the best and brightest administration in history.

Annie Liebowitz didn't stick around to take "HISTORIC PORTRAITS" of the unraveling of "WASHINGTON'S NEW ESTABLISHMENT." There's no room in her perfectly airbrushed portfolio to commemorate the unglamorous reality of Team Obama's meltdown. But posterity demands that the discards be framed and memorialized. Call it *Calamity Fair*.

THE RISE AND FALL OF
"DOLLAR BILL" RICHARDSON

He denied it was a "consolation prize." They both did. But the odd couple of New Mexico Democrat Governor Bill Richardson and Barack Obama fooled no one. On December 3, 2008, the former rivals for the White House appeared at a news conference in Chicago to announce Richardson's nomination to head the Commerce Department. "Governor Richardson is uniquely suited for this role as a leading economic diplomat for America," Obama asserted. "As governor of New Mexico, Bill showed how government can act as a partner to support our businesses," said Obama, adding that Richardson would "bring a leadership style all his own."[14]

"In the end, Bill Richardson is a leader who shares my values," the President-Elect concluded. More to the point: Richardson was owed. After abandoning his own presidential bid in January 2008, Richardson ditched the Clintons, his old friends and former bosses, to offer a timely endorsement of Obama in March 2008.[15]

Richardson happily accepted the nomination with a boilerplate speech about the importance of commerce, spiced up with a bit of Spanish ("*Al resto de la comunidad Latina, gracias por su apoyo y su confianza*") to show off his identity-politics contribution of vibrant "diversity." Challenged by a Latino reporter on whether the nomination was meant to appease Hispanics, Obama bristled: "Well, Commerce secretary is a pretty good job, you know. It's a member of my key economic team that is going to be dealing with the most significant issue that America faces right now—and that is, how do we put people back to work and rejuvenate the economy? Bill Richardson has been selected because he is the best person for that job....I think the notion that somehow the Commerce secretary is not going to be central to everything we do is fundamentally mistaken."

Obama further rejected the suggestion that he was engaging in ethnic tokenism. "I think that when people look back and see the entire slate, what they will say is, not only in terms of my Cabinet but in terms of, but in terms of my White House staff, I think, people are going to say, this is one of the most diverse Cabinets and White House staffs of all time. But more importantly they're going to say, these are all people of outstanding qualifications and excellence." Protesting too much, Obama argued "that there's no contradiction between diversity and excellence. I'm looking for the best people, first and foremost, to serve the American people. It just so happens that Bill Richardson is one of those people."[16]

"Best people?" Richardson's business experience consisted of serving on several corporate boards after leaving a lifetime of government employment in Washington. Oh, and he was the son of a Citibank executive. His claim to fame during his years as U.N. ambassador under Bill Clinton? Going out of his way to extend a job offer to presidential plaything, Monica Lewinsky.[17] His claim to fame during his years as Energy Secretary under Clinton? Botching the espionage case against nuclear scientist Wen Ho Lee.[18]

"Shared values?" Richardson was infamous for inflating and fudging his personal and political biographies. For almost forty years, he stoked the myth that he had been drafted as a young pitcher for the Kansas City Athletics. His hometown newspaper, the *Albuquerque Journal*, reported in 2005 that it never happened.[19] In another disturbing glimpse at his flawed character, Richardson repeatedly exploited the tale of a fallen Marine for self-aggrandizement while on the campaign trail. He told a stump anecdote about a young American Marine from New Mexico, Lance Corporal Aaron Austin, who was killed in Iraq. His mother, Richardson claimed, personally thanked him for obtaining federal death benefits. However, Richardson got the fallen Marine's name and age wrong and completely fabricated the conversation, according to Austin's mother. She demanded an apology. Instead, on *Meet the Press*, Richardson stood by his story and patted himself on the back again for standing up for veterans.[20]

"Excellence?" Richardson's heavy-handed cronyism had been documented for years by both the Right and the Left in his home state. His political horse-trading with private businesses—campaign donations for infrastructure projects, patronage jobs, and board appointments—was so notorious it earned him the moniker "Dollar Bill." And as the New Mexico GOP documented in

March 2007, Richardson's role in the bankruptcy and securities fraud scandal of fraud-ridden software company, Peregrine Systems, had been widely publicized:

> Richardson served on the board of directors of Peregrine Systems from February 2001 to June of 2002, during a period when the company was covering up accounting fraud to the tune of $509 million in overstated profits and $2.6 billion in understated losses. Gov. Richardson resigned two months after the fraud conspiracy was uncovered by the Securities and Exchange Commission. Gov. Richardson is a close family member of former Peregrine president and CEO, Stephen P. Gardner, who pleaded guilty on March 13, 2007, to three felony charges of defrauding the company and shareholders out of millions of dollars.
>
> The company bankruptcy cost thousands of employees their jobs.
>
> Gardner is married to [the governor's wife] Barbara Richardson's sister, Dorothy Flavin Gardner.
>
> ...Richardson, who in the past has tried to minimize his role in the implosion of Peregrine, has said he was "unaware of the accounting irregularities" and only attended "about five" board meetings during his 16 months on the board. Yet according to [*San Diego Reader* veteran financial reporter] Don Bauder, Richardson was briefed several times on the accounting meltdown inside the company.
>
> According to Bauder, Richardson attended 15 board meetings either in person or by telephone. Bauder has nicknamed Gov. Richardson "Dollar Bill."
>
> "In those meetings, directors were hearing that the company might get caught cooking the books. For example, Richardson attended the meeting of July 18, 2001. The company's chief executive, Stephen Gardner (the brother-in-law of Richardson's

wife), informed board members of a barter transaction that had occurred with Critical Path, a Bay Area company headed by a Rancho Santa Fe executive known around Peregrine as a FOJ (Friend of John Moores)."

In the same article, Bauder also wrote: "The directors were told that the Securities and Exchange Commission had questioned three Peregrine top executives and a national business magazine was on the story. Directors discussed how to spin it."

John Moores, a real estate mogul and the owner of the San Diego Padres, had also reportedly been a campaign contributor to Richardson's re-election campaign. According to an article in the *San Diego Union-Tribune*, Moores sold or transferred more than $487 million worth of Peregrine shares, though he hasn't been charged or implicated in the government's investigation. [21]

On the other side of the political aisle, liberal magazine *Mother Jones* had also called attention to Richardson's shady role in the Peregrine Systems scandal, which the publication in 2007 dubbed "a financial scam in the Enron style."[22] On top of all that, Richardson was the subject of a high-profile probe and ongoing grand jury investigation into whether he traded New Mexico government contracts for campaign contributions. The White House transition team knew about the pay-to-play scandal involving a California company, CDR Financial Products, well before Obama unwisely fêted Richardson's ability to show "how government can act as a partner to support our businesses." FBI and federal prosecutors launched their probe of CDR's activities in New Mexico in the summer of 2008.

The feds had been digging into a nationwide web of favor-trading between financial firms and politicians overseeing local government bond markets. CDR was tied to a doomed bond deal in Alabama which, according to Bloomberg News, threatened to cause the biggest municipal bankruptcy in U.S. history.[23] CDR raked in nearly $1.5 million in fees from a New Mexico state financial agency after donating more than $100,000 to Richardson's efforts to register Hispanic and American Indian voters and to pay for expenses at the 2004 Democratic National Convention, the news service reported. The state agency that awarded the money consisted of five Richardson appointees and five members of his gubernatorial cabinet. CDR made contributions both shortly before and after securing consultant work with the state of New Mexico. CDR's president also contributed $29,000 to Obama's presidential campaign.

It took thirty-three days before Team Obama threw Richardson and his ethical baggage off the bus. On January 4, 2009, Richardson announced his withdrawal. "Let me say unequivocally that I and my Administration have acted properly in all matters and that this investigation will bear out that fact," he told NBC News. "But I have concluded that the ongoing investigation also would have forced an untenable delay in the confirmation process." [24] Obama gave the obligatory send-off: "It is a measure of his willingness to put the nation first that he has removed himself as a candidate for the Cabinet to avoid any delay in filling this important economic post at this critical time."[25]

But it is a measure of Obama's obliviousness that he nominated the ethically-challenged Richardson in the first place. *Mother Jones* writer James Ridgeway's comment on the day of Richardson's withdrawal proved quite prescient: "It may be premature to say that Obama and his team have too high a tolerance for corruption. But this first self-destruct among his cabinet picks could well prove all the more damaging because it's something they should have seen coming from miles away."[26]

DRIVING TOM DASCHLE

In 1998, then Minority Leader Tom Daschle read a bold statement on the Senate floor condemning tax cheats. "Make no mistake," the Democrat politician said emphatically, "tax cheaters cheat us all, and the IRS should enforce our laws to the letter."[27] He also crusaded righteously against "Benedict Arnold corporations" that earned income overseas to avoid high corporate tax rates in the United States.[28] Daschle had zero tolerance for tax evaders.

Fast-forward to January 31, 2009. The *New York Times* reported that Daschle "was aware as early as last June [2008] that he might have to pay back taxes for the use of a car and driver provided by a private equity firm, but did not inform the Obama transition team until weeks after Mr. Obama named him to the health secretary's post" in mid-December 2008.[29] Daschle was on the cusp of attaining enormous power to reshape the American economy and implement his sweeping universal health care proposals. He wasn't going to let a pesky tax omission get in the way. On January 2, 2009, he had been forced to amend his 2005 and 2007 tax returns to reflect $255,256 for the use of the car service, $83,000 in unreported consulting income, and $14,963 in charitable contributions. In addition, the would-be Health and Human Services Secretary failed to pay $6,000 in Medicare taxes for the driver. On February 1, 2009, Daschle groveled before his former Senate colleagues to explain away the back payments he owed, as well as dubious charitable deductions worth an estimated $146,000, including interest and penalties.

"Sorry" worked for tax cheat Treasury Secretary Tim Geithner. Why not Daschle, too? His hang-dog letter read:

> As you can well imagine, I am deeply embarrassed and disappointed by the errors that required me to amend my tax returns. I apologize for the errors and profoundly regret that you have had to devote time to them.
>
> Last fall, when I was being considered for this position, the Presidential Transition Team's vetters reviewed my records. During the course of those reviews, the vetting team flagged charitable contributions they felt were deducted in error. When my

accountant realized I would need to file amended returns, he suggested addressing another matter I had raised with him earlier in the year: whether the use of a car service offered to me by a close friend might be a tax issue. In December, my accountant advised me that it should be reported as imputed income in the amended returns.

At about the same time, the friend's company, a consulting client, informed my accountant of a clerical error it had made on the Form 1099 it provided to me and reported to the IRS for 2007. In an effort to ensure full compliance and the most complete disclosure possible of my personal finances, we remedied these issues by filing amended tax returns with full payments, including interest. We provided all this information to the Committee in addition to the completed Committee questionnaire and my responses to your staff's questions. I disclosed this information to the Committee voluntarily, and paid the taxes and any interest owed promptly. My mistakes were unintentional.

The national media seemed ready to downplay the unbelievable lapses. A *Washington Post* headline characterized the problem as a "tax glitch."[30] A glitch is checking off the wrong box or misspelling a name. This was an ethical morass. The donor and personal friend who provided the chauffeured services, Leo Hindery Jr., had also made Daschle chairman of the executive advisory board of InterMedia Advisors, a high-flying investment firm. Daschle raked in a million-dollar salary from the arrangement in addition to his private chariot. Asked why he hadn't disclosed the cozy arrangement, Daschle "told committee staff he had grown used to having a car and driver as majority leader and did not think to report the perk on his taxes, according to staff members."[31] It was a perfect expression of the culture of Beltway entitlement.

Obama stuck by Daschle—one of his earliest champions and closest advisers—that day. "Absolutely," the president-elect responded when asked if he still supported the nomination. At a press briefing that afternoon, White House spokesman Robert Gibbs dismissed Daschle's tax evasion: "Nobody's perfect." But in twenty-four short hours, Obama was singing a different tune. CBS News rounded up the White House "I'm Sorry" Media Tour:

> During interviews with CBS, ABC, NBC, FOX and CNN, President Obama was asked about the cabinet staffing hiccup. The typically confident president repeatedly said that the appointment scandal was his responsibility and apologized over (and over) again.
>
> "I believe, on Tom's part, that, you know, ordinary people are out there paying taxes everyday and whether it's an intentional mistake or not, it was sending the wrong signal," he told Couric, "so again, this was something that was my fault."
>
> "I've got to own up to my mistake which is that ultimately it's important for this administration to send a message that there aren't two sets of rules. You know, one for prominent people and one for ordinary folks who have to pay their taxes," Mr. Obama told NBC.
>
> "I'm frustrated with myself, with our team," he added, "and I'm here on television saying I screwed up and that's part of the era of responsibility, is not never making mistakes; it's owning up to them and trying to make sure you never repeat them and that's what we intend to do."
>
> ABC's Charles Gibson asked President Obama what type of message he thought investigations into three of his appointee's taxes sent. Responded the president: "Well, I think it sends the wrong one. And that's, you know, something I take responsibility for."

"I think I made a mistake. And I told Tom that. I take responsibility for the appointees," Mr. Obama told CNN. "I think my mistake is not in selecting Tom originally.... But I think that, look, ultimately, I campaigned on changing Washington and bottom-up politics. And I don't want to send a message to the American people that there are two sets of standards, one for powerful people, and one for ordinary folks who are working every day and paying their taxes."

And, just to make sure no audience members were missed, the apologetic president told Fox News, "I take responsibility for this mistake." He promised to "make sure we're not screwing up again."

In total, President Obama said the word "mistake" twelve times during the five interviews. He also used the phrase "I take responsibility" three times and the word "regret" twice.[32]

It was a little late to be worrying about sending a bad message to the American people about double standards. But only the blessed Barack Obama could have national media outlets describing this fiasco of the first order as a "cabinet staffing hiccup." The Daschle nomination was a Shrek-sized stink bomb from start to finish. The limousine liberal's tax evasions were the least of his problems. Tom Daschle is the personification of all that Obama professed to detest during his campaign of Hope and Change—a consummate Beltway insider who parlayed his public service (where he earned a $158,000 yearly salary) into a $5.2 million personal fortune as one of Washington's biggest influence peddlers along with his lobbyist wife.

Did Obama forget that GOP Senator John Thune defeated Daschle the Dodger in 2004 after news broke of Daschle's bogus property-tax homestead exemption claim on his $1.9 million D.C. mansion—which he listed as his primary residence despite voting in South Dakota, claiming it in order to run for re-election? Did

Obama forget that Daschle worked for the legal and lobbying firm Alston & Bird, scratching backs, making phone calls, offering advice, trading on his name and connections, and doing everything short of registering as a lobbyist? President Obama bashed corporate executives for flying in lavish planes—even as the Senate Finance Committee was investigating his HHS nominee's repeat flights on the $31 million luxury jet of a scandal-ridden educational charity called Educap, owned by one of the Daschles' closest friends, Catherine Reynolds.[33] "Even without the tax issue," the UK Telegraph's Toby Harnden correctly noted, "Daschle is the kind of guy who epitomises the Washington way of doing things, the 'broken politics' that during his campaign Obama promised to sweep away."[34]

Nevertheless, Obama steadfastly praised Daschle's devotion to "public service." The president expressed "sadness and regret" that his nominee got tripped up by his "mistake," but not an iota of remorse to the American people for his lack of good sense and judgment in nominating his wheeler-dealer Beltway buddy in the first place.

PERFORMANCE CZAR
NANCY KILLEFER TAKES A DIVE

Just hours before the jaw-dropping Daschle announcement came the withdrawal of Nancy Killefer. She was tapped to be President Obama's "Chief Performance Officer" overseeing compliance, organizational effectiveness, and waste management across every federal agency. Obama had also asked her to serve as deputy director at the Office of Management and Budget. But the former Clinton Treasury official and head of the Washington office of the prestigious management consulting firm McKinsey & Company, Inc., couldn't be bothered to manage her own household help effectively. While she climbed the corporate ladder, she hired two nannies and a personal assistant to manage affairs at home, where her economics professor husband and two children lived. The management guru failed for a year and a half to pay employment taxes on her household help and had an outstanding $1,000 tax lien on her home.

Degrees out the wazoo, the woman whose reputation rested on her meticulousness with numbers did not have enough smarts or care to dot her I's and cross her T's on her own tax forms in a town that had been through several infamous Nannygate crises during the past two administrations. Mimicking her would-be boss's penchant for playing the "distraction" card when caught in an ethical pickle, Killefer issued a withdrawal statement that deflected blame to those who took tax lapses seriously: "I recognize that your agenda and the duties facing your Chief Performance Officer are urgent. I have also come to realize in the current environment that my personal tax issue of D.C. Unemployment tax could be used to create exactly the kind of distraction and delay those duties must avoid."[35]

White House spokesman Robert Gibbs blithely insisted the day after the Killefer and Daschle withdrawals, "The bar that we set is the highest that any administration in the country has ever set."[36]

It was getting harder to listen to such lofty claims every week without hearing a laugh track or drum rimshot.

BAILING OUT AT TREASURY

Treasury Secretary Tim Geithner probably savored the *Vanity Fair* photo shoot more than any of the other Cabinet members. He hasn't had that much company since taking office. By mid-March 2009, only one of fifteen key Treasury Department positions requiring Senate confirmation had been filled.[37] Treasury officials denied there were any vetting problems. But Mr. Lonely saw at least five staff picks withdraw before the Obama administration had reached the 100-day mark:

On March 5, Geithner's choice for chief deputy, Annette Nazareth, dropped out of the running after drawing criticism of "what some considered to be a lax oversight of the banking industry," the Associated Press reported.[38] She had served as a former senior staffer and commissioner with the Securities and Exchange Commission (SEC), where she founded the Consolidated Securities Entities program. According to the *Wall Street Journal*, the Consolidated Supervised Entities program "was created in 2004 to coax global investment banks to voluntarily submit to regulation." The five major investment banks that participated in the program no longer exist. The program was abandoned in September 2008, the *Journal* reported, after then SEC Chairman Christopher Cox declared it "fundamentally flawed from the beginning."[39] In addition, SEC Inspector General David Kotz faulted the SEC program for failing to respond to "numerous, potential red flags" at Bear Stearns, which collapsed in 2008.[40] It also failed to detect the $50 billion Ponzi scheme engineered by convicted mega-swindler Bernie Madoff.

The same day, White House aides acknowledged that Caroline Atkinson, the Treasury pick for Undersecretary for International Affairs, had withdrawn after a "tax problem" was discovered in the vetting process.[41]

A week after Nazareth and Atkinson bowed out, New York Attorney H. Rodgin Cohen withdrew his bid to replace Nazareth. Cohen was a preeminent counsel to Wall Street firms and a partner at prestigious Sullivan & Cromwell LLP, which had donated nearly $242,000 to the Democratic National Committee during the 2008 campaign cycle.[42] Democratic sources told ABC News, "An issue arose in the final stages of the vetting process."[43] The "issue" may well have been Cohen's hands-on role as a primary engineer of the very banking crisis he was nominated to help fix.

The *Wall Street Journal* noted in the fall of 2008 that Cohen "helped mold the financial system that is now under assault," "helped draft the rules that led to the emergence of powerful national banks, waged the first hostile bank takeover in the U.S.," "lobbied...to expand the Federal Reserve's power to provide the emergency loans now being employed by the government," and "helped broker the deal that put Fannie [Mae] and Freddie [Mac] into conservatorship."[44] Yes, it certainly would have been an "issue" if Geithner's top deputy pick were approved for office— only to be forced to recuse himself from every aspect of his job over conflicts of interest.

On March 24, 2009, hedge fund manager Frank Brosens withdrew his name from consideration for the Treasury job overseeing the $700 billion bank bailout program, surprising many who expected him to take the position. Obama economic adviser Larry Summers lobbied on Brosens's behalf.[45] Brosens, a Goldman Sachs alum who was a $200,000-plus fund-raising bundler for Obama and actively campaigned for the candidate, abruptly jumped ship citing "personal" reasons.[46]

On March 26, 2009, another Treasury official took a fall—at a time when Tim Geithner could ill afford to lose any of the few staffers actually working in the department with him. Scott Polakoff, the acting director of the Office of Thrift Supervision, was put on an underdetermined leave "pending a review of the agency's role in the backdating of capital infusions by some banks."[47] The late-night announcement indicated that Polakoff's office allowed at least six instances of apparent book-cooking on behalf of IndyMac and other banks so that earlier quarterly financial statements looked healthier than they would have. In addition, Polakoff's agency was faulted for lax oversight of bailout behemoth AIG. President Bush originally appointed Polakoff to his post. But this wasn't merely an "inherited" problem. President Obama made the decision to promote Polakoff in February 2009.

In early March 2009, Polakoff testified before a Senate Banking Committee that his office should have exercised its authority in 2004 to stop AIG's troubled financial products division from engaging in risky derivatives and credit default swaps. Polakoff hasn't been heard from publicly since.[48]

EPA DEPUTY NOMINEE
JON CANNON'S ROUGH WATERS

And the hits kept coming. On February 23, 2009, the White House heralded the nomination of Jon Cannon for the Deputy U.S. Environmental Protection Agency Administrator slot. Cannon was a law professor at the University of Virginia. Less than a month later, Cannon voluntarily removed his name from consideration for the post. "It has come to my attention that America's Clean Water Foundation, where I once served on the board of directors, has become the subject of scrutiny," he acknowledged in a brief statement. "While my service on the board of that now-dissolved organization is not the subject of the scrutiny, I believe the energy and environmental challenges facing our nation are too great to delay confirmation for this position, and I do not wish to present any distraction to the agency."[49] The withdrawal was abrupt and curious. For the past month, he had been working in Washington as a member of the Obama transition team and had prepared to leave his job in academia.

An EPA report from 2007 documented how America's Clean Water Foundation mishandled three huge government grants totaling nearly $26 million:

> The Foundation (1) could not provide support for any of its general journal entries; (2) included duplicate transactions in its accounting system; (3) recorded labor charged to EPA grants incorrectly; (4) could not support the recorded indirect costs; (5)

claimed unallowable preaward costs; (6) recorded EPA cash draws inaccurately; (7) did not submit required indirect cost proposals to EPA; (8) did not complete the required single audits for fiscal years ended June 30, 2003, June 30, 2004, and June 30, 2005; and (9) did not submit a Federal Cash Transactions Report when required.

The Foundation's procurement practices and procedures did not comply with the grant regulations. The Foundation awarded sole source contracts without performing the cost/price analysis required by Title 40 CFR 30.45. It also awarded a contract to a member of its Board of Directors, contrary to the conflict of interest provisions at Title 40 CFR 30.42, and reimbursed a contractor for billings above contractual ceilings. Because the Foundation did not adequately document its costs and did not comply with the EPA regulations, we questioned the Federal share claimed of $25,372,590.[50]

The America's Clean Water Foundation disappeared soon after the discovery of financial shenanigans:

> While performing the single audit for the year ended June 30, 2004, RAFFA, the Foundation's accounting firm, discovered accounting irregularities and a potential embezzlement of funds.
>
> . . . In a July 14, 2006, letter, the Foundation's attorney notified EPA that the Foundation was formally dissolved. The letter stated that all members of the Board of Directors had resigned, the Foundation filed dissolution papers with the District of Columbia, and it no longer had any employees or an office location. The stated reason for the dissolution was the lack of program funding; the Foundation could no longer operate effectively or respond to Agency inquiries. The letter indicated that Foundation records and files had been moved to a storage facility in Standardsville, Virginia, that access to the records can

be arranged, and that the Foundation retained its right to initiate and maintain claims.[51]

The investigation also uncovered a smelly arrangement between the foundation and the pork industry. One of the foundation's contractors, which raked in tens of millions in federal EPA grants through no-competition bids, was a firm called Validus Services LLC—a for-profit subsidiary of the National Pork Producer Council. Agricultural journalist Alan Gubert originally broke the story of how the pork lobby collaborated with the not-so-clean Clean Water Foundation to set up federal environmental assessments funded through the EPA—and from which they both profited.[52] The agency gave up efforts to recover the taxpayer money squandered by the foundation.

Cannon remained tight-lipped about his withdrawal. Supporters portrayed him as a victim of guilt-by-association.[53] "I appreciate your interest in this," Cannon told *The Hook*, a Charlottesville weekly newspaper, "but I said what I wanted to say in the statement I released, and I want to leave it at that."[54]

CHARLES FREEMAN:
AN UN-INTELLIGENT CHOICE

The directorship of the National Intelligence Council is not a position for the thin-skinned, paranoid, or ethics-compromised. Or at least, it shouldn't be. Somehow, however, President Obama nominated former U.S. ambassador to Saudi Arabia Charles Freeman to the post in late February 2009. Freeman's responsibilities would include preparation of important National Intelligence Estimates about potential threats to our national security. Both the left and right in Washington balked at Freeman's baggage. Once again, Obama supporters were left wondering why the Ivy League geniuses in the White House didn't see this coming.

His conflicts of interest abounded. Freeman had served for four years on the board of the China National Offshore Oil Corp, a company owned by the Chinese communist government. The state-owned firm has invested in Sudan and Iran. Freeman also led the Middle East Policy Council, a Washington, D.C.-based group funded by the Saudi government. *Washington Times* reporter Eli Lake also disclosed that Freeman chaired Projects International, a consulting firm that has worked with foreign companies and governments.[55]

To compound those ethical concerns, Freeman was a Jew-basher and tyrant-coddler with a Blame America axe to grind. Liberal writer Jonathan Chait called Freeman an "ideological fanatic" of the realist school blinded to morality.[56] Freeman endorsed hyperbolic attacks on "Zionist political influence" and wrote in a leaked e-mail obtained by the *Weekly Standard* that China's problem in handling the Tiananmen Square Massacre was that it was *too restrained*:

> [T]he truly unforgivable mistake of the Chinese authorities was the failure to intervene on a timely basis to nip the demonstrations in the bud, rather than—as would have been both wise and efficacious—to intervene with force when all other measures had failed to restore domestic tranquility to Beijing and other major urban centers in China. In this optic, the Politburo's response to the mob scene at 'Tian'anmen' stands as a monument to overly cautious behavior on the part of the leadership, not as an example of rash action. . . .
>
> I do not believe it is acceptable for any country to allow the heart of its national capital to be occupied by dissidents intent on disrupting the normal functions of government, however appealing to foreigners their propaganda may be. Such folk, whether they represent a veterans' "Bonus Army" or a "student uprising" on behalf of "the goddess of democracy" should

expect to be displaced with despatch [sic] from the ground they occupy.[57]

On the right, the editors of *National Review* ripped the appointment as an abject "intelligence failure":

> He has distinguished himself as a rabid Israel-hater who regards the Jewish state's defensive measures as the primary cause of jihadist terror. He is a shameless apologist for Saudi Arabia (where he once served as U.S. ambassador) despite its well-documented record of exporting terrorists and jihadist ideology. And he is a long-time sycophant of Beijing, where he served as Richard Nixon's interpreter during the 1971 summit and later ran the U.S. diplomatic mission.[58]

In 2002, Freeman echoed President Obama's former Pastor, the Reverend Jeremiah Wright Jr., waxing indignant: "And what of America's lack of introspection about September 11? Instead of asking what might have caused the attack, or questioning the propriety of the national response to it, there is an ugly mood of chauvinism. Before Americans call on others to examine themselves, we should examine ourselves."[59]

Doing the vetting the Obama administration wouldn't do, critics examined the Saudi government's $1 million grant to Freeman's Middle East Policy Council. National security journalist Gabriel Schoenfeld quoted Freeman acknowledging that the group owed its endowment to the "generosity" of Saudi King Abdullah bin Abdul Aziz.[60] The panel also paid Freeman nearly $90,000 in 2006. "Whatever else you think of the Saudis, they spare no expense in rewarding their lap dogs," syndicated columnist Rich Lowry noted.[61] But instead of the regular vetting process, Freeman's advocate, Director of National Intelligence Dennis Blair, assigned a special inspector general to probe Freeman's foreign financial ties. The White House claimed ignorance of the matter. For his part, Blair insisted on praising Freeman's "inventive mind" (that's one way to put it) at a Senate hearing just hours before the withdrawal was announced.[62]

On March 10, 2009, Freeman's "inventive mind" was on full, festering display in an open letter blasting the "Israel Lobby" for "character assassination" upon his withdrawal:

> I have concluded that the barrage of libelous distortions of my record would not cease upon my entry into office. The effort to smear me and to destroy my credibility would instead continue. I do not believe the National Intelligence Council could function effectively while its chair was under constant attack by unscrupulous people with a passionate attachment to the views of a political faction in a foreign country. I agreed to chair the NIC to strengthen it and protect it against politicization, not to introduce it to efforts by a special interest group to assert control over it through a protracted political campaign.
>
> The libels on me and their easily traceable email trails show conclusively that there is a powerful lobby determined to prevent any view other than its own from being aired, still less to factor in American understanding of trends and events in the Middle East. The tactics of the Israel Lobby plumb the depths of dishonor and indecency and include character assassination, selective misquotation, the willful distortion of the record, the fabrication of falsehoods, and an utter disregard for the truth. The aim of this Lobby is control of the policy process through the exercise of a veto over the appointment of people who dispute the wisdom of its views, the substitution of political correctness for analysis, and the exclusion of any and all options for decision by Americans and our government other than those that it favors.[63]

The screed says less about Freeman than it does about the Obama administration's AWOL vetting system. Where were the watch-dogs to guard against terror-friendly, conspiracy-minded kooks slipping into sensitive intelligence positions? Like so many of the other withdrawal cases that plagued the White House, Freeman's appointment never should have happened in the first place. Incompetence, inattention to detail, and apathy were common threads—running stitches—that carried through the Richardson and Daschle cases to the Killefer ship-jumping to the Treasury and EPA dropouts. The Center for Security Policy's Frank Gaffney summed up the Freeman fiasco in four words: "Garbage in, garbage out."[64] This was fast becoming the epigram for the White House. And no amount of media photoshopping, airbrushing, and diversionary fluff could cover the stench.

Which brings us to Michelle Obama. Behind the glamorous exterior and soft-focus lens is a hardened influence-peddler on par with Obama's dropouts. Lucky for the Mrs. Obama, first ladies don't require Senate confirmation.

CHAPTER 2

BITTER HALF
FIRST CRONY MICHELLE OBAMA

Whoopi Goldberg was giddy with laughter in June 2008 as she introduced "our very special guest co-host, who actually could be the next first lady of the United States of America, Michelle Obama!" After the studio audience for ABC's *The View* had given her a standing ovation, the honored guest said, "I have to be greeted properly—fist-bump, please," exchanging the gesture with her hostesses. The first question went to Barbara Walters, who asked about that day's *New York Times* story that Mrs. Obama's appearance on the show was aimed at "softening her reputation."[1]

Hard-hitting questions aren't what *The View* is about, but the chummy treatment Michelle Obama got from Whoopi, Barbara, and the gang was hardly different than the adulatory coverage she has received from the rest of a supposedly skeptical press corps. Nothing revealed the news media's love-struck idolization of Barack Obama more than the way they constantly compared him to their favorite president JFK, with Michelle cast in the role of the media's favorite first lady. In January 2008, shortly after

Obama was endorsed by the Kennedy clan—Teddy, his son Patrick, and JFK's daughter Caroline—Helena Andrews of *Politico* invoked the Jacqueline Kennedy comparison: "Michelle cut the faultless figure of the quintessential president's wife last Saturday in South Carolina—the president, of course, being John F. Kennedy and the wife being Jackie."[2] CBS News gushed after the election: "Change is definitely coming to 1600 Pennsylvania Ave., as our next first lady, Michelle Obama, is bringing a new sense of style to the White House. Obama follows in the fashion footsteps of first ladies like Jackie Kennedy, who was known for her sophistication and elegance." [3]

The glamorous "Camelot" aura of the Kennedy administration was obviously what the media had in mind with this comparison, rather than more recent revelations about JFK's ties to the Chicago mob. As with her husband, however, the new First Lady's media-generated image doesn't quite match the reality of her life.

Beneath the cultured pearls, sleeveless designer dresses, and false eyelashes applied by her full-time makeup artist, Michelle Robinson Obama is a hardball Chicago politico. Star-struck liberal journalists swoon over Michelle O.'s bare arms, but it's her bare knuckles they should be watching. Anyone who criticizes her is at risk of being labeled a racist. The First Lady long ago showed a willingness to employ accusations of racial oppression as a defense against criticism. Mrs. Obama's senior thesis at Princeton University, titled "Princeton-Educated Blacks and the Black Community," bemoaned her racial otherness. The aggrieved Ivy Leaguer accused her university of pushing her down the dreaded path toward "further integration and/or assimilation into a white cultural and social structure that will only allow me to remain on the periphery of society; never becoming a full participant."[4]

Rather than remaining "on the periphery," however, Mrs. Obama climbed the crooked Chicago ladder on a rapid ascent to the top. She hopped from Princeton to Harvard to prestigious law firms, cushy non-profit gigs, and an exclusive Hyde Park manse, before landing at 1600 Pennsylvania Avenue with the greatest of ease. While regaling campaign crowds with complaints about her burdensome education loans and unhappiness with the lily-white corporate world, she neglected to mention that it was a white male Princeton alum, Sidley & Austin corporate law partner Stephen Carlson, who went beyond the call of duty to bring her from her imagined "periphery" to the center of power. He gave her career advice and summer work suggestions while she was an undergrad, and then reached out to her again when she was at Harvard Law. She had a grand time as a summer associate in 1987, accepted a full-time job upon graduation, and never looked back.[5]

In the Chicago patronage culture that made Michelle Obama, the color that matters most is neither black nor white, it is green— the color of money. Mrs. Obama was literally born into the Chicago political corruptocracy. Her father, Fraser Robinson, was a volunteer precinct captain for the Democrat Party. *Washington Post* writer Liza Mundy called him "an essential member of the powerful political machine run by [Richard J.] Daley, who, in addition to being mayor, was the chairman of the Cook County Democratic Central Committee, meaning he controlled both the government and the political party, and could use one to do the other's bidding." Former alderman Leon Despres bluntly told Mundy that it was "overwhelmingly likely" that Robinson's job at the city water department was a reward for his loyalty. "The water department, where Fraser Robinson worked, was a renowned repository of patronage jobs."[6]

Why such little scrutiny of Michelle the Merciless (or "That *Other* Michelle," as she's known in my house) and her crony-aided rise to power? Like her husband, Mrs. Obama is quick to play the victim card when her ill-considered statements and her dealings come under scrutiny. I don't call her President Obama's bitter half for nothing.

Remember when the Tennessee Republican Party ran a hard-hitting ad in spring 2008 skewering Mrs. Obama's patriotism-impaired remark at a Wisconsin campaign rally ("For the first time in my adult life, I am proud of my country")? The Obamas took to ABC's *Good Morning America* to bemoan the "low class" and "detestable" criticisms. Obama insisted indignantly that "these folks should lay off my wife." Mrs. Obama laughed softly at his side.[7]

Perhaps the self-proclaimed "South Side girl" chuckled because she knew how transparently ridiculous her hubby's spousal defense really was. Mrs. Obama, he argued to *Glamour* magazine, was an innocent bystander untrained in the rough and tumble ways of political life:

> SENATOR OBAMA: It's infuriating, but it's not surprising, because let's face it: What happened was that the conservative press—Fox News and the *National Review* and columnists of every ilk—went fairly deliberately at her in a pretty systematic way...and treated her as the candidate in a way that you just rarely see the Democrats try to do against Republicans. And I've said this before: I would never have my campaign engage in a concerted effort to make Cindy McCain an issue, and I would not expect the Democratic National Committee or people who were allied with me to do it. Because essentially, spouses are civilians. They didn't sign up for this.[8]

Mrs. Obama most certainly signed up for heightened public scrutiny of her public words and deeds. She signed up for it the minute she voluntarily stepped on the campaign trail to sell her husband as America's soul-fixer. She signed up for it when she made herself a public spokeswoman for working mothers and chief public surrogate for her husband's legislative agenda. She signed up for it when she consciously and continuously milked liberal bitterness on the campaign trail to drum up votes for her husband. If she couldn't stand what little heat she was exposed to during the presidential election season, she should have refrained from grabbing the closest microphone to complain repeatedly about America's health care, lack of compassion, and the evil lure of corporate America.

Exposing the First Lady's crony history is vital to understanding the depth and breadth of her hubby's ethical corruption. The couple's political and financial fortunes have been intertwined since their earliest days together in Chicago. Their marital partnership is a business partnership that has profound domestic policy consequences. Like Hillary Clinton, Michelle Obama intends to play a hands-on role as a policy advocate the next four years— and she has filled her staff with seasoned Chicago operatives like herself with longtime big business ties and left-wing agendas. (As you'll see throughout this book, the two are far from mutually exclusive.)

Even the most seemingly innocuous of Mrs. Obama's aides in the White House is a credentialed crony. Take the First Lady's social secretary, Desirée Rogers. Mrs. Obama heaped praise on her dear friend's "phenomenal job" of creating a "People's House."[9] Fawning profiles of Rogers focused on the aide's taste in clothes and art. But in true Obama fashion, the First Lady chose a hometown political pal who is an expert in much more than china patterns and scheduling matters. Rogers sees herself not merely as a party planner, but as the overseer of the White House "strategy for events." While she pays lip service to exercising restraint in Washington ("As we go through our struggle, there is a need to be prudent"), Rogers defended the lavish "Camelot" scene that quickly became an Obama hallmark in the economically stressed first 100 days. The celebrity-filled cocktail nights and conga lines are a means to end, she explained to National Public Radio:

My belief is that we don't always get everything accomplished over a meeting table," Rogers says. "Many times it's over cocktails, it's over dinner and so the other piece to our work will be what kind of events can we create?[10]

Fittingly, Ms. Rogers's personal motto is *laissez les bon temps rouler*: Let the good times roll.[11] With her savvy fundraising skills, she helped keep Team Obama rolling in dough during the 2008 presidential campaign. According to left-wing watchdog Public Citizen, Rogers bundled more than $200,000 for Obama and contributed $28,500 to committees supporting her good friend.[12] A Harvard MBA and former Allstate Financial executive, Rogers spent 2004 to 2008 as head of Peoples Gas and North Shore Gas, a $1.1 billion natural gas utility in Chicago. During her tenure, the utility's parent company was sued for artificially inflating gas prices; a settlement with Illinois regulators required the firm to refund $100 million to consumers. Separate actions resulted in fines of $500,000 for a backlog of overdue meter safety inspections and $1 million for failing to properly inspect distribution pipes.[13] In April 2009, financial disclosure forms revealed that Rogers "collected more than $1 million for her work as president of two gas companies for part of 2008. Later, she earned a $350,000 salary from Allstate Financial as president of its social-networking division, and $150,000 in board fees from Equity Residential, a real-estate investment trust in which she also holds at least $250,000 in stock."[14]

Rogers has known Mr. and Mrs. O. for more than a decade. How did they meet? You can thank those Ivy League connections—the same connections that Michelle Obama griped would keep her "on the periphery." Rogers's ex-husband, John W. Rogers Jr., chief executive of multi-billion-dollar Ariel Capital Management, played basketball with Michelle O.'s brother, Craig Robinson, at Princeton. Mr. Rogers also served as a campaign finance bundler for Team Obama. The Rogerses were among 79 top fundraisers who, according to the *Washington Post*, tapped their personal networks to raise at least $200,000 each. The bundlers recruited a total of more than 27,000 donors to write maximum-limit checks for $2,300 each.[15]

These deep-pocketed rainmakers represent one of the endless, glaring examples of Obama-pocrisy. In 2007, then Senator Barack Obama boldly declared in a *Chicago Tribune* op-ed piece:

> To set an example in the 2008 presidential election, I am refusing to accept campaign contributions from registered federal lobbyists, political-action committees, and I won't take contributions bundled by lobbyists. I'm also reporting any contributions that are bundled—whether it's from a small-town doctor or a chief executive officer. If we can open up the system and pull aside the curtain of secrecy, then we might be able to start changing the way Washington works.[16]

But of course, "no lobbyist money" depends on the meaning of "lobbyist." The Obama campaign sheepishly "clarified that the policy of Obama's campaign is to not accept campaign contributions from registered federal lobbyists. He is accepting contributions from registered state lobbyists." Ah. Obama himself explained the quid pro quos of bundled donations, put together by "bundlers" who amass campaign contributions for politicians, in his column assailing this disclosure-evading campaign finance practice: "These lobbyists are delivering millions in bundled contributions to the very politicians from whom they are seeking favorable votes or legislation. . . . It is no coincidence that the best bundlers are often granted the greatest access, and access is power in Washington."

Indeed, "it is no coincidence" that Mrs. Obama is now using her perch in the White House to reward wheeler-dealers like

Desirée Rogers who helped pave her husband's path to power—
and her own. And it is no coincidence that the Obamas' water-car-
riers in Congress are fighting reasonable proposals to keep the
First Lady's public policy-related meetings transparent to the public. Preemptively playing the victim card on Mrs. O.'s behalf,
Democrat Congressman William Clay argued in a heated House
debate in March 2009 that a Republican open-meetings amendment would be seen by the president as "an attack on his wife."[17]

Remember: In Chicago politics and in Obama-land, there are
no coincidences.

VALERIE JARRETT:
GODMOTHER, CONFIDANTE, SLUMLORD

After graduating from Princeton University and Harvard Law
School, the bitterly oppressed Michelle Obama headed back to her
native Chicago to join the high-powered law firm of Sidley
Austin—the fifth-largest in the world. There, she griped about
having to do the duties of a second-year associate while she was a
second-year associate—demonstrating the trademark attitude of
entitlement and inflated ego that led the law partner who recruited
her to later describe her as "perennially dissatisfied."[18] At Sidley
Austin, she mentored and dated Barack Obama. She also
schmoozed an elite mover and shaker who would become the
Obamas' consigliere for life.

Democrat activist and real estate mogul Valerie Jarrett was a
protégée of Chicago mayor Richard Daley. A member of Hyde
Park's upper crust who hobnobbed with other wealthy black families in Martha's Vineyard, Jarrett later closely consulted with her
great uncle and Clinton crony super-lobbyist Vernon Jordan for
campaign advice. The Obamas don't make a move without Jarrett. She has been dubbed "the other side of Barack's brain"[19] and
"Barack's Rock."[20] In an October 2008 interview with the

Chicago Tribune, President Obama said of his relationship with Jarrett: "I trust her completely."[21]

Michelle Obama shares that same reverence and devotion. "I can count on someone like Valerie to take my hand and say, 'You need to think about these three things,'" she told the *New York Times.* "Like a mom, a big sister, I trust her implicitly."[22] Fellow Chicago crony Rahm Emanuel said on ABC News's *This Week with George Stephanopoulos*: "People should know that Valerie Jarrett is—and people do know—she is a very dear friend of the president-elect and a valuable ally of his, not only prior to running for president, in his Senate life, and just personally for Michelle and Barack."[23] Jarrett is also tight with Desirée Rogers. *Chicago Magazine* reported in 2000 that Jarrett and Rogers were two-thirds of a "high-profile Chicago sisterhood," along with publishing heir Linda Johnson Rice (who featured Mrs. Obama on the covers of *Ebony* and *Jet* magazines, donated $18,500 to the Obama Victory Fund, and kicked in $50,000 for the presidential inauguration). *Chicago Reporter* publisher Laura Washington called the women "politically savvy, tough-as-nails operators."[24]

After serving as finance committee chair for Obama's 2004 Senate campaign, senior advisor to the presidential campaign, and co-chair of the Obama-Biden presidential transition team, Jarrett was named "Senior Advisor and Assistant to the President for Intergovernmental Affairs and Public Liaison."[25] Whatever her title, Jarrett is the Obamas' political godmother.

Jarrett's father was a renowned hematologist/pathologist, her mother a child development expert. Her maternal grandfather, Robert Rochon Taylor, was the first black man to head the Chicago Housing Authority, and his father was the first black graduate of M.I.T., who went on to hold a top position at the Tuskegee Institute.[26] Educated at Stanford and University of Michigan Law School, Jarrett eschewed corporate law after a stint in the 1980s and instead became immersed in the Chicago political scene. As Daley's deputy chief of staff, Jarrett met Michelle Robinson (then engaged to Barack Obama) and persuaded her to leave her private law firm for a public-sector stint as Assistant Commissioner of Planning and Development. According to Obama lore, Michelle didn't take the job until Jarrett agreed to meet Barack for a two-hour "grilling" in July 1991.[27] With characteristic narcissism, Mrs. Obama reportedly told Jarrett: "My fiancé wants to know who is going to be looking out for me and making sure that I thrive."[28] Ask not what you can do for your law firm, but what your law firm can do for you!

From then on, everywhere that Jarrett went, Michelle Obama was sure to go. As the *New York Times* admiringly put it: "Ms. Jarrett swept the young lawyers under her wing, introduced them to a wealthier and better-connected Chicago than their own, and eventually secured contacts and money essential to Mr. Obama's long-shot Senate victory." As we shall see, those contacts were also essential to Michelle Obama's career. When Jarrett left Mayor Daley's office to chair the Chicago Transit Authority, Mrs. Obama trailed her and finagled a job as head of a citizens' advisory board. When Daley promoted Jarrett to head the Department of Planning and Development, Obama (with no expertise or training in planning or development) followed her again.

Jarrett served on numerous boards, including a prestigious position as Chairman of the Board of Trustees of the University of Chicago Medical Center. She began serving on the board in 1996, ascended to Vice-Chair in 2002, and took the helm as Chair in 2006. Jarrett was also Vice-Chair of the Board of Trustees at the University of Chicago, which she first joined in 2001. It is no coincidence that Mrs. Obama soon found herself smack dab in the middle of the university/corporate/community-organizing nexus forged by Jarrett.

What fawning social magazine profiles and fashion photo spreads of Jarrett leave out is the abominable history of her fail-

ures and neglect as a developer and manager of low-income housing. Jarrett's official White House biography proclaims that she
"became the President and Chief Executive Officer of The Habitat Company on January 31, 2007. She had served as Executive
Vice President of Habitat for 12 years."[29] You will not, however,
find pictures on the White House website of the dilapidated Grove
Parc Plaza apartment complex that Jarrett's Habitat Company
oversaw. Located just south of the University of Chicago, the federal Section 8 residential development had been built in the 1960s
to address affordable housing demands. Today, the Grove Parc
units are virtually uninhabitable and facing demolition.

Three cheers for community organizing, eh?

In an uncommonly hard-hitting investigative piece, the *Boston
Globe's* Binyamin Appelbaum blew the whistle on the rodent-
infested, sewage-clogged Chicago slums run by the Obamas' most
trusted confidante. Jarrett refused to answer any questions about
Grove Parc, "citing what she called a continuing duty to Habitat's
former business partners." A "continuing duty," presumably, to
whitewash the inconvenient truth about the failed public-private
partnerships the Obamas continue to promote in the White House:

> "They are rapidly displacing poor people, and these companies
> are profiting from this displacement," said Matt Ginsberg-
> Jaeckle of Southside Together Organizing for Power, a commu-
> nity group that seeks to help tenants stay in the same
> neighborhoods.
>
> "The same exact people who ran these places into the
> ground," the private companies paid to build and manage the
> city's affordable housing, "now are profiting by redeveloping
> them."[30]

In 2006, while Valerie Jarrett was executive vice president of Grove
Parc's management firm Habitat Company, federal inspectors

graded the condition of the complex a bottom-of-the-barrel 11 on a 100-point scale. Another Habitat-mismanaged property called Lawndale Restoration was so run-down that city officials urged the federal government to take over the complex.

Jamie Kalven, a veteran Chicago housing activist, told the *Boston Globe* about Barack Obama: "I hope there is not much predictive value in his history and in his involvement with that community." Kalven's hopes will likely be dashed. As Chicago goes, so goes the nation. Obama has made a career of rewarding failure, and no amount of overhyped "Hope" will change that. He sponsored a plethora of bills in the state Senate benefitting afford-able housing developers.[31] In February 2009, he unveiled a plan to set up a $1 billion Housing Trust Fund "to rehabilitate hous-ing in the nation's poorest neighborhoods."[32] "Trust Fund?" Try slush fund, bottomless pit, and eternal stimulus for the real estate moguls posing as saviors of urban America.

In one of those endless Chicago coincidences, Grove Parc Plaza Apartments—now targeted for demolition as a result of years of neglect by Obama's developer friends—sits in the shadows of the proposed site of the city's 2016 Olympics Stadium. Valerie Jarrett is vice chair of Chicago's Olympics committee.[33]

MRS. O. SCREWS THE POOR

Speaking of uncanny timing: It is no coincidence that Mrs. Obama found herself named to another University of Chicago Medical Center post—Executive Director of Community Affairs—the year her friend and mentor Valerie Jarrett became vice-chair of the medical center's board of trustees.

Nor is it a coincidence that Mrs. Obama found herself pro-moted in 2005 after her husband won his U.S. Senate race with Jarrett's invaluable aid. As "vice president for community and external affairs" and head of the "business diversity program," her annual salary nearly tripled from $122,000 in 2004 to $317,000 in 2005.[34] Even after she went on leave in 2007 to help her husband campaign, the hospital paid Mrs. Obama $62,709 in 2008,[35] prompting one skeptic to ask: "We know this is Chicago, but isn't $63,000 quite a lot for a no-show job?"[36]

Hospital officials asserted that Mrs. Obama was "worth her weight in gold,"[37] singling out her special relationship with—and her "new level of compassion"[38] for—the city's poor. But it was undoubtedly her relationships with her husband and political god-mother that held far greater value.

"[S]he just has a way about her, a real kindness," gushed the hospital's general counsel, Susan Sher.[39] But Sher was no disinterested observer. Her personal friendship with Mrs. Obama began years ago when the women worked together at Chicago City Hall; Sher headed up Mayor Daley's legal department when Michelle O. came on board.[40] In January 2009, Sher was tapped to serve as White House associate counsel.[41]

The high-paying "community affairs" post was another make-work job no one else at the university needed to do until Michelle Obama came along. And it was a job no one else needed to fill after she left. In January 2009, Mrs. Obama's indispensable job was eliminated as part of a massive restructuring to cut annual budget costs by 7 percent.[42] Naturally, Mrs. Obama's remnant duties were taken over by another old pal—Dr. Eric Whitaker, vice president at the University of Chicago Medical Center and an Obama basketball buddy from their Harvard grad student days.[43] Whitaker previously served as director of the Illinois Department of Public Health. Obama enthusiastically recommended him for that job. And, mother of all coincidences, you'll never guess to whom Obama made the recommendation:

> …Obama, then an Illinois state senator, gave a "glowing" reference for Whitaker to Tony Rezko, the now-convicted political

fixer who helped Gov. Blagojevich find people to run state agencies. Blagojevich hired Whitaker to be the state's public health
director.

Obama has said that's the only time he can recall talking to
Rezko—who was a major campaign fund-raiser for him and for
Blagojevich—about getting anyone a state job.

"Somebody who I do remember talking directly to Tony
about was Dr. Eric Whitaker," Obama told the *Sun-Times* in
March. "He and I played basketball together when he was getting his master's in public health at Harvard, while I was in law
school there. He had expressed an interest in that job. I did contact Tony, or Tony contacted me, and I gave him a glowing recommendation because I thought he was outstanding."[44]

"Outstanding?" Well, his ability to escape scrutiny and accountability for his sleazy ties to Rezko certainly is outstanding. Rezko
pulled the strings at the Illinois Health Facilities Planning Board
overseeing medical construction projects. Dr. Whitaker sat as the
stooge-in-charge of the board's budget. Rezko and his cronies controlled the board, "which they used to solicit kickbacks and payoffs, according to testimony at Rezko's trial," the *Chicago Tribune*
reported. Rezko is in jail. Whitaker remains the Obamas' close
confidante.

Crony out, crony in.

Unfortunately for many of Chicago's poor, Mrs. Obama didn't
depart until after she helped engineer a rather un-progressive and
unkind plan to dump low-income patients with non-urgent complaints from the medical center. Like the unfortunate residents of
Valerie Jarrett's slums, the unfortunate patients at Michelle
Obama's University of Chicago Medical Center got to see the real
meaning of Chicago liberal compassion. Under the Orwellian
banner of an "Urban Health Initiative," Mrs. Obama sold the
scheme to outsource low-income care to other facilities as a way

to "dramatically improve health care for thousands of South Side residents." The program guaranteed "free" shuttle rides to and from the outside clinics. It was old-fashioned cost-cutting and favor-trading repackaged as minority aid. Clearing out the poor freed up room for insured (i.e., more lucrative) patients. If a Republican had proposed the very same program and recruited black civic leaders to front it, Michelle Obama and her grievance-mongering friends would be screaming "RAAAAAAAAACISM!" at the top of their lungs:

> To ensure community support, Michelle Obama and others in late 2006 recommended that the hospital hire the firm of David Axelrod, who a few months later became the chief strategist for Barack Obama's presidential campaign.
>
> Axelrod's firm recommended an aggressive promotional effort modeled on a political campaign—appoint a campaign manager, conduct focus groups, target messages to specific constituencies, then recruit religious leaders and other third-party "validators." They, in turn, would write and submit opinion pieces to Chicago publications.
>
> The medical center's initiative provides a window into the close relationship between the Obamas, their associates at the University of Chicago and Axelrod, the strategist most central to Barack Obama's rise.

Some health care experts saw through Mrs. Obama and her public relations man, David Axelrod—yes, the same David Axelrod who is now Mr. Obama's senior adviser at the White House. The patient-dumping scheme was as transparent as Scotch tape. The University of Chicago Medical Center hired Axelrod's public relations firm, ASK Public Strategies, to promote Mrs. Obama's Urban Health Initiative. Axelrod had the blessing of Valerie Jarrett. His great contribution: Re-branding! Axelrod's firm recommended re-naming the initiative after "[i]nternal and external respondents expressed the opinion that the word 'urban' is code for 'black' or 'black and poor'.... Based on the research, consideration should be given to re-branding the initiative."[45] Axelrod and the Obama campaign refused to disclose to the *Washington Post* how much his firm received for its genius re-branding services.

No amount of repackaging could get around these bottom-line facts determined by the *Post*: As a hospital with non-profit tax status, the University of Chicago Medical Center receives special tax breaks for providing charity care. It spent a measly $10 million on charity care for the poor in fiscal 2007 when Mrs. Obama was employed there—"1.3 percent of its total hospital expenses, according to an analysis performed for *The Washington Post* by the bipartisan, nonprofit Center for Tax and Budget Accountability. That is below the 2.1 percent average for nonprofit hospitals in Cook County." Prominent South Side physician Quentin Young called the finding "shameful.... They are arguably, if not defrauding, then at least taking advantage of a public subsidy."

In February 2009, outrage in the community Mrs. Obama was supposedly so in tune with exploded after a young boy covered by Medicaid was turned away from the University of Chicago Medical Center. Dontae Adams's mother, Angela, had sought emergency treatment for him after a pit bull tore off his upper lip.[46] Mrs. Obama's hospital gave the boy a tetanus shot, antibiotics, and Tylenol and shoved him out the door. The mother and son took an hour-long bus ride to another hospital for surgery. I'll guarantee you this: You'll never see the Adams family featured at an Obama policy summit or seated next to the First Lady at a joint session of Congress to illustrate the failures of the health care system.

The *Chicago Tribune* reported that Mrs. Obama's hospital was "one of the only hospitals in the county that decreased its contribution to caring for uninsured patients from 2006 to 2007."

"New level of compassion," indeed.

Following the Adams incident, the American College of Emergency Physicians (ACEP) blasted Mrs. Obama and Mr. Axelrod's grand plan. The group released a statement expressing "grave concerns that the University of Chicago's policy toward emergency patients is dangerously close to 'patient dumping,' a practice made illegal by the Emergency Medical Treatment and Active Labor Act (EMTALA), and reflected an effort to 'cherry pick' wealthy patients over poor."[47]

Favoring the wealthy over the poor while posing as guardians of the downtrodden? Hey, it's the Chicago way. Just ask the tenants in Valerie Jarrett's tax-subsidized slums.

The shady business of Michelle Obama's non-profit hospital may not have garnered widespread national interest, but someone in the U.S. Senate was paying attention. In August 2008, Senate Finance Committee minority ranking member Republican Charles Grassley of Iowa pressed Mrs. Obama's employer for more information about its glaringly obvious patronage positions and the "troubling" patient- dumping scheme. Senator Grassley has investigated the lack of adequate charity care and financial accountability at tax-exempt medical institutions for years. Non-profit hospitals receive billions in tax benefits at the local, state, and federal levels in exchange for providing "community benefit" to earn the tax-exempt status. Yet, many of those institutions routinely deny uninsured patients charitable care. "We need to get a better handle on how nonprofit hospitals are fulfilling their requirement to serve the community in exchange for the generous tax breaks they receive," Senator Grassley concluded in April 2007 after congressional hearings found a lack of monitoring and standards. "This is especially important as policymakers talk about helping the uninsured."[48]

Senator Grassley pressed the University of Chicago Medical Center (UCMC) with pointed questions concerning the Urban

Health Initiative, another related "South Side Health Collaborative" program created by Mrs. Obama and funded with a federal grant in 2005, and Mrs. Obama's position. Among the requests for information he made in his 11-page, August 29, 2008, letter:

- Please describe each of these programs including their history, mission, accomplishments, and revenues and losses since inception as well as the reduction in emergency room visits resulting from these programs;
- Provide minutes of board or other executive meetings documenting the decision to launch these programs;
- Describe how UCMC funds these programs;
- Describe UCMC's marketing and outreach efforts for these programs....[49]

And regarding Mrs. Obama's position as Vice President of Community and External Relations: "[D]escribe the hiring and selection process for this position, including when the position was created, whether the vacancy was publicly announced, and the criteria for selection."

The hospital's response was due last fall. To date, it remains "under review" and unavailable for public consumption. And that's the way Illinois Democrats would like to keep it. The Senate's number two Democrat, Dick Durbin, bristled at Senator Grassley's pointed questions. After Senator Grassley expressed concern that the medical center was "culling the least profitable patients from its emergency room" and "losing sight of the public service that comes with tax-exempt status,"[50] Durbin huffed in September 2008: "The fact that Senator Grassley is questioning the work of the University of Chicago Medical Center—especially those programs aimed at reducing emergency department overcrowding and promoting preventive health—is troubling and shows that he simply doesn't understand the problems facing our hospitals today."[51]

To the contrary, Senator Grassley seems to understand the racket all too well.

DOCTORING THE BIDDING PROCESS

In his request for information from the University of Chicago Medical Center, Senator Grassley also raised the issue of the hospital's policy governing political activity, given its numerous ties to the Obamas: its policy regarding management salaries; its criteria for hiring and compensating public relations firms; and its process for selecting contractors.[52]

One of those contractors was businessman Robert Blackwell Sr., who owned an information technology firm, Blackwell Consulting Services. After Mrs. Obama received her promotion at the University of Chicago Medical Center, the hospital made unprecedented changes to its regular bidding process in order to include Blackwell in a competition to upgrade the center's internal computer network. Lo and behold, Blackwell Consulting won the contract and received a whopping $600,000-plus for its work. The university touted Mrs. Obama's minority vendor expansion as evidence of her neighborhood outreach accomplishments.[53] But Blackwell wasn't any ordinary minority business owner in need of a leg up.

Coincidentally, Chicago-style, Blackwell Sr. had served on a local literacy group board with Mrs. Obama for years.

Coincidentally, Chicago-style, Blackwell Sr. is a longtime friend of Barack Obama.

Coincidentally, Chicago-style, Blackwell Sr. and his namesake son had bailed out Barack Obama during hard times after his failed 2000 congressional campaign. At the time, Obama was earning less than $58,000 a year as a state senator. His total income from practicing law that year: zero. In 2001, his fortune took a turn for the better. He drummed up nearly $99,000 in lawyer's fees—$80,000 of it from the Blackwells. The Blackwell family, owners of the largest minority-owned consultancy in Chicago, had hired Obama to do legal work for the son's tech business, Electronic Knowledge Interchange (EKI), on an $8,000 per month retainer.[54] In 2002, the state senator reported $34,000-plus from legal services and speeches. Of that, $32,000 came from EKI—a relationship that ended when Obama set his sights on the U.S. Senate.

Coincidentally, Chicago-style, Obama had lobbied the Illinois legislature to give another Blackwell-owned business, Killerspin, a tourism promotion grant worth $50,000. The elder Blackwell's son, Robert Jr., owned the table tennis manufacturer and event producer and worked with longtime Obama aide Dan Shomon. The grant subsidized ping-pong tournaments at the University of Illinois-Chicago. Coincidentally, Chicago-style, Blackwell Jr. was one of Team Obama's top campaign financiers and a transition team member for former corruptocrat Governor of Illinois Rod Blagojevich.

Hospital officials vigorously denied any favoritism in the hospital contract award. But Blackwell Sr. himself admitted that the circumstances surrounding the work were "really fuzzy."[55] Besides, he explained to the *Washington Post*, Michelle Obama's "diversity program [was] critical because minorities don't always enjoy the informal social connections available to others." Some minorities may not enjoy those informal social connections. But the millionaire Blackwells certainly did.

Health care analyst David Catron points out a major disparity in what Blackwell's company was paid versus the normal market price for similar services. "It doesn't help appearances," Catron noted, "that the going rate for intranet upgrades rarely exceeds 10 percent of what Blackwell Consulting was evidently paid for the project in question."[56] Moreover, Catron observed, the preferential treatment actually put the hospital's status as a Medicare and Medicaid provider in jeopardy:

> Ironically, the Blackwell Consulting deal could have more lasting consequences for the University of Chicago Medical Center than for Michelle or Barack Obama. For a hospital, particularly one with UCMC's history, the appearance of impropriety associated with such a transaction has far more serious implications than it would for a garden variety corporation. Even if the bidding process broke no state or federal ethics statutes, it could well have violated the "conditions of participation" stipulated by the Centers for Medicare and Medicaid (CMS).
>
> CMS conditions of participation (COP) are standards to which health care providers must adhere in order to receive payment for services rendered to Medicare and Medicaid patients. The most basic COP, for hospitals, is to remain in good standing with the Joint Commission on Accreditation of Healthcare Organizations (JCAHO), which imposes stringent conflict of interest rules requiring a hospital to vet the "relationships" of medical staff, directors, and upper management "to ensure that its mission and responsibility to the clients and community it serves is not harmed by any professional, ownership, contractual or other relationship."
>
> ...According to financial reports released pursuant to its bond obligations, audits conducted in 2000 and 2001 found UCMC wanting: "CMS notified the corporation that it is not in compliance with certain of the Medicare Conditions of Participation for Hospitals...."
>
> UCMC still participates in the Medicare and Medicaid programs, which suggests that the hospital eventually cleared up its COP deficiencies. But another unsatisfactory CMS audit could

well be disastrous. As the financial reports mentioned above dryly phrase it, "Approximately 28.8% and 24.8% of the gross payment revenues of the corporation were derived from Medicare and Medicaid patients, respectively. As a result, any termination from the Medicare and Medicaid programs would adversely affect the corporation's financial position."

Of course, such a termination is not bloody likely with the Obamas running the health care show from the White House now. Pay for play, play for pay: it's the protection racketeers' code.

EARMARKS AND EDIFICE COMPLEX

In 2005, Barack Obama nearly tripled the amount of federal earmarks flowing to his wife's employer to over $310,000. In 2008, United States Senator Barack Obama raised eyebrows even further after disclosing his $1 million request for federal earmark money to help pay for the construction of a new hospital pavilion at his wife's place of work.[57]

When asked by the *Chicago Tribune* about the inherent impropriety of his water-carrying for Mrs. Obama's employer, the Agent of Hope and Change shrugged:

> I don't think that I was obligated to recuse myself from anything related to the university. When it comes to earmarks because of those concerns, it's probably something that should have been passed on to [Democrat Senator] Dick Durbin, and I think probably something that slipped through the cracks. It did not come through us, through me or Michelle, and Michelle has been very careful about staying separate and apart from any government work. But you could make a good argument that this is something that slipped through our cracks, through our screening system.[58]

Note the passivity and the pass-the-buck diffidence with which Obama met the question. It "should have been passed on" to someone else. It "slipped" through the cracks. It was the screeners' fault. But most importantly: "I don't think that I was obligated to recuse myself." Spoken like the faux reformer he has always been—and will continue to be during his presidency.

CORPORATE PERKS FOR ME, BUT NOT FOR THEE

Two-faced-ness is a trademark of the Obama power couple. While she profited handsomely from her crony corporate ties, Mrs. Obama earned the adoration of liberal women, the indulgent press, and capitalism-bashers across the country by ostentatiously "abandoning" the corporate life for motherhood, public service, and devotion to her husband's ambitions. "I wanted to have a career motivated by passion and not just money," she told the *New York Times*.[59] *Time* magazine marveled at how "this tough, razor-smart Chicago native had to sacrifice many of her own career ambitions along the way."[60] The *Washington Post* quoted her Best Friend Forever Valerie Jarrett lamenting her protégé's decision to step down from the University of Chicago Medical Center job in 2007: "It's a sacrifice for her to give that up."[61]

Vanity Fair reported that Mrs. Obama "sigh[ed] and roll[ed] her eyes as she recounted making the family decision to enter the presidential race. "Before I signed on, I had to know, in my mind and my heart, how is this going to work for me, and would I be O.K. with that? He wouldn't have done this if he didn't feel confident that I felt good about it, because it is a huge sacrifice. The pressure and stress on the family isn't new. But we entered this thing knowing it was going to be really, really hard." Once again, power-enabling Jarrett is quoted without a hint of irony extolling poor Michelle's hardships: "[S]he was willing to walk away from a huge salary potential and all the trappings of power that go along with it."[62]

The Great Goddess of Sacrifice shared her distastes and complaints about her financial and professional plights repeatedly on the campaign trail—moaning about her college debts here, sighing about the constant "struggle" to balance home and work life there. In Zanesville, Ohio, in February 2008, she complained to working women at a child care center about the Ivy League career track. Mrs. Obama made a special effort to bash those who pursue corporate law and hedge-fund management. Bear in mind: the median income for female workers in Zanesville and the surrounding county last year was $20,142, according to professor Ralph Reiland, and nearly a quarter of the city's population lives below the poverty line. Not exactly an audience at risk of jumping en masse into corporate law or hedge fund management. But the tin-eared Mrs. Obama is an incurable kvetch. Moreover, the remarks and visit struck many as opportunistic pretexts for her own therapy and passive-aggressive attack on rival Hillary Clinton (corporate law) and her daughter, Chelsea (hedge fund management employee). Reporter Byron York recounted the grievance-fest:

> "The salaries don't keep up with the cost of paying off the debt, so you're in your 40s, still paying off your debt at a time when you have to save for your kids," she says. "Barack and I were in that position," she continues. "The only reason we're not in that position is that Barack wrote two best-selling books. . . . It was like Jack and his magic beans. But up until a few years ago, we were struggling to figure out how we would save for our kids." A former attorney with the white-shoe Chicago firm of Sidley & Austin, Obama explains that she and her husband made the choice to give up lucrative jobs in favor of community service. "We left corporate America, which is a lot of what we're asking

young people to do," she tells the women. "Don't go into corporate America. You know, become teachers. Work for the community. Be social workers. Be a nurse. Those are the careers that we need, and we're encouraging our young people to do that. But if you make that choice, as we did, to move out of the money-making industry into the helping industry, then your salaries respond."[63]

"Don't go into corporate America?" Easy for you to say, sister. Mrs. O. parlayed her brief corporate stint into a cascading series of ever-more lucrative positions and promotions in the "helping industry." In turn, her hospital gig paid off sweetly thanks to the synergistic relationships she and her husband had with other corporate and political cronies. Here is a stark graph of Michelle Obama's "sacrifice" while working for the "helping industry" with a little help from hubby:[64]

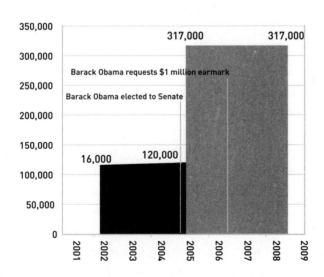

University of Chicago Expenditure on "Vice President for Community and External Affairs"

Chart used courtesy of Director Blue

While she played the martyr-ific about "leaving" the business world, Mrs. O. was quite happy to serve on a plethora of community and corporate boards that pumped up her income to $500,000 in 2007. Boo-freaking-hoo. Despite her great "sacrifices," the Obamas were able to afford pricy, five-figure private school tuition for both their daughters, and four-day-a-week personal training sessions for long-suffering mom. Feigning modesty, she downplayed her hefty contribution as bread-winner and filler of the family coffers: "Me? No! Barack had, like, four jobs, always," she laughs. "No, really. Barack's a hustler. I shouldn't say hustler, but he's a humper in terms of work."[65] The lady doth protest too much.

In June 2005, a few months after her husband was elected to the United States Senate, Mrs. Obama hustled a seat on the corporate Board of Directors of TreeHouse Foods, Inc. The food-processing company is "a leader in supplying high quality products and services to the private label and food service industries" including pickles, non-dairy creamer, and other items. The chairman of the board, Sam K. Reed, was a top executive at Kellogg and Keebler Foods. Other board members had decades of impressive business experience in packaging, food services, financial services, and corporate management. Mrs. Obama had her law degree, "community service," and her husband's last name. In fact, she took the position for exactly the opposite reason regular executives get on such boards. Instead of assuming the job to share corporate expertise and experience, she took the seat to acquire what she did not have. Reporting in spring 2007 on her re-election to the board, the UK *Telegraph* said that she took the position "to gain experience in the private sector."[66] The company put her on its audit and nominating and corporate governance committees. For her on-the-job-training and the privilege of putting her name and face on their literature, the company forked over $45,000 in 2005 and $51,200 in 2006—

as well as 7,500 TreeHouse stock options worth more than $72,000 for each year.

Must have been "really, really hard" for Mrs. Obama to pocket such easy cash for such little "work" without laughing all the way to the bank.

The corporation-bashing Mrs. Obama would have continued collecting her corporate TreeHouse money for nothing if it hadn't been for her husband's pesky pledge to pander to Big Labor and swear off Wal-Mart. The retail giant, you see, happens to be TreeHouse's biggest customer. And Wal-Mart is to Big Labor as sunshine is to Dracula. In May 2007, Obama told AFL-CIO workers in Trenton, New Jersey, that Wal-Mart was dead to him. "I won't shop there," he pledged with an eye toward embarrassing chief rival Hillary Clinton, who had served on Wal-Mart's board from 1986–1992. The AFL-CIO has waged relentless attacks on Wal-Mart, dubbing it the "Poster Store for Greed."[67] That, by extension, would make Mrs. Obama—all-too-happy recipient of a Wal-Mart dependent compensation package worth more than $100,000 in 2008, according to Securities and Exchange Commission records—a Poster Child for Ancillary Avarice.

Once again, Barack Obama took a diffident, passive view of the glaring conflict of interests his wife's professional position posed. In November 2006, he told the left-wing "Wake Up Walmart.com" organization that there was a "moral responsibility to stand up and fight" the company and to "force them to examine their own corporate values and what their policies and approaches are to their workers and how they are going to be good corporate citizens."[68] But as for walking the walk in their own household, neither of the Obamas felt any real moral responsibility to forego Wal-Mart-tainted cash. "Michelle and I have to live in the world and pay taxes and pay for our kids and save for retirement," Obama shrugged when questioned by Crain's

Chicago Business magazine about his wife's involvement with TreeHouse while he crusaded for corporate reform.[69]

Political expediency, alas, required that the candidate's wife step down when the issue reared its head after Obama's Wal-Mart-bashing during the presidential campaign cycle. True to form, Mrs. Obama turned the decision into an ostentatious display of self-sacrifice. "As my campaign commitments continue to ramp up, it is becoming more difficult for me to provide the type of focus I would like on my professional responsibilities," said Chicago's Joan of Arc in a resignation statement eight days after her husband declared his boycott of the stores stocked with food items processed and distributed by her TreeHouse colleagues. "My priorities, particularly at this important time, are ensuring that our young daughters feel a sense of comfort and normalcy in this process, and that I can support my husband in his presidential campaign to bring much needed change to this country."[70] Quick, get her a Purple Heart.

Instead of acknowledging her husband's rank hypocrisy, Mrs. Obama turned it into another moment of hero worship: "Barack is gonna say what needs to be said, and it's not going to, you know, necessarily matter...what I'm doing if it's not the right thing. He's going to do what's right for...the country. He's going to speak out. And he's going to, you know, implement his views as he sees fit....I see no conflict in that."

The see-no-conflict Obamas also saw no dissonance in the campaign's loud drumbeat for executive compensation reform. Obama made it a signature issue in the U.S. Senate and milked populist sentiment for limiting CEO pay as a Democratic presidential campaign. In February 2009, he took a grand stand to take "the air out of golden parachutes" and announced pay caps on company executives who received federal bailout funds[71] (just a first step toward nationwide pay caps for all corporate heads, as advocated by top House Democrat Barney Frank).[72]

Yet, while the CEO of Wal-Mart received $8.7 million in total compensation in 2005, the CEO of TreeHouse—a company dwarfed in size by Wal-Mart—received $26 million in total compensation in the same year. What is the definition of "excessive compensation"? It all depends on who's supplying the butter for your bread—and putting the pickles on the side plate.

THE OBAMAS AND THE AYERS: VERY FRIENDLY NEIGHBORS

Cronies come in all colors: White, black...and pinko, too. In 1997, Mrs. Obama launched the "University of Chicago Community Service Center" for "service learning, volunteerism and civic engagement." Her position of Associate Dean of Student Services and Director of the University of Chicago Community Service Center had not existed until it was created shortly after Barack Obama won the Democratic nomination in his first campaign for Illinois State Senate. The project provides training for the next generation of left-wing community organizers and "social justice activists." Investigative journalist Stanley Kurtz summed up the racket:

> In short, just after Barack Obama effectively secured a seat in the State Senate, the University of Chicago invented a new job, for which it hired Michelle Obama. In that job, Michelle would be able to channel University of Chicago students into the radical anti-American groups that she and her husband worked with, and whose ideology has received far too little scrutiny....
>
> So we see here an unusual arrangement between the University of Chicago and its new teacher/State Senator. The Senator's wife provides political cover for the university with the community, in return for which the university provides a previously non-existent and prestigious position to the Senator's wife,

which allows her to funnel students into hard-left political groups that sometimes provide campaign workers to the Senator. At any rate, that's how it looks.[73]

It was during her first year overseeing the program that Mrs. Obama arranged an eyebrow-raising panel on juvenile justice. The featured speakers? Barack Obama, newly elected Illinois State Senator and lecturer at the University of Chicago Law School, appeared with friend, neighbor, and unrepentant Weather Underground terrorist Bill Ayers. From the November 1997 university press release touting this grievance-mongering, crime-excusing event:

> The juvenile justice system was founded by Chicago reformer Jane Addams, who advocated the establishment of a separate court system for children which would act like a "kind and just parent" for children in crisis.
>
> One hundred years later, the system is "overcrowded, underfunded, over-centralized and racist," Ayers said.
>
> Michelle Obama, Associate Dean of Student Services and Director of the University of Chicago Community Service Center, hopes bringing issues like this to campus will open a dialogue between members of the University community and the broader community.
>
> "We know that issues like juvenile justice impact each of us who live in the city of Chicago. This panel gives community members and students a chance to hear about the juvenile justice system not only on a theoretical level, but from the people who have experienced it."[74]

A month after Ayers graced Mrs. Obama's summit with his radical presence, Mr. Obama wrote a glowing book review of Ayers's book about the juvenile court system, *A Kind and Just Parent: The*

Children of Juvenile Court. Mr. Obama called it "[a] searing and timely account of the juvenile court system, and the courageous individuals who rescue hope from despair."[75]

Not coincidentally, Ayers name-dropped his Hyde Park pal Barack Obama on page 82 of the book, along with Nation of Islam racial demagogue Louis Farrakhan—their own militant Neighborhood Watch captain:

> Our neighbors include Muhammad Ali, former mayor Eugene Sawyer, poets Gwendolyn Brooks and Elizabeth Alexander, and writer Barack Obama. Minister Louis Farrakhan lives a block from our home and adds, we think, a unique dimension to the idea of a "safe neighborhood watch": the Fruit of Islam, his security force, has an eye on things twenty-four-hours a day. I pass Farrakhan's mansion, offer a cheery wave to the Fruit, get a formal nod in response, and turn north two blocks across 47th Street, into the lap of urban blight.[76]

In another noteworthy Chicago coincidence, Ayers's Weather Underground terrorist partner and wife Bernardine Dohrn was hired in 1984 by the same white-shoe law firm, Sidley Austin, that later recruited Michelle Obama. Former federal prosecutor Andrew McCarthy reported:

> Ayers's father, Tom Ayers, a prominent Chicago businessman, was also deeply involved in the [education] reform effort. Interestingly, in 1988, while Obama and Ayers toiled on the same education agenda, Bernadine Dohrn worked as an intern at the prestigious Chicago law firm of Sidley Austin—even though she could not be admitted to the bar due to her contempt conviction for refusing to cooperate in a terrorist investigation. How could that happen? It turns out that Sidley was the longtime outside counsel for Tom Ayers's company, Commonwealth Edison. That

is, Ayers's father had pull at the firm and successfully pressed for the hiring of his daughter-in-law.[77]

Like Mrs. Obama's father, Ayers's father was a cog in the Daley political machine. Mrs. Obama and the elder Ayers's Commonwealth Edison shared another common bond: David Axelrod. Just as Mrs. Obama had relied on Axelrod's signature re-branding skills to sell an unpalatable program to Chicago's poor, Commonwealth Edison hired Axelrod's same public relations firm, ASK Public Strategies, to repackage a huge utility rate hike. *Newsweek* magazine reported that the company "took a creative lobbying approach, concocting a new outfit that seemed devoted to the public interest: Consumers Organized for Reliable Electricity, or CORE." This front group ran fear-mongering ads warning of a "California-style energy crisis" if the utility rate increase wasn't approved. Axelrod failed to disclose that the ads were funded by Commonwealth Edison. Transparency for thee, but not for Team Obama.

Now, hum with me to the tune of that famous Sesame Street ditty:

> *Oh, these are cronies in Michelle and Barry's neighborhood.*
> *They're the people that they met (and did business with, and socialized with, and traded favors with) each day...*

CHAPTER 3

VETTING THE VEEP
THE MYTH OF
"AVERAGE JOE" BIDEN

M ore than 30,000 people gathered in front of the Illinois Statehouse in Springfield in August 2008 to see Barack Obama announce his new running mate. Obama introduced his partner as an insider's outsider, a "working class kid from Scranton and Wilmington" who "has always been a friend to the underdog." Obama praised his choice for the vice presidency as a "unique public servant who is at home in a bar in Cedar Rapids and the corridors of the Capitol; in the VFW hall in Concord, and at the center of an international crisis." Above all, Obama said, "Joe Biden is that rare mix—for decades, he has brought change to Washington, but Washington hasn't changed him."

Biden was only too eager to claim the mantle of Working Class Hero in his acceptance speech. "Ladies and gentlemen, your kitchen table is like mine," he said. "You sit there at night after you put the kids to bed and you talk, you talk about what you need. You talk about how much you are worried about being able to pay the bills." Your kitchen table, however, is probably not like the one in the Biden family's $3 million, custom-made, lakefront home—built and paid for with generous help from wealthy banking executives and developers. As for worrying about paying the bills, Biden might imagine that he feels your pain, but he's a struggling Average Joe only in his own mind.

Non-delusional observers in Wilmington and Washington regard Biden's "Ordinary Man" mythology as a joke. Even the *New York Times* was forced to conclude: "A review of his finances found that when it comes to some of his largest expenses, like the purchase and upkeep of his home and his use of Amtrak trains to get around, he has benefited from resources and relationships not available to average Americans."[1] Like the Naked Emperor of Hope and Change in the Oval Office, the Court Jester of Reform in the vice president's office has no clothes. Lunch bucket Joe, ridin' the train to work, rubbin' elbows with the unwashed masses, stayin' true to his hard-scrabble upbringin', pinchin' pennies, and keepin' it real in D.C.? Guffaw. Biden's "just folks" image is one of Capitol Hill's most farcical false narratives.

His hometown newspaper, the *Wilmington News Journal*, snickered at a typical example of the Delaware senior senator's bluster on the campaign trail. Brandishing his blue-collar credentials during the vice presidential debate in October, Biden exclaimed: "Look, all you have to do is go down Union Street with me in Wilmington and go to Katie's Restaurant or walk into Home Depot with me where I spend a lot of time and you ask anybody in there whether or not the economic and foreign policy of this administration has made them better off in the last eight years."[2]

Just a few tiny problems with Average Joe's folksy anecdote, the *News Journal* pointed out.

Katie's Restaurant in Wilmington's Little Italy "closed in the 1980s"—and it wasn't on Union Street.[3] Home Depot Joe spending "a lot of time" shopping for garden tools and barbecue grill accessories? Not likely.[4] Biden's supporters brushed off the bogus brag as an innocent error. But this small gaffe epitomized Biden the blowhard. *News Journal* readers—the small-town folks Joe Biden claims to represent—tore into their dissembling senator:

> Joe Biden reminded us that "the Past [is] Prologue" and then went on to prove it by again resorting to the type of bizarre, completely made up, life experience tale that got him into trouble 20 years ago.... The past truly is prologue. [Twenty] years ago Biden lied about his academic record and assumed (with conviction and sincerity) the life story of a British Politician (Neil Kinnock).

> He tells these tales with such wonderful conviction and sincerity—but they are all lies—he just makes things up and seems to really believe what he makes up. That seems borderline delusional to me.

> Remember please that few of us have as high of an IQ as Joe Biden. He told us that in 1988 when he claimed to be an academic superstar (before his mediocre transcript was released). He also told us that the "Bidens were coal miners"—but that was actually the British Kinnock's story that Ol' Joe stole.

> It's not just that he lies, it's that he lies SO well that you think he really believes the stuff he makes up. That is a bit scary. But there is no better way to hone the art of lying with sincerity than 35 years in the Senate. I see the Obamabots are furiously scrambling to treat this as "just a minor" issue, nothing important. Come on people! In an attempt to appear all "folksy," ol' Just

Joe told a whopper, pretending that he regularly goes someplace to be with the regular folks. His dropping of a name that no longer exists in the locale (and hasn't for many years) proves he's lying about it. Now, I realize that, to the liberal (sorry, "progressive") mind set, what's a little lying in order to get the power to do good things for us all (whether we want it or not?) Still, a man who lies so blatantly about so-called little things (especially when it is so un-necessary) is a man who can't be trusted to be straight with us about anything.

I hate these politicians that claim to give straight talk and then can't even name a restaurant in their own back yard. I'm completely disgusted by him. And it only goes to show just how out of touch this man really is. Pathetic attempt to touch the heart strings of America and a pathetic attempt at seeming human.

Joe makes things up, and repeats them even when he knows they are not true. The worst one was about the truck driver who was driving when Neilia [Biden, Joe Biden's first wife] was killed in 1972. He maliciously lied when repeatedly saying that the (now-deceased) driver was drinking.[5] Lying about a dead man is the lowest of the low things one can do. That is not "being human" or "flubbing the facts." That is just plain evil. What worries me, as someone else said, is that this kind of pathological "straying from the truth" is evidence of a much more serious problem.

Biden's buffoonery continues to provide us with endless comic relief. Who can forget his assertion that "J-O-B-S" is a three-letter-word; that FDR promoted his economic recovery program on television in 1929 when only experimental TVs existed; or his mortifying call for a Democrat official in a wheelchair to rise and be recognized at a campaign event ("Stand up, Chuck, let 'em see ya.")? His serial denials of reality and Team Obama's whitewashing of his backroom enrichments, however, are no laughing matter.

While Biden boasts of being one of the Senate's least wealthy members, he has profited mightily from the perks of entrenched incumbency—earmarks, sweetheart real estate deals, and lucrative positions for his children. Biden prides himself on shaking up business as usual in Washington, but he used his clout to install his sons in positions of influence and fill the family coffers. While his running mate's wife admonished voters to spurn selfish jobs in corporate law and hedge-fund management, Biden helped grease the wheels for his son Hunter's entry into . . . er, corporate law and hedge-fund management. While he paid lip service to change, Beltway Joe engaged in business-as-usual string-pulling to set up son Beau to succeed him in the Senate. The elder Biden arranged for seat-warmer and former Biden chief of staff Ted Kaufman to hold the seat until 2010, by which time Beau Biden is scheduled to return from National Guard duty in Iraq in order to succeed his father.

Rest assured that the man who is a heartbeat from the presidency is every bit as self-serving a hypocrite as his boss.

MBNA: MAKING BIDEN'S NEPOTISM APPARENT

Thanks to friendly tax laws and corporate governance rules, the state of Delaware is a business haven.[6] For two centuries, the E. I. Du Pont de Nemours chemical empire dominated the landscape. Hundreds of thousands of corporations and other business entities flocked to incorporate in Delaware—from Chrysler and Coca-Cola to Google and Walt Disney—and take advantage of the enterprise-embracing climate. State legislation passed in the 1980s particularly encouraged the growth of credit card subsidiaries, including what would become the world's largest independent issuer of credit cards: MBNA. (The company was bought out by Bank of America in 2006.)

Former MBNA president Charles Cawley pioneered the "affinity card" concept by marketing credit cards branded by sports teams, business associations, unions, and other special interest groups. The 1990s saw business boom and jobs skyrocket. Spending ballooned, too: MBNA splurged on private golf courses, vintage cars, expensive watercraft, Lear and Gulfstream jets, a helicopter, a lavish $56 million downtown Wilmington headquarters, New England and Florida resorts, and even an in-house barbershop and nail salon. Managers gave away cars to top call-center employees.[7] The company amassed a $65 million art collection, including one of the biggest caches of Andrew Wyeth's work.[8] In 2001, MBNA surpassed DuPont as the state's largest private employer.[9]

MBNA spread the wealth in other ways, too. United States Senator Joe Biden was a prime beneficiary of the credit card behemoth's largesse. Since 1993, the company has been the number one donor to his campaigns.[10] (The overall partisan split of MBNA's political contributions was about 65 percent to Republicans and 35 percent to Democrats.) In 1996, Biden sold his two-decades-old mansion (a fixer-upper that had been slated for demolition) to MBNA vice chairman John Cochran. The asking price was $1.2 million. Cochran forked over the full sum. Biden then paid $350,000 in cash to real estate developer Keith Stoltz for a 4.2-acre lakefront lot. Stoltz had paid that same amount five years earlier for the undeveloped property. Stoltz told the *Wilmington News Journal* that "the residential real estate market was soft" at the time he sold the land to Biden. But "soft" for whom?

Stoltz was a well-off businessman who didn't appear to be in such financial dire straits that he needed to unload the property quickly in a weak market.

Reporter Byron York looked at comparable properties in Biden's neighborhood and found three cases where homes in the area went "for a good deal less than their appraised value. In comparison, it appears Cochran simply paid Biden's full asking price." Moreover, York's sources told him, "the house needed quite a bit of work; contractors and their trucks descended on the house for months after the purchase." Biden's office denied any sweetheart deals took place, but York noted:

> It appears that MBNA indirectly helped Cochran buy the Biden house. According to a statement in the company's filing with the Securities and Exchange Commission—in which it is required to detail the compensation of top officers—in 1996 MBNA reimbursed Cochran $330,115 for expenses arising from the move. The statement says $210,000 of that was to make up for a loss Cochran suffered on the sale of his Maryland home. An MBNA official declined to comment on the payment.
>
> Was the home sale a sweet deal for Biden? If you talk to people involved in real estate in the Wilmington area, you'll quickly find that few want to approach the question. "I wouldn't touch that with a ten-foot pole," said one agent. Another declined to say anything. And a third agent said only, "In my opinion, (Cochran) overpaid." None wanted to be identified by name.[11]

The Bidens' custom-built new home, with an adjacent carriage home for his mother, was built in Delaware's ritziest Chateau Country neighborhood. It is now worth at least $2.5 million ($1.8 million more than the couple owes) and is the Bidens' most valuable asset. Biden tapped campaign funds to pay for his home's lawn needs—worth a few thousand dollars every year.[12] A Biden spokesman attempted to wrap his boss in populist clothing, insisting that Biden's real estate transactions represented "a snapshot of life in America that I think folks can relate to."[13]

If "folks" means other politicians who have benefited from cozy deals followed by a shower of campaign donations, then the "snapshot" is certainly clear enough. Those "folks" can "relate." Developer Keith Stoltz, who sold the Bidens the land where his current house is built, has donated some $9,000 to Biden's campaigns; his parents, wife, and brother pitched in nearly $25,000 more to Biden since 1994. Not long after he sold his old house to MBNA's vice chairman, Quid Pro Joe started rolling in a new infusion of company cash. In the 1996 election season, MBNA forked over nearly $63,000 in bundled primary and general contributions from its employees to Biden.[14] Biden refused to answer questions about the deal through his campaign spokesman David Wade, who cited "time constraints."[15] Ordinary Joes don't have room in their schedules to answer pesky reporters.

To be clear, no laws were broken. These arrangements were simply a continuation of Biden's mutually beneficial, Beltway business-as-usual relationships with corporate benefactors. And that's just the tip of a massive iceberg.

Soon after Senator Biden's 1996 reelection, MBNA hired Biden's son, Hunter. The younger Biden graduated from Georgetown University and Yale Law School. There were no late-night, kitchen table sessions worrying about where the young Biden kid would find a job. MBNA apparently stands for "Making Biden's Nepotism Apparent." The company, described in its heyday as having a "cult"-like atmosphere, remained tight-lipped about Hunter Biden's duties, job description, and salary. He started out as a management trainee and quickly moved up at the firm, becoming a senior vice president by early 1998. Hunter Biden then clocked in with the Clinton administration's Commerce Department, specializing in "electronic commerce" issues for three years before returning to MBNA as a "consultant" in 2001. According to various reports, Hunter Biden received a $100,000 yearly retainer from MBNA to offer advice on "Internet and privacy law." He received consulting fees from MBNA from 2001 through 2005.[16] The consulting arrangement ended when Bank of America acquired MBNA in January 2006.

What was Hunter Biden's dear old dad up to during this time frame? Not coincidentally, Senator Biden was distinguishing himself as one of the few Democrats on Capitol Hill in favor of the credit card giant's pet project: bankruptcy reform. (Biden would end up voting four times in favor of the company's agenda in 1998, 2000, 2001, and in March 2005, when the Senate passed a new bankruptcy law by 74 to 25.)[17] The changes MBNA pushed for would make it more difficult for credit card holders to abandon their debt. (That's not a bad thing, in my opinion, but the bill hardly matches Biden's class-warfare populist rhetoric about the "rich.") Senator Biden took the unusual step of stuffing the MBNA-backed package into a foreign relations bill in 2000. Left-wing consumer groups blasted him for providing cover to other Democrats doing the credit industry's bidding. Congress passed the bill, but then-President Clinton vetoed it. In 2005, Biden was back championing another MBNA-supported bill to stiffen personal bankruptcy standards. Left-wing consumer groups lambasted the proposal. Like Senator Biden, Republican Senator John McCain supported the bill. One of their fellow Senate colleagues, however, singled out McCain for criticism:

> Like the president he hopes to succeed, Sen. McCain does not believe the government has a real role to play in protecting Americans from unscrupulous lending practices.... He would continue to allow the banks and credit card companies to tilt the playing field in their favor, at the expense of hardworking Americans.[18]

The 2005 bankruptcy measures, this Senator said in his aggressive attacks on McCain, amounted to "siding with banking industry lobbyists" and against the downtrodden. Who was this vocal senator opposed to the bankruptcy law changes championed by McCain and Biden? None other than Barack Obama, who would later pick Joe Biden as his running mate.

Notwithstanding Biden's legislative victories, MBNA's credit card operations (taken over by Bank of America in 2006) began to run into trouble after the U.S. economy cratered in late 2007. As a result of rising defaults, Bank of America's credit card services unit lost $373 million in the third quarter[19] and $204 million in the fourth quarter[20] of 2008. But don't feel too badly for Biden's MBNA pals. Bank of America has received $45 billion of taxpayer money via the Treasury Department's Troubled Asset Relief Program.[21]

The Obama campaign team knew Biden's MBNA ties would cause trouble and acknowledged that the relationship "was one of the most sensitive issues they examined while vetting the senator for a spot on the ticket."[22] But they pressed forward anyway. Glossing over the cognitive dissonance, Team Obama vehemently denied any ethical improprieties on Biden's part. But the incestuous entanglements do not pass the smell test.

MEET THE RAINMAKERS

Hunter Biden raked in the MBNA consulting payments while serving as a founding partner of the Washington, D.C., lobbying firm, Oldaker, Biden & Belair, which opened shop in 2002. While Biden's son was raking in the bucks as a well-connected lobbyist, Barack Obama was boasting that lobbyists "won't find a job in my White House." In November 2007, Obama vowed at a campaign event in Spartanburg, South Carolina:

One year from now, we have the chance to tell all those corporate lobbyists that the days of them setting the agenda in Washington are over. I have done more to take on lobbyists than any other candidate in this race—and I've won. I don't take a dime of their money, and when I am President, they won't find a job in my White House. Because real change isn't another four years of defending lobbyists who don't represent real Americans—it's standing with working Americans who have seen their jobs disappear and their wages decline and their hope for the future slip further and further away. That's the change we can offer in 2008.[23]

But those evil corporate lobbyists found plenty of room in Joe Biden's coffers—and offered *him* plenty of change. "He's no stranger to how the system works," David Williams, vice president of policy for Citizens Against Government Waste, put it politely.[24] According to the Center for Responsive Politics, the lobbying industry kicked in $344,400 for Biden's campaigns since 1989, making lobbyists his tenth largest contributing industry. During the 2008 election cycle, he took in $43,000 more than the average $81,700 that lobbyists gave senators. One of Biden's top 20 most generous contributors over time was lobbying firm Blank Rome LLP, whose employees donated $68,200.[25]

What was the effect of these lobbying contributions? Joe Biden himself said it best at a campaign event in December 2007 addressing a supporter named "Lynn":[26]

Lobbyists aren't bad people. Special interest groups are not bad people, but guess what? They're corrosive. People who accept the money from them aren't bad people. But it's human nature. You go out, Lynn, and bundle $250,000 for me—all legal—and then you call me after I'm elected and say, "Joe I'd like to come and talk to you about something." You didn't buy me, but it's human nature. You helped me. I'm going to say, "sure, Lynn, come on in."

Obama and Biden spokespeople repeatedly emphasized that the younger Biden never lobbied his father directly—which is entirely beside the point. No direct lobbying is necessary. The buying of access works by wink and nods. Carrying the Biden name greased the wheels. As Biden the Elder said, "It's human nature." Or, as transparency advocate Bill Allison of the Sunlight Foundation explained: "It's not necessarily that the father's going to do favors for the child's clients, but that every other member knows who his father is and what the connection is and that can carry a lot of influence as well."[27]

ABC News reported that, since 2003, Hunter Biden has lobbied for drug companies, universities, and other clients who have paid his firm "a total of $3.8 million, jumping from $20,000 in 2003 to $1.6 million in 2007," including "drug research companies Achaogen and Pulmatrix, Sharp & Barnes on internet gambling, and six universities: Regis University, St. Joseph's University, St. Xavier University, University of Detroit Mercy, Xavier University, and University of Scranton which is located in his father's home-town."[28] In the first half of 2008 alone, Hunter Biden worked on accounts worth nearly a half million dollars for the firm.

Coincidentally, some of the educational earmark projects brought lobbyist Hunter Biden into contact with that outspoken foe of lobbyists and earmarks, Senator Barack Obama. Obama secured $192,000 for Hunter Biden's client St. Xavier University, which is located in suburban Chicago. Hunter Biden first contacted the small Roman Catholic institution in 2005 with the promise of winning federal earmark funding. An official for the school told the *Washington Post* that he "found Biden's parentage a selling point."[29] Nepotism has its privileges. Biden took school officials around to members of the Illinois delegation. Small world! Senator Barack Obama was on their earmark itinerary.

Another Hunter Biden client in Chicago: Thorek Memorial Hospital. Senator Obama went to bat for the cancer treatment center, seeking $2 million in federal funding. Hunter Biden represented Thorek Memorial and earned $120,000 representing the hospital. In all, Senator Obama pursued more than $3.4 million in congressional earmarks for clients who just happened to be represented by Hunter Biden.[30] Small world!

One major client of Hunter Biden's, biotech firm Achaogen, nailed a $24.7 million Pentagon contract for anthrax-threat mitigation in October 2006[31] and a $26.6 million contract for biodefense research in March 2009.[32] Lobbyist disclosure filings show that Achaogen paid Oldaker, Biden & Belair $20,000 in the last quarter of 2006 and a total of $90,000 in 2008.

Two days after Obama tapped Biden for the vice presidential slot, Hunter Biden quit the "corrosive" lobbying business.[33] But the son's resignation did not end questions about the family's influence peddling racket. In fact, the "resignation" was partial. While foregoing any more lobbying fees for his work with one firm, he continues to lobby at Oldaker, Biden & Belair on behalf of medical and academic clients.[34]

The "Oldaker" in "Oldaker, Biden & Belair" is William Oldaker. Oldaker represented everything Barack Obama purported to detest. Nicknamed "The Rainmaker," Oldaker had served as Biden's former fundraiser/campaign treasurer/general counsel and presidential campaign adviser before establishing his lobbying shop with Hunter Biden as co-partner.

Oldaker's Democrat machine days stretched back to 1980, when he served as top counsel for Teddy Kennedy's 1980 Democratic presidential bid. What distinguished Oldaker was his special expertise in campaign finance law. From 1968 to 1975, Oldaker served as general counsel at the Federal Election Commission. He parlayed that niche into a lucrative, double-dealing career. As a *Legal Times* profile in 2006 noted, "Oldaker is one of the gurus of election law, and over the past quarter-century as a lobbyist, he has advised campaigns and handled the financial books for more than 20 politicians. He also has signed off on quarterly statements as treasurer for 26 political action committees, according to FEC records."[35]

The mingling of lobbying and campaign work raised red flags on Capitol Hill, but not enough for Biden to completely cut himself off from Oldaker. He dropped Oldaker as his campaign treasurer, but retained him to do election law work. Biden's chief of staff in 2006, Alan Hoffman, said he spoke with Oldaker "for campaign advice almost weekly."[36] The employees of Oldaker's firm earned more than $140,000 in legal fees incurred by Biden's failed presidential bid in 2008.[37] Other Oldaker staffers held positions as Biden's PAC treasurer or assistant treasurer until early 2009, according to the *Wilmington News Journal*.[38]

In addition, Oldaker created another lobbying arm that worked out of the same office as the firm he co-founded with Biden's son. The National Group specialized in securing federal earmarks—taxpayer funds for lawmakers' pet projects—from Oldaker's former employer and lobbying client, Sen. Biden. Oldaker helped drum up hefty sums for the University of Delaware, which has paid his firm $1.5 million in legal fees. Oldaker also helped secure tens of millions in earmarks for university projects including defense research, a student-exchange program, and a drug-and-alcohol-studies program.[39]

The *Wilmington News Journal* reported in June 2008 that Oldaker garnered nearly $70 million from the Delaware congressional delegation for the University of Delaware. Though the university's main source of federal funding is still annual grants of about $100 million, the university has secured another $68 million from the Delaware delegation in the five years since The National Group's lobbyists began working for UD. In the three years before The National Group began lobbying for UD, the university averaged about $7.4 million a year in earmarks obtained through the Delaware delegation, according to Sen. Biden's office. The firm's price tag for UD is listed in federal reports as $240,000 a year.[40]

Another notable National Group client: the Adler Planetarium in Chicago. None other than Senator Barack Obama requested $300,000 in federal earmark funding for the institution, which he jacked up by 900 percent to $3 million, between 2006 and 2008. The planetarium's board of trustees chairman was Frank Clark—a top Obama donor and mega-bundler who raised between $200,000 and $500,000 for Obama's presidential campaign.[41] Several other officers and trustees of the planetarium had also contributed to Obama's campaigns. The non-profit planetarium was hardly needy; it had more than $33 million in assets at the end of 2006. Obama had sought, but was unsuccessful in securing, money to replace the planetarium's projector and other theater equipment. Happily for the planetarium, former Illinois Representative Rahm Emanuel—who subsequently became White House chief of staff—stuffed a $900,000 earmark for the planetarium into the $410 billion spending bill President Obama signed in 2009.[42] And the benefit to Biden buddy Oldaker? In 2008, the planetarium paid the National Group $120,000 for lobbying services—triple its lobbying expenses from 2002.[43]

The working relationship between Senator Biden's office and his close advisor and son's lobbying firm was so intimate that staffers grew accustomed to receiving phone calls from The National Group at the beginning of every appropriations cycle— with expected follow-up calls later.[44] On speed-dial, no doubt.

THE BIDEN FAMILY AND
TRIAL LAWYERS: BFF!

"Average Joe" Biden wants you to believe he hangs with the regular guys at Home Depot. But the BFFs (Best Friends Forever!) of the Bidens wear pin-striped suits, not coveralls. They carry briefcases, not toolboxes. And you can bet they're not driving pick-up trucks.

One lucrative cloud seeded by "rainmaker" William Oldaker showered generous benefits on both Hunter Biden and his dad. In 2005–06, the Chicago-based personal injury law firm of Cooney and Conway paid Oldaker, Biden & Belair $220,000 to push its tort reform proposals.[45] At the same time, Cooney and Conway gave Senator Biden's political campaigns more than $70,000.[46] The firm's founding co-partner John Cooney told the *Chicago Daily Law Bulletin* that he struck up a friendship with Biden in 2004 over a legislative battle before Biden's Senate Judiciary Committee. Cooney was part of a small group that strategized with Biden on campaign matters at his Delaware home.[47] Cooney and Conway represent clients claiming asbestos-related injuries. Biden sided with the trial lawyers, actively opposing measures to reduce frivolous lawsuits and reduce the returns on future lawsuits.

Other heavy-hitting law firms that pitched in to Biden's campaigns: Baltimore-based Peter Angelos, whose law firm gave Biden $156,250; Wilmington-based Young Conaway Stargatt & Taylor, which kicked in $127, 979; and Pachulski Stang Zielhl & Jones, which donated $145,625, according to *The American Lawyer*.[48] Philip Howard, author and founder of Common Good, a bipartisan coalition that advocates for legal reform, summed up his record: "Senator Biden has a pretty clear record of being close to the trial lawyers. To people who are interested in restoring reliability to the legal system, he's probably unlikely to be the champion."[49]

Disgraced trial lawyer Richard Scruggs donated $11,500 to Biden in 2008. After Scruggs was convicted of attempting to bribe a federal judge, Biden tried to show his ethical bona fides by donating the money to a worthy charity. But Biden couldn't steer clear of nepotism. The money ended up with the National Prostate Cancer Coalition—a charity where, *The American Lawyer* pointed out, Biden's son Hunter sits on the board of directors.[50]

Another Biden family pal in the trial lawyers' community: Jeff Cooper. With his partner John Simmons, the 39-year-old Cooper built one of the biggest asbestos litigation firms in the country. SimmonsCooper, based in Madison County, Illinois, has donated a whopping $196,050 to Biden's campaigns since 2003, according to the nonpartisan Center for Responsive Politics in Washington, D.C. In that same time frame, the firm poured $6.5 million into lobbying against the same tort reform bill that fellow asbestos litigators Cooney and Conway opposed—and which Senator Biden worked hard to defeat.[51] Without a hint of irony, Cooper extolled Biden's anti-tort reform stance: "He understands the plight of the little guy and is against huge corporate interest."[52] But what Biden did was help fuel lucrative business for the tort bar. When courts in SimmonsCooper's home base in Illinois finally started cracking down on what had become "America's No. 1 judicial hellhole" for filing out-of-control tort claims, the firm turned east. And in Joe Biden's Delaware, they created a new sanctuary. The *Wall Street Journal* explained:

> SimmonsCooper is a big asbestos player, and Madison County was until recently one of America's meccas for jackpot justice. But the story gets better: Mr. Biden has been helping the tort bar turn his home state of Delaware into a statewide Madison County.

SimmonsCooper made hundreds of millions of dollars on asbestos cases in Madison County, but that started to change in 2004. The business community helped to elect conservative Lloyd Karmeier to the Illinois Supreme Court. Madison County Circuit Judge Daniel Stack also took over the asbestos docket, was determined to clean house, and began dismissing suits filed by residents outside his jurisdiction.

SimmonsCooper and other firms started shopping for a new legal goldmine. And where better than Delaware? Many companies incorporate there, which means a list of defendants usually includes a Delaware target. Beginning in mid-2005, SimmonsCooper began transferring its suits to Bidenland.

The trial bar's strategy has been to overwhelm Delaware's once-sensible legal system, taking advantage of rules that pressure companies to settle. In the 22 months following Simmons-Cooper's first asbestos filing in Delaware, the state was hit with 412 suits, primarily from SimmonsCooper and fellow asbestos giant Baron & Budd.

According to the *Madison County Record*—a legal journal that has doggedly followed this story—clerks in Wilmington were "working nights and weekends to keep up" with the filings. The trial lawyers drew sympathetic judges that have already overseen big verdicts against defendants, primarily Detroit auto makers. Plaintiffs have obtained certain procedures that raise the costs of defense, and restrict defendants' ability to take discovery.[53]

Cooper first befriended Biden's sons, Hunter and Beau, before deepening his financial and political relationship with their dad. There's a personal connection: Cooper's wife went to high school with Hunter Biden's wife, Kathleen. And as Biden the Elder was carrying water for the trial lawyers in the U.S. Senate, SimmonsCooper was working another Biden channel through the Wilmington,

Delaware, law firm of Bifferato, Gentilotti & Biden, where Joe's son and Hunter's brother, Beau, was a partner. SimmonsCooper found Delaware an attractive new magnet for its asbestos litigation racket, because many of the firm's defendants included clients who had incorporated in the state.

SimmonsCooper recruited Beau's firm to work as co-counsel on Delaware asbestos litigation cases. The Illinois firm steered dozens of cases Beau Biden's way. He dropped an asbestos defense client to accommodate his deep-pocketed family friend.[54] Simmons-Cooper then forked over $35,000 to Beau Biden's successful run for state attorney general in 2006. Steve Hantler, president of the American Justice Partnership Foundation, observed, "Delaware is fast becoming asbestos lawsuit central.... A tsunami of lawsuits being filed by the SimmonsCooper firm, along with the flow of campaign dollars to Delaware politicians, is quite the troubling coincidence."[55]

Even more troubling was the financial partnership Hunter Biden and his Uncle James (Senator Biden's brother) attempted to forge with SimmonsCooper. The Bidens approached Simmons-Cooper with a proposition: Team up with the family to buy a hedge fund investment firm for $21 million. Cooper agreed to chip in $2 million in exchange for 10 percent interest. The Bidens negotiated the hedge fund buyout of Paradigm Global Advisors with business partner Anthony Lotito Jr. in 2006.[56] As Paradigm chairman, Hunter Biden oversaw half a billion dollars of client money invested in hedge funds while remaining a lobbyist at Oldaker, Biden & Belair.

But things fell apart. In their haste to clean up the Biden image, they ended up with dirtier hands. According to Lotito, the Bidens pursued the venture to help get Hunter Biden out of the lobbying business before Dad launched another presidential campaign. The *Madison County Record*, which tracked the dealings of the Bidens and SimmonsCooper closely, laid out the timeline:

According to court records filed by Lotito, Joe Biden wanted Hunter Biden to find a different line of work because he couldn't afford to run for president as father of a lobbyist.

Lotito claims he and James Biden discussed Hunter Biden's job prospects.

Lotito met James Biden in 2002 and they invested together in 2005, according to Lotito.

Lotito introduced James Biden and Hunter Biden to lawyer John Fascian[a], and the four began planning to buy Paradigm Capital Management.

Majority owner James Parks had started Paradigm in 1991 and successfully promoted it as less volatile than most hedge funds.

Everyone agreed that the Bidens and Lotito would form a corporation to buy 54 percent of Paradigm for $21.3 million in cash.

They would install Hunter Biden as chief executive officer at a salary of $1.2 million.

In April 2006, they formed LBB Limited Liability Corporation.

In May 2006, SimmonsCooper invested $1 million.

In June 2006, according to Lotito, the Bidens told him to stay away.

In August 2006, according to Lotito, the Bidens formed a corporation, executed a promissory note for $8.1 million, and purchased Paradigm's assets.

In September 2006, Lotito signed an agreement relinquishing his third of LBB.

He sued the Bidens in January 2007, alleging fraud and breach of fiduciary duty.[57]

Lie down with shady partners, get up with a public relations nightmare. Lotito maintained that the Bidens cut a secret deal and tried to fraudulently trick him into signing away his interest in the LLC that they had formed together. In court filings, Lotito's lawyer asserted that the Bidens used their political clout to intimidate his client: "Ultimately, the Bidens threatened to use their alleged connections with a former U.S. Senator to retaliate against counsel for insisting that his bill be paid, claiming that the former Senator was prepared to use his influence with a federal judge to disadvantage counsel in a proceeding then pending before that court."[58]

The Bidens shot back that Lotito had neglected to mention that the lawyer he connected them with, John Fasciana, was a crook. Fasciana had been convicted in July 2005 on federal charges of conspiracy and wire and mail fraud over a scheme to cheat Electronic Data Systems (Ross Perot's computer services company) of millions of dollars. Fasciana was sentenced in 2008 to four years in prison, but has appealed the case.[59] He sued the Bidens for nearly $200,000 in legal fees; they countersued Fasciana for overbilling them and committing fraud by concealing his criminal conviction. Hunter and James Biden also countersued Lotito in February 2007 seeking $10 million. The Bidens asserted that Lotito "hid debts and falsely claimed he held securities licenses to lure them as partners in the planned $21.3 million acquisition," the *Washington Post* reported.[60] "Had James and Hunter Biden known the truth about Anthony Lotito, they never would have gone into business with him," their complaint alleged.

Where did this leave SimmonsCooper, which had kicked in half of a $2 million investment at the request of the Bidens? The Illinois firm had withdrawn from the deal after watching $1 million of its investment allegedly squandered by Lotito. The investment "converted to debt,"[61] which Hunter and James Biden then attempted to shift to Lotito. A New York judge didn't go along with the Bidens' attempt to play the victim card. In May 2008, he rejected their bid after concluding they should have vetted the fund more carefully and performed their own due diligence. Cutting through the ploy, the judge ruled that the Bidens' counterclaims "seek only to foment uncertainty and chaos between the parties in the event that plaintiff is successful in presenting the main claims.... Such pleading will not be countenanced." Moreover, he ruled, "Certainly defendants do not claim that the law permits sophisticated investors to rely on whatever representations a potential advisor makes without the need for a diligent inquiry by defendants, and that such representations are actionable if they wind up to have been faulty."[62]

In January 2009, court papers announced that the legal fracas had been settled confidentially[63]—preventing any disclosure or discussion whatsoever regarding the nature of the settlement or the subject matter of the action. The record did note that the lawsuit was resolved "without cost to any party." For anyone paying close attention, however, the cost to the Biden family's "just folks" reputation was clear. Alas, the settlement didn't end the sordid story for the Bidens.

They and Lotito were named defendants in yet another lawsuit, this one filed by investor Stephane Farouze, global head of fund derivatives for Deutsche Bank. Farouze alleges in his $10 million suit that the defendants agreed to buy his membership interest in Paradigm knowing they didn't have the money to back up their promise.[64] Farouze asserts that the Bidens "engaged in an elaborate scheme to defraud" him. In February 2009, Manhattan Supreme Court Judge Bernard Fried halted court proceedings for 45 days and ordered the two parties to submit to mediation.[65]

Adding yet another layer of taint, the *Wall Street Journal* reported in February 2009 that the Bidens' sketchy hedge funds were marketed exclusively by scandal-plagued Texas financier R. Allen Stanford, who is facing Securities and Exchange Commission charges of engaging in an $8 billion fraud scheme. Stanford-related companies marketed the Bidens' funds to investors, the *Journal* disclosed, "and also invested about $2.7 million of their own money in the fund, according to a lawyer for Paradigm."[66] Stanford's investment in Paradigm was set aside for a special court-appointed receiver after the SEC probe was launched. The news "triggered a few client defections," according to the Bidens' hometown *Wilmington News Journal*.[67] The Bidens responded, as always when questions were raised about their dubious associates, with defensive denials issued through intermediaries: "There is no connection between the Bidens and Allen Stanford or Stanford period, full stop," Biden lawyer Marc LoPresti said. "There never was any meeting between any member of the Biden family, no phone calls, zero correspondence."

And yet, LoPresti told the paper that the Bidens' hedge funds worked out an agreement with Stanford entitling him to share in a portion of their fund's management and performance fees. Either LoPresti is lying, or the Bidens failed to vet their high-risk business partners.

There's more: Financial blogger John Hempton reported that Paradigm was closely connected with a separate hedge fund accused of fraud. Ponte Negra Capital shared its main New York City address with Paradigm's office, Hempton wrote, and also shared a few staffers between the two firms.[68] Ponte Negra Capital had its assets frozen by the Securities and Exchange Commission in April 2009 after the panel obtained an emergency court order "to freeze the assets of a Connecticut-based money manager and the hedge funds that he controls, alleging that he forged documents, promised false returns, and misrepresented assets managed by the funds to illicitly raise more than $30 million from investors."[69] Ponte Negra Capital was marketed by a company called Onyx, which also handled marketing duties for both Paradigm and Ponzi king Allen Stanford.[70]

BIDEN'S SLEAZY REZKO CONNECTION

Perhaps the Bidens' unfortunate interlude with Paradigm was an anomalous case of bad luck. Or perhaps it was symptomatic of the company the Bidens keep. Senator Biden's good friend of thirty years, Joseph Cari, served as Biden's Midwest field director for the 1988 Biden for President campaign. Cari raised money for the Democratic Party for decades, serving as a key fundraiser for former president Bill Clinton, former vice president Al Gore, the Democratic Senatorial and Congressional Campaign Committees, the Democratic National Committee, and scores of individual candidates. Biden returned to Cari for advice on his second presidential run in 2008. Cari's advice should have been: Stay away from me, buddy.

Three years earlier, Cari had confessed to his role in an $850,000 kickback scandal tied to the political fund-raising operation of Illinois Governor Rod Blagojevich (who was later impeached). The scheme was directed by Barack Obama's old Chicago crony, Tony Rezko. Cari pleaded guilty to attempting to commit extortion in his role as a partner and managing director of a private equity firm that had received $35 million from the Illinois state teachers' public pension plan.[71] Cari threatened to withhold $85 million in teacher retirement system funds from a real estate investment firm unless it hired a consultant of his choosing. At the behest of co-defendant Stuart Levine, who sat on the Teachers Retirement System board, Cari executed a plan to squeeze political or charitable contributions from their cherry-picked consultants, who were to be hired by the private firms in exchange for public pension fund investments.[72]

A superseding indictment from February 2005 illuminates the Rezko connection in this convoluted fraud scheme:

> The Scheme To Defraud: 2. Beginning no later than in and
> about the spring of 2003 and continuing through at least in or

about July 2004, in the Northern District of Illinois, Eastern Division, and elsewhere, STUART LEVINE and ANTOIN REZKO, also known as "Tony Rezko," defendants herein, together with Joseph Cari, Steven Loren, Jacob Kiferbaum, Individual A, and others known and unknown to the Grand Jury, devised and intended to devise, and participated in, a scheme and artifice to defraud the beneficiaries of TRS [The Teachers' Retirement System of the State of Illinois] and the people of the State of Illinois, of money, property, and the intangible right to LEVINE's honest services, by means of materially false and fraudulent pretenses, representations, and promises, and material omissions, and in furtherance thereof used the United States mails and other interstate carriers, and interstate and foreign wires, which scheme is further described below.

Overview of the Scheme: 3. It was part of the scheme that defendants REZKO and LEVINE, with the assistance of Cari, Loren, Kiferbaum, Individual A, Individual B, and others, fraudulently used and sought to use the position and influence of LEVINE and other members of the TRS Board of Trustees and the Planning Board to obtain financial benefits for REZKO, LEVINE, and their nominees and associates. In the course of the scheme, REZKO and LEVINE solicited and demanded millions of dollars in undisclosed kickbacks and payments, and received and directed hundreds of thousands of dollars in actual undisclosed kickbacks and payments, for the benefit of REZKO, LEVINE, and their nominees and associates, from investment firms seeking to do business with TRS, and from Kiferbaum.[73]

The *Chicago Sun-Times* reported this gem of a coincidence:

On the day Cari's name first surfaced in the federal probe of the state Teachers Retirement System, the former finance chairman for the Democratic National Committee and for the Democratic

Senatorial Campaign Committee was to have hosted a Biden fund-raiser in Chicago. Cari was a no-show at that July 25, 2005, event.

Offering Cari a vote of confidence at the time, Biden said, "All I know is Joe Cari is a friend, and he's an honorable guy, but I don't know anything beyond that."[74]

"Honorable guy?" In the midst of his extortion scheme, federal prosecutors quoted Cari telling a target: "This is how things are done in Illinois."[75] Cari would move on to testify at the federal corruption trial of Obama pal Tony Rezko, shining light on pay-to-play promises offered to Cari by disgraced Illinois Governor Rod Blagojevich.

Birds of a feather corrupt the system together. But as usual, Go Along-Get Along Joe don't know nuthin'.

RIDING THE RAILS

One thing Joe does know is trains. And he made sure everyone in America knew about his love for taxpayer-subsidized Amtrak. He repeatedly told the folksy story of riding the rails from Wilmington to Washington, D.C., and back—just your ordinary working dad taking public transportation daily to earn a living and get back home to his family. He brought journalists with him on the journey and schmoozed with passengers to demonstrate his Everyman cred. Citing his train travel, Beltway journalist turned Obama flack Linda Douglass gushed about Biden: "He's not a creature of Washington."[76] She dug deeper: "He goes home on the train, eats dinner with his family, he's the epitome of a regular guy."

This Joe the Commuter narrative demonstrates the exact opposite—that Biden is indeed the consummate creature of Washington. As an Amtrak-designated Champion of the Rails, he has lobbied for decades to preserve the government-funded, money-losing Amtrak operation. He signed on as a co-sponsor of legislation reauthorizing the beleaguered government enterprise, which received $1.3 billion in federal subsidies in 2008. Former President George Bush signed the bill in October 2008, doubling funding for Amtrak to an estimated $13 billion over five years. The rail line is important to Biden's home state's economy; the tiny state of Delaware doesn't have commercial air service.[77]

Joe Biden's daily trips to D.C. on the high-speed Acela line were out of reach for your average blue-collar Joes. It's a $172 round trip from Wilmington, or more than $1,000 for a monthly pass. Unlike ordinary folks, U.S. Senate members are eligible for a federal discount—or, like Joe Biden, they can use campaign money to pay for trips if they involve a campaign-related meeting or event. The *New York Times* found that Biden's Amtrak campaign expenses "have remained high even in years without elections, when he was not actively campaigning and his committee retained a handful of part-time staff members and almost no consultants. In 2003, for instance—after he had just easily won re-election to another six-year term—his committee spent $10,874 on Amtrak tickets; that same year, the campaigns of Senator [Tom] Carper and Representative [Mike] Castle spent $1,257 and $589, respectively."[78]

Another perk not available to the average rider: When Biden was late getting to the station, his friends at Amtrak waited for his arrival—causing the trains on the Eastern corridor to run late.[79]

Making it a family affair once again, Biden's son Hunter was nominated to serve on the Amtrak reform board in 2006. Like his father, Hunter extolled the virtues of the government rail service, which he used to commute to New York for his hedge fund job before it went awry. As a quasi-governmental institution, Amtrak is forbidden by law from lobbying Congress. But as *Politico* reported, Hunter served as an "effective advocate" for the government railroad system.[80]

In February 2009, President Obama signed the $787 billion, pork-stuffed "economic stimulus" package into law. During his address to a Joint Session of Congress after signing the bill, Obama designated Vice President Biden the stimulus spending watchdog to be perched at a new website—*www.recovery.gov*—and in charge of ensuring the money is spent wisely. A few weeks later, spending cop Biden announced that his beloved sinkhole Amtrak would get $1.3 billion of stimulus funds to expand passenger rail capacity and boost Delaware's economy.[81] Biden couldn't be bothered to remember the name of his own website (he created a gaffe-tastic TV moment in late February 2009 when he blanked out on the Internet address of recovery.gov). But Joe the Back-Slapper never forgot to take care of his Amtrak cronies. "Amtrak is not bent at the trough. Amtrak has been left out," Biden complained at an event celebrating the stimulus bounty. "I'm tired of apologizing for help for Amtrak." And now, as head of the appropriately named "RAT" Board (Recovery Accountability and Transparency Board), Biden will have wide-ranging powers over the inspectors general who've been tasked to independently investigate stimulus waste, fraud, and abuse. He'll have the power to initiate such probes, but more importantly for entrenched Democrats protecting powerful constituencies, the power to forestall such probes.[82] "Nobody messes with Joe," he bragged.[83]

Apparently, the rich irony of appointing a deal-making, big government Washington insider who shuns transparency and accountability to head up stimulus monitoring efforts was completely lost on the White House. It was not, however, lost on local officials who heard Vice President Biden threaten them if they squandered the funds on things like bike paths, swimming pools, and golf courses. (Which is, of course, precisely what's happening.)

JOSEPH BIDEN, Vice President of the United States: Because of the rules, the president and I can't stop you from doing some things, but I'll show up in your city and say, "This was a stupid idea." You think I'm kidding? This is the only part the president was right about: Don't mess with Joe, because I mean it. I'm serious, guys. I'm serious. I'm absolutely serious.[84]

Biden's audience did what more and more audiences are doing when he opens his mouth: They laughed at him. Why? Because as his lifelong public record shows, when it comes to ethical self-policing that puts taxpayer interests above electoral and special interests, Joe Biden doesn't have a serious bone in his body.

CHAPTER 4

MEET THE MESS
INSIDE THE CROOKED CABINET

When asked why they were voting for Barack Obama, young people across the country cited his outsider status. José Villanueva, twenty-one, a senior at Claremont McKenna College in California, told *Time* magazine: "He's new and modern and breaking with the past." Eighteen-year-old Neil Stewart, a freshman at the University of Colorado in Boulder, echoed this sentiment. "I like that he's new," Stewart enthused. "We need some freshness in our government right now."[1] Internet entrepreneurs cranked out Obama t-shirts emblazoned with "Hope is the New Black" and "Change is fresh."

A comprehensive look at the men and women serving Barack Obama, however, exudes the freshness of a bologna sandwich left in a Lincoln Town Car parked in the muggy heat of Washington, D.C., in the middle of August with the windows rolled up for a week. Within days of President Obama's swearing in, the lemon-fresh scent of "Hope and Change" had been overpowered by the fetid odor of Beltway swamp business as usual.

Without further ado, I have compiled for you a handy guide to Obama's team of moldy oldies, rancid hacks, and rank tax evaders. Perform an act of public service and share it with your favorite starry-eyed young Obama supporters.

This is not the "new" they thought they knew.

CIA INTELLIGENCE DIRECTOR LEON PANETTA: LIFESTYLES OF THE RICH AND ENTRENCHED

New York Democrat Senator Charles Schumer once called Leon Panetta "the perfect government servant."[2] He's also the perfect illustration of the Beltway swamp creature. After serving sixteen years in Congress, four years in the Clinton administration as budget director and chief of staff, and a lifetime schmoozing in the halls of power, Panetta cashed in big. According to *Washingtonian* magazine, Panetta, seventy, is one of the administration's wealthiest members with up to $4 million in assets—"demonstrating once more how lucrative government positions can be once they're no longer held (see also: Clinton, Bill)."[3]

While he has zero experience in intelligence matters, he has extensive experience in how to parlay his past political tours of duty into lucrative speaking gigs, consulting fees, and stock options. Indeed, the only central intelligence-gathering duties Panetta has performed are at D.C. cocktail parties and corporate boardroom meetings picking up gossip.

Team Obama wanted a nominee unstained by ties to Bush-era War on Terror policies. What they settled for was a nominee unstained by any intellectual, managerial, or hands-on operational record on War on Terror policies at all—unless you count his nasty office battles with former CIA director James Woolsey over agency budget cuts during the Clinton era[4] or his op-ed against torture in the *Washington Monthly* in 2008.[5]

It wasn't only Republican partisans who questioned the crony CIA appointment. Senate Select Committee on Intelligence chair

Democrat Diane Feinstein of California was so dumbfounded by Panetta's nomination to helm the agency that she released a biting statement noting that her own position "has consistently been that I believe the Agency is best-served by having an intelligence professional in charge at this time." An aide to Democrat Senator Jay Rockefeller pronounced his boss "puzzled by the selection" because "he has always believed that the director of CIA needs to be someone with significant operational intelligence experience, and someone outside the political realm."[6] Defense analyst Michael O'Hanlon of the left-leaning Brookings Institution frowned on Panetta for never holding down a single "major job in national security." The nomination, he said, "seems to be Obama's weakest appointment in that sphere."[7]

Forced to disclose his financial assets and interests before his Senate confirmation, Panetta at least helped to inform the public of the lifestyles of the rich and entrenched. His disclosure forms show that he earned more than $1.2 million in investment, speaking, and consulting fees since the beginning of 2008, including:

- $56,000 from Merrill Lynch & Co. for two speeches;
- $28,000 for a speech for Wachovia Corp;
- $28,000 for an honorarium from the Carlyle Group, a private-equity firm whose companies do business with national security bureaucracies within the federal government;
- $60,000 in "Governmental Advisory Fees" from the shipping lobbyists of the Pacific Maritime Association;
- $130,000 in director's fees from big-time lobbying firm Fleishman Hillard;
- $150,000 in consulting fees from California State University, which hosts the Leon & Sylvia Panetta Institute for Public Policy, a nonprofit think tank run by Mr. Panetta and his wife[8]—which, coincidentally enough,

just happened to publish a survey showing wide support for Obama among college students in spring 2008
and disapproval of rival Republican John McCain and
President George W. Bush;[9]

- $125,000 in director fees from BP Corporation North
  America;
- $93,000 from Blue Shield of California; and
- $170,000 from Zenith National Insurance (in which he
  also owns up stock worth up to $350,000).[10]

Technically speaking, lobbyist-lite Panetta never registered as a
federal lobbyist, so technically speaking, Obama did not violate
his no-lobbyists-in-charge hiring rule. But HopeAndChange™ was
supposed to be about the most qualified officials meeting the highest standards, not the most unqualified political hacks eking by on
technicalities, wasn't it?

Offering the emptiest reassurance, White House spokesman
Tommy Vietor said Panetta's income and investments "have been
thoroughly reviewed by the Office of Government Ethics."
Vietor instead touted Mr. Panetta's views about how to
strengthen our intelligence gathering and keep our nation safe.
But a vetting of Panetta's income and investments illustrates the
fundamental problem with Obama's choice: he's an access trader
whose expertise lies not in national security, but in Washington
job security.

COMMERCE SECRETARY GARY LOCKE:
CHINAGATE-TAINTED,
INTEREST-CONFLICTED CRONY

After two botched attempts to fill the top post at the Commerce
Department, the Obama White House finally settled on the former Democratic governor of Washington state, Gary Locke. Team

Obama regarded Locke as, well, a lock. The national media dutifully toed the Good Gary line.

The *Washington Post* quoted officials touting him as a "safe choice" because of his "long history in public life, his strait-laced reputation and his bipartisan governing credentials."[11] The *New York Times* "reported" that Locke, "the nation's first and only Chinese-American governor and now an expert on China issues as a partner in a prominent Seattle law firm, brings something new: an international focus, centrist pragmatism, strong skills in public policy and a largely scandal-free résumé."[12] "Obama's New Commerce Pick Has Clean Reputation," declared National Public Radio.[13]

But repeating the Mr. Clean claim doesn't make it so. Locke's laces ain't tied so straight. I covered Locke when I worked at the *Seattle Times* in the late 1990s. I dealt with his campaign and gubernatorial staffs. "Strait-laced" and "clean reputation" are not the phrases I'd use from my dealings with him and his people. Those in his home state who know Locke best paint a far grimier picture of a crony politician with a serial habit of skirting campaign finance laws and conflict-of-interest rules. In other words: Locke's spotty record made him a good fit for the ethically-impaired Obama administration.

The left-leaning *Seattle Weekly* newspaper notes that Locke presided over a $3.2 billion tax break for Boeing as governor, while "never disclosing he paid $715,000 to—and relied on the advice of—Boeing's own private consultant and outside auditor for advice."[14] The state paid the auditor, Deloitte Consulting, the $715,000 in taxpayer funds to help land the Boeing Dreamliner assembly plant with the largest tax incentive in Washington state history. Oh, and Boeing just happened to be a $5 million Deloitte client.[15] Great coinky-dinks!

Then there's the tainted matter of Locke's "favors for his brother-in-law (who lived in the governor's mansion), including a tax break for his relative's company, personal intervention in a company dispute, and Locke's signature on a federal loan application for the company."[16] Republicans inquiring into the contract determined there was no illegality, but it was just too close for comfort for some ethics watchdogs. The *Seattle Weekly's* Rick Anderson reported that Locke's brother-in-law, Judd Lee, served as chief financial officer for SafeHarbor Technology. The company snagged a master contract from the state after Locke promoted it and championed nearly $12.7 million in tax breaks and state economic aid to benefit the company and its industry. In addition, Governor Locke aided his brother-in-law's company by funneling federal aid to it through a public corporation pipeline.[17]

Locke denied any conflict of interest and maintained that he never spoke about business to the brother-in-law who lived in his gubernatorial mansion (and frequently brought guests to tour the stately home). Well, duh. He didn't have to say a word. The language of nepotism is always spoken with winks and nudges.

Most alarming, the glowing profiles of Locke largely glossed over his troubling ties to the Clinton-era Chinagate scandal. As the nation's first Chinese-American governor, Locke aggressively raised cash from ethnic constituencies around the country. Convicted campaign finance money-launderer John Huang helped grease the wheels and open doors. In the same time period he was drumming up illegal cash for Clinton-Gore at the federal level, Huang organized two 1996 galas for Locke in Washington, D.C. (where Locke hobnobbed with Clinton and other Chinagate principals); three fund-raisers in Los Angeles; and an extravaganza at the Universal City, California, Hilton in October 1996 that raised upwards of $30,000. Huang also made personal contributions to Locke—as did another Clinton-Gore funny money figure, Indonesian business mogul Ted Sioeng, and his family and political operatives. Sioeng, whom Justice Department and intelligence officials suspected of acting on behalf of the Chinese government, illegally donated hundreds of thousands of dollars to both Democrat and Republican coffers.[18]

Checks to Locke's campaign poured in from prominent Huang and Sioeng associates, many of whom were targets of federal investigations, including: Hoyt Zia, a Commerce Department counsel, who stated in a sworn deposition that Huang had access to virtually any classified document through him; Melinda Yee, another Clinton Commerce Department official who admitted to destroying Freedom-of-Information-Act-protected notes on a China trade mission involving Huang's former employer, the Indonesia-based Lippo Group; Praitun Kanchanalak, mother of convicted Thai influence-peddler Pauline Kanchanalak; Kent La, exclusive distributor of Sioeng's Chinese cigarettes in the U.S.; and Sioeng's wife and son-in-law.[19] Bank records from congressional investigators also indicated that an associate of Sioeng made a maximum individual contribution to Locke that was then illegally reimbursed by Sioeng's daughter.

Locke eventually returned[20] a token amount of money from Huang and Kanchanalak, but not before bitterly playing the race card and accusing critics of his sloppy accounting and questionable schmoozing of stirring up anti-Asian-American sentiment. "It will make our efforts doubly hard to get Asian-Americans appointed to top-level positions across the United States," Locke complained. "If they have any connection to John Huang, those individuals will face greater scrutiny and their lives will be completely opened up and examined—perhaps more than usual."[21]

That scrutiny (such as it was) was more than justified. On top of his Chinagate entanglements, Locke's political committee was fined the maximum amount by Washington's campaign finance watchdog for failing to disclose out-of-state New York City Chinatown donor events.[22] One of those events was held at NYC's Harmony Palace restaurant, co-owned by Chinese street gang thugs. And then there were Locke's not-so-squeaky-clean fund-raising trips to a

Buddhist temple in Redmond, Washington, which netted nearly $14,000 from monks and nuns—many of whom barely spoke English, couldn't recall donating to Locke, or were out of the country and could never be located. Of the known temple donors identified by the Locke campaign, five gave $1,000 each on July 22, 1996—paid in sequentially-ordered cashier's checks. Two priests gave $1,000 and $1,100 respectively on August 8, 1996. Three other temple adherents also gave $1,000 contributions on August 8. Internal campaign records show that two other temple disciples donated $2,000 and $1,000 respectively on other dates. State campaign finance investigators failed to track down some of the donors during their probe.[23]

But while investigating the story for the *Seattle Times*, I interviewed temple donor Siu Wai Wong, a bald, robed, 40-year-old priest who could not remember when or by what means he had given a $1,000 contribution to Locke. He also refused to say whether he was a U.S. citizen, explaining that his "English [was] not so good."[24] Although an inept state campaign-finance panel absolved Locke and his campaign of any wrongdoing, the extensive public record clearly shows that the Locke campaign used Buddhist monks as conduits for laundered money.[25]

The longtime reluctance to press Locke—who became a high-powered attorney specializing in China trade issues for international law firm Davis, Wright & Tremaine after leaving the governor's mansion—on his reckless, ethnic-based fundraising extended to the politically correct and cowed Beltway. Instead of questioning his abysmal judgment, supporters touted Locke's cozy relations with the Chinese government as a primary reason he deserved the Commerce Department post. He sailed through the Senate confirmation process, with GOP Senator Kay Bailey Hutchison cluelessly concluding that Locke's background check was "boring."[26]

Thanks to Republicans asleep at the wheel, Teflon Gary evaded tough scrutiny once again. Like Panetta, he skirted Obama's no-lobbyist-rule, despite having lobbied the Chinese government on behalf of Microsoft, Starbucks, Weyerhauser timber, and other Washington state businesses. He traveled five times to China seeking loosened restrictions and favors for his clients, including an American bank seeking to establish a presence in the Communist regime. He also served as a fixer for Chinese nationals demanding streamlined visa applications and as a travel agent for Chinese President Hu Jintao when he visited the United States in 2006.[27]

But since Locke didn't lobby the U.S. government, Obama didn't count his lobbying work as "lobbying." See no lobbying, hear no lobbying, speak no lobbying. "We are confident," a White House aide insisted, "that Governor Locke will be able to continue to advocate on behalf of American businesses and workers while at the same time adhering to the administration's ethics policy."[28] Confidence built on delusion—an unmistakable mark of the Obama administration beast.

HUD'S NO. 2 MAN RON SIMS: ENEMY OF TRANSPARENCY

If you need a simple, shining example of the utter disingenuousness of Barack Obama's commitment to government transparency, I have two words for you: Ron Sims. This lifelong political hack is to transparency what sunlight is to Dracula, what salt is to a slug, what kryptonite is to Superman, what *The View* is to intelligent debate.

That is: lethal.

In its press release announcing the nomination of the Seattle-area county executive to the number two post at the U.S. Department of Housing and Urban Development, the White House described Sims as a "visionary urban leader." The White House also touted Sims's "willingness to make the tough choices necessary to ensure that American tax dollars are spent wisely." But his key accomplishments in the Pacific Northwest have involved illegally keeping taxpayers in the dark. Despite his long-known notoriety in Washington state as an incompetent manager and obstinate campaign finance law-breaker, President Obama has entrusted Sims to oversee the day-to-day operations of a federal agency with 8,500 employees, a $39 billion yearly budget, and a chronic history of corruption and cronyism.

Here's what fellow Seattle liberal Ted Van Dyk, a veteran Democratic strategist who supported Obama, said when Sims's nomination was announced:

> It is hard to imagine someone less qualified as Deputy Housing and Urban Development Secretary than Ron Sims. Sims' weak suit, as King County Executive, was his administrative competence. His troubles with the county jail, elections office, sewage-treatment facility and transportation planning are well known. Like [former Washington state governor-turned-Obama-Commerce-Secretary Gary] Locke, he is personable; a nice guy. But the HUD Deputy's job is to administer and run day-to-day a department notorious for its scandals, corruption, and screw[-]ups while the Secretary serves as outside man. Unless he is careful, HUD will eat Sims alive.[29]

The folks who have fought the real Ron Sims in his own backyard know he is the very antithesis of an open, accountable public servant. Ask Armen Yousoufian. In 1997, the former Boeing engineer embarked on what would be a twelve-year legal battle to force Sims to obey public disclosure rules. Instead of making the "tough choices necessary to ensure that American tax dollars are spent wisely," Sims did everything in his power to ensure that King

County, Washington, taxpayers were deprived of vital information on how their money was being spent.

Yousoufian wanted access to government documents related to a sports stadium subsidy plan up for a vote in Washington in the summer of 1997. The records he requested at the end of May 1997 pertained to the fiscal impact of a massive tax-hike proposal to build a new football palace for the Seattle Seahawks. Time was of the essence: County residents were preparing to vote on a ballot initiative package worth $300 million on June 17, 1997. Boosters of similar "public-private stadium partnerships" had made dubious claims of economic windfalls that never transpired. Yousoufian—serving as the watchdog that Sims failed to be for his constituents—was absolutely right to question the numbers.

But Sims, a leading stadium subsidy booster and corporate water-carrier for Microsoft billionaire and Seahawks owner Paul Allen, didn't put an informed citizenry first. His office deliberately stonewalled Yousoufian's request—at first, failing to deliver the documents, then claiming they didn't exist, and then admonishing him to bug off because he had been given everything he requested. All lies. While Sims's deputies gave Yousoufian the grand runaround, Referendum 48 passed by a margin of 51–49.

Yousoufian launched a one-man crusade to hold Sims accountable to taxpayers. He sued under Washington's open-records law in 2000. He spent $330,000 of his own money in legal fees and 4,000 hours of his own time. A lower court ruled in his favor, dinging the county's obstructionism as "egregious," but skimped in awarding him the minimum $5 a day for each of the 8,252 days that Sims's office withheld the documents. The courts found "hundreds" of instances where Sims's office deceived Yousoufian or refused to tell the truth. To deter future abuse, Yousoufian appealed for higher fines. A lower court came back and awarded him $15 a day—for a total of $124,000 in penalties and attorney fees of $171,100.

The largest fine of its kind ever assessed under the law, it was still not enough for public officials to treat it as anything other than a minor cost of doing business. Yousoufian pointed out after that ruling that he still did not receive all the documents he requested, and that the outcome meant "most people will never get a lawyer to take such a case without being paid hourly, as there just isn't enough potential for penalties to make a contingent fee arrangement worthwhile."[30]

Yousoufian appealed again to the state Supreme Court. In January 2009, just weeks before President Obama tapped Sims for the number two HUD post, the high court issued an historic ruling in Yousoufian's favor, damning Sims's "blatant violations of the state Public Records Act." From the majority opinion in *Yousoufian v. Office of Ron Sims*:

> To summarize, the unchallenged findings of fact demonstrate King County repeatedly deceived and misinformed Yousoufian for years. King County told Yousoufian it produced all the requested documents, when in fact it had not. King County told Yousoufian archives were being searched and records compiled, when in fact they were not. King County told Yousoufian the information was located elsewhere, when in fact it was not. After years of delay, misrepresentation, and ineptitude on the part of King County, Yousoufian filed suit; nevertheless, it would still take another year for King County to completely and accurately respond to Yousoufian's original request, well past the purpose of his request, the referendum on public financing of a sports stadium.
>
> ...King County failed to reply to Yousoufian's clear request promptly or accurately. King County failed to train its responding personnel or supervise its response. King County did not comply strictly to the procedures set forth in RCW 42.56.520,

failing to seek clarification from Yousoufian when necessary, failing to give any reason for its delay, failing to set forth an exception for its refusal, failing to provide any estimate of its delayed response time, and making Yousoufian contact King County more than 11 times over the course of two years to obtain the requested information when under the statute only one request should suffice.... King County either made no explanation of its noncompliance or misrepresented the truth. As the trial judge found, with proper diligence and attention, King County could have responded accurately to Yousoufian within five days. The potential for public harm was high; the requested records tested the veracity of King County's assertions regarding a pending referendum on a $300 million public financing scheme. The request was time-sensitive, seeking documents relevant to the upcoming referendum, whereas the disclosure of these documents was delayed years beyond the election day without justification.[31]

This travesty is the singular responsibility of Ron Sims. It dragged on through his entire tenure as King County executive—and beyond. The state Supreme Court remanded the case back to the lower courts to determine a final fine that may exceed some $1 million in taxpayer funds.

Sims's pattern of evasion was no anomaly. In 2005, another citizen filed suit against Sims for violating public disclosure rules. Seattle resident and blogger Stefan Sharkansky had requested documents related to the November 2004 election, which at the gubernatorial level was marked by fraud allegations across Washington state. The election records revealed that Sims's office unlawfully counted hundreds of ineligible ballots in the governor's race. As Sharkansky alleged in his complaint, which was scheduled to go to trial in April 2009:

[1] On December 27, 2004 I submitted a public records request to the County for "a list of all King County voters who submitted ballots in the Nov. 2 election." The County did not satisfy this request in full until September 12, 2005.

It took me at least four more letters and the presentation of irrefutable evidence from other documents to override King County's insistence that they didn't have the documents I was asking for, and which revealed the existence of dozens of unlawfully counted ballots, among other things.

[2] On April 7, 2005 I submitted through my attorney a public records request...[for] copies of "both the absentee ballot outer envelope and the provisional ballot envelope" for [91] known voters who submitted both types of ballots...As of July 5, 2005 the County had not produced any of the absentee and provisional ballot envelopes I had requested, so I renewed my request and asked to examine all the original absentee ballot envelopes...The County finally responded July 14, 2005 stating that only 27 (out of 91) of the provisional ballots were found and estimating that other documents would be produced July 22, 2005...I appeared at the elections office July 25, 2005, and received only 27 provisional ballots out of 91 identified... On September 2, 2005 the County informed me that only 1 additional provisional ballot envelope responsive to my request had been located....On September 16, 2005 I obtained permission to examine the contents of a box marked "provisional ballot envelopes November 2004"...Inside were approximately 59 more envelopes responsive to my request of April 7, 2005.

If King County had released the documents that other folks and I requested 6—10 months ago in a complete and timely fashion, [losing GOP gubernatorial candidate Dino] Rossi's legal team would have been able to present a much stronger argument that official misconduct occurred. What we've seen is not just a lazy agency dragging its heels to respond to document requests, but an organized effort to cover-up official misconduct and to obstruct justice.[32]

On April 24, 2009, King County settled out of court with Sharkansky for $225,000, one of the largest settlements for public records violations in state history.[33]

Less than a week after the January 2009 ruling against the man he would elevate to manage day-to-day operations at HUD, President Obama signed with great fanfare a Freedom of Information Act memorandum declaring his commitment to open government:

> The Freedom of Information Act should be administered with a clear presumption: In the face of doubt, openness prevails. The Government should not keep information confidential merely because public officials might be embarrassed by disclosure, because errors and failures might be revealed, or because of speculative or abstract fears. Nondisclosure should never be based on an effort to protect the personal interests of Government officials at the expense of those they are supposed to serve. In responding to requests under the FOIA, executive branch agencies (agencies) should act promptly and in a spirit of cooperation, recognizing that such agencies are servants of the public.
>
> All agencies should adopt a presumption in favor of disclosure, in order to renew their commitment to the principles embodied in FOIA, and to usher in a new era of open Government.[34]

As veteran open-records attorney Greg Overstreet, another Washington state citizen's advocate who knows Sims best, jibed: "Let's hope President Obama is not relying on Ron Sims to carry out the president's transparency agenda."[35] Irony doesn't just abound. It reeks.

ATTORNEY GENERAL ERIC HOLDER:
CRIME-CODDLING CORPORATE LAWYER

"Don't go into corporate America," First Lady Michelle Obama admonished supporters on the campaign trail. Remember? She extolled the rewards of public service over the material perks of life at a high-powered law firm.[36] She certainly didn't take her own advice—and neither did her husband's own Attorney General. If he hadn't pulled out all the stops campaigning for the president, raising money at lavish celebrity events, and offering his strategic and legal advice—and if Eric Holder had an "R" by his name instead of a "D"—he might have served as the perfect poster boy for Mrs. O.'s caustic campaign against white-shoe corporate law.

After a quarter-century as a government lawyer, Holder joined the prestigious Covington & Burling business and corporate law firm. He represented a gallery of the Left's fattest targets in Big Pharma and Big Business, defending them in fraud and discrimination cases that drove progressives mad. Holder has served both his corporate and government masters well—and he has the bank account and stock portfolio to prove it. His salary jumped from under $200,000 as deputy U.S. Attorney General for the Clinton administration, to more than $2 million a year as a Covington & Burling senior partner. During 2008, Holder spent countless hours away from his corporate office working for the Obama campaign—raising money, fielding calls, making speeches. "I hope the management committee is going to be real understanding when they see my billable hours this year," Holder joked to *The American Lawyer*. It's an investment, of course, and the law firm will get its political dividends later.

Holder returns to a more modest $186,000 salary as Obama's Attorney General. But parting has its perks, too. The Washington revolving door pays. Covington & Burling will make a separation payment valued at between $1 million and $5 million, plus a repayment of up to $1 million from the firm's capital account, plus a retirement plan of up to $500,000.[37] His net worth: $5.7 million.[38] Reflecting on his past eight years raking in the dough and watching him schmooze friends and clients from his "elegant new Manhattan offices," an *American Lawyer* profile observed: "Life is good for private citizen Eric Holder, Jr."[39] President Obama and the missus, such outspoken detractors of climbing the corporate ladder and influence-peddling, were unavailable for comment.

One wonders what the Obamas would say about Holder's lucrative work for Chiquita Brands International if it had been performed by, say, John McCain's top lawyer? As chief counsel for the global company, Holder won a "slap-on-the-wrist plea deal to charges that it had paid off" Colombian paramilitary death squads.[40] Liberal critics of Holder point out that he used his influence as a former Clinton Justice Department official to negotiate a sweetheart deal for Chiquita. The company pleaded guilty to illegally doing business with the "Autodefensas Unidas de Colombia" or AUC (designated as an international terrorist organization by the State Department in 2001). Chiquita admitted negotiating with and forking over $1.7 million in protection racket money to the guerillas beginning in 1997. AUC terrorists slaughtered thousands of civilians to gain control of Colombia's banana fields. The company ignored the advice of outside counsel (not Holder or anyone else at Covington & Burling) to stop the illegal payments in 2003:

- "Must stop payments."
- "Bottom Line: CANNOT MAKE THE PAYMENT."
- "Advised NOT TO MAKE ALTERNATIVE PAYMENT through CONVIVIR."
- "General Rule: Cannot do indirectly what you cannot do directly."

- Concluded with: "CANNOT MAKE THE PAY-MENT."
- "You voluntarily put yourself in this position. Duress defense can wear out through repetition. Buz [business] decision to stay in harm's way. Chiquita should leave Colombia."
- "[T]he company should not continue to make the Santa Marta payments, given the AUC's designation as a foreign terrorist organization[.]"
- "[T]he company should not make the payment."[41]

Even after disclosing the payments to the Justice Department in the spring of 2003, Chiquita continued funneling money to the terrorists. According to the Justice Department: "From April 24, 2003 (the date of Chiquita's initial disclosure to the Justice Department) through February 4, 2004, Chiquita made 20 payments to the AUC totaling over $300,000." And yet, despite knowingly and repeatedly breaking the law, not a single Chiquita official was prosecuted or jailed. The $25 million criminal fine was written off as the cost of doing business. And, stunningly, the plea agreement forged by Holder and the DOJ succeeded in protecting the identities of the executives involved in the bloody terrorist payoffs.[42]

Putting on the best terrorist defense is a Covington & Burling specialty. Among the firm's other celebrity terrorist clients: Seventeen Yemenis held at the Guantanamo Bay detention facility. The law firm employed dozens of radical attorneys such as David Remes and Marc Falkoff to provide the enemy combatants with more than 3,000 hours of pro bono representation. Covington & Burling co-authored one of three petitioners' briefs filed in the *Boumediene v. Bush* detainee case, and secured victories for several other Gitmo enemy combatants in the U.S. Court of Appeals for the D.C. Circuit.[43] Falkoff went on to publish a book of poetry, *Poems from Guantanamo: The Detainees Speak*, which he dedicated to the suspected terrorists: "For my friends inside the wire, Mahmoad, Majid, Yasein, Saeed, Abdulsalam, Mohammed, Adnan, Jamal, Othman, Adil, Mohamed, Abdulmalik, Areef, Adeq, Farouk, Salman, and Makhtar. Inshallah, we will next meet over coffee in your homes in Yemen."[44]

How sweet. One of the class of Yemeni Gitmo detainees that Falkoff described as "gentle, thoughtful young men" was released in 2005—only to blow himself up (gently and thoughtfully, of course) in a truck bombing in Mosul, Iraq, in 2008, killing thirteen soldiers from the Second Iraqi Army division and seriously wounding forty-two others.[45]

The Senate shrugged at the glaring conflict of interest Attorney General Holder presents in handling Gitmo legal issues. Lieutenant Colonel Gordon Cucullu, author of *Inside Gitmo: The True Story Behind the Myths of Guantanamo Bay*, makes the ethical problem plain:

> As a senior partner, he undoubtedly had significant input on what kind of charity cases his firm picked up. He surely knew that dozens of lawyers from his firm were among the 500-plus civilian lawyers representing the 244 or so remaining detainees (on top of military-court-appointed defenders). Even now, his Covington colleagues continue to allege rampant torture at Gitmo. They're fighting hard to have detainees tried through the US court system—essentially given the same rights as US citizens. And their arguments and plans hinge largely on having Holder issue a bad report card.
>
> Recent polls indicate that at least half of Americans disagree with affording the detainees legal rights on US soil. Will they have the same access to Holder's ears as his former colleagues do?[46]

The White House says that Holder will formally recuse himself from charging decisions and prosecutions affecting any of Covington &

Burling's clients, but he will have unfettered oversight over Obama's order to close the facility within a year.[47] Moreover, there's a gaping loophole in the Obama administration ethics rules that will allow Holder to participate in decision-making despite his conflicts of interests if he can show that his participation in a matter outweighs an appearance or actual conflict of interest.[48] If you think Holder's professional connections won't have any influence on the outcome of these decisions, I have a Colombian banana farm to sell you.

Among the other eyebrow-raising cases Holder took on at Covington & Burling:

- Signing up to assist then Illinois Governor Rod Blagojevich in a casino license battle in 2004. The state's gaming board had approved the construction of a disputed casino, overruling the recommendation of the board's staff. Rank-and-file investigators had qualms over the casino developer's alleged mob ties and over Blago's appointment of a crony fundraiser to oversee the state's deal-making with the casino. The fundraiser, Christopher Kelly, turned out to be a business partner of convicted Obama/Blago confidante and real estate mogul Tony Rezko. The *Chicago Sun-Times* reported that Rezko "held an option to lease a hotel site next to the proposed casino site." Holder held a public press conference with Blago to announce his role as a special "independent" investigator into the matter. The dog-and-pony show produced no report, but Holder and his law firm had contracted to conduct the probe for a tidy $300,000.[49] Somehow, the foul-smelling case slipped Holder's mind; he failed to mention it in his Senate Judiciary Committee questionnaire.
- Forging a massive settlement for Purdue Pharma, manufacturer of the addictive painkiller OxyContin, with

the state of West Virginia in 2004. The state accused the drugmaker of deceptively marking OxyContin as safe and effective for minor pain. The firm's marketing practices, the state maintained, led to West Virginia users becoming addicted to the drug. State Attorney General Darrell McGraw Jr., a Democrat, filed suit. In an article entitled, "Why Eric Holder Represents What's Wrong with Washington," liberal columnist David Corn described Holder's pivotal role in negotiating a settlement that spared executives a criminal trial:

"This suit was a serious threat to the drugmaker, and it eventually called in Holder. And in November 2004, the morning that the case was about to go to trial, Holder helped negotiate a settlement. Working in the judge's chambers in West Virginia, he forged an agreement under which the firm would have to pay $10 million over four years into drug abuse and education programs in West Virginia. Purdue would not have to admit any wrongdoing. (Days earlier, the firm had offered the state about $2 million to settle; McGraw had turned down Purdue and had not bothered to produce a counter-offer.)

"The settlement was a big win for the company. Ten million dollars was a piddling amount compared to what Purdue was reaping from OxyContin sales. More important, this settlement helped keep the lid on the firm's criminal activities. There would be no trial—and no public release of documents or testimony about the company's actions, which were already being investigated by federal prosecutors. In late 2002, the feds had begun an investigation of Purdue, with the first of what would be nearly 600 subpoenas for corporate records related to the manufacturing, marketing, and distribution of OxyContin.

"In May 2007, the company and its three top executives pleaded guilty to federal charges of fraudulently marketing

OxyContin by claiming it was less addictive, less subject to abuse, and less likely to cause withdrawal symptoms. Purdue and the three execs agreed to pay fines of $634.5 million."[50]

■ Brokering a settlement for pharmaceutical kingpin Merck, which had been besieged by multiple state lawsuits over Medicaid overbilling and doctor kickbacks involving four popular drugs.[51] Merck admitted no wrongdoing, paying $671 million to make whistleblowers, state probes over their pricing, and bribery charges go away.[52]

In his tony Manhattan offices, Holder did what any corporate lawyer worth his multi-million-dollar salary and benefits package would do: Represent his clients to the best of his ability. But in his first tours of duty as a government lawyer, Holder repeatedly put politics above the national interest. During his Senate confirmation hearing, Holder's infamous roles in issuing pardons to Clinton crony Marc Rich and clemency to convicted bank robbers and bombers of the Puerto Rican terrorist group FALN (*Fuerzas Armadas de Liberación Nacional*) received the most heat. In both cases, the government servant played a far more active role in intervening than he ever cared to admit.

The *Los Angeles Times* added new information to the terrorist clemency case by disclosing before the hearing that Holder had "repeatedly pushed some of his subordinates at the Clinton Justice Department to drop their opposition to" the FALN commutations. Holder, the paper determined from whistleblower interviews and documents, "played an active role in changing the position of the Justice Department" to facilitate President Clinton's commutations for sixteen violent terrorists from the group. The FALN had waged a bloody bombing campaign that maimed dozens of New York City police officers and resulted in the deaths or injuries of scores of other victims.[53] Holder forged ahead with his meddling on behalf of the president against the protests of the FBI, NYPD, federal prosecutors, and victims.

The nation's top law enforcer did not pay the bombing victims or their families the courtesy of notifying them of the decision to release the unrepentant terrorists until after the clemencies were publicized in the media.

As for the Marc Rich case, former federal prosecutor Andrew McCarthy accurately described it as "one of the most disgraceful chapters in the history of the Justice Department."[54] Congressional investigators called it "unconscionable." Fugitive commodities trader Marc Rich, on the run for evading nearly $50 million in taxes, found the best lawyer he could buy: former Democratic White House counsel and intimate friend of Eric Holder, Jack Quinn. Despite his denials, memos showed Holder knew of the pardon in advance, failed to notify prosecutors and the FBI that it was coming, "and even gave Quinn public-relations advice on getting out the 'legal merits of the case.'"[55] The evidence clearly shows Holder and Quinn violated department protocols and colluded to keep the Justice Department out of the pardon deal.

Appearing contrite at his Senate confirmation hearing, Holder confessed:

> I've accepted the responsibility of making those mistakes. I've never tried to hide. I've never tried to blame anybody else.
>
> What I've always said was that, given my—given the opportunity to do it differently, I certainly would have.
>
> I should have made sure that everybody, all the prosecutors in that case, were informed of what was going on. I made

assumptions that turned out not to be true. I should have not spoken to the White House and expressed an opinion without knowing all of the facts with regard to that matter.

That was and remains the most intense, most searing experience I've ever had as a lawyer. There were questions raised about me that I was not used to hearing.

I've learned from that experience. I think that, as perverse as this might sound, I will be a better attorney general, should I be confirmed, having had the Mark Rich experience.

...It was something that I think is not typical of the way in which I've conducted myself as a careful, thoughtful lawyer. As I said, it is something where I made mistakes, and I learned from those mistakes.[56]

Washington, alas, was determined to repeat the mistakes of the past. The Senate, including nineteen Republicans, confirmed Holder on February 2, 2009. A month later, the *Washington Post* reported that Holder politicized the legal review process involving the contentious issue of D.C. voting rights. After careful study, the DOJ's Office of Legal Counsel (OLC) had issued an opinion that a House bill on the matter was unconstitutional. Holder, who supports D.C. voting rights along with President Obama, overrode his staff lawyers' ruling—and simply ordered up an alternative opinion that fit the White House agenda.[57] Despite assuring the Senate that he would not change OLC opinions "simply because a new administration takes over" and pledging that legal reviews "would not be a political process, [but] will be one based solely on our interpretation of the law," Holder did exactly that. Former OLC principal deputy Edward Whelan noted that Holder refused to make the OLC opinion on D.C. voting rights available and did not issue a signed opinion explaining his grounds for reversal.[58]

No transparency, no accountability, no surprise.

U.S. TRADE REPRESENTATIVE
RON KIRK: TAX CHEAT

"I think Barack Obama is a genius," late night talk host Jay Leno joked amid a flurry of tax-cheating Obama nominations. "I think this is part of the plan. Do you ever notice when Barack Obama nominates someone, the first thing they do is pay their taxes? He's found a way to pay off the deficit. Nominate every single person in the country one at a time, until they pay off the deficit."[59] Unfortunately, the White House didn't need comedians to come up with more laughs. They just kept producing new punchlines. In March 2009, Obama tapped former Dallas mayor Ron Kirk to take the U.S. Trade Representative's post. Investigators determined that Kirk owed close to $10,000 in back taxes on claimed deductions for Dallas Mavericks sports tickets and donated speaking fees in 2005, 2006, and 2007.

In the most egregious instance, Kirk improperly deducted more than $17,000 as entertainment expenses for the cost of Mavericks' tickets, nearly half of which was not substantiated.[60]

Why Kirk's tax troubles were deemed "minor" by the White House, while those of would-be performance czar Nancy Killefer—who withdrew from her nomination over unpaid household taxes worth a tenth as much as Kirk's—became a major issue, is a question Obama's feminist supporters curiously failed to ask.[61] In any case, Capitol Hill fell in line and agreed with the White House that he was the "right man for the job."[62] And Jay Leno's mockery of the party of tax cheats hit the nail on the head:

"I guess the Democrats think I.R.S. means, 'I'm really sorry.'"

HHS SECRETARY KATHLEEN SEBELIUS:
THE NOMINEE WHO COULDN'T COUNT

She was supposed to be a "safe" choice after the Daschle debacle. But Democrat Kansas Governor Kathleen Sebelius came with her own set of tax troubles and accounting problems. In March 2009, she admitted in a letter disclosed to the press that she had made "unintentional errors" on her taxes and corrected her returns from three different years. The Democrat head of the Senate Finance Committee rushed to support her: "There is absolutely no doubt in my mind that Governor Sebelius has the political experience, determination, and bipartisan work ethic to get the job done with Congress this year," Senator Max Baucus wrote. "She's the right person for the job."[63] By now, the public was learning that "right person for the job" was code for tax scofflaw in the age of Obama. Sebelius coughed up $7,000 in back taxes, along with $878 in interest for debt owed between 2005–2007.

Two weeks later, more trouble with math: Sebelius was forced to admit that she lowballed the amount of political contributions she had received from infamous late-term abortion doctor George Tiller. In a letter to the Senate Finance Committee dated April 2, 2009, Sebelius revealed that she had received nearly three times as much cash from Tiller as she had initially disclosed. Here is the full question and response between GOP Senator Jon Kyl and Sebelius:

> There has been a lot of attention concerning your relationship with George Tiller, a doctor who has performed late term abortions in Kansas. Can you describe your relationship with Mr. Tiller? Has he ever contributed to your campaign or has your PAC ever received money from Mr. Tiller or a PAC related to Mr. Tiller? Have you ever hosted Mr. Tiller at an event during your tenure as Governor of Kansas?
>
> Answer: I regret that there was an inadvertent omission in my previous response to this question. The oversight led to an incomplete listing of certain PAC contributions as well as contributions from Dr. Tiller's business. After further review of the records at the Kansas Governmental Ethics Commission, including electronic records and all available paper records dating back to 1986, I have provided an updated answer below.

I have been familiar with Dr. Tiller for many years because he lives and works in Kansas. Like many Kansans, he contributed to my campaign for Insurance Commissioner; he also contributed to the Bluestem Fund, a leadership PAC established primarily to support candidates for the Kansas Legislature.

Between 1990 and 2001, my campaign received $11,100 from Dr. Tiller. In addition, my campaign also received $2,250 from Mrs. Tiller, $2,250 from Women's Health Care Services, and $1,000 from the Pro Choice Action League, which in media reports has been associated with Dr. Tiller.

In 2000, the Bluestem Fund received $10,000 from Dr. Tiller. In addition, between 2001 and 2002, the Bluestem Fund received $13,000 from Women's Health Care Services. I am aware of no donations from Dr. Tiller, from any PAC related to him, from Mrs. Tiller, or from Women's Health Care Services since 2002.

Throughout the course of my career, I have donated a lunch, dinner, or reception to non- profit organizations at their annual auctions. I did so every year as Insurance Commissioner and have done so every year as Governor. In 2006, I donated a reception at Cedar Crest to the Greater Kansas City Women's Political Caucus for their annual fundraiser, the Torch Dinner. Dr. Tiller bid on and won that auction item. As a result, an afternoon event lasting approximately one hour was held at Cedar Crest, with Dr. Tiller and his staff in attendance. All costs were reimbursed to the state.[64]

Funny how all these unintentional "goofs," "errors," and financial misstatements always err on the side of understating the problem.

LABOR SECRETARY HILDA SOLIS: SELF-LOBBYING UNION LACKEY

Upon presenting her with the 2000 "Profile in Courage Award," Senator Ted Kennedy praised California Democrat Congresswoman

Hilda Solis for her "ability and dedication to overcome the entrenched opposition of special interest groups." Solis, Kennedy waxed, was "the fulfillment of the American dream."[65] If your dream is for an America where cronies can come in all colors and climb the political ladder with the patronage of Big Labor, indeed, Hilda Solis certainly fits the bill.

Solis's father, Raul, was a Teamsters Union shop steward from Mexico. Her mother, Juana, was an assembly-line worker from Nicaragua. Born in Los Angeles, Solis served in the state legislature for eight years before winning a congressional seat against a fellow Democrat, 71-year-old, nine-term incumbent Matthew Martinez, in 2000. Martinez angered powerful unions in southern California with his support of the North American Free Trade Agreement. Solis eagerly carried the organized labor banner. Organized labor, in return, showered her with financial affection.

To help ensure her upset defeat of Martinez, the political action committee of the Service Employees International Union (SEIU) gave her a maximum $5,000 donation[66]—but more important, it supplied her with nearly 300 rank-and-file canvassers and ground troops. "I wouldn't be here, were it not for my friends in the labor movement," she gushed at her victory speech. A look at Solis's campaign coffers underscores that debt of gratitude. Over four terms in Congress, Solis has pocketed more than $900,000 in campaign contributions from unions—including $264,300 from building trade unions, $180,500 from industrial unions, $162,550 from public sector unions, and $153,500 from transportation unions.[67]

Labor bosses turned cartwheels when the White House tapped her on December 18, 2008, for the Cabinet post. SEIU godfather Andy Stern called it "extraordinary."[68] (See chapter seven for more on the Obama/SEIU/Stern axis.) Democrats extolled Solis's knowledge and leadership on work issues. But during her confirmation hearing, Solis dodged questions from Republicans on right-to-work laws that prevent requiring membership in a union as a condition of employment. Solis hemmed and hawed before asserting: "I don't believe that I am qualified to address that at this time." Solis also punted on questions about the number one agenda item of her union patrons: the so-called Employee Free Choice Act (or "card check" bill), which would obliterate secret ballot elections in union organizing and increase pressure on workers to organize against their will: "My position as a nominee for President-elect Obama to serve as secretary of labor doesn't, in my opinion, afford me the ability to provide you with an opinion at this time."[69]

Solis acted more like a Supreme Court nominee than a Cabinet appointee, bobbing and weaving as if direct answers would jeopardize a future court case:

> "Senator, I would just say to you that that is an item of great interest to me. I think that that is something that I am not able to speak to you [about] at this time but will like to review and then come back to you personally on that matter....
>
> "I would like to explore that more with this committee.... But that's something that I think I'm not prepared to give you a complete answer on at this time."[70]

Republican Senator Mike Enzi of Wyoming blasted Solis's evasions. "What answers? She doesn't even recognize her own record when giving the answers."[71]

Indeed, Solis was a co-sponsor of the very card-check legislation she refused to talk about at her hearing! Moreover, she served as director and treasurer of a union-promoting lobbying group, American Rights at Work, which was pushing her card-check bill. On top of that, Solis failed to disclose those positions to the House on her financial disclosure forms. In effect, she was lobbying herself, as former Federal Election Commissioner and Justice Department official Hans A. von Spakovsky put it.[72] Neat trick, huh?

Wait, that's not all. Solis's self-lobbying group took in at least "$1 million in contributions from labor unions" and spent "thousands of dollars on television spots described by the group in its report to the FEC as 'electioneering communications.'"[73] Those ads targeted Republican incumbent Senators Norm Coleman, Lisa Murkowski, Susan Collins, Gordon Smith, and John Sununu. The scheme circumvented vaunted McCain-Feingold campaign finance reforms barring so-called soft money donations from unions and corporations alike.

Despite apparent violations of both basic disclosure and campaign finance rules, Solis skated. She signed an affidavit stating that she didn't control her lobbying group's funds—even though she was its treasurer and a board member.[74] The GOP was ready to roll over. And then, just hours before the nomination vote, the Obama White House sheepishly disclosed that Solis's husband had just paid 16-year-old tax liens worth about $6,400. According to *USA Today*: "Los Angeles County records showed 15 outstanding state and county tax liens against Sam Sayyad and his auto repair business, totaling $7,630. Two other liens worth $981 were released in 1999 after Sayyad repaid the taxes owed, according to county records."[75] After the requisite eyebrow-furrowing, Solis coasted to victory. Or rather, her special-interest patrons in Big Labor coasted to victory: the union bosses' dream fulfilled.

TRANSPORTATION SECRETARY
RAY LAHOOD: EARMARK MAN

There was much ado about President Obama's "unprecedented"[76] choice of Republican Congressman Ray LaHood to lead the Department of Transportation. (Er, never mind that GOP President George W. Bush tapped Democrat Norm Mineta in the previous administration.) Paeans to "reaching across the aisle" and "working together" resounded among the chattering classes.

"Ray's appointment reflects that bipartisan spirit—a spirit we need to reclaim in this country to make progress for the American people," Obama said in cheerleading himself and his pick.[77]

But donkeys and elephants have always come together in the spirit of expanding government, rolling logs, and barreling pork. Seven-term Congressman LaHood may have an "R" by his name, but it's his political DNA that matters more than the partisan label. LaHood is a card-carrying member of the Chicago Political Machine. And as an Illinois congressman from 1995 to 2009, he reveled in his power as a House appropriator: He chose the assignment on the House Appropriations Committee, he told the *Peoria Journal Star*, because he and his fellow pork-slingers "know that it puts them in a position to know where the money is at, to know the people who are doling the money out and to be in the room when the money is being doled out."[78]

LaHood is an especially intimate crony of fellow Illinois king-maker and Obama Chief of Staff Rahm Emanuel. Their public displays of affection abound. In a House floor speech last fall, Emanuel hailed his GOP colleague as "someone the framers of the Constitution would have 'had in their mind's eye' when they 'thought of a member of Congress...He is an individual who, while firm in his principles, was very flexible about his opinions.'"[79]

"Flexibility" is easy when you have no fiscal conservative spine.

Emanuel and LaHood teamed up to push the massive expansion of the State Children's Health Insurance Program in 2007, funded through huge cigarette tax hikes and reaching far beyond the scope of the original plan towards the goal of universal health care.[80] They co-hosted a series of bipartisan dinners for members of Congress to forge a consensus on spending your money. LaHood also crusaded for federal funding to pay for a $20 billion O'Hare International Airport expansion at the behest of Chicago Mayor Richard Daley. And when the White House sought

Republican support for the trillion-dollar stimulus bill, LaHood was the go-to guy.

Not a single House Republican voted for the stimulus, but former Republican Congressman LaHood got the last laugh. He now has $48 billion in stimulus money for the Department of Transportation to play with—including $8 billion for his pet transportation cause, high-speed rail. Next to Joe the Train Rider Biden, LaHood is the loudest Capitol Hill advocate for government-subsidized money loser Amtrak. "The subsidies need to continue," LaHood protested in response to a 2005 Bush plan by Democrat Transportation Secretary Norm Mineta that called for reducing the feds' role in Amtrak operations. "These subsidies are the lifeblood of Amtrak continuing the kind of service they have to the college towns and the small communities in Illinois and around the country. I don't see us really tinkering with that."[81] The stimulus funds for transportation represent what's been called the "largest wave of federal transportation spending since the Eisenhower administration launched the creation of the interstate highway system."[82]

LaHood is a klieg-light shining example of Obama's anti-earmark disingenuousness. The *Wall Street Journal* dubbed the Transportation Secretary the "Earmark King."[83] But that title belongs solely to the man in the White House who pledged to "ban all earmarks" in the stimulus—and then promptly broke the pledge by rubber-stamping billions of dollars worth of earmarks. President Obama is the Earmark King. Transportation Secretary LaHood is the Earmark Courtier.

Taxpayers for Common Sense reported that in fiscal year 2008, LaHood scored $62.7 million in federal earmarks for his district, either solo or with other colleagues. The *Washington Post* added that LaHood directed at least $9 million of that oft-hidden, last-minute pork project money to campaign donors.[84] LaHood has a special fetish for road-building earmarks—doling out millions to home state paving companies and projects, including an unsolicited $245,000 check in December 2007 to fix roads leading to a Springfield, Illinois, cemetery where Abraham Lincoln is buried.

One of LaHood's top back-scratching donors was Republican William Cellini Sr., an Illinois pal who shares the bipartisan Chicago spirit of pay-to-play. *Chicago Tribune* columnist John Kass introduces you:

> Obama selected outgoing Illinois U.S. Rep. Ray LaHood (R-Combine) for the post of secretary of transportation, putting LaHood in charge of Obama's planned trillion-dollar public works bonanza being sold as a jobs bill. "Every dollar that we spend, we want it spent on projects that are there, not because of politics, but because they're good for the American people," Obama said. "If we're building a road, it better not be a road to nowhere." Not because of politics? What does the great reformer take us for, a bunch of chumbolones? What Obama forgot to mention is that with LaHood in charge of the roads, they'll lead to one place: Bill Cellini.
>
> Cellini, the Republican boss of Springfield who has been indicted in the Blagojevich scandal for allegedly shaking down the producer of the movie "Million Dollar Baby," is a strong LaHood ally. Cellini runs Sangamon County, and LaHood has enjoyed Cellini's political support. They also joined to help oust the last true reformer in Illinois politics, former Sen. Peter Fitzgerald, the Republican who was denied an endorsement from his own state party after he brought federal prosecutors to Illinois with no connection to the bipartisan Combine that runs things here. Republican money man Cellini is not only the Chicago political connection to machine Democrats and Mayor Richard Daley's City Hall—and a Blagojevich fundraiser—he's also the boss of the Illinois Asphalt Pavement Association. They're the guys behind the guys who pour that hot sticky stuff

on the roads, but don't get their cashmere sweaters dirty and drive black Escalades to the job site, before wheeling off for some osso bucco at Volare or other fine restaurants.[85]

Cellini was indicted in the fall of 2008 after a criminal investigation spearheaded by Northern District U.S. Attorney Patrick J. Fitzgerald. The charges? Shaking down government vendors to raise money for—wait for it—disgraced Democratic Governor Rod Blagojevich. Asked to explain how a lifelong Republican had insinuated himself into Blago World, Cellini once quipped before his indictment: "When we're in, we're in. And when you're in, we're in."[86]

The autumn 2008 indictment cited thirty charges of conspiracy to commit mail and wire fraud, conspiracy to commit extortion, attempted extortion, and soliciting. A new indictment released in March 2009 dropped the bribery solicitation, but the basic pay-to-play allegations should sound eerily familiar: A financial firm called Capri Capital wanted a piece of the state government pie— control and management of $200 million worth of state teachers' pension money. The Chicago Political Machine named its price. Cellini and others, including convicted Obama/Blago real estate mogul Tony Rezko, "agreed to demand that Thomas Rosenberg, the owner of Capri Capital, arrange to raise or donate substantial funds to Friends of Blagojevich, and to threaten that if such funds were not forthcoming, they would block" a proposed investment by the state teachers' pension fund of $220 million with Capri Capital, according to impeached former Illinois governor Rod Blagojevich's criminal indictment.[87]

These are the friends of Obama's Transportation Secretary, an earmark-addicted influence peddler born and raised on the politics of pay-to-play. For his "disregard for the taxpayers' money and an abundance of concern over how he will administer the Department of Transportation," the non-partisan Citizens Against

Government Waste designated LaHood its "Porker of the Month" in January 2009.[88] "Change?" It's all we'll have left after Ray LaHood gets done plundering the stimulus coffers for his pet projects and pals.

EPA CHIEF LISA JACKSON: CLEAN
AS SHE SAYS, NOT AS SHE CLEANS

President Obama's choice to head the Environmental Protection Agency (EPA), Lisa Jackson, racked up a controversial record as chief eco-regulator for the state of New Jersey. But national journalists seemed more interested in her skin color than the dark spots on her resume. Diversity consultants cheered and the Associated Press trumpeted: "Lisa Jackson in line to be first black EPA chief."[89]

Jackson stressed her green credentials while posing as an adherent of sound science and regulations. In her Senate confirmation testimony, Jackson promised that "Science will be the backbone of what EPA does."[90] But some of her own scientists and the EPA's own inspector general say Jackson did not practice in New Jersey what she now preaches. Critics on both the left and right pointed to an EPA inspector general's report lambasting Jackson's state agency for failing to clean up toxic sites in a timely manner and for "not implement[ing] agreements on cleanup milestones, Agency responsibilities, and enforcement actions."[91]

A former senior scientist who worked for Jackson, Jeff Ruch of the activist Public Employees for Environmental Responsibility, lambasted Jackson's oversight (or rather, lack of oversight) when the OIG report was released:

> The new EPA OIG report blasts inordinate delays and mismanagement of state-supervised Superfund clean-ups performed under the authority of federal law. The report focuses on several

toxic clean-up operations that had been going on for more than 20 years without completion and concludes that—

- New Jersey has the worst track record in the nation, accounting for more than one quarter of all unresolved Superfund clean-ups more than 20 years old;
- Delays are primarily due to the state department of Environmental protection (DEP) not using legal tools available to them to force responsible parties to clean up pollution; and
- The U.S. EPA should step in and take over mired state-supervised clean-ups.

"New Jersey used to have the strongest clean-up program in the country but now it is among the worst," stated New Jersey PEER Director Bill Wolfe, a former DEP analyst. "We should be embarrassed that George Bush's EPA has to step in and take over pollution control in our state."[92]

In 2008, a Justice Department investigation led to several guilty pleas from New Jersey Department of Environmental Protection contractors under Jackson's watch who were involved in a Superfund clean-up kickback conspiracy: "The owner of a Camden County wastewater treatment supply company and a former contracts administrator pleaded guilty to big rigging, fraud and tax charges involving work at two Superfund sites in New Jersey, according to the U.S. Department of Justice." More than $410,000 in kickbacks was exchanged "in the form of checks, cash, cruises, home renovations, boat trailers and airline flights, as well as inflated invoices."[93] Another co-conspirator was ordered to pay a $1 million criminal fine related to the conspiracy. And in March 2009, as Jackson settled in to her new position at EPA, the Justice Department secured still more guilty pleas related to the kickback scheme.[94]

Risk and environmental policy analyst Jonathan Tolman of the free-market Competitive Enterprise Institute in Washington, D.C., stated the obvious: "If a Republican president had nominated a former Republican State DEP head with the exact same environmental record as Lisa Jackson, environmental groups in Washington would be howling. But all one seems to be hearing from the major environmental groups is the sound of one hand clapping."[95]

As the official Cabinet nominees stumbled, bumbled, or greased their way through the nomination process, the Obama administration was installing a shadow cadre of unaccountable advisers and regulators pulling the strings. If at first you don't succeed, the White House learned, circumvent the democratic process.

CHAPTER 5

BACKROOM BUDDIES
DANCING WITH THE CZARS

There seems to be an unwritten mandate in the Obama White House: If you can't beat 'em, czar 'em. The nomination process has proved to be a dangerous landmine for one too many Obama picks. So the vetters found a convenient way to circumvent the problem—by creating a handful of new posts through presidential executive orders that require no Senate approval.

No Senate review, no questions. No questions, no problems. Viva la transparency.

In effect, the Obama administration has created a two-tiered government—fronted by Cabinet secretaries able to withstand public scrutiny (some of them, just barely) and run behind the scenes by shadow secretaries with broad powers beyond the reach of congressional accountability.

A few lawmakers aren't too crazy about Obama's czar-mania. Democrat Senator Robert Byrd (yes, even a broken clock is right twice a day) warned the White House in a February 2009 letter about his worries regarding the new czar positions in health care, urban affairs, energy and climate policy, and technology and management performance. "I am concerned about the relationship between these new White House positions and their executive branch counterparts," Byrd wrote. "Too often, I have seen these lines of authority and responsibility become tangled and blurred, sometimes purposely, to shield information and to obscure the decision-making process."[1] GOP Senator James Inhofe questioned whether hearings on Obama's pick to chair the Council on Environmental Quality, which requires Senate confirmation, were directed at the wrong person: "I'm quite concerned that the chair's role has been diluted by the addition of former EPA Administrator Carol Browner as White House climate and energy czar."[2]

It's one thing to create a White House coordinator slot to handle sensitive tasks that no other agency is handling. Ten days after the September 11 terrorist attacks, the Bush administration appointed a new domestic security czar to coordinate the counter-terrorism efforts of more than forty federal agencies, including the CIA, FBI, and National Guard.

But Obama's key czars all have Cabinet counterparts already in place. While past administrations dating back to the Nixon era have designated such "super aides," none has extended the concept as widely as Obama has—which raises another bureaucratic concern: sheer chaos. New York University professor Paul Light, who has written extensively on government organization, said that in addition to Byrd's constitutional concerns, "there are so many czars in this White House, they'll be constantly bumping into each other."[3]

That chaos could serve as useful smokescreen to obscure the true source of decision-making. "If the czars are working behind the scenes and the secretaries will be the mouthpieces of the administration, it calls into question who is actually making the policy decision," Senator Byrd concluded. "Whoever is making the policy decisions needs to be accountable and available to Congress and the American public."[4] Obama's czar class, however, operates by different rules and different ethics. Unchecked, these shadow despots with spotty records could wreak major havoc on the economy.

CAROL BROWNER: ETHICALLY CHALLENGED ENERGY CZAR

In December 2008, the Obama White House wheeled out yet another moldy old Clinton/Gore corruptocrat to serve in the administration of Hope and Change. Obama named Carol Browner, a neon green extremist who headed the Environmental Protection Agency from 1993 to 2000 and served as former Senator Al Gore's legislative director, to the post of "Assistant to the President for Energy and Climate Change." The control freaks preferred the title "Energy Czar." Perhaps they should have called her "Energy Commissar" given her membership in a Socialist International organ called the Commission for a Sustainable World Society. By February 2009, she had already announced radical plans to declare carbon-dioxide emissions a danger to the public—a move that could potentially subject not just power and chemical plants, refineries, and vehicles, but also schools, hospitals, and any other emitters of carbon dioxide to costly new regulations and litigation.[5] Initially, the White House pegged the cost of the cap-and-trade program supported by Browner at $646 billion over eight years. In March 2009, Senate staffers learned the true cost would be closer to $2 trillion.[6]

The Browner appointment (which, like other czar appointments, bypassed the Senate confirmation process) came despite concerns about her ideological zealotry. As the *Washington Examiner* reported, the Socialist International organization responded to exposure of Browner's membership by scrubbing its web site to remove Browner's photo and biography.[7] Such whitewashing is par for the course for Browner. On her last day as Clinton's EPA chief, nearly eight years ago, Browner oversaw the destruction of agency computer files in brazen violation of a federal judge's order requiring the agency to preserve its records. This from a public official who bragged about her tenure: "One of the things I'm the proudest of at EPA is the work we've done to expand the public's right to know."[8]

Asked to explain her track-covering actions, the savvy career lawyer Browner played dumb. Figuratively batting her eyelashes, she claimed she had no clue about a court injunction signed by U.S. District Judge Royce Lamberth on the same day she commanded an underling to wipe her hard drives clean. Golly gee willikers, how could that have slipped by her?

According to testimony in a freedom of information lawsuit filed against EPA by the Landmark Legal Foundation, a Virginia-based conservative legal watchdog group, Browner commanded a computer technician on January 19, 2001: "I would like my files deleted. I want you to delete my files."[9] Not coincidentally, the Landmark Legal Foundation had been pressing Browner to fully and publicly disclose the names of any special interest groups that might have influenced her wave of last-minute regulatory actions. Two days before she told her technician to purge all her records, EPA had gone to court to file a motion opposing the federal court injunction protecting those government documents.

Plausible deniability? Not bloody likely.

Incredibly, Browner asserted that there was no work-related material on her work computer. She explained she was merely cleaning the hard drive of computer games she had downloaded for her son, and that she wanted to expunge the hard drive as a "courtesy" to the incoming Bush administration. How thoughtful.[10]

Later, her agency admitted that three other top EPA officials had their computers erased despite the federal court order and ongoing Freedom of Information Act case. (The record is silent on whether Browner's son was playing games on their desktops, too.) A further belated admission revealed that the agency had failed to search Browner's office for public documents as required by Landmark's public disclosure lawsuit.[11]

Not only were all the top officials' hard drives cleared and reformatted, but e-mail backup tapes were erased and reused in violation of records preservation practices.[12]

After a two-year legal battle, Judge Lamberth finally held the EPA in contempt of court for the systemic file destruction—actions Lamberth lambasted as "contumacious conduct."[13] As is typical in Washington, Browner weaseled out of any serious repercussions. Lamberth inexplicably decided that slapping the agency as a whole with contempt—rather than any individual—would deter future cover-ups.

Browner has crossed the line and violated public trust before in her capacity as eco-chief. Early in her first term as EPA head, Browner got caught by a congressional subcommittee using taxpayer funds to create and send out illegal lobbying material to over 100 grassroots environmental lobbying organizations. Browner exploited her office to orchestrate a political campaign by left-wing groups, who turned around and attacked Republican lawmakers for supporting regulatory reform.[14] These are the very same groups—anti-business, anti-sound science, pro-eco-hysteria—that Browner will be working with arm in arm as Obama's "energy czar." A bipartisan subcommittee of the House Government Reform and Oversight Committee reprimanded Browner, concluding: "The concerted EPA actions appear to fit the definition of prohibited grass-roots lobbying.... The prima facie case is strong that some EPA officials may have violated the criminal law."[15]

Manhattan Institute scholar Max Schulz also points out that Browner "was the driving force behind the federal government's effort to force General Electric Co. to spend $490 million to dredge New York's Hudson River to rid it of polychlorinated biphenyls (PCBs) that—because they were buried under layers of silt—posed no environmental harm." Some of her employees, Schulz recalled, "wound up facing criminal charges for falsifying evidence and manipulating lab results."[16]

Then there's Browner's husband, Tom Downey. While Team Obama pays lip service to breaking old Washington lobbying habits, Browner and Downey represent the prototypical influence-peddling power couple. In 2006, the pair teamed up on behalf of infamous Dubai Ports World—the United Arab Emirate-owned company that unsuccessfully sought to take over operations of six major U.S. ports. Browner was a principal in the "international consulting firm" of her old Clinton pal, and former secretary of state, Madeline Albright. Browner and Downey, whose own firm lobbied for Dubai Ports World, met with New York Senator Charles Schumer to try and quell congressional opposition. All deny that lobbying took place. It was "for informational purposes," an Albright Group spokeswoman told the *Wall Street Journal*.[17] Yet Downey was named by *Washingtonian* magazine as one of Washington's top 50 lobbyists. His clients have included foreign governments, drug and insurance companies, and major energy companies including Chevron and the Standard Renewable Energy Group, which will no doubt come under the regulatory purview of his broadly-empowered "energy czar" wife. Obama's stringent lobbying rules do not apply to spouses. The White House blithely claims that "administration officials will recuse themselves from any issue involving a spouse,"[18] but how exactly can Browner recuse herself from the very core duties of her job, which include targeting carbon emissions, enacting onerous global warming reduction policies, and regulating the very industry her husband represented for years?[19]

This is particularly troubling given Browner's husband's past. Conflict of interest and abuse of power seem to be Downey's specialty. He was a Democrat congressman in New York for nearly two decades before losing his seat during the House banking scandal. Downey racked up overdrafts on 151 checks worth $83,000 at the House bank while his wife held a patronage job as an auditor in the House office that ran the House bank.[20] An undercover ABC News investigation in 1990 showed him lolling on a beach during a congressional junket to Barbados. Reflecting on Downey's defeat in 1992 and the loss of his long-ago image as an upstart reformer, one of Downey's congressional colleagues told the *New York Times*: "You live in Washington, you just get sucked into Washington."[21]

Thanks to Barack Obama, two more old crony players have been sucked back into the Beltway swamp to wield their joint power and influence.

ADOLFO CARRIÓN: ETHICALLY STAINED URBAN CZAR

Former Bronx Borough President Adolfo Carrión Jr. is a man in Barack Obama's own image: Son of immigrants. Check. Young. Check. Charismatic. Check. Ambitious. Check. Oh, and embroiled in pay-for-play scandals that would make convicted Obama crony developer Tony Rezko and the Chicago political machine proud. Checkity-check-check. A perfect fit for the Obama administration.

As with energy czar Carol Browner, the Obama White House circumvented the normal confirmation process for Carrión by creating a new executive position and office for him: head of the White House Office of Urban Affairs. Voilà: urban czar! But doesn't the president already have a Secretary of Housing and

Urban Development? Why, yes. Yes, he does. That spot went to Harvard grad and former Clinton HUD official Shaun Donovan, who moved up from his role as New York City commissioner of housing and development. Grievance groups, however, were miffed that the HUD job didn't go to a racial or ethnic minority. (Donovan is white; HUD is a notorious bastion of cronyism of color.)

Enter Carrión.

The Puerto Rican Democrat initially supported Hillary Clinton in the presidential primaries, but threw his whole being into campaigning for Obama after Clinton bowed out. As a reward for turning out the Latino vote, Obama handed him the keys to the urban czar's office—where he will have the power to shower federal dollars on urban areas and "coordinate urban policy in traditional areas such as education, health care and public safety," as he described the position to the *Washington Post*.[22] The budget and staffing for the office are unknown. According to the executive order establishing the office, Carrión's purview is sweeping. His mission:

- to provide leadership for and coordinate the development of the policy agenda for urban America across executive departments and agencies;
- to coordinate all aspects of urban policy;
- to work with executive departments and agencies to ensure that appropriate consideration is given by such departments and agencies to the potential impact of their actions on urban areas;
- to work with executive departments and agencies, including the Office of Management and Budget, to ensure that Federal Government dollars targeted to urban areas are effectively spent on the highest-impact programs; and

- to engage in outreach and work closely with State and local officials, with nonprofit organizations, and with the private sector, both in seeking input regarding the development of a comprehensive urban policy and in ensuring that the implementation of Federal programs advances the objectives of that policy.[23]

In practice, the job empowers Carrión to carry out the pay-to-play schemes that sullied his tenure in the Bronx on a nationwide scale. It's Obama-approved old school patronage dressed up as the new, new urban renewal.

The *New York Daily News* did the work the Obama vetters failed to do and spearheaded the investigation into Carrión's cash-and-carry arrangements with a slew of Big Apple developers. The Bronx "beep," as borough presidents are known, took tens of thousands of dollars in donations from the real estate firms just before and after the developers snagged lucrative deals or crucial zoning changes for their projects. In turn, he made millions in public tax dollars available to his cronies. Most of the contributions, the *Daily News* reported, were "organized and well-timed."[24] The quid pro quos couldn't be more obvious. One developer, Jonathan Coren, was gunning for a deal to build 166 units of affordable housing in the Parkchester neighborhood. He did something he had never done before in order to grease the wheels: Coren registered as a fund-raiser for Carrión.

Three weeks after Coren drummed up more than $2,500 from multiple contributors, Carrión green-lighted his project. The *Daily News* added that on another single day he raised an additional $1,255 for Carrión—less than a month before the Planning Commission, which includes a Carrión appointee, approved the deal. Next, Coren raised $6,532 for Carrión from forty-three donors: "Asked about the purpose of fund-raising for Carrión just before he reviewed the project, Coren replied, 'None, other than, to be perfectly honest with you, at that time I became aware of his campaign. It is what it is.'"[25]

"It is what it is." And there was plenty more where that came from.

Two of the largest Carrión donors were Atlantic Development Group and Latino-themed Boricua College. The developer sought approval, regulatory changes, and funding for a public project to construct housing and a college tower called Boricua Village. Atlantic and Boricua chipped in nearly $70,000 to Carrión's campaign coffers as they negotiated the deal. Eight donations from college officials totaling $8,750 arrived for Carrión one spring day in 2006—not long after the first application for the construction project had been filed. More would follow. For their share, Atlantic's employees contributed a total of $52,400, the largest single source of Carrión campaign money, the *Daily News* reported.[26]

Another firm that paid to play: BTM Development Partners. The developers sought a critical zoning change for a project that had raised community ire over traffic and other complications. BTM executives started dashing off $1,000 checks to Carrión. Not long after, they announced plans for a hotel-retail complex, and just a few months later, Carrión and Bronx officials approved the zoning changes necessary. Payoffs pay.

Carrión went even further by bringing his cash-and-carry deal to his front doorstep—literally. In 2006, he hired an architect to renovate his City Island Victorian home. The architect was Hugo Subotovsky, who just happened to be seeking approval for a number of development projects in Carrión's realm. Once again, the *Daily News* broke the details. Once again, the Obama administration shrugged.

Over two years, the paper reported, Carrión rubber-stamped three separate Subotovsky housing projects, including the Boricua Village plan. Carrión delivered $3 million in taxpayer funds to one of the developments in May 2008. During the time period that he approved the deals, Carrión failed to pay Subotovsky for the renovation work on his home, which included the addition of a porch and balcony at a reported cost of about $36,000, including $3,627.50 in architectural fees. It is illegal for an elected official to accept home improvement renovations as a gift from an architect seeking business from the city. Carrión claimed in March 2009 that he hadn't paid the bills because he was waiting for a "final survey" that had not yet been filed with the city. The work was finished in early 2007.[27]

Similar arrangements involving home renovation freebies from corporate suitors resulted in multiple criminal convictions for entrenched Alaska GOP Senator Ted Stevens and forced the resignation of Republican former Connecticut Governor John Rowland. But there was barely a peep from the Beltway's clean government types about Carrión's smelly deals. On March 11, 2009, White House Press Secretary Robert Gibbs was asked about the growing scandal. Gibbs glibly brushed it off:

> Question: Robert, two things. What's the concern from the White House about Adolfo Carrión—this current controversy about him, this possible conflict of interest?
>
> MR. GIBBS: Well, I think—I don't have a whole lot to add from what was in—has been in the papers and what Mr. Carrion has said about this.
>
> Question: But are you concerned that he has not, or will not, pay this alleged $32,000 for this porch and balcony? I mean, is that—is that all he needs to do? What does he need to do to clear up this controversy in the White House's opinion?
>
> MR. GIBBS: Well, I think—again, I think the quote says, that when the work is complete, that the bill will be paid, and certainly that would be the expectation.[28]

Fortunately, the Obama administration's apathy did not infect the Bronx District Attorney's office. "The facts, as reported, raised questions that we are looking to get answers to," Steven Reed, a spokesman for the Bronx DA, told the Associated Press. Citizens for Responsibility and Ethics in Washington (CREW), generally a left-leaning government watchdog group, pressed Attorney General Eric Holder to investigate Carrión. "If the era of pay-to-play politics is over, Adolfo Carrión did not get the message," Melanie Sloan, executive director of CREW, said in a statement. And Dick Dadey, executive director of another watchdog group, Citizens Union, challenged Carrión's judgment: "It is irresponsible for an elected official not to conduct his personal affairs above board and avoid any perceived conflict.... He should have paid the architect before now, given his role as borough president and the architect's involvement with development projects."

Compensating the architect, however, would not allay doubts and concerns about Carrión's ethics and fiscal responsibility. City records showed that in his last two years as Borough President, he squandered nearly $20,000 on a Teleprompter, stage equipment, and lights to conduct lavish "State of the Borough Tours"; spent $24,000 on overnight travel and conferences, including $5,295 at a four-star San Juan Resort and Casino; charged a satellite radio subscription to taxpayers because it was important to keep him "mobile"; $8,000-plus for picture frames and mats; and was the only borough president in New York City to stick the public with his $13,000 bill for membership to a county executive organization.[29]

Lucas Herbert, a community urban planner who had dared to oppose Carrión's aggressive push for the city's taxpayer-funded Yankee Stadium development, summed up Carrión's appointment most succinctly: "I thought when people voted for Obama they were voting for change, but Carrión is just more of the same."[30]

NANCY DEPARLE: HEALTH CZAR
WITH DEEP CORPORATE TIES

In early March 2009, following the humiliating debacle involving corruption-plagued nominee Tom Daschle, President Obama announced the appointment of Kansas Democrat Governor Kathleen Sebelius as Health and Human Services Secretary. But Sebelius couldn't have been completely thrilled. Along with her nomination requiring Senate confirmation, the White House unveiled a new health czar to direct the "White House Office for Health Reform." No hearings necessary, no questions asked. The position went to Nancy-Ann Min DeParle, a Clinton-era official who ran Medicare and Medicaid as head of the Health Care Financing Administration (now known as the Centers for Medicare and Medicaid Services). DeParle oversaw $600 billion in annual federal spending on health care to 74 million Americans. She then parlayed her government experience into a lucrative private-sector stint. In 2007, she and husband Jason DeParle, a *New York Times* reporter, spent nearly $3 million for a six-bedroom, six-bath Colonial in exclusive Chevy Chase, Maryland.[31]

Despite President Obama's loud denunciations of the revolving-door lobbyist culture in Washington, DeParle's industry ties didn't bother the White House in the least. DeParle served as an investment advisor at JP Morgan Partners, LLC, a private equity division of JP Morgan Chase & Co; sat on the board of directors at Boston Scientific Corporation and Cerner Corporation; and held directorships at Accredo Health Group Inc. (now owned by Medco Health Solutions Inc.), Triad Hospitals (now part of Community Health Systems), Guidant Corporation (now part of Boston Scientific), and DaVita Corporation, among others. In all, she sat on at least ten boards while advising JP Morgan and working as managing director at a private equity firm, CCMP Capital. From 2002 to 2008, while holding all those titles, DeParle also served as a member of the government-chartered Medicare Payment Advisory Committee (MedPAC), an influential panel that advises Congress on what Medicare should cover and at what price.[32]

In 2006 and 2007 alone, DeParle collected at least $3.5 million from fees and the sale and awards of stock from health-care businesses whose businesses will likely fall under her jurisdiction, according to the *Chicago Tribune*. That amount probably represents a small portion of DeParle's corporate earnings since 2001.[33]

Philip Klein of *The American Spectator* concluded: "[DeParle's] journey from the public sector to the private sector and back again would seem to represent the type of revolving-door relationship between Washington and corporate America that President Obama pledged to put an end to during the campaign and in an executive order."[34] The point is not that administration officials should be barred if they have any ties to business or any past lobbying experience that might raise conflict-of-interest questions. Indeed, DeParle's significant private-sector experience could be a strength. The point is that the Obama administration has taken a self-aggrandizing stand against hiring such players . . . while hiring them left and right.

As with previous czar questions, White House press secretary Robert Gibbs shrugged off concerns about DeParle's industry ties:

> Question: Robert, I just wanted to ask about Nancy DeParle and the fact that she sits on corporate boards that have health and medical-related interests. Is that—does the administration view that as any potential conflict of interest? Are there any potential problems there?
>
> MR. GIBBS: No. I mean, obviously, the White House has confidence in her and her abilities as part of the health care reform effort here.[35]

DeParle, the White House announced, would not need a waiver to the president's famous executive order requiring appointees to pledge not to participate "in any particular matter involving specific parties that is directly and substantially related to any former employer or former clients, including regulations and contracts" for a period of two years from the date of his or her appointment. The health czar will simply resign from all her corporate boards and directorships and recuse herself from any issue that "would directly impact in a significant way any of the companies for which she was a director," according to an anonymous administration official quoted by *Politico*.[36] White House spokesman Tommy Vietor stated that "Nancy will recuse from each and every particular matter involving a specific company on whose board she served."[37]

Unfortunately, it's not so simple. It's hard to imagine any health care reform-related issue that *won't* involve one of DeParle's vast array of former employers, clients, and corporate boards in the health care industry.

She earned at least $376,000 from Cerner Corporation, for example, which specializes in health information technology. As health czar, DeParle will have unmeasured clout in directing $19 billion of federal stimulus money earmarked for, yes, health information technology. GOP Congressman Darrell Issa of California stated the obvious: "There's no question that there will be a large presidential earmark for integrating a data system to try to reduce costs to try to put people's health records all into a single data base. A lot of these efficiencies, although merited, are going to lead to picking very large multibillion dollar winners, and she's going to be at the center of it all."[38] Financial writer Richard Gibbons notes that Cerner's annual revenues are about $1.7 billion, "so even a fraction of the $19 billion can make a huge difference to Cerner's bottom line."[39]

Nevertheless, liberal Beltway supporters see no reason for concern. An article in *The Hill*, quoting various ethics experts giving the health czar a pass, declared "DeParle's industry ties a non-issue."[40] Would these ethics experts have been equally sanguine if the Bush Administration had appointed a drug industry official to head up the Food and Drug Administration or an oil executive to head up the Department of Energy?

Jonathan Cohn at *The New Republic* wrote that he "found no examples of worrisome behavior. And one assumes the White House checked her private sector career a lot more carefully than I did. If their vetting had turned up anything even remotely disqualifying, it seems unlikely that they would be tapping her."[41] Because, you know, all of Obama's other appointees were vetted with such meticulous care.

"It is our view, and the view of counsel here, that the incidence of that will be very low," an Obama administration official reassured the *New York Times* when asked how frequently DeParle might have to recuse herself.[42]

The *Times,* which employs DeParle's husband, neglected to point out the obvious: If she were, in fact, to recuse herself from such issues—if she were to abide not just by the letter, but by the spirit of Obama's conflict-of-interest policy—Nancy DeParle would not have very much left to do.

STEVE "CHOOCH" RATTNER: THE AUTO CZAR'S SHADY TINSELTOWN TRADE

Before heading up the Obama Administration's auto bailout task force, Steven Rattner was a money manager at the Quadrangle Group, a high-octane Wall Street investment fund. In October 2004, Rattner paid a visit to then deputy comptroller of New York, David Loglisci, to solicit an investment for Quadrangle from the New York State Retirement Fund, according to an April

2009 Securities and Exchange Commission complaint and the *Wall Street Journal*.[43]

In January 2005, Loglisci arranged a meeting between one of his brothers and Rattner to discuss acquiring the DVD distribution rights to a low-budget comedy called *Chooch* for $88,841. Of course, it's neither unethical nor illegal to finance a movie, even a really bad one. But *Chooch* wasn't produced by just anyone. It was produced by David Loglisci and his brothers: the same David Loglisci who at the time was the deputy comptroller of New York; the same David Loglisci whom Rattner had solicited for a pension fund investment just three months earlier.

A few weeks after the DVD deal was completed, David Loglisci personally informed Rattner that the New York Retirement Fund would be making a $100 million investment in the Quadrangle Fund.[44] According to the SEC complaint, Loglisci never disclosed the *Chooch* deal to either the Retirement Fund's Investment Advisory Committee or to other members of the comptroller's staff. [45]

Loglisci is now under indictment, but neither Quadrangle nor Rattner has been accused of wrongdoing. The investigation by Securities and Exchange Commission (SEC) officials and the New York Attorney General, however, is not over. According to the *Journal*, the next phase of the investigation will focus on Quadrangle and other investment firms that received state retirement money.[46]

In addition to the DVD deal, federal and state investigators are looking at a $1.1 million "finder's fee" paid by Quadrangle to an agent named Henry Morris even though, according to the SEC complaint, Loglisci was already negotiating the investment directly with Quadrangle by the time the firm "retained" Morris.[47]

A spokesman for the Treasury Department said Rattner disclosed the SEC-Quadrangle investigation before his appointment.[48] A White House spokesman in April 2009 said President Obama remains fully supportive of Rattner.

Naturally, New York wasn't the only state in which Rattner worked his magic. In 2005, Quadrangle won a $20 million contract from the New Mexico State Investment Council, headed by New Mexico Governor Bill Richardson, later to be a disgraced Obama Commerce Secretary nominee. Rattner donated a total of $20,000 to Richardson's 2002 and 2006 gubernatorial campaigns.[49] From 2004 to 2009, Quadrangle employed New Mexico Senator Jeff Bingaman's son.[50] At some point during that period, Rattner had lunch with Senator Bingaman at Quadrangle's offices in New York.[51]

No word on whether they discussed *Chooch*.

TECHNOLOGY CZAR VIVEK KUNDRA: PETTY THIEF, CLUELESS CHIEF

Whoever thinks putting a shoplifter in charge of the entire federal government's information security infrastructure is a good idea? Raise your hands. Anybody? Well, the Obama White House has complete confidence in Vivek Kundra, the 34-year-old "whiz kid" named Federal Chief Information Officer (CIO) in March 2009 despite his criminal history. As first reported by blogger Ed Morrissey at HotAir.com, Kundra was convicted of misdemeanor theft.[52] He stole a handful of men's shirts from a J.C. Penney's department store and ran from police in a failed attempt to evade arrest.[53]

Morrissey, a former call center manager for the burglary and alarm business, points out that his employees in the private workforce had to be licensed; in some of those states, "any adult theft conviction at all would be disqualifying."[54] But such high standards for technology security czars in the government workforce apparently do not exist. Only after Morrissey pestered the White House—and only after mainstream media outlets picked up on Morrissey's reporting—did the White House finally acknowledge

Kundra's criminal past.[55] Kundra was a 21-year-old adult at the time of his attempted thievery and attempted escape from the police. From the White House's pooh-poohing of the incident as a "youthful indiscretion," you might have thought the digits in his age were reversed.

You will find no acknowledgment of Kundra's troubles on the official White House website. Instead, President Obama effuses about his technology czar's "depth of experience in the technology arena" and "commitment to lowering the cost of government operations." As the nation's CIO, Kundra "will play a key role in making sure our government is running in the most secure, open, and efficient way possible."[56]

But the aura of security and openness was further thrown into doubt in March when an FBI search warrant was issued at Kundra's office. He was serving as the Chief Technology Officer of the District of Columbia before moving over to the White House. During the transition, two of Kundra's underlings, Yusuf Acar and Sushil Bansal, were charged in an alleged scheme of bribery, kickbacks, ghost employees, and forged timesheets. Kundra was put on leave for five days and then reinstated after the Feds informed him that he was neither a subject nor a target of the investigation.[57]

Team Obama emphasized that Kundra had no idea what was going on in his workplace, which employed about 300 workers. But if his claimed ignorance is supposed to exonerate Kundra, what does it suggest about his ability to police government technology operations across the entire federal government? And what responsibility and oversight exactly did Kundra have over the indicted employees in his office? The buck stops where? Veteran D.C. newspaper columnist Jonetta Rose Barras reported that Acar "was consistently promoted by his boss, Vivek Kundra, receiving with each move increasing authority over sensitive information and operating with little supervision, according to government sources familiar with activities inside the Office of the Chief Technology Officer, or OCTO." The raid was no surprise to city and federal watchdogs, who identified a systemic lack of controls in the office, Barras reported.[58]

Eric Krangel at technology trade publication *Silicon Alley Insider* called on Kundra to resign:

> No one has accused Vivek of direct wrongdoing. But Vivek's apparent obliviousness to the alleged criminal behavior in his office hardly testifies to his managerial skills. Especially not given Vivek's self-promotion as a crusader against corruption. If Vivek couldn't keep tiny DC clean, can he handle the responsibility of an exponentially larger federal budget?
>
> Even if Vivek is clean as a whistle, his effectiveness as a reformer has already been crippled. Who won't question Vivek's motives should the new CIO call for a radical reform of our government's IT infrastructure? Is there any chance Vivek can implement real reform while we wait—over the course of months and years—for more information about what he knew to dribble out of an ongoing criminal investigation?
>
> Reforming the federal government's bloated web presence is a huge job, one we once thought Vivek Kundra was an inspired choice to tackle. But surely Vivek isn't the only person capable of taking on the dot-gov mess.[59]

No, but he may be one of the few convicted petty thieves in the country who has gone on to testify, as Kundra did in 2007, on how to create "a culture of accountability and innovation" in order to prevent "theft and fraud."[60] The anti-crime prevention strategy of Obama's technology security chief: Takes one to know one.

CHAPTER 6

MONEY MEN
LIFESTYLES OF THE RICH AND LIBERAL

Man of the People Barack Obama was on fire. Playing to a crowd in Chester, Virginia, with his shirt sleeves rolled up, the Democratic presidential candidate took his rhetorical piñata-stick to GOP rival John McCain and whacked him repeatedly for his personal wealth. Obama told the crowd that reporters had asked McCain how many houses he owned. Obama pretended to be aghast at McCain's answer:

> "He said, 'I'm not sure. I'll have to check with my staff.' True quote!"

Obama performed a righteous head wag and mocked McCain's answer again:

> "'I'm not sure, I'll have to check with my staff.' So they asked his staff and he said, 'at least four.'"

Barry Q. Public wrinkled his nose in disapproval and repeated McCain's words:

"At least four."

The One True Guardian of the Everyman paced back and forth across the outdoor stage, working himself into a thick, bash-the-rich lather: "Now think about that! I guess if you think that being rich means you've got to make $5 million, and if you don't know how many houses you have, then it's not surprising that you might think the economy was fundamentally strong."

The Peeved Populist paused for applause and laughter, then thrashed McCain again: "But if you're like me, and you got one house, or you were like the millions of people who are struggling right now to keep up with their mortgage so they don't lose their home, you might have a different perspective."

He Who Is Like You wasn't finished yet: "By the way, the answer is, John McCain has seven homes. There's just a fundamental gap of understanding between John McCain's world and what people are going through every single day here in America. You don't have to be a Nobel Prize-laureate economist, you just have to have a little bit of a sense of what ordinary people are going through to understand that we can't afford eight more years or four more years or one more year of the failed economic policies that George Bush has put in place."[1]

How audacious of Obama to carry on about other politicians' homes. He seemed to have forgotten that his own $1.7 million Chicago manse was financed with a discounted mortgage from Northern Trust and infamously included a shady land swap with convicted felon donor/developer Tony Rezko.[2] A report released by the Federal Election Commission in February 2009 under-scored that the Obamas received reduced loan rates (saving $300 a month, or $108,000 over the life of a 30-year loan) because of their high-profile positions. Northern Trust offered the super jumbo loan to the Obamas in anticipation of entering "long-term financial relationships" with the successful couple.[3]

This preferential treatment is not available to average Joes (with last names other than Biden) shopping for a new home.

In response to a complaint by Washington, D.C.-based watch-dog Judicial Watch, the FEC refused to call the Obama's mortgage deal an illegal corporate contribution, but it was an obvious act of favor-trading. Northern Trust employees had contributed $71,000 to Obama since 1990. "This was a business proposition for us," the lender's president bluntly told the *Washington Post* when asked about the below-market benefits of the Obamas' home loan deal. As is so often the case in political life, the scandal isn't necessarily what's illegal—the scandal is what's legal.[4]

Prominent members of Team Obama benefited from similar special home deals. *Politico* reminded readers that the Clintons secured a $1.35 million loan from Democrat pal and fundraiser Terry McCauliffe for their New York estate; PNC Mortgage further supplied the Clintons "several fee deductions and waivers to its policies"; Obama special envoy Richard Holbrooke snagged a sweetheart loan to refinance his Telluride, Colorado, ski vacation home from embattled Countrywide Financial as part of its "Friends of [CEO] Angelo [Mozilo]" V.I.P. program;[5] and Obama's close confidante Jim Johnson accepted more than $7 million in below-market-rate loans from Countrywide.

Obama had tapped and then dropped Johnson from his vice presidential search committee in June 2008 after his Countrywide ties became public. Johnson, who had served as CEO of government-sponsored mortgage behemoth Fannie Mae from 1991 to 1998, had failed to disclose his Countrywide perks in violation of Fannie's code of conduct, perks which increased after his departure from Fannie Mae. Informal Obama economic consultant and fellow Fannie Mae chief Franklin Raines also failed to disclose his arrangements with Countrywide. The *Wall Street Journal* broke the story:

> Property records show Mr. Johnson has received more than $7 million in loans from Countrywide since 1998, the first coming in the waning days of his Fannie Mae tenure. He borrowed $392,950 on a row house in Washington's Dupont Circle neighborhood, with the rate set for the first five years at 6.375%.
>
> At the time, initial rates for such loans ranged from about 6.2% to 6.5%, according to data compiled for The Wall Street Journal by HSH Associates Inc., which surveys lenders. Rates depend partly on how much borrowers pay in points, if any, to lower their interest charge. Records don't show whether Mr. Johnson paid points or if so how many.
>
> Mr. Johnson returned to Countrywide several times to finance his growing real-estate holdings. In November 2001, he received a Countrywide loan of $1.3 million for a home in Palm Desert, Calif. The rate was 5.250% for five years, then became adjustable. Rates on such loans averaged about 6% to 6.2% about that time....
>
> In June 2003, Mr. Johnson obtained a $971,650 mortgage on a house in upper northwest Washington, D.C., with a rate of 3.875% for the first five years. About that time, the market average was about 4.3% to 4.9%....
>
> In January 2006, Mr. Johnson got a $5 million home-equity line of credit from Countrywide on a residence in Ketchum, Idaho, near the Sun Valley ski resort. And in December 2007 he received a Countrywide home-equity line of credit for $1.01 million and executed a $1 million promissory note in connection with that home.
>
> ...Mr. Raines, who succeeded Mr. Johnson at Fannie's helm at the end of 1998, became a repeat customer of Countrywide while he was CEO. Two days before Christmas in 1999, Mr.

Raines got a $1 million loan on his house in upper northwest Washington, D.C., refinancing it in November 2001. Property records don't show the interest rate in either case.

In April 2003, Mr. Raines refinanced again with Countrywide, this time getting a 5.125% rate for the first 10 years... the average rate for such a loan around that time was about 5.5% to 5.7%.[6]

Yes, this is the same Countrywide that Obama had endlessly excoriated for its role in the subprime mortgage crisis. Obama likened the demonized lender's CEO Angelo Mozilo to a dangerous virus in March 2008: "These are the people who are responsible for infecting the economy and helping to create a home foreclosure crisis.... These executives crossed the line to boost their bottom line." Instead of focusing on Obama's hypocrisy, liberal *Time* magazine journalist Karen Tumulty cried RAAACISM!—denouncing an ad that spotlighted Raines's fraud-ridden tenure at Fannie Mae. Raines, who happens to be black, presided over the mother of all financial accounting scandals at Fannie Mae in which the institution misstated profits for years, yet escaped with a golden parachute worth an estimated $240 million in benefits.

No matter to Tumulty. She decried the McCain camp's anti-Raines ad because it depicted "sinister images of two black men" (Obama and Raines).[7] The ad's photos of Obama and Raines were standard headshots—some with dour expressions, others smiling. The fact that Tumulty perceived them as "sinister" suggested that she should perform a racism self-exam before diagnosing anyone else.

Race-card distractions aside, Obama campaign manager David Plouffe soldiered on with the Clean Hands Narrative: "If we're really going to crack down on the practices that caused the credit and housing crises, we're going to need a leader who doesn't owe these industries any favors." A leader above the fray. A leader unsullied by crony connections. A leader who would usher in a "new kind of politics" that represented the little people and abandoned the old ways of doing business. Barack Obama did a very fine job of paying lip service to such leadership. In his open letter to the public announcing his presidential candidacy, Obama lamented that Washington had become "so gummed up by money and influence."[8] He has since taken every opportunity to separate himself rhetorically from evil industry and greedy capitalists:

"I want to be absolutely clear that the reason I'm in public life, the reason I came to Chicago, the reason I started working with unions, the reason I march on picket lines, the reason that I am running for president is because of you, not because of folks who are writing big checks," Obama declared at an AFL-CIO debate in August 2007.

On Super Tuesday 2008, he expounded on his folksy We the People theme. The *New York Times* transcribed the euphoria:

> Maybe this year, this time can be different. (Cheers, applause.)
>
> Their voices echoed from the hills of New Hampshire to the deserts of Nevada, where teachers and cooks and kitchen workers stood up to say that maybe Washington doesn't have to be run by lobbyists anymore. (Cheers, applause.) Maybe the voices of the American people can finally be heard again. (Cheers, applause.)
>
> They reached the coast of South Carolina, when people said that maybe we don't have to be divided by race and region and gender—(cheers, applause)—that the crumbling schools are stealing the future of black children and white children—(cheers, applause)—that we can come together and build an America that gives every child everywhere the opportunity to live out their dreams. This time can be different. (Cheers, applause.)

And today, on this Tuesday in February, in states north and south, east and west, what began as a whisper in Springfield has swelled to a chorus of millions calling for change. (Cheers, applause.) It's a chorus that cannot be ignored, a chorus that cannot be deterred. This time can be different because this campaign for the presidency of the United States of America is different. (Cheers, applause.)

(Chants of "Yes, We Can! Yes, We Can!")[9]

"Too often," Obama lectured Wall Street in March 2008, "we've excused and even embraced an ethic of greed, corner cutting and inside dealing that has always threatened the long-term stability of our economic system. Too often, we've lost that common stake in each other's prosperity."[10]

In June 2008, Obama railed against credit card companies: "This has to stop. We cannot let the rules of the game continue to be rigged against ordinary Americans. We need a President who will look out for the interests of hardworking families, not just their big campaign donors and corporate allies."[11] Immediately after the speech, he headed to a campaign fundraiser at the Manhattan headquarters of Credit Suisse, one of the major investment companies caught up in the subprime lending debacle.

In March 2009, Obama assailed the corporate bonuses handed out by bailout recipient AIG—which had been approved by his own handpicked Treasury Secretary and AIG bailout architect Tim Geithner. But let's not get distracted.

Obama blamed "the system and culture that made them possible—a culture where people made enormous sums of money, taking irresponsible risks that have now put the entire economy at risk."[12] The irresponsible risk-takers at AIG donated $104,332 to Barack Obama in the 2008 federal election cycle.[13] Since 2004, AIG has donated 60 percent of its $2.6 million in political donations to Democrats. Obama kept the corrupted cash. But I digress.

"We don't need these house of cards, these Ponzi schemes, even when they're legal, where a relatively few do spectacularly well while the middle class loses ground," Obama inveighed. "I want to describe to you the kind of economy that we want to build: an economy that rewards hard work and responsibility, not high-flying finance schemes." He vowed to "make sure we don't find ourselves in this situation again, where taxpayers are on the hook for losses in bad times, and all the wealth generated in good times goes to those who are at the very top of the income ladder. That's the kind of ethic we've had for too long. That's the kind of approach that led us into this mess."

However, a close look at the high-flying financiers whom Barack the Commoner has surrounded himself with in Washington shows how deeply embedded the "ethic of greed" is in Obama World. The Wall Street gamblers that Obama and his wife carped about on the campaign trail were shoveling money to his campaign hand over fist. According to the Center for Responsive Politics, hedge funds and private equity firms donated $2,992,456 to the Obama campaign in the 2008 cycle. Obama, erstwhile critic of the campaign finance practice known as "bundling," happily accepted more than $200,000 in bundled contributions from billionaire hedge-fund manager James Torrey, more than $100,000 in bundled contributions from billionaire hedge-fund manager Paul Tudor Jones, and more than $50,000 in bundled contributions from billionaire hedge-fund manager Kenneth C. Griffin, chief executive officer of Citadel Investment Group in Chicago.

No fewer than 100 Obama bundlers are investment CEOs and brokers: nearly two dozen work for financial giants such as Lehman Brothers, Goldman Sachs, or Citigroup.[14]

By comparison, multi-house dweller and Evil Republican Rich Guy John McCain received $1,699,525 from the industry—that's over forty percent less than Obama took.[15]

Now, the hedge fund managers, statist bankers, corporate lob-byists, and lax regulators Obama incessantly cursed are the same ones whom he has appointed to "fix" the "system and culture" they created—and from which they all profited greatly.

"We can't afford eight more years or four more years or one more year of the failed economic policies that George Bush has put in place," Obama proclaimed on the campaign trail. But just like George Bush, Barack Obama is relying on Goldman Sachs/Wall Street power brokers to engineer massive government interventions to "rescue" failing businesses with the tax dollars of ordinary Americans. Obama had assailed John McCain for being "in cahoots" with CEOs and hedge fund managers. How are the myriad "public-private partnerships" Obama has embraced between government and corporate interests any different?

LARRY THE HEDGE FUND MANAGER

In the final weeks of the 2008 election season, the Man of the People met his match. Campaigning in Ohio, Barack Obama came upon Joe Wurzelbacher, who had been playing football with his son in his front yard. "Your new tax plan is going to tax me more, isn't it?" the plumber asked the candidate. "It's not that I want to punish your success," Obama replied. "I just want to make sure that everybody who is behind you, that they've got a chance at success, too. My attitude is that if the economy's good for folks from the bottom up, it's gonna be good for everybody. If you've got a plumbing business, you're gonna be better off if you've got a whole bunch of customers who can afford to hire you, and right now everybody's so pinched that business is bad for everybody and I think when you spread the wealth around, it's good for everybody."[16]

The McCain campaign seized on Obama's wealth redistribu-tion gospel; the videotaped confrontation between Obama and

Wurzelbacher went viral on YouTube and was invoked in a presidential debate. Obama lashed back. At a late October 2008 rally in Richmond, Virginia, Obama snarked:

> I had a nice conversation the other day with Joe the plumber. Joe's cool, I got no problems with Joe, all I want to do is give Joe a tax cut, but let's be clear who Senator McCain's fighting for. *He's not fighting for Joe the Plumber; he's fighting for Joe the Hedge Fund Manager. John McCain likes to talk about Joe the Plumber but he's in cahoots with Joe the CEO [emphasis added].*[17]

A month later, Obama appointed Lawrence Summers—let's call him Larry the Hedge Fund Manager—as director of the White House National Economic Council. Yes, Obama is "in cahoots" with a king of Wall Street. Summers, an academic economist turned Clinton Treasury official turned Harvard University president, gained notoriety in 2005 after feminists protested his remarks on how women might not have the same genetic ability as men in the sciences and engineering. He was drummed out of academia in a ridiculous hissy fit of political correctness. But the episode had a multi-million-dollar silver lining. Summers landed on his feet at New York City-based D. E. Shaw—one of the world's largest hedge funds. Between late 2006 and late 2008, he worked there one day a week for two years providing private consultations and serving as a "sounding board" for Shaw's traders. In 2008, he earned nearly $5.2 million working for the $30 billion hedge fund management company. One day a week. The *New York Times* provided a glimpse of his schmooze-filled work life:

> In addition to his salary at Shaw, Mr. Summers enjoyed growing wealth through investments in the firm's funds. Unlike most hedge funds, which lost money as the markets plunged in 2008,

Shaw posted returns of about 7 percent in its so-called macro-economic fund. . . . When investors rushed en masse to withdraw their money from hedge funds last year, Shaw asserted its right to block redemptions from its fund. An exception was made for Mr. Summers, however, because the White House job he was taking required him to divest.

A spokesman for Shaw said Mr. Summers's main job was not to act as a salesman. But in the fall of 2007, as the financial crisis simmered, Mr. Summers traveled to Dubai for a series of meetings with Shaw's marketing staff and potential investors. Bankers from across the region flew in for the event. Mr. Summers spoke at several lavish dinners and met with local parties involved in Shaw's real estate investments in the area, people briefed on his trip said.

Last September, Mr. Summers explained to Shaw traders what appeared to be an aberration in a key interest rate, the London interbank offered rate, or Libor, thus helping its traders avoid losses. He spoke at the firm's 20th anniversary gathering for its investors and at a prominent hedge fund investor conference in Boston, weeks before the presidential election. In December, he attended the firm's annual holiday party, held in the American Museum of Natural History in New York, beneath the giant model of a blue whale. [18]

Summers also remained on the faculty at Harvard University.

In Beltway business-as-usual form, the Obama White House minimized press attention by performing a late Friday afternoon document dump disclosure—of Summers's financial assets forms. The records showed that in addition to his massive hedge fund salary and $590,000 in Harvard pay, Summers reaped nearly $2.8 million in speaking fees from many of the major financial institutions and government bailout recipients he now polices, including J.P. Morgan, Citigroup, Goldman Sachs, and Lehman Brothers.[19]

A single speech to Goldman Sachs in April 2008 brought in $135,000. A Nigerian media conglomerate, Leaders & Company Ltd., shelled out $225,000 to hear Summers speak at an October 2008 gig. A week after Election Day 2008, Summers spoke to Merrill Lynch for $45,000. A week and a half after that, Obama appointed Larry the Hedge Fund Manager to his top economic advisory post—circumventing the Senate confirmation vetting process. Summers donated the Merrill Lynch speaking fee to charity. But whatever highly sought after advice and counsel he gave the failing company was non-refundable. On the side, Summers made $34,000 in spare change writing a column for the *Financial Times*—weighing in weeks before Election Day on the $700 billion bailout that he was undoubtedly being paid to speak about to clients.[20] Nice work if you can get it.

Summers has experience negotiating government-sponsored bailouts that benefit private concerns. In 1995, he spearheaded a $40 billion Mexican peso bailout that bypassed Congress. Summers personally leaned on the International Monetary Fund to provide nearly $18 billion for the package. His boss, then Secretary of the Treasury Robert Rubin, was former co-chairman of Wall Street giant Goldman Sachs—the Mexican government's investment banking firm of choice. Rubin had personally lobbied former Mexican President Carlos Salinas de Gortari to allow Goldman to handle the privatization of Teléfonos de México, *The Multinational Monitor* financial newsletter reported. Rubin also shepherded the $2.3 billion global public offering of mega-media television company Grupo Televisa.[21] Rubin acknowledged in his financial disclosure forms that he had

> 42 Goldman Sachs clients with whom he had had 'significant contact,' including six powerful Mexican clients. The public sector clients were the Mexican government, Mexico's finance ministry, and Mexico's central bank. The private sector clients were

Teléfonos de México, Cemex S.A., the largest cement firm in the Americas, and Desc, Sociedad de Fomento Industrial, Mexico's seventh largest manufacturing conglomerate. Rubin reaped $25 million in compensation from Goldman, Sachs & Co. in 1992 alone.[22]

In 1997, the Clinton administration announced with great fanfare that Mexico had repaid $12.6 billion in loans. Clinton, Rubin, and Summers openly joked about how the Treasury Secretary had profited. The *New York Times* captured the jubilation:

> The usually understated former investment banker was clearly reveling in the success of the bailout today.
>
> In the Roosevelt Room at the White House, Mr. Clinton side-stepped a question about a recent decline in the value of the peso and deferred to Mr. Rubin, explaining "you've made so much more money than I have."
>
> "There is a point to that!" said Mr. Rubin, who usually makes no references—even in jest—to his huge fortune.
>
> Back at the Treasury later in the day Mr. Rubin raised an eyebrow when his deputy, Lawrence H. Summers—who was the first to recognize the possible ripple effects of the crisis in emerging markets and who organized much of the loan effort—joked that he would settle for just 1 percent of the Treasury's $580 million profit on the deal.
>
> "Larry, anything you can negotiate, I'm happy to split with you," Mr. Rubin shot back.[23]

Not everyone was so jovial and sanguine about the moral hazard the Summers-Rubin bailout created. GOP Congressman James Leach of Iowa, chairman of the House banking committee, warned that "great caution is going to have to be exercised in assuming that this is the only or best way to proceed . . . [American taxpayers cannot be] placed disproportionately in jeopardy" as the world's lender of last resort.[24]

More than a decade later, Summers was back in D.C. helping guide another Democrat administration down the road to bailout hell. Perhaps that explains why he was caught literally napping not once,[25] but twice,[26] at economic summits hosted by President Obama. At a "fiscal responsibility" summit in late February 2009 and at a meeting with credit card CEOs in mid-March 2009, photographers captured Summers slumbering while bureaucrats and businessmen collaborated on creating new taxpayer pipelines to prop up failing enterprises. Been there. Done that. Zzzzzz.

Some liberal journalists and bloggers did try and wake up the public to Summers's role in helping engineer the current fiscal meltdown while he served as Clinton Treasury Secretary. "It was Summers, as much as anyone, who in the Clinton years prevented the regulation of the hedge funds that are at the center of the explosion of the derivatives bubble, and the fact that D. E. Shaw, a leading hedge fund, paid the Obama adviser $5.2 million last year does suggest a serious conflict of interest," Robert Scheer wrote in *The Nation*.[27] The left-leaning ProPublica online investigative journalism website explained that in 1998, "an obscure federal agency, the Commodity Futures Trading Commission, raised the prospect of regulating the burgeoning market in complex financial instruments." Who led the charge against such oversight? "The nation's leading financial officials—[Securities and Exchange Commission chairman Arthur] Levitt, Federal Reserve Chairman Alan Greenspan, Secretary of the Treasury Robert Rubin, and his deputy Lawrence Summers—pummeled the proposal, saying it was dangerous to even discuss the idea."[28]

Double standards, anyone? Scheer acknowledged them: "If this was happening in a Republican administration, scores of Democrats in Congress would be all over it, asking tough questions about what exactly did Summers do to earn all that money from the D. E. Shaw hedge fund. As it is, with their silence they are complicit in this emerging scandal of the banking bailout." [29] Another epiphany hit *Washington Post* blogger Dan Froomkin: "It's become increasingly clear over the last several months that despite the Obama administration's generally progressive economic views and sporadic bouts of populist rhetoric, the White House has something of a soft spot for Wall Street." [30]

You don't say.

TIMMY THE TAX-CHEATING, BAILOUT-BUNGLING BUREAUCRAT

They called Tim Geithner an indispensable "whiz kid" [31] and "wonder boy." [32] "They" are the bipartisan establishmentarians in Washington. Geithner's mentor, President George W. Bush's Treasury Secretary Hank Paulson, called him a "very unusually talented young man" who "understands government and understands markets." [33] Geithner's longtime mentor and tennis camp partner Larry Summers affectionately calls him "young Tim." [34] GOP Senator Orrin Hatch declared him "a very competent guy." [35] Democrat Senator Harry Reid concurred: "Tim Geithner is exactly the man for the job.... From his time as the President of the Federal Reserve Bank of New York, and in leadership roles at the Treasury Department, IMF and the Council on Foreign Relations, Mr. Geithner knows...how to navigate the complex financial world." [36]

Announcing Geithner's nomination as Treasury Secretary on November 24, 2009, President Obama hailed the genius civil servant as uniquely qualified: "With stellar performances and outstanding results at every stage of his career, Tim has earned the confidence and respect of business, financial and community leaders; members of Congress; and political leaders around the world—and I know he will do so once again as America's next

Treasury Secretary, the chief economic spokesman for my Administration."[37]

Golden Boy seemed to have it all. The Dartmouth and Johns Hopkins-educated president of the New York Federal Reserve Bank had studied Japanese and Chinese, and had lived in East Africa, India, Thailand, China, and Japan. His father ran the Ford Foundation's Asian grants, and once crossed paths with Obama's mother, who worked on developing Ford programs for Indonesia.[38] Geithner's maternal grandfather was an adviser to President Dwight D. Eisenhower. But all the public service pedigrees and Ivy League degrees in the world couldn't save him from basic tax-cheating stupidity. In mid-January 2009, before his confirmation hearing, the Senate Finance Committee discovered that Geithner had failed to pay some $43,000 in federal self-employment taxes for four separate years—and only coughed up $26,000 of that debt when he was named Obama's Treasury Secretary-designate in November 2009. Somehow, brilliant and meticulous Geithner didn't catch the lapses.

Recall that Joe the Plumber, an average guy with no Ivy League degrees in business or finance, was crucified for his $1,200 Ohio tax lien (the state had sent a notification to a prior residence he had vacated).[39] One might give a common man some leeway for making common mistakes. But Tim Geithner, as all his cheerleaders in Washington reminded us, is no "common" man. The Obama/Geithner defense—"$43,000 in unpaid taxes is a common occurrence"—simply is not a credible alibi. Nor was his sheepish admission during his Senate confirmation hearings that he used Turbo Tax to prepare his taxes.

Supporters dubbed Geithner "too big to fail." Try "too smart to care."

In addition to his failure to pay four years' worth of federal taxes—you try getting away with that without getting thrown behind bars!—Geithner also illegally employed an immigrant maid for three months after her work authorization papers had expired. But wait. That wasn't all. Geithner's employer at the time of his serial tax-dodging was the International Monetary Fund. The agency reimburses its employees for their self-employment taxes. The allowance was made to keep IMF and World Bank workers' salaries on par with other foreign peers. IMF employees receive an Employee Tax Manual outlining their obligations. (Maybe if it were written in Japanese or Chinese, Geithner would have paid closer attention?)

Employees also file an Annual Tax Allowance Request promising to "pay the taxes for which I have received tax allowance payments." The Senate Finance Committee released one of those forms signed by Geithner. A Senate source confirmed to *National Review's* Byron York that Geithner pocketed the cash: "He was getting the money. He was being paid a tax allowance to pay him for tax payments that he should have made but had not."[40] IRS employment application packets notify potential workers that the Treasury Inspector General for Tax Administration vets all candidates and current employees "who have violated or are violating laws, rules, or regulations related to the performance of their duties." Obama stood by his nominee who would oversee the IRS, but might not even qualify for a lesser job at the agency.

Obama spokesman Robert Gibbs calls Geithner's transgressions "honest mistakes." Media outlets like the Associated Press attempted to downplay his snubbing of the law as mere "tax goofs." (When Democrats like Geithner, Al Franken, and Charlie Rangel fail to pay up what they legally owe, they're just "goofs." When you or I object to forking over more than what we're already paying, Vice President Joe Biden calls us unpatriotic.) The condescension towards ordinary Americans incensed by Geithner's tax evasion was bipartisan. "These are not the times to think in small political terms," Senator Lindsey Graham, a South Carolina Republican, sniffed. "He has a great résumé."[41]

No, Senator Graham, he does not.

Left out of the glowing endorsements: Geithner's disastrous track record while working at the IMF in the 1990s. Former Australian prime minister and Labor Party leader Paul Keating blasted Geithner for botching Indonesia's economic troubles: "Tim Geithner was the Treasury line officer who wrote the IMF [International Monetary Fund] program for Indonesia in 1997–98, which was to apply current account solutions to a capital account crisis." The *Sydney Morning Herald* explained the debacle:

> In other words, Geithner fundamentally misdiagnosed the problem. And his misdiagnosis led to a dreadfully wrong prescription.
>
> Geithner thought Asia's problem was the same as the ones that had shattered Latin America in the 1980s and Mexico in 1994, a classic current account crisis. In this kind of crisis, the central cause is that the government has run impossibly big debts.
>
> The solution? The IMF, the Washington-based emergency lender of last resort, will make loans to keep the country solvent, but on condition the government hacks back its spending. The cure addresses the ailment.
>
> But the Asian crisis was completely different. The Asian governments that went to the IMF for emergency loans—Thailand, South Korea and Indonesia—all had sound public finances.
>
> The problem was not government debt. It was great tsunamis of hot money in the private capital markets. When the wave rushed out, it left a credit drought behind.
>
> But Geithner, through his influence on the IMF, imposed the same cure the IMF had imposed on Latin America and Mexico. It was the wrong cure.[42]

Geithner fared no better as president of the Federal Reserve Bank of New York—a position he attained thanks to heavy lobbying by his Wall Street mentors Robert Rubin and Larry Summers, both of whom sat on the New York Fed's selection committee. Their cronyism had multi-billion-dollar consequences for taxpayers. Rubin, you see, was also an executive at New York-based Citigroup, which Geithner regulated. Or was *supposed* to regulate. Instead, he helped foster Citi's spending binge and engineered the teetering company's $52 billion federal bailout.

An investigation by ProPublica found that the New York Fed under Geithner "had lifted some restrictions on Citigroup, allowing it to engage in risky ventures with insufficient capital."[43] In response to questions from the Senate Finance Committee about his failure to police Citigroup, Geithner acknowledged: "Citigroup's supervisors, including the Federal Reserve, failed to identify a number of their risk management shortcomings and to induce appropriate changes in behavior." He called his own initiatives to strengthen the financial system ahead of the crisis "inadequate."[44] Geithner had a hand in the $30 billion Bear Stearns bailout and the multi-level AIG bailouts ($85 billion and $38 billion under President Bush and another $30 billion in March 2009 under Obama). Handsome sums of that taxpayer money went to major financial institutions that had employed Obama's money men and their closest confidants. Goldman Sachs, for example, raked in nearly $13 billion in December 2009 from AIG in federal TARP funds. It is money the company's chief financial officer said he did not need or expect.[45]

Those who saw Geithner work up close provided the most damning criticisms. Aaron Ross Sorkin reported in the *New York Times*'s Dealbook page that, "Behind the scenes, Mr. Geithner was the point person for weeks of sleep-deprived Bailout Weekends. It was Mr. Geithner, not Mr. Paulson, for example, who put together

the original rescue plan for the American International Group."
Said one executive who attended several confidential meetings on
the bailouts: "He was in the room at every turn of the crisis. You
can look at that both ways."[46] In other words, Geithner's intellectual DNA is embedded in these failed financial rescues.
"Failed" and "inadequate" in his own words. Superfluous and
harmful in the eyes of many on Wall Street. And yet, senators on
both sides of the political aisle lavished praise on his "great
resumé" before installing him as the next bank-beholden bureaucrat to steer Barack Obama's savior-based economy.

By March 2009, Geithner had become a running national
joke—eliciting scorn in the conservative blogosphere after
announcing he would be chasing after international tax deadbeats
while he was a tax deadbeat himself, and evoking snickers from
Capitol Hill over his inability to fill top slots at the Treasury. The
conservative *New York Post* editorial board remarked on the
irony of tax cheat Geithner testifying before the House Ways and
Means Committee of tax cheat Charlie Rangel, Democrat Congressman from New York, on how "to reduce...tax evasion and
avoidance."[47]

Meanwhile, the liberal *Huffington Post* reported that lawmakers and congressional staff on both sides of the aisle laughed in dis-
belief at a briefing on Geithner's latest financial rescue plan: "The
laughter was at its height when Obama officials explained that the
White House planned to guarantee a wide swath of toxic assets—
which they referred to as 'legacy assets'—but wouldn't be asking
Congress for money," the site noted. "Rep. Brad Sherman (D-CA),
a bailout opponent in the fall, asked the officials to give Congress
the total dollar figure for which they were on the hook. The officials said that they couldn't provide a number, a response met by
chuckling that was bipartisan, but tilted toward the GOP side."[48]

Soon after, the Grand Kabuki Theater of Outrage erupted over
AIG bonuses that Geithner had approved. Geithner claimed he

didn't find out about the AIG bonus issue until March 10, 2009. This was contradicted by AIG president Edward Liddy's testimony a week earlier. Liddy was right. Geithner was wrong. A House hearing broadcast on C-SPAN on March 3 showed Geithner being questioned directly about the bonuses—a full week before Geithner claims he was made aware of the impending controversy.[49]

Geithner probably wished he had lost his appointment book on February 10, 2009, when he unveiled his vaunted, vague financial stability "plan" on Capitol Hill. In stark contrast to the lovefest at his confirmation hearing, Senators openly mocked the not-so-golden boy. "So you have no clue," retorted Senator Lindsay Graham—who only a few months ago chastised Geithner's critics for "playing gotcha"[50] and engaging in "small" politics. The Dow dropped 382 points after Geithner's big fail.[51]

A month later, Geithner caused the dollar to decline in international trade after he suggested at a major forum that the United States was "quite open" to a suggestion from Chinese officials to move to a new global currency.[52] Former Clinton Treasury colleague Roger Altman tried to rescue Geithner from his blunder with painful prompting ("I'd like to ask one final question, in effect, *on behalf of the market* [emphasis added]. It might be useful if you tried to clarify your earlier comment on the reaction to the central bank governor of China's idea..."). But by the time Geithner took the hint, it was too late.[53] It was actually the second time Geithner had roiled the markets with public comments about China; in January 2009, during his confirmation hearings, his suggestion that China was manipulating its currency resulted in a sharp sell-off of U.S. bonds (in which China has a large stake).[54] "He came right out and said Obama believes China is manipulating their currency," Maryann Hurley, a bond market strategist, told the *Wall Street Journal*. "It's very easy to pick another country to be your whipping boy. In an era where we're looking at deficits as far as the eye can see...[what] we don't need is somebody starting to dump our debt." The *Wall Street Journal*'s "MarketBeat" reporter David Gaffen pleaded with Geithner: "Will you please be quiet, please?"[55]

By May 2009, the whiz kid was the nation's whipping boy. Geithner had the "eyes of a shoplifter," a cable TV talking head cracked. "Think Bambi looking into the headlights on an 18-wheeler," quipped veteran risk analyst Christopher Whalen to Portfolio.com reporter Gary Weiss.[56] Treasury Department vacancies and key policy decisions piled up as a result of what the *Washington Post* called "Treasury's ad-hoc management," ruled by Geithner's unofficial advisors.[57] "In over his head" was the new conventional wisdom. White House chief of staff Rahm Emanuel swooped in at President Obama's urging, according to the *Wall Street Journal*, to bail out the Bailout King. Emanuel "has been so involved in the workings of the Treasury that 'Rahm wants it' has become an unofficial mantra among some at the Treasury, according to government officials," the paper reported.[58]

But well before he set foot in office, clear-eyed critics had pegged Geithner for a career bureaucrat buoyed by the Wall Street old boys' network with a track record of misreading financial crises, pandering to failing banks, and playing fast and loose with his taxes.

It's not like Washington hadn't been warned.

IN CAHOOTS WITH CITICORP

By late November 2008, taxpayers came to expect midnight bailouts from feckless feds "in cahoots"—to borrow our president's words—with Big Business. At 1 a.m. Eastern on November 24, 2008, Citicorp got its share of the bailout pie: $306 billion in government backing and $20 billion from the TARP banking bailout rammed through Congress a month earlier. The Citi "rescue" was the result of intense collaboration between Citigroup board member and former Clinton Treasury Secretary Robert Rubin; then Bush Treasury Secretary Henry M. Paulson Jr.; and then president of the Federal Reserve Bank of New York/Paulson-Rubin protégé/soon-to-be Obama Treasury Secretary Tim Geithner.[59]

"[I]s it too much to ask Washington to develop a policy that isn't crafted in a scramble of private phone calls?" an exasperated *Wall Street Journal* editorial board wondered the next day.[60]

In January 2009, the Obama administration flexed its faux populist muscle in demanding that Citigroup drop its plans to spend $50 million for a luxury French jet. The same month Rubin resigned from the company—walking away from the wreckage with $150 million after ten years at the company. Behind the scenes, more Citi men were sitting in the catbird's seat. They included Jacob Lew, former chief financial officer of Citigroup Alternative Investments, who was appointed Obama's number two at the Department of State and will oversee interagency economic policy matters, and Michael Froman, another former CFO in the same division, who is now deputy assistant to the president and deputy national security adviser for international economic affairs. Obama and the bonus-bashers refrained from demagoguing Lew's $1.1 million-plus salary and bonus and Froman's $7.4 million-plus salary and 2008 year-end bonus of $2.25 million.

Both Lew and Froman now work closely with Wall Street crony and former Robert Rubin co-worker Larry Summers at the National Economic Council. *National Journal* connected more Rubin/Citi dots: "Director of the Office of Management and Budget Peter Orszag, and Summers's deputy, Jason Furman, both served as directors of the Hamilton Project, a Brookings Institution initiative the [*sic*] produces research and policy positions on economic issues, where Rubin was a founding member of the advisory council. If that isn't enough, Froman served as Rubin's chief of staff during Rubin's stint as Secretary of Treasury."[61]

Three months after the Bush-Obama team engineered the first Citi bailout in November 2008, the Obama administration announced it was raising its stake in the failing company from 8 percent to 38 percent.

"We need a President who will look out for the interests of hardworking families, not just their big campaign donors and corporate allies," candidate Barack Obama insisted in the halcyon days of his campaign. Still waiting. He promised Hope, but his Wall Street friends and backers got the Change—billions and billions of dollars worth of change.

THE SUBPRIME GANG

Former Fannie Mae corruptocrats Jim Johnson and Franklin Raines may not have official positions with the administration, but other subprime crisis-connected beneficiaries do.

Louis Caldera, director of the White House Military Office, earned a hefty six-figure sum for serving on various corporate boards, including $227,155 in board fees and deferred compensation from IndyMac Bancorp, the California-based savings and loan company that collapsed in 2008; IndyMac was seized by the federal government and investigated by the FBI for subprime loan fraud.[62] (Fun fact: Caldera was responsible for freaking out New York City residents in late April 2009 after approving a "mission" to allow low-flying planes that resembled Air Force One to zoom past the Statue of Liberty for an aerial photo op.[63] City officials were not warned. Hundreds of New Yorkers, under the quite reasonable impression that it was a terrorist attack, panicked, and several were hurt in the rush to evacuate their buildings.)

Obama's close hometown crony, campaign finance chief, and senior adviser Penny Pritzker was head of Superior Bank of Chicago, a subprime specialist that went bust in 2001, leaving

ABOVE: Barack Obama, impeached Democrat Gov. Rod Blagojevich, and Chicago Mayor Richard Daley yuk it up. Blago's secretly taped musings on how to profit from his power to appoint Obama's Senate replacement roped in key members of Team Obama, including White House Chief of Staff Rahm Emanuel, White House senior adviser Valerie Jarrett, and the Service Employees International Union.

LEFT: Vice President Joe Biden and First Lady Michelle Obama share an intimate moment. Both also share common histories of nepotism and liberal hypocrisy—bashing the corporate world and influence-peddling industries from which they and their relatives benefited mightily.

Vice President Biden's corporate lobbyist son, Hunter, raked in consulting payments from credit card giant MBNA while dad championed the company's bankruptcy reform legislation. Two days after Obama tapped Biden as his running mate, Hunter Biden officially quit the registered lobbying business, but continued working on behalf of medical and academic clients at the corporate law and lobbying firm he co-founded with his father's old campaign treasurer and consummate Democrat influence peddler, William Oldaker. Hunter Biden and his Uncle James (Senator Biden's brother) later entangled themselves in a messy business deal with shady partners at Paradigm Companies LLC—a hedge fund that failed amid massive fraud allegations and litigation.

Chicago political machine protégé-turned Clinton crony-turned Freddie Mac profiteer-turned-investment banker Rahm Emanuel is the fifth wealthiest member of the Obama administration, with assets between $5,023,000 and $13,170,000 in 2007, according to *Washingtonian* magazine. The former Goldman Sachs money man helped spearhead the $700 billion TARP banking bailout law in Congress and has assumed a lead role in overseeing Treasury Secretary Tim Geithner. Emanuel's signature motto: "Never allow a crisis to go to waste."

Lawrence Summers, the Clinton Treasury Secretary-turned-multi-million-dollar hedge fund manager, falls asleep on the job as Obama's director of the White House National Economic Council. The White House circumvented the regular Senate confirmation process to appoint Summers while avoiding scrutiny of his dubious corporate bailout track record and myriad financial conflicts of interest.

"Auto czar" Steven Rattner is one of nearly twenty unaccountable bureaucrats installed by the White House—again without Senate confirmation—to influential policy positions despite serious ethical baggage and conflict-of-interest questions. Rattner, a wealthy investment banker, is tied to a vast pension fund scandal involving his former company, the Quadrangle Group investment firm.

Hillary Clinton and her husband fought for years to keep donors to the former president's global mega-charity, the William J. Clinton Foundation, secret. To secure Hillary's Secretary of State nomination, the couple cut a deal to release partial information on the wealthy crony capitalists and foreign governments who have filled the Clinton coffers. The pay-to-play potential remains huge and essentially unchecked.

President Obama, agent of Hope and Change, has vowed to support the re-election of Connecticut Senator Chris Dodd despite the Democrat's mounting corruption scandals, sweetheart deals with favor-currying lender Countrywide and convicted insider trader Edward Downe, and his intimate ties with government bailout recipient AIG. It's audacious business as usual in Washington.

more than 1,400 people stripped of their savings after bank officials falsified profit reports.

Pritzker's lawyer at O'Melveny & Myers, Tom Donilon, is now deputy national security adviser. He earned just shy of $4 million representing her and other high-profile meltdown clients including, yep, Citigroup and Goldman Sachs.[64]

In April 2009, the White House tapped former Fannie Mae executive Donald Remy to be the Army's top lawyer. He submitted a bio that stated that he had "worked as a senior vice president for a 'major U.S. company' for an unspecified number of years." The employer was Fannie Mae. He worked there from 2000 to 2006, during the height of the government-sponsored mortgage giant's accounting scandals. Remy wasn't just any low man on the totem pole. Among his job titles at Fannie, according to *Congressional Quarterly*: Vice president and deputy general counsel for litigation; senior vice president and deputy general counsel; senior vice president and chief compliance officer; and senior vice president, housing and community development. When questioned by Republicans in the Senate about these rather glaring omissions on his bio, Remy protested: "My time at Fannie Mae was a time period where I am personally proud of all the work that I did." Omissions speak louder than words.[65]

Austin Goolsbee, named head of Obama's Economic Advisory Board, was a champion of extending credit to the uncreditworthy. In a 2007 op-ed for the *New York Times*, he derided those who called subprime mortgages "irresponsible." He preferred to describe them as "innovations in the mortgage market" to expand the pool of homebuyers.[66] Now this wrong-headed academic who espoused government policies that fed the housing feeding frenzy is in charge of fixing the loose-credit mess he advocated.

Goolsbee, by the way, is the fifteenth wealthiest member of the Obama administration, with assets valued at between $1,146,000 to $2,715,000. He also pulled in a University of Chicago salary of $465,000 and additional wages and honoraria worth $93,000, according to the *Washingtonian*. If you've got the right connections, being wrong pays.

RAHM-BO THE RICH

White House Chief of Staff Rahm Emanuel's most famous dictum is this: "Rule one: Never allow a crisis to go to waste.... They are opportunities to do big things."[67] Emanuel certainly didn't let the housing crisis go to waste. During the Clinton years, he was appointed to the Freddie Mac board of directors at a time when its oversight manager called the quasi-governmental agency "so pliant" that it enabled rampant book-cooking. Freddie Mac's stock skyrocketed; its CEOs helped themselves to massive bonuses. Emanuel's hometown paper, the *Chicago Tribune*, exposed how Emanuel's "profitable stint" during this corruption-plagued period entailed almost no work:

> The board met no more than six times a year. Unlike most fellow directors, Emanuel was not assigned to any of the board's working committees, according to company proxy statements. Immediately upon joining the board, Emanuel and other new directors qualified for $380,000 in stock and options plus a $20,000 annual fee, records indicate.
>
> On Emanuel's watch, the board was told by executives of a plan to use accounting tricks to mislead shareholders about outsize profits the government-chartered firm was then reaping from risky investments. The goal was to push earnings onto the books in future years, ensuring that Freddie Mac would appear profitable on paper for years to come and helping maximize annual bonuses for company brass.

The accounting scandal wasn't the only one that brewed during Emanuel's tenure.

During his brief time on the board, the company hatched a plan to enhance its political muscle. That scheme, also reviewed by the board, led to a record $3.8 million fine from the Federal Election Commission for illegally using corporate resources to host fundraisers for politicians. Emanuel was the beneficiary of one of those parties after he left the board and ran in 2002 for a seat in Congress from the North Side of Chicago.

The board was throttled for its acquiescence to the accounting manipulation in a 2003 report by Armando Falcon Jr., head of a federal oversight agency for Freddie Mac. The scandal forced Freddie Mac to restate $5 billion in earnings and pay $585 million in fines and legal settlements.[68]

Freddie lost tens of billions of dollars and cost billions more after both major parties in Washington engineered a gargantuan Fannie/Freddie bailout. The former ballet dancer-turned-Chicago pol, meanwhile, pirouetted off the Freddie stage—and then cashed-in again. The *Tribune* reported that he sold more of his Freddie Mac stock for an easy $100,001 to $250,000.[69] Displaying their continued disregard for their own transparency pledges, White House officials refused to fulfill the newspaper's request for public documents related Emanuel's tenure as a Freddie Mac director.

The revolving money machine brought Emanuel a combined $51,000-plus in campaign contributions from Fannie Mae and Freddie Mac when he ran for the House. *Chicago Sun-Times* columnist Lynn Sweet pointed out that as a member of the same House subcommittee that has oversight of Fannie/Freddie, Emanuel (with outstanding options for 2,500 shares of Freddie) had a major conflict of interest. When Emanuel responded that he put the shares in a trust and would recuse himself from voting on any issues related to Freddie Mac, Sweet shot back: "Emanuel's trust is supposed to be blind, not stupid."[70]

Emanuel's savvy ability to flit in and out of the government-corporate revolving door paid huge dividends. *Washingtonian* magazine lists him as the fifth wealthiest member of the Obama administration, with assets between $5,023,000 and $13,170,000 in 2007.

"According to congressional disclosures, Emanuel made $16.2 million in his 2½ years as an investment banker at Wasserstein Perella, in between advising Bill Clinton and taking Rod Blagoje-vich's vacant seat in the 5th District of Illinois—or roughly $740 an hour 24 hours a day, 365 days a year."[71]

While Barack and Michelle Obama assailed greedy bankers and hedge fund managers and advised hopeful young followers to stay away from Wall Street, Emanuel happily absorbed hedge fund cash. OpenSecrets.org reported that Emanuel "was the top House recipient in the 2008 election cycle of contributions from hedge funds, private equity firms and the larger securities/investment industry" with $1.5 million filling his campaign coffers.[72] They only call them "ill-gotten gains" when the cash is going in some-body else's pocket.

Emanuel cut his teeth in the mega-fund-raising business under the Daley machine in Chicago and then under the Clinton machine in Washington. Goldman Sachs kept Emanuel on a $3,000 monthly retainer while he worked as Clinton's chief fundraiser, leading *Washington Examiner* reporter Timothy P. Carney to speculate about whether "Goldman may have been fun-neling money to Clinton's campaign through the back door...and the front door. By March of 1992, the heart of that dramatic pri-mary season, Goldman partners had sent $54,000 to the Clinton campaign." The financial titans threw in another $50,000 to become the Clinton administration's top funder. Emanuel received nearly $80,000 in cash from Goldman Sachs during his four terms in Congress[73]—investments which have reaped untold rewards as Emanuel assumed a leading role championing the $700 billion TARP banking bailout law.

It's all about nurturing past, present, and future lucrative relationships for Rahm-bo. Perhaps that explains why the fifth wealthiest member of Team Obama chooses to live rent-free in the Washington, D.C., home of close friend Democrat Congresswoman Rosa DeLauro of Connecticut. DeLauro's husband, Stan Greenberg, owns a polling firm employed by an Emanuel campaign committee and by the Democratic Congressional Campaign Committee, which Emanuel headed in 2005 and 2006, the *Chicago Tribune* reported.[74] Ethics watchdogs raised disclosure and tax liability red flags about the arrangement. But nothing came of the complaints. The revolving door grants immunity to Wall Street's best-connected.

LOUIS THE VACUUM CLEANER

Ambassadorships have long been used as patronage rewards for deep-pocketed donors. Clinton did it. Bush did it. And before his first 100 days had passed, Obama embraced business-as-usual, too. In May 2009, the *UK Telegraph* broke the news that Obama would appoint one of his biggest campaign fundraisers for the post of U.S. ambassador to Britain.[75] Louis Susman has no diplomatic experience. But he has beaucoup bucks. The Chicago lawyer and banker (who worked for Solomon Brothers and retired as a Citigroup vice chairman in February 2009) gallivants with the Kennedys and the Kerrys in Hyannisport and Nantucket. He has raised massive amounts for Democrats since the Carter era. He bundled between $200,000 and $500,000 for Team Obama and is known as "The Vacuum Cleaner" and "The Big

Bundler" for his fundraising prowess.[76] (Research indicates that no reporter has ever asked how many homes Susman owns.)

The *Washington Post*'s Al Kamen tallied up more ambassadorial candidates from the money pit: Entertainment mogul Charlie Rivkin—who headed up Obama's California fundraising operations, raking in $500,000 for the campaign and another $300,000 for the inaugural—was the leading candidate for a post in France. Boston money man Alan Solomont, who also bundled the same amounts for the campaign and inaugural, was the leading candidate for the ambassadorship in Spain.

About one-third of all ambassadorships are political appointees. Barack the Change Agent told the press he would not abandon historical precedent and that it would be "disingenuous" to commit to anything less.[77]

GARY THE GOLDMAN SACHS GUY

Yes. Another one. It's like another eight years of "failed Bush economic policies" all rolled into the first 100 days! In March 2009, the Senate Agriculture Committee approved Goldman Sachs partner Gary Gensler as head of the Commodity Futures Trading Commission—despite heated grilling over his role, as Reuters described it, "as a high-level Treasury official in a 2000 law that exempted the $58 trillion credit default swap market from oversight. The financial instruments have been blamed for amplifying global financial turmoil."[78]

Gensler said sorry—which worked for Tim Geithner, so why not? *Washingtonian* magazine named Gensler the wealthiest member of the Obama administration, worth an estimated $15,533,000 to $61,745,000.[79] In announcing his nomination, Obama said Gensler "brings a wealth of expertise from both the public and private sectors to this position."[80] Well, he was right about the wealth.

JIMMY THE MUNI BOND MAN

Chicago investment banker James Reynolds raised more than $200,000 for the Obama campaign while chief executive of Loop Capital Markets. The municipal bond specialist was a longtime friend of Obama—feting the rising star in his Hyde Park home and convincing friends and associates to open up their wallets more than a decade ago. In 2003, *USA Today* reported, Reynolds was caught on FBI wiretaps arranging what prosecutors called a "sham" consulting contract with a gal pal of a Philadelphia mayoral adviser. After the conversations, Reynolds snagged $300,000 in no-bid city contracts for Loop Capital Markets.[81] City officials went to jail over the scam. Reynolds skated. The Obama campaign's only statement?

"Jim Reynolds has admitted that he made mistakes, but he has not been charged with any wrongdoing."[82]

Only the highest ethical standards for Hope and Change.

GEORGE THE GENEROUSLY PAID GENERAL COUNSEL

Corporate lawyer George W. Madison worked for retirement management company TIAA-CREF before the Obama administration tapped him for the general counsel position at the Treasury Department. The firm has spent big bucks lobbying in Washington. But Treasury ethics bureaucrats saw no conflict of interest problems. In fact, they approved a deal allowing Madison to collect a government salary of $153,200 while receiving an additional $955,000 next year from TIAA-CREF as part of a corporate buyout. Madison is slated to receive another $1.6 million from TIAA-CREF in 2011 and $333,000 in 2012, according to the *Washington Times*.[83] Obama officials state blithely that Madison will simply recuse himself from any matter affecting TIAA-CREF. The company, however, has lobbied every corner of the

federal government on every major corporate financial issue rang-
ing from the banking bailout to executive compensation to
accounting and securities regulations to mortgage reform, and the
stimulus. What would be left for Madison to counsel the Treasury
Department on?

MARK THE CORPORATE LOBBYIST

There's always room for another Goldman Sachs water-carrier in
the House of Barack. Even if it means breaking Obama's own no-
lobbyist rules. In January 2009, Treasury Secretary Tim Geithner
chose former Goldman Sachs lobbyist Mark Patterson to serve as
his top deputy and overseer of the $700 billion TARP banking
bailout—$10 billion of which went to Goldman Sachs. In the
understatement of the year, left-leaning government watchdog
Melanie Sloan of the Citizens for Responsibility and Ethics in
Washington responded: "It makes it appear that they are saying
one thing and doing another."[84] Give her the Sherlock Holmes
Award!

Paul Blumenthal of the Sunlight Foundation noted that, while
at Goldman Sachs, Patterson lobbied against executive pay limits
that Obama had crusaded for as Senator (before, that is, his
administration carved out exemptions for AIG). While Patterson
agreed to recuse himself on any Goldman Sachs-related issues or
related policy concerns, Blumenthal wrote, it "still creates a serious conflict for Geithner, as Treasury is being partly managed by
a former Goldman lobbyist. Geithner is also placed in a tough
position considering that his chief of staff is limited in the areas in
which he can work (supposedly)."[85]

As if that weren't enough baggage, *Washington Examiner*
columnist Timothy P. Carney reported that Patterson was also a
former Tom Daschle acolyte and adviser who carved out a niche

in alternative energy mandates and subsidies. He championed an ethanol firm in Canada, Iogen Corporation, which received $30 million from Goldman Sachs in a bid to boost its green image. The logs started rolling. Iogen soon received an $80 million Bush Energy Department grant and millions more in energy bill set-asides. "So now you see how it works," Carney demonstrated. "A well-connected company invests in a technology that is currently unprofitable. That company then uses its high-dollar lobbyists and friends inside government to subsidize or mandate that product into profitability. Goldman similarly invested in—and lobbied for—greenhouse gas credits, which are literally worthless without climate change legislation that caps emissions. A good lobbyist is like an alchemist, turning lead into gold. Mark Patterson and Goldman Sachs may not have figured out how to turn switchgrass into energy, but they did figure out how to turn it into profit. Patterson is a rainmaker, leveraging his government connections into private profit. He's emblematic of both the 'green revolution' Obama touts, and the 'revolving door' Obama assails."[86]

Yes, so much for Obama's "close the revolving door between K Street and Capitol Hill."[87] So much for ridding Washington and Wall Street of "excess greed, excess compensation, excess risk taking."[88] So much for giving the American people "more than window-dressing when it comes to ethics reform." [89]

It's not that *bona fide* capitalism is evil, or that lawyers, lobbyists, hedge fund managers, or corporate executives should have no role in government. It's the cognitive dissonance. This is the same Obama, remember, who said, "Let's be clear who Senator McCain's fighting for. He's not fighting for Joe the Plumber; he's fighting for Joe the Hedge Fund Manager. John McCain likes to talk about Joe the Plumber but he's in cahoots with Joe the CEO."

Words. Just words. Words that were, in fact, the reverse of the truth.

And, as we'll see, not only do the titans of Wall Street enrich themselves at the House of Obama, but so do the president's fat-cat union friends, with the added unctuousnesses of claiming to save America's workers while screwing them over.

CHAPTER 7

SEIU

LOOK FOR THE UNION LABEL

Barack Obama donned a purple silk tie for one of his most important campaign speeches in the fall of 2007. "It's time to turn the page on the old way of doing business," he urged the rowdy crowd. Extending thanks to "Andy and Anna," his "Illinois crew," and the rest of his "homies," Obama told attendees he was "so grateful to them for their unbelievable love and support." It was, he gushed, "so good to be among friends."

A hyperkinetic Obama adopted the tone, accent, and swagger of a Chicago street preacher at the event, which turned into an unabashed revival meeting as his forty-minute speech progressed. "We look after each otha!" he shouted. Supporters responded with "Amens" and "Uhm-huhms." With finger jabbing and voice rising, Obama vowed: "I will open up the doors of government and ask you to be involved in your democracy again!" Audience members interrupted repeatedly with whoops, applause, and standing ovations.

Recounting his early years as a community organizer, Obama reminded the crowd that he had walked with them before—"I've been there, done that," he boasted—and he would do it again if he needed to as president. "The White House is the people's house," he bellowed. "It's our time!" The crowd went wild.

"Fired up?" Obama asked at the climax of his speech. "Fired up!" the crowd shouted in response. "Ready to go?" he hollered. "Ready to go!" they shouted. "Let's go change the world!" he exhorted them, and they broke into a deafening chant: "Obama! Obama!"[1]

This was no ordinary reunion of family and friends. The setting was the 1.8 million-member Service Employees International Union's political action conference in Washington, D.C. Obama's purple tie was a nod to the "spirit color" of the labor organization. And his effusive shout-outs went to SEIU's heaviest hitters:

"Andy" is militant left-wing social worker-turned-union heavy Andy Stern, who broke off SEIU from the old guard AFL-CIO to consolidate low-skill service workers and create a twenty-first century labor empire.

"Anna" is Anna Burger, Stern's partner at SEIU. Known as the "Queen of Labor," she climbed from welfare caseworker in Pennsylvania to strategist for old-guard union king John Sweeney to "the most powerful woman in the labor movement.[2]

The "Illinois crew" to which Obama referred repeatedly is SEIU's Local 880, the Chicago chapter of home care and hotel workers, which Obama assisted in his early activist days.

The "homies" Obama personally thanked are Tom Balanoff (Illinois President of SEIU Local 1, with 40,000 janitors and security guards), whom Obama worked with as a community organizer; Keith Kelleher, president of SEIU's Local 880; and Christine Boardman, president of SEIU's Local 73, which represents 25,000 public service workers in Illinois and Indiana.

"I've spent my entire adult life working with SEIU. I'm not a newcomer to this," Obama bragged—a remark that reporter Marc Ambinder saw as a dig at Democratic rival John Edwards, who had been diligently courting SEIU officials. "Obama didn't just promise to walk with SEIU members on picket lines. He vowed to "play offense," to reclaim the Bush Administration's Labor Department for Big Labor ("we're gonna take it back!"), and to deliver a radical legislative agenda pushed by the unions. Obama promised to pass universal health care "by the end of my first term" and the Orwellian-titled "Employee Free Choice Act" (EFCA) to do away with private-ballot union elections in the workplace. In 2007, he co-sponsored EFCA (also known as "card check") legislation in 2007 and pledged to SEIU members to "make it the law of the land when I am president of the United States."

Obama's fierce support from the SEIU rank and file convinced Stern and the union bosses (who had favored Edwards) to delay a primary endorsement. Obama "rocked the house," one union official admitted.[3] Five months later, after Edwards abandoned his campaign and Obama was battling Hillary Clinton for the nomination, the SEIU crowned its torch-bearer. "There has never been a fight in Illinois or a fight in the nation where our members have not asked Barack Obama for assistance and he has not done everything he could to help us," Andy Stern, the union's president, said at his February 2008 press conference announcing the decision.[4]

Stern put his membership's dues money where his mouth was. The SEIU political action committee poured an estimated $80 million worth of independent expenditures into the campaign coffers of Democratic candidates in 2008—more than $27 million of which went to Barack Obama.[5] The union proudly claimed that its members "knocked on 1.87 million doors, made 4.4 million phone calls, registered 85,914 voters and sent more than 2.5 million pieces of mail in support of Obama," in addition to sending SEIU leaders to seven states in the final weekend before the election to get out the vote for Obama and other candidates.[6] SEIU's

enforcers have set aside another $10 million to spend on un-elect-
ing any of its political beneficiaries who abandon their pledges to
do the union's legislative bidding. The campaign money was
raised by slapping an extra $6 per-member fee on top of regular
dues payments—which was funneled straight to the union's political action committee.

What major private company could escape scrutiny or criticism
for forcing all of its employees to subsidize its political activities,
whether they agreed with them or not?[7] And what does it say
about Obama's credibility as a reformer that the massive infusion
of union dues into his campaign treasury didn't trouble him in the
least?

SEIU paid—and Obama played. Within two weeks of moving
into the White House, Obama immediately signed a series of executive orders championed by union bosses. The new rules author-
ized sweeping powers for the Labor Secretary that essentially
blackball non-union contractors targeted by labor organizers and
blacklist non-union employees in the private sector from working
on taxpayer-funded projects.[8] Such regulatory favoritism limits
freedom in the workplace and raises the cost of doing business.
Another measure immediately adopted by President Obama
requires that when a government service contract runs out—and
there's a new contract to perform the same services at the same
location—the new contractor must retain the old workers. Mickey
Kaus of the left-leaning *Slate* magazine dubbed the move the
"Labor Payoff of the Day."[9]

President Obama and Vice President Biden invited labor leaders to join them for a public ceremony unveiling the executive
orders repealing Bush policies that had reined in Big Labor. "Welcome back to the White House," Biden gloated.[10] Who authored
the orders? Carter Wood of the National Association of Manu-
facturers traced the original executive order files to Craig Becker,

legal counsel for the SEIU and member of Obama's transition team for labor issues.[11]

In May 2009, the *Los Angeles Times* reported that the White House had included the SEIU in a conference call with California government officials over federal stimulus money. State officials said the union pressured them to repeal a bipartisan-approved wage cut for home health care workers as a condition for receiving the federal funds.[12] An Obama lawyer for the Centers for Medicare and Medicaid Services (which regulates home health care) sided with the SEIU and concluded that California arguments in defense of the wage cuts were "unsupportable." (The feds later backed off, but not before Andy Stern's union received unprecedented access to negotiations.)[13]

When Obama promised at the SEIU conference to "open up the doors of government and ask you to be involved," he meant it.

Patrick Gaspard, former chief lobbyist for SEIU's behemoth New York health care affiliate, Local 1199, served as Obama's campaign national political director and transition deputy director of personnel. During the 2004 election cycle, he had led the radical, left-wing, George Soros-funded group, America Coming Together (ACT) as national field director. SEIU poured $23 million into ACT in a costly, unsuccessful attempt to put Democratic Senator John Kerry in the White House.[14] Under Gaspard's tenure at ACT, the get-out-the-vote group employed convicted felons as canvassers and committed campaign finance violations that led to a $775,000 fine by the Federal Election Commission—the third largest civil penalty levied in the panel's history.[15] Gaspard was appointed White House political director shortly after Election Day 2008.[16]

Obama named two of SEIU's favored candidates to top Cabinet posts—Kansas Democrat Governor Kathleen Sebelius to head the Department of Health and Human Services and California

Democrat Representative Hilda Solis to head the Department of Labor. "She probably will be the labor secretary that has been on more picket lines and rallied more in support of workers rights than potentially anyone in American history," Stern gushed in his endorsement of the SEIU's hand-picked candidate Solis.[17] When the Solis nomination ran into trouble over her husband's unpaid tax liens and lobbying activities (see Chapter 4 for more details),[18] the SEIU war machine turned up the heat[19]—blasting e-mails,[20] petitions,[21] and a YouTube protest video from Stern.[22] Republicans yielded. Upon her confirmation on February 24, 2009, the union crowed: "SEIU pushed for Hilda Solis to be confirmed as Secretary of Labor and took action to urge others to join in. More than 10,000 people called for Hilda Solis to be confirmed as our next Secretary of Labor—and now, she has been.[23]

Less than a month after taking the oath of office in January, Obama awarded SEIU President Stern with a prominent place at the table for a "fiscal responsibility summit" focusing on health care. (A delighted Stern basked in presidential approval at the summit when Obama called on him to make a statement and then complimented the union boss on his jaunty purple scarf.) Stern also boasted via Twitter (the micro-blogging social network) that he was a special guest at one of the first White House Wednesday cocktail parties.[24] The social gathering of union leaders and other left-wing groups was organized by Obama crony and chief adviser Valerie Jarrett[25] to coordinate the message on "progressive" legislation such as card-check. A few weeks later, Stern was invited to speak at Vice President Biden's "Task Force on the Middle Class" kick-off. Not long after that, Stern, SEIU Secretary-Treasurer Anna Burger, and SEIU Healthcare Chair Dennis Rivera gave input during the White House health care summit.

Obama also appointed Burger to the President's Economic Recovery Advisory Board to provide advice on "boosting the sagging U.S. economy."[26] The SEIU secretary-treasurer praised Obama as a politician who "does not turn a deaf ear to the hurts and hopes of working people. He is a president who sees members of labor unions as part of the solution too." She complimented Team Obama for showing the leadership necessary to "address the challenges working families face in a twenty-first century global economy, and create economic recovery that works for everyone—not just those at the top."[27]

So much for the lofty rhetoric. But for all the talk of "change," SEIU represents the very essence of top-down corruption and business-as-usual funded by the compulsory dues of its workers. The Competitive Enterprise Institute's Ivan Osorio reported that, since abandoning the AFL-CIO in 2005, SEIU's Stern "has sought to assert his union's influence over private equity firms, centralize his authority within the union by forcing various locals to merge, and negotiate large deals with employers without member participation."[28] Three of Stern's hand-picked operatives were forced to step down in 2008–2009 over financial scandals.

The union's own rank-and-file members have revolted in disgust over mismanagement and thuggery. In March 2009, the SEIU notified the local that represents its Washington, D.C.-based national field staff and community organizers that a third of them would be laid off. The "Union of Union Representatives," as the local is known, lodged an unfair labor practices complaint against the SEIU, alleging that it laid off workers without proper notice, banned union activities, and hired temporary workers. SEIU's top brass insisted with straight faces that, after burning through $85 million of workers' dues to elect Barack Obama, the powerful union can't afford to keep paying seventy-five of its national field staffers because of budget troubles. In a delicious, petard-hoisting moment, the laid-off union workers protested outside SEIU headquarters in Washington, chanting: "How do you spell hypocrisy? S-E-I-U!"

Like the Obama White House, SEIU's brass embraces a policy of self-exemption on ethics, transparency, and fiscal responsibility: Do as they say, not as they do.

THE BLAGO-SEIU-OBAMA CONVERGENCE

The "Illinois crew" and the SEIU friends that Obama so effusively praised are integral parts of the tainted Chicago political machine. In December 2008, those ties came under national scrutiny when federal prosecutors publicly released their criminal complaint against disgraced former governor of Illinois, Democrat Rod Blagojevich. SEIU figured prominently in Blago's secretly taped musings on how to profit from his power to appoint Obama's Senate replacement. So did a larger union umbrella federation, Change to Win, led by SEIU secretary-treasurer Anna Burger. Blago hatched a plan to snag a $300,000-a-year job as head of Change to Win in exchange for appointing a union-friendly successor to Obama.

The SEIU backed Blago for governor in 2002. SEIU's political action committee donated $821,294 for his successful gubernatorial bid. In the 2005–2006 season, the SEIU Illinois Council PAC was the governor's top contributor in his re-election effort, with $908,382 in donations. All told, according to research by the National Right to Work Foundation, "union PACs poured more than $8 million into Blagojevich's two gubernatorial campaign coffers"—1.7 million from the SEIU alone. In return, Blagojevich delivered an executive order clearing the path for SEIU to unionize nearly 50,000 home child care providers subsidized by taxpayers.[29] He signed another executive order facilitating union organizing on public university campuses. At the time of his arrest, Blago was preparing another executive order to expand the union organizing abilities of an even larger portion of home health care workers targeted by the SEIU.[30]

Blagojevich did the country an extraordinary unintended favor. As health care analyst David Catron wrote: "He has made it clear to the meanest intelligence that [President] Obama emerged from a hopelessly corrupt political culture. Barack Obama oozed from the same stinking Chicago swamp that produced Blagojevich, and a man whose formative years were spent wallowing in the muck with such creatures isn't likely to be long in White House before the stench of pay-to-play politics begins to pervade the place."[31]

FBI Special Agent Daniel W. Cain detailed Blago's conversations with Chief of Staff John Harris revolving around the SEIU in the federal criminal complaint, which documented a laundry list of charges of conspiracy to commit fraud and solicitation to commit bribery:

> 98. On November 7, 2008, ROD BLAGOJEVICH talked with Advisor A about the Senate seat. ROD BLAGOJEVICH stated that he is willing to "trade" the Senate seat to Senate Candidate 1 in exchange for the position of Secretary of Health and Human Services in the President-elect's cabinet.
>
> 99. Later on November 7, 2008, ROD BLAGOJEVICH discussed the open Senate seat in a three-way call with JOHN HARRIS and Advisor B, a Washington D.C.-based consultant. ROD BLAGOJEVICH indicated in the call that if he was appointed as Secretary of Health and Human Services by the President-elect, then ROD BLAGOJEVICH would appoint Senate Candidate 1 to the open Senate seat. HARRIS stated "we wanted our ask to be reasonable and rather than...make it look like some sort of selfish grab for a quid pro quo." ROD BLAGOJEVICH stated that he needs to consider his family and that he is "financially" hurting. HARRIS said that they are considering what will help the "financial security" of the Blagojevich family and what will keep ROD BLAGOJEVICH "politically viable." ROD BLAGOJEVICH stated, "I want to

make money." During the call, ROD BLAGOJEVICH, HAR-
RIS, and Advisor B discussed the prospect of working a three-
way deal for the open Senate seat. HARRIS noted that ROD
BLAGOJEVICH is interested in taking a high-paying position
with an organization called "Change to Win," which is connected to Service Employees International Union ("SEIU").

HARRIS suggested that SEIU Official make ROD BLAGO-
JEVICH the head of Change to Win and, in exchange, the President-elect could help Change to Win with its legislative agenda
on a national level. Advisor B asked why SEIU Official cannot
just give the job to ROD BLAGOJEVICH. HARRIS responded
that it would be just a big "give away" for SEIU Official and
Change to Win since there are already individuals on the
Change to Win payroll doing the functions of the position that
would be created for ROD BLAGOJEVICH. HARRIS said that
Change to Win will want to trade the job for ROD BLAGOJE-
VICH for something from the President-elect. HARRIS suggested a "three-way deal," and explained that a three-way deal
like the one discussed would give the President-elect a "buffer
so there is no obvious quid pro quo for [Senate Candidate 1]."
ROD BLAGOJEVICH stated that for him to give up the gover-
norship for the Change to Win position, the Change to Win
position must pay a lot more than he is getting paid right now.
Advisor B said that he liked the idea of the three-way deal. ROD
BLAGOJEVICH stated that he is interested in making $250,000
to $300,000 and being on some organization boards. Advisor B
said they should leverage the President-elect's desire to have Senate Candidate 1 appointed to the Senate seat in order to get a
head position with Change to Win and a salary. Advisor B
agreed that the three-way deal would be a better plan than ROD
BLAGOJEVICH appointing Senate Candidate 2 to the Senate
seat and getting more done as Governor.

The conniving governor contemplated an SEIU position for his wife, Patty, as well:

100....Also, ROD BLAGOJEVICH wanted to know whether SEIU could do something to get his wife a position at Change to Win until ROD BLAGOJEVICH could take a position at Change to Win.

Harris mapped out a "three-way deal" to give the White House a "buffer" obscuring the obvious *quid pro quo*. SEIU would assist Obama with Blago's appointment of a union-friendly candidate, Blago would get his cushy union job, and SEIU would be rewarded down the road with favors from the White House:

[101](c): ROD BLAGOJEVICH said that the consultants (Advisor B and another consultant are believed to be on the call at that time) are telling him that he has to "suck it up" for two years and do nothing and give this "mother f###er [the President-elect] his senator. f### him. For nothing? f### him." ROD BLAGOJEVICH states that he will put "[Senate Candidate 4]" in the Senate "before I just give f###ing [Senate Candidate 1] a f###ing Senate seat and I don't get anything." (Senate Candidate 4 is a Deputy Governor of the State of Illinois). ROD BLAGOJEVICH stated that he needs to find a way to take the "financial stress" off of his family and that his wife is as qualified or more qualified than another specifically named individual to sit on corporate boards. According to ROD BLAGOJEVICH, "the immediate challenge [is] how do we take some of the financial pressure off of our family." Later in the phone call, ROD BLAGOJEVICH stated that absent getting something back, ROD BLAGOJEVICH will not pick Senate Candidate 1. HARRIS re-stated ROD BLAGOJEVICH's thoughts that they should ask the President-elect for something

for ROD BLAGOJEVICH's financial security as well as maintain his political viability. HARRIS said they could work out a three-way deal with SEIU and the President-elect where SEIU could help the President-elect with ROD BLAGOJEVICH's appointment of Senate Candidate 1 to the vacant Senate seat, ROD BLAGOJEVICH would obtain a position as the National Director of the Change to Win campaign, and SEIU would get something favorable from the President-elect in the future.

(d). One of ROD BLAGOJEVICH's advisors said he likes the idea, it sounds like a good idea, but advised ROD BLAGOJE-VICH to be leery of promises for something two years from now. ROD BLAGOJEVICH's wife said they would take the job now. Thereafter, ROD BLAGOJEVICH and others on the phone call discussed various ways ROD BLAGOJEVICH can "monetize" the relationships he is making as Governor to make money after ROD BLAGOJEVICH is no longer Governor.

A few days later, Team Blago reached out to the SEIU. An unnamed SEIU official agreed to float their plan and "see where it goes":

109. On November 12, 2008, ROD BLAGOJEVICH spoke with SEIU Official, who was in Washington, D.C. Prior intercepted phone conversations indicate that approximately a week before this call, ROD BLAGOJEVICH met with SEIU Official to discuss the vacant Senate seat, and ROD BLAGOJEVICH understood that SEIU Official was an emissary to discuss Senate Candidate 1's interest in the Senate seat. During the conversation with SEIU Official on November 12, 2008, ROD BLAGOJEVICH informed SEIU Official that he had heard the President-elect wanted persons other than Senate Candidate 1 to be considered for the Senate seat. SEIU Official stated that he would find out if Senate Candidate 1 wanted SEIU Official to

keep pushing her for Senator with ROD BLAGOJEVICH. ROD BLAGOJEVICH said that "one thing I'd be interested in" is a 501(c)(4) organization. ROD BLAGOJEVICH explained the 501(c)(4) idea to SEIU Official and said that the 501(c)(4) could help "our new Senator [Senate Candidate 1]." SEIU Official agreed to "put that flag up and see where it goes."

110. On November 12, 2008, ROD BLAGOJEVICH talked with Advisor B. ROD BLAGOJEVICH told Advisor B that he told SEIU Official, "I said go back to [Senate Candidate 1], and, and say hey, look, if you still want to be a Senator don't rule this out and then broach the idea of this 501(c)(4) with her."

"Senate Candidate 1" was top Obama adviser and Chicago political godmother Valerie Jarrett, who removed herself from the running when she took a top White House adviser post instead. Who was the "SEIU official" Team Blago spoke with and met? The *Wall Street Journal* obtained an internal communication in December 2008 fingering President Obama's homeboy, SEIU Local 1 president Tom Balanoff.[32] The *New York Times* then followed up with a report that several union officials in Chicago and Washington also identified Balanoff as the official who spoke to Blago.[33] Balanoff, not coincidentally, had been appointed by Blago to the llinois Health Facilities Planning Board.

Two days before Christmas 2008, legal counsel Greg Craig released an official report outlining contacts between Team Obama and Team Blago. Balanoff, it turns out, had spoken with Jarrett:

On November 7, 2008—at a time when she was still a potential candidate for the Senate seat—Ms. Jarrett spoke with Mr. Tom Balanoff, the head of the Illinois chapter of the Service Employees International Union (SEIU). Mr. Balanoff is not a member of the Governor's staff and did not purport to speak for the Governor on that occasion. But because the subject of the Governor's interest in a cabinet appointment came up in that conversation, I am including a description of that meeting. Mr. Balanoff told Ms. Jarrett that he had spoken to the Governor about the possibility of selecting Valerie Jarrett to replace the President-Elect. He told her that Lisa Madigan's name also came up. Ms. Jarrett recalls that Mr. Balanoff also told her that the Governor had raised with him the question of whether the Governor might be considered as a possible candidate to head up the Department of Health and Human Services in the new administration. Mr. Balanoff told Ms. Jarrett that he told the Governor that it would never happen. Jarrett concurred. Mr. Balanoff did not suggest that the Governor, in talking about HHS, was linking a position for himself in the Obama cabinet to the selection of the President-Elect's successor in the Senate, and Ms. Jarrett did not understand the conversation to suggest that the Governor wanted the cabinet seat as a quid pro quo for selecting any specific candidate to be the President-Elect's replacement. At no time did Balanoff say anything to her about offering Blagojevich a union position.[34]

It strains credulity to believe that a seasoned Chicago pol such as Jarrett "did not understand" that a gobsmackingly obvious *quid pro quo* was being suggested to her at the behest of Blagojevich. Jarrett claims complete ignorance of any scheming, but note from the criminal complaint cited above that Blagojevich "understood that [the] SEIU Official was an emissary to discuss Senate Candidate 1's [Valerie Jarrett's] interest in the Senate seat" and that the "SEIU Official stated that he would find out if Senate Candidate 1 wanted [the] SEIU Official to keep pushing her for Senator with" Blagojevich.

Obama counsel Greg Craig stuck to the story in a media conference call discussing the Obama administration's self-exonerating report:

Q Okay. And then why did Valerie Jarrett characterize this as a ridiculous proposition?

MR. CRAIG: This was—she thought it was ridiculous for the governor of Illinois to be talking about being appointed to Barack Obama's Cabinet at a time when he was under investigation, widely reported in the newspapers—under investigation for a variety of problems. And the reason that I believe that she thought it was ridiculous and said so was because that's what she told her counsel, and that's what her counsel told me.

Q And did she at that point or did anyone else in the course of their communications with, you know, folks perceived to be communicating for Blagojevich raise a red flag and say, "Hey, you know, guess what. Balanoff just told me that, you know, this ridiculous thing, that Blagojevich wanted to be HHS secretary"?

MR. CRAIG: Well, she did not perceive Balanoff to be communicating as an emissary of Governor Blagojevich.

She conceived of him as being a union official who had met with the governor. And this topic came up. But it was not presented to her as a quid pro quo.[35]

In January 2009, the Associated Press, *Wall Street Journal*, and other news organizations reported that SEIU president Andy Stern and Balanoff had met personally with Blagojevich on November 3—right around the time the feds allege the governor was hatching his pay-for-play schemes.[36] Balanoff spoke with Blago a total of three times—on November 3, November 6 (the day before Balanoff met with Jarrett), and November 12. Balanoff announced in mid-February 2009 that he was cooperating with the feds.[37]

SEIU flacks have taken pains to emphasize that no one has yet alleged any illegality on the union's part. Defiantly standing by his union's past support of the impeached governor, Stern insisted he had "no reason to believe anyone did anything wrong."[38] But blanket denials can't cover the cesspool stench.

Does the SEIU deserve the benefit of the doubt? A review of the union's sordid history of corruption over the past few years suggests otherwise. Stern has been responsible for installing a cabal of hand-chosen officers who exploited their cash-infused fiefdoms for personal gain and presided over rigged elections—in the process, becoming all that they had professed to stand against as representatives of the downtrodden worker.

LIVING LARGE IN L.A.

Andy Stern rallied the Illinois delegation to the 2008 Democratic National Convention in August 2008 with an impassioned salute to the working man. Flanking Stern on stage at the Denver celebration: Chicago political machine kingpins Rahm Emanuel and Richard Daley. Stern roared about "rebalancing power between wealth and work" to "make sure everyone shares in the wealth of a growing economy."[39] Echoing Obama's 2007 speech to the SEIU political action conference, union boss Stern condemned the old way of doing business and called on America to "turn the page" on behalf of hard-working Americans and their families.

But just two weeks before Stern and company gathered in the Mile High City to celebrate Obama's coronation, the *Los Angeles Times* published an explosive investigative series about the SEIU. Although the series got surprisingly little attention from national news organizations, *L.A. Times* reporters exposed how one of Stern's top protégés "shared in the wealth"—by siphoning off hundreds of thousands of dollars in dues money for his personal enrichment and pleasure. Moreover, the paper alleged, Stern helped cover up the scandal. No wonder they keep urging us to "turn the page."

The *L.A. Times* investigation zeroed in on Tyrone Freeman who, like Barack Obama, began his career as an urban community organizer. In Atlanta, Freeman quickly ascended the SEIU ladder.

In 1994, Stern found him at a small Georgia chapter of the union, Local 1985, and brought him westward. Stern set his loyalist Freeman up as head of Local 6434, the sprawling home care workers' chapter in southern California that represents an estimated 160,000 workers who make about nine dollars an hour caring for the elderly and disabled. Stern chose Freeman as part of his administration slate at the SEIU convention in 2008 and named him a national vice president in addition to the L.A. appointment. The move wasn't an altruistic act of affirmative action. It was part of Stern's grander plan to consolidate power by merging locals into statewide chapters.

With bigger membership rolls came bigger coffers, and with bigger coffers came irresistible temptations.

Freeman, the *L.A. Times* discovered, had piped $600,000 in union contracts to his wife's video production and entertainment ventures. The local also paid his mother-in-law $8,000 a month to babysit his daughter and other union employees' children, footed a $13,000 bill for membership at a Beverly Hills cigar club, covered $12,500 in tabs at upscale Morton's restaurant in Burbank, and forked over $8,000 in union dues to cover expenses for Freeman's Hawaiian wedding. Freeman's spending orgy didn't end there.

Stern's protégé created a non-profit training shop called the "Homecare Workers Training Center"—ostensibly to provide educational opportunities for nurses. In practice, the non-profit served as a conduit to subsidize a childcare business operated by Freeman's mother-in-law. "Her business had been receiving more than $90,000 annually for the past several years from the training center that Freeman founded as a separate nonprofit and chairs, according to IRS filings and interviews," as reported by the *L.A. Times*. The funding from her son-in-law constituted more than 10 percent of the nonprofit's total yearly expenditures. Freeman's wife, Pilar, and brother-in-law, Hernando Planells Jr., are listed in state documents as officers in the mother-in-law's business.[40] Free-man's ransacking of Local 6434's treasury didn't end with nepo-tistic favoritism. The *Times* also reported:

- A housing corporation that Freeman helped found as a nonprofit has not been granted the IRS tax-exempt sta-tus it sought and was suspended from doing business in California. It also has claimed on its website to have a "strong relationship" with the prominent California Community Foundation, which says it has no such rela-tionship.
- The union spent at least $123,000 more on a fund-raising tournament at the Four Seasons Resort in Carls-bad than it received in reimbursements, according to Labor Department filings and interviews. Freeman said the event made money for the charity. The union's expenditures included $100,000 in payments to entities associated with former professional football star Eric Dickerson, which have been suspended from doing business in California. The payments were listed as donations to nonprofits, not as fund-raising expenses.
- And a now-defunct minor league basketball team coached by Freeman's brother-in-law received $16,000 for what the union described as public relations.[41]

Freeman's local also paid nearly $106,000 to a company called "The Filming Inc."—for which the *Times* could find no state incorporation record or IRS nonprofit listing, no business license, and no legitimate address—and another $106,000 to Hollywood talent agency William Morris for "advice and counsel" in such areas as media and "membership awareness.[42]

Even more troubling, Freeman allegedly rigged his own elec-tion. In August 2008, the Labor Department began investigating charges from rank-and-file members that Freeman's union local "made it nearly impossible for candidates not on his slate to qualify for the ballot, according to people familiar with the probe. The FBI and the U.S. Attorney's office also opened investigations. Former employees of Freeman's nonprofit charity also alleged that the Stern protégé forced them to work on campaigns of political candidates in violation of federal law."[43]

Even more damning, a key union source told the *Times* that, contrary to the denials of union brass, SEIU's top officials were warned of Freeman's plundering six years before the paper blew the whistle:

> In response to the July [2008] inquiries, [union spokesman Steve] Trossman had issued a statement on behalf of Stern that said the union had received no allegations about Freeman's local. Freeman denied any wrongdoing.
>
> The source, who said he was party to internal conversations about Freeman in 2002, told The Times last week: "The international knew that there were allegations of impropriety many years ago. This is not news to them.[44]

On August 20, 2008, just days before Stern would join Democrats in toasting Barack Obama at the party convention in Denver, Stern's protégé Tyrone Freeman stepped aside as head of Local 6434, and the chapter was placed in a temporary trusteeship. Stern's office in Washington, D.C., released the announcement. "These allegations are of serious concern to all of us and we support Mr. Freeman's decision to put the best interests of the members first," Stern spokeswoman Michelle Ringuette wrote in an e-mail to the *Times*.[45] But even as he relinquished his position, Freeman was apparently engaging in the strong-arm tactics he learned from Stern. Ten employees told the *Times* that they suffered retaliation after refusing to sign a petition supporting him as the scandal exploded. "Freeman's lieutenants" at Local 6434 essentially pressured other members to sign a "loyalty oath," one union member disclosed.[46]

After dragging its feet and being forced to act to quell public embarrassment over the *Times* investigations, SEIU finally announced formal charges against Freeman "for engaging in self-dealing and financial malpractice in violation of SEIU's Constitution and Local bylaws."[47] In November, Stern threw his underling under the bus. Freeman, whom Stern had groomed in his own image, was banned for life from the SEIU and ordered to provide $1.1 million in restitution to the union. A sanctimonious Stern issued a statement lamenting Freeman's downfall: "Today's decision sends a clear message across our Union....We are all accountable. Our members do some of the toughest jobs anywhere, and we will not tolerate any actions violating their trust or putting their interests at risk."[48]

But rank-and-file members weren't fooled or mollified. An insurgent group called S.M.A.R.T.—SEIU Member Activists for Reform Today—blasted the union leadership:

> Freeman didn't come from nowhere. He was appointed by Andy Stern—for the third time.... And there are many other locals where Stern has installed unaccountable appointees and, sometimes ignoring reports that they were out for personal gain.... So Stern's message to us is clear—he cares more about expanding control for himself and an ever shrinking inner circle than he does about building real power for working people, creating solid organizations, coming through on SEIU's political pledges for the fall, or even the perception of our union and our movement as real, democratic, valuable and clean. He will only act when there is no other option, and he will never apologize.[49]

As for Freeman, he glided into a new life as a Los Angeles sports agent—where he uses his criminal involvement in defrauding low-wage workers as a selling point. His shameless biography on the website of the SMWW Sports Agency touts his "tireless commitment to lead the struggle for livable wages, decent housing and health care for all." Burnishing his scandal credentials, Freeman adds: "I believe my recent personal experience evolving from turmoil, can be a testimony shared in preparing any athlete for the trials and tribulations of being a star."[50]

Ruthless Andy Stern taught Tyrone Freeman and his southern California peers all too well. Rickman Jackson, another Stern administration protégé and former chief of staff to Tyrone Freeman, headed Michigan's largest SEIU chapter before being "reassigned" for three years to a staff organizing job, after the revelation of financial shenanigans tied back to L.A.'s Local 6434.[51] While collecting a six-figure annual salary in Michigan, Jackson was drawing a second salary in California and accepted $33,500 in housing payments on a residence listed as the business address of Freeman's bogus housing non-profit corporation.[52]

Another Stern administration protégé, Annelle Grajeda, rose to power after the SEIU president installed her as president of the 80,000-member Local 721 in Los Angeles. She ascended to positions on the union's state council and international executive board. Like Freeman and Jackson, Grajeda had been voted onto Stern's official administration slate at the SEIU convention in 2008.[53] The *Times* published damning details of how Grajeda's ex-boyfriend, SEIU official Alejandro Stephens, collected multiple salaries and consultant fees from the union while also pocketing a salary as a Los Angeles County health services employee. Grajeda had arranged for her ex-lover to get an eight-month leave of absence from the job. He was fired after he refused to return to work.[54] Grajeda quit her California posts after catching public flak and found a new job—as special assistant to SEIU secretary-treasurer Anna Burger in Washington, D.C.! Her former chapter heralded the move up. Grajeda will now oversee efforts to "partner with the Obama administration" to secure more public funds for SEIU projects. What could go wrong?

> Former SEIU 721 President Annelle Grajeda assumed her new role as special assistant to the International Secretary-Treasurer Anna Burger for the Public Sector Mar. 9.
>
> According to a staff announcement from the International Union in Washington, D.C.: "With more than two decades of service, Annelle has played a critical role in winning strong contracts for tens of thousands of union members, preserving trauma centers in Los Angeles County, fighting for health care reform, defeating ballot initiatives in 2005 that challenged working families' livelihoods and uniting more than 80,000 workers into SEIU 721 for greater strength and a stronger voice for public service providers. She brings this wealth of experience and talent to the national level in her new role."
>
> ...The International's announcement went on to state "While there has been no finding of wrongdoing on Annelle's part, she has decided to change the capacity in which she serves the Union in order to take on the challenge of developing quality public services at a time when funding is threatened like never before."
>
> In her new role, Annelle will expand SEIU's work in the public sector partnering with the Obama Administration to secure more funds for key infrastructure projects and core public services including care for the elderly, health care, education and social services.[55]

Tyrone Freeman, Rickman Jackson, and Annelle Grajeda were all groomed by Stern and personally appointed by him to the posts they exploited. But there's no "three-strikes" policy in labor management. Like Obama, Stern has managed to pass the buck while pretending it stopped at his desk. Birds of a feather evade accountability together.

A SEA OF PURPLE PAYOFFS

The L.A. SEIU debacles were just one stinking layer of Stern's rotten onion. Corruption isn't an anomaly at the SEIU. It's a contagion. Cronyism isn't the exception. It's the rule. *L.A. Times* reporter Paul Pringle relentlessly exposed additional cases of nepotism and back-scratching—worth millions of dollars in compulsory union dues—that benefitted the consulting businesses, political nonprofits, and individuals with family or personal ties to top SEIU officials in southern California and beyond:

- The SEIU and its political affiliate contributed $3 million to America Votes, an advocacy organization that was headed by Cecile Richards, wife of an aide to SEIU President Andy Stern, at the time the payments were made.
- Melissa Mullinax was an SEIU political director when the political consulting firm in which she held a 20-25 percent stake, The Edison Group, was paid more than $1 million, including expenses, by the union. In addition, the SEIU has spent about $41,000 on a graphic design company owned by Mullinax's husband, Jason Abbott.
- The union paid about $520,000 to a consulting firm co-founded by Democratic Party and labor strategist Steve Rosenthal, the husband of another SEIU director, Eileen Kirlin. Rosenthal, a longtime friend of Stern, also headed America Coming Together, a get-out-the-vote nonprofit that received $23 million from the union.

- Pamela Kieffer, wife of a third union director, David Kieffer, has received about $70,000 in consulting fees and in separate payments from a firm that provided recruitment services to SEIU.
- In addition, the SEIU and an associated nonprofit paid roughly $210,000 in consulting fees over four years to Don Stillman, husband of the union's outside legal counsel, Judith Scott. Stillman helped edit a 2006 book written by Stern, a publication that has generated controversy because of how the union president profited from it. Although she is not an SEIU staffer, Scott disclosed her husband's relationship with the union on U.S. Labor Department disclosure forms filed by officers.[56]

A separate corruption case in the Bay Area uncovered another SEIU double-dipper, James Bryant, who used a nonprofit run out of his home to line his pockets and his family's with extra union-funded income—while also collecting a salary as a government transit worker.

> A Bay Area officer of the scandal-clouded Service Employees International Union has collected double salaries, one as a city transit worker and the other from a charity that receives much of its funding from the labor organization and corporate interests, records show.
>
> In addition, the nonprofit paid more than $16,000 in rent for the officer's home in 2007, the most recent year for which the charity's tax return is available, according to his son, who is also on the charity's payroll. James Bryant, who earned just under $68,000 as a transit station agent in 2007, received about $117,000 that year as president of the San Francisco chapter of the A. Philip Randolph Institute, according to the tax return and the city's Municipal Transportation Agency. He was also paid

or reimbursed about $10,000 as an executive board member for SEIU Local 1021, whose political committee he chairs, the union's financial statements show.[57]

Bryant's son received $62,000 from the "charity." His wife is also an employee of SEIU Local 1021. Compulsory union dues directly and indirectly paid the Bryant family's salary and rent with the help of the nonprofit, which was later decertified but continued to operate. The self-dealing scheme smelled as foul as the sea lion hangout at San Francisco Bay's Pier 39. But the local cleared Bryant of any wrongdoing and vowed to "move forward on behalf of the working men and women of Northern California."[58]

The union nicknamed the "Purple Ocean" is awash in purple payoffs and personal enrichment scams. Yet another high-ranking SEIU official was nabbed in February 2009 for bilking the union out of $9,000 for personal expenses. Adding salt to the wound: the officer, Byron Hobbs, who served as an executive vice president of the SEIU's 90,000-member Illinois-Indiana healthcare local, had been assigned to serve as watchdog over a local in St. Louis that had been placed in trusteeship (basically a takeover of a local labor organization by its parent organization, which suspends the local chapter's autonomy and installs an outside monitor).[59] In other words, Hobbs stole from the local chapter he had been assigned to help clean up. A smug SEIU spokeswoman concluded that the case showed "the system works."[60]

"The system," however, has long enabled a den of union thieves to embezzle workers' dues for political and personal gain. In 2006, former Los Angeles City Councilman Martin Ludlow was sentenced to five years' probation and 2,000 hours of community service for his role in conspiring to scam SEIU Local 99, which represents nearly 40,000 public school teachers. Ludlow "admitted to improperly using union money to pay six people who were put on the union payroll but who actually worked on his City

Council election campaign.... The money also covered the cost of a cell phone he used in the campaign. Nearly $37,000 was diverted to his 2003 election campaign to underwrite the phantom union employee scheme."[61]

A year later, former president of SEIU Local 99 Janett Humphries was sentenced to five years probation and ordered to perform 1,000 hours of community service for her role in the embezzlement conspiracy. In addition to using teachers' dues to support Ludlow's campaign, Humphries (a delegate to the 2004 Democratic National Convention) pleaded guilty to using union funds to pay for a trip to the Virgin Islands for her daughters and a family friend.[62] She too had been installed to oversee a trusteeship at the local—and left it under a darker cloud than when she arrived.

As United States Attorney Debra Wong Yang said in a statement following Humphries's guilty plea: "Corruption in organized labor strikes at the very heart of the benefits that unions bring. We owe working men and women our full commitment to root out corruption in public office and in organized labor."[63]

"THE PERSUASION OF POWER"

Asked about his organizing philosophy, Andy Stern summed it up this way: "[W]e prefer to use the power of persuasion, but if that doesn't work we use the persuasion of power."[64]

Stern and his shock troops have bullied companies—from private equity firms to Burger King to food management company Aramark—who have resisted SEIU's attempts to organize their workers. The Purple People have staged aggressive protests and a "War on Greed" campaign to intimidate employers into submission.[65] One of the besieged targets, security provider Wackenhut Services, battled SEIU's attempts to gain exclusive representation for its employees. The company already had ten other unions representing its workers. Initially unbowed by a massive, malicious negative publicity campaign against them, Wackenhut blew the whistle:

> The SEIU seeks membership growth through aggressive "corporate campaigns" that have a blunt message to employers, "Let us unionize your workforce or we will destroy your reputation." This tactic has been used against a number of organizations to include Wal-Mart, Kaiser Permanente, Advocate Health Care, Catholic Healthcare West, and Sutter Health.
>
> SEIU is attempting to coerce The Wackenhut Corporation and WSI to recognize it as the "exclusive" collective bargaining representative throughout Wackenhut. Wackenhut declined to enter into such an agreement. The SEIU responded with a corporate campaign that is intended to damage WSI's reputation and relationships with our clients. Their campaign tactics include distributing misinformation, distortion and omission of fact through the media, conducting demonstrations in proximity of work sites in an effort to disrupt normal client operations, and aggressively attempting to intimidate or influence clients.[66]

But after filing a racketeering lawsuit against the SEIU, a weary and drained Wackenhut entered into an agreement allowing its employees in nine cities to choose SEIU as its bargaining representative. Behold the "persuasion of power."

Showing an appalling lack of concern for the well-being of its members, the SEIU upped the ante in a representation battle with the University of Miami in 2006, where Stern's organizers mounted a campus hunger strike. The union fought tooth and nail against a true, democratic unionizing election for campus janitors using a secure, federally monitored secret ballot. Stern personally escalated the dispute, joined the fasters,[67] and demonized then university president Donna Shalala (yes, the same Donna Shalala who served in President Clinton's cabinet). She lashed back:

> We are devastated that the union is risking the health and well-being of our students and the Unicco employees by sanctioning an activity as drastic as a hunger strike. Hunger strikes have never been used in this country to oppose an election. We have urged both parties to continue daily discussions until this issue is resolved. A free election for or against unionization is a federal statutory right.[68]

In the end, the SEIU relented to a federally monitored election. But at what price? Five SEIU members were hospitalized, one with a minor stroke.[69] Wackenhut Corporation chief operating officer Paul Donahue, expressing sympathy for the University of Miami's plight, saw the big picture:

> The bullying, protesting, harassment, contrived events and demands will continue indefinitely because the union has millions of dollars in dues money from hard working janitors and other service workers which can be spent on ruining the reputation of businesses instead of bettering the lives of those workers that contributed.[70]

Indeed, no one has felt the blunt force—and physical danger—of Stern's "persuasion of power" more than workers themselves.

In Oakland, Stern and his Washington crew imposed a trusteeship on a 150,000-member local that had publicly opposed SEIU strong-arm tactics. The D.C. headquarters (knee deep in ethical mud) accused the local—known as SEIU United Healthcare Workers West (UHW West)—of financial malpractice and misconduct.

The local fought back, charging the Beltway union leaders with manufacturing the allegations to retaliate and to distract from Washington mismanagement. The UHW West president, Sal Rosselli, quit the SEIU Executive Board and formed a new union in February 2009, which declared:

> We're tired of SEIU's hostile tactics, threatening phone calls, their collusion with employers and governors like Blagojovich, and the corruption of Stern's appointees like Local 6434 head Tyrone Freeman in Los Angeles, disgraced SEIU Executive Vice President Annelle Grajada, and the appointees who have just taken over what had been our local. We don't trust them with our contracts, we don't trust them with our dues—we just don't trust them.[71]

In Philadelphia, Stern engineered the hostile takeover of a 150,000-member union representing garment and hospitality workers. Workers United had broken off from the national UNITE HERE union of 450,000 workers. Progressive *New York Daily News* columnist Juan Gonzalez, citing SEIU's agreement with Workers United, called Stern "hellbent on using classic corporate raider tactics to bring a huge portion of the U.S. labor movement under his absolute control." The pact included discounted member dues and legal and financial assistance to aid the breakaway group's efforts to take control of the Amalgamated Bank, the nation's only union-owned bank. One union official called the power grab "a breathtaking form of imperialism.[72]

In Portland, Oregon, Ryan Canney, who worked for silicon chip manufacturer Siltronic, was subjected to union coercion and deception by labor organizers using a card-check scheme. According to the National Right to Work Foundation, which successfully represented Canney, SEIU Local 49 union officials

allegedly tricked Canney and his coworkers into signing "information flyers" that were later counted as votes favoring unionization. Canney also charged that Siltronics overlooked outdated
cards, promised benefits, and otherwise deceived and coerced
employees into supporting unionization. The National Labor
Relations Board intervened, ordering the local to abandon its
fraudulent methods.[73] The same union was involved in a similar
attempted hijacking at Kaiser Permanente in Portland. Kaiser
employee Karen Mayhew also staved off the deceptive takeover,
winning an NLRB settlement that forced SEIU Local 49 officials
to "renounce their illegally obtained monopoly bargaining
power over Kaiser employees" and to "issue notices to employees alerting them of their legal rights (including the right to
refrain from formal union membership)" and to "inform workers that the company will not bargain with union officials unless
the employees chose to do so through the less-abusive NLRB
secret-ballot election process."[74]

The abusive system that workers like Ryan Canney, Karen
Mayhew, and their colleagues suffered is what Andy Stern wants
imposed nationwide—and what Barack Obama has promised to
"make the law of the land as president of the United States"
through the Orwellian-titled "Employee Free Choice Act." It's a
system that would dragoon hundreds of thousands of unsuspect-
ing workers into Stern's platoons to transform the political landscape in the most radical and perhaps irreversible way. If
Wal-Mart's workforce alone were unionized and captured by
SEIU, it would provide an additional 1.4 million bodies and $500
million more in forced dues.[75] As SEIU Queen of Labor Anna
Burger herself put it at the SEIU convention in 2008: "It is the
fuel—the opening—for SEIU to change our growth curve from
100,000 to a million or more workers a year."[76]

Unchecked corruption. Gagged dissenters. Corporate black-mail. A massive new infusion of coerced dues spent on Big Labor lackeys in Washington to seal the deal on a permanent political majority.

This is the change they seek.

CHAPTER 8

OBAMACORN
A COMMUNITY OF ORGANIZED RACKETEERS NATIONWIDE

Donna Hanks gathered friends in front of her foreclosed house in Baltimore to bemoan the ravages of the subprime crisis. Greedy lenders hiked her mortgage payments by "$300 in one month," the despondent hotel restaurant worker told a local reporter for WJZ-TV. The bank refused to work with her, she explained, and cruelly kicked her to the curb. She was exactly the kind of downtrodden victim Barack Obama had promised to help if elected.

One of Hanks's friends, Louis Beverly, stood beside her on the porch. Beverly sported a distinctive acorn patch on his shirt—and wielded a pair of red-handled bolt cutters in his hands. With cameras rolling, Beverly used the tool to break a padlock on the front door. He then used his body as a battering ram to bust the door open and boldly declared:

"This is our house now!"

Hanks and her friends, many wearing identical T-shirts declaring a "foreclosure free zone" and advertising a hotline number, streamed into the home. The cameras followed. Hanks wistfully toured her old residence, lashed out at the bank for a few more minutes, and then put her own lock on the door to cap off the reclamation.

Bertha Lewis, the national president of ACORN, the Association of Community Organizations for Reform Now, praised Hanks for taking action to "liberate her home from the bank."[1]

Louis Beverly, ACORN's chief Baltimore housing activist, called it "civil disobedience" and "the right thing to do."[2]

The Baltimore police called it fourth-degree burglary and charged both Beverly and Hanks with criminal trespassing.

President Obama, the community organizer-in-chief who cut his teeth as a street activist working with ACORN and its inextricably linked SEIU allies in Chicago, made no public comment. But the Left's ground troops know exactly where their comrade in the White House stands. As Obama reminded ACORN leaders after its political action committee endorsed his presidential candidacy in February 2008:

> I come out of a grassroots organizing background. That's what I did for three and half years before I went to law school. That's the reason I moved to Chicago was to organize. So this is something that I know personally, the work you do, the importance of it. I've been fighting alongside ACORN on issues you care about my entire career. Even before I was an elected official, when I ran Project Vote voter registration drive in Illinois, ACORN was smack dab in the middle of it, and we appreciate your work.[3]

The Baltimore home invasion was part of ACORN's aggressive pressure campaign for a nationwide foreclosure moratorium. It just happened to coincide with the White House launch of massive new government interventions in the housing market unveiled in February 2009. This was a cunning public relations stunt, complete with ACORN banners and apparel to intimidate lenders and recruit new members (the protesters' T-shirts blared "1-866-67-ACORN.") Donna Hanks was a seasoned ACORN activist who had successfully pimped her subprime sob story to national media outlets without even minimal vetting.

It would have been an opportune moment for the professionals in the mainstream media to illuminate ACORN's trademark shakedown methods and shady activists. It would have been an opportune moment to remind the taxpaying public of how President Obama guaranteed these government-subsidized political operatives a seat at his table of power. "Before I even get inaugurated, during the transition, we're going to be calling all of you in to help us shape the agenda," Obama promised ACORN activists at a December 2007 Democratic presidential rally. "We're going to be having meetings all across the country with community organizations so that you have input into the agenda of the next presidency of the United States of America."[4]

But the mainstream media, continuing a decades-old pattern of whitewashing the radical left-wing outfit's activities, failed to report the unvarnished truth about ACORN's racketeers in Baltimore. Here are the facts:

Hanks bought the two-story home in the summer of 2001 for $87,000. At some point during the next five years, she re-financed the original home loan for $270,000. Where did all that money go? (Hint: Think house-sized ATM.) The property initially went into foreclosure proceedings in the spring of 2006. Hanks soon filed for bankruptcy and agreed to a Chapter 13 plan to pay back her bank and other creditors. In September 2006, the bankruptcy court ordered Hanks's employer to deduct $340 per month from her salary to pay down the debt. Hanks did not comply with the legally binding plan. In December 2007, the loan servicer issued a notice of default on nearly $7,000 past due. While she was reneging on her mortgage IOUs, she managed to collect rent on her basement and rack up a criminal record on charges of theft and second-degree assault. The house was sold only after two years of court-negotiated attempts to allow Hanks to dig herself out of her debt hole.[5]

Baltimore ACORN leader Louis Beverly, who also claims to be a foreclosure victim, is a housing thug. He was charged with separate second-degree assault and property destruction in early 2009 and battery, assault, handgun possession, and possession of a deadly weapon with intent to injure in 1992. In 2006, he was slapped with a peace order. According to court records, he owned several rental properties in the Baltimore area and has for years been involved in civil cases alleging failure to maintain property, dumping, and uninhabitable conditions.[6]

The *Washington Post* spotlighted Beverly and Hanks's activism without ever following up on their criminal records and financial negligence. The paper also shilled for ubiquitous ACORN foreclosure "victim" Veronica Peterson of Columbia, Maryland, recycling uncritically her accusation that she had been tricked into buying a $545,000 home by a broker who inflated her income and misrepresented her assets. "These loans were weapons of mass destruction," the single mom of three and home daycare provider told the *Post* reporter on not being able to keep up with her mortgage bills. "They destroyed our credit, our lives, and they blew up in our face."[7]

But a look at court and real estate records exposed the truth. Edward Ericcson, Jr., a reporter for the independent *Baltimore City Paper*[8] discovered that the "victim"—who took out a full mortgage with no down payment on a house she couldn't afford—looks more like a predatory borrower.[9] Amazingly, Peterson lived in the home more than year without paying rent or mortgage:

> The online court and land records show that Peterson closed on
> the house on Nov. 3, 2006, with two loans from Washington

> Mutual. The main mortgage, for $436,000, had a starting inter-
> est rate of 8.5 percent, adjusting in December. . . . The second
> loan, often called a 'piggyback,' totaled $109,000 with an inter-
> est rate of 11.25 percent. . . . Those two payments together
> would have totaled $3,386.17 per month. That's before prop-
> erty taxes, upkeep, utilities, etc. Peterson would have to earn at
> least $50,000 per year just to make her house payments.[10]

The foreclosure was filed in July 2007. "The balance on the main
note then was $435,735.86," Ericcson reported, plus unpaid
interest and late fees—suggesting she made at most one payment
on the house. "Had she made all of her payments, Peterson would
have spent about $64,335 so far. Had she rented a similar place,
she would have been charged around $2,500 per month—a total
of $47,500—since January 2007. Instead, she apparently paid
nothing."

These foreclosure con artists are just the tip of ACORN's fraudulent enterprises. The non-profit ACORN, which takes in 40 percent of its revenues from American taxpayers after four decades
on the public teat, has a long history of engaging in voter fraud,
corporate shakedowns, partisan bullying, and pro-illegal immi-
gration lobbying.[11] This is the bread and butter work that
ACORN does. President Obama knows it, and he appreciates it.
He said so himself.

Despite his numerous on-the-record remarks tying himself to
ACORN over the years, candidate Obama asserted on its "Fight
the Smears" campaign website that he "never organized with
ACORN."[12] According to ACORN, however, Obama trained its
Chicago members in leadership seminars; in turn, ACORN vol-
unteers worked on his campaigns.[13] Obama also sat on the boards
of the left-wing Woods Fund (with Weather Underground terrorist Bill Ayers) and Joyce Foundation, both of which poured money
into ACORN's coffers. ACORN head Maude Hurd gushed that

Obama is the candidate who "best understands and can affect change on the issues ACORN cares about"[14]—like ensuring their massive government pipeline to your hard-earned money.

Under the guise of "consumer advocacy," ACORN has lined its pockets with both public and private money. The Department of Housing and Urban Development funds hundreds, if not thousands, of left-wing "anti-poverty" groups across the country with ACORN as a leading recipient of the agency's subsidies. In October 2008 under the Bush administration, HUD announced more than $44 million in new housing counseling grants to over 400 state and local efforts. The Bush White House increased funding for housing counseling by 150 percent since 2001, despite the role most of these recipients play as activist satellites of the Democratic Party. The ACORN Housing Corporation received more than $1.6 million.[15] ACORN is eligible for untold millions more in taxpayer funds from the trillion-dollar stimulus package that President Obama signed into law in February 2009 and the $6 billion National Service Act passed the following month.

Moreover, the ACORN Housing Corporation has worked to obtain mortgages for illegal aliens in partnership with Citibank. It relies on undocumented income, "under the table" money, which may not be reported to the Internal Revenue Service.[16] Whistleblower documents reveal internal discussions among the group that blur the lines between its tax-exempt housing work and its aggressive electioneering activities. The group also targets corporate interests with relentless PR attacks, and then enters "no lobby" agreements with bullied corporations after receiving payment.[17]

The profound threat the group poses is not merely ideological or economic. It's electoral. In March 2009, the Obama White House made good on its promise to give ACORN a hand in shaping the administration's agenda when it designated the group an official partner of the U.S. Census Bureau. President Obama has entrusted ACORN—infamous for voter fraud scandals spanning more than a decade—to assist with the recruitment of the 1.4 million temporary workers needed to go door-to-door to count every person in the United States.[18] At first, the administration denied that ACORN would play a substantial role in the census process. But documents obtained by Washington, D.C.-based watchdog Judicial Watch revealed in May 2009 "that the Census Bureau offered ACORN the opportunity to 'recruit Census workers' who would participate in the count. Moreover, as an 'executive level' partner, ACORN has the ability to 'organize and/or serve as a member on a Complete Count Committee,' which, according to Census documents, helps 'develop and implement locally based outreach and recruitment campaigns.'"[19]

What could possibly go wrong?

SEE NO EMBEZZLEMENT, HEAR NO EMBEZZLEMENT, SPEAK NO EMBEZZLEMENT

At the intersection of the SEIU and ACORN stands Wade Rathke. The New Orleans-based activist was the founder of SEIU's Local 100 chapter in Louisiana, Texas, and Arkansas, which represented hotel workers. He also launched a social justice initiative in Arkansas that would become the mega-umbrella conglomerate of community organizers known today as ACORN. After 38 years, the association now claims more than 400,000 dues-paying members with more than 1,200 chapters across the country.

On his website, Rathke bills himself as a lifelong progressive who has been "dedicated to winning social justice, workers rights, and a democracy over the last 40 years, where the people shall rule."[20] Rathke recently became "chief organizer" of "ACORN International," which now operates in "Canada, Peru, Mexico,

Argentina, Dominican Republic, and India," along with "emerging projects in Kenya and Ecuador and partnerships in Indonesia, Korea, and the Philippines."

Like so many of his foot soldiers breaking into homes and registering cartoon characters to vote,[21] ACORN's founder isn't telling the whole truth. His do-gooder image is a far cry from the ugly reality exposed not by right-wing radio or Republican Party operatives as might be expected, but by internal ACORN whistleblowers themselves, disgusted with the corrupt organization.

In June 2008, Rathke was forced to step down from the powerhouse association he founded. A month later, the *New York Times* (in a rare bit of investigative journalism against a left-wing sacred cow) exposed ACORN's dirty laundry, prolonged cover-up, and complicated network of pass-through organizations. Reporter Stephanie Strom boiled it down:

> Acorn chose to treat the embezzlement of nearly $1 million eight years ago as an internal matter and did not even notify its board.... A whistle-blower forced Acorn to disclose the embezzlement, which involved the brother of the organization's founder, Wade Rathke.
>
> The brother, Dale Rathke, embezzled nearly $1 million from Acorn and affiliated charitable organizations in 1999 and 2000, Acorn officials said, but a small group of executives decided to keep the information from almost all of the group's board members and not to alert law enforcement.
>
> Dale Rathke remained on Acorn's payroll until a month ago, when disclosure of his theft by foundations and other donors forced the organization to dismiss him.[22]

Rathke admitted he suppressed disclosure of his brother's massive theft—first discovered in 2000—because "word of the embezzlement would have put a 'weapon' into the hands of enemies of Acorn." In other words: The protection of ACORN's political viability came before protection of members' dues (and taxpayers' funds). Rathke's supporters on ACORN's board helped cover up the crime by carrying the amount his brother embezzled—$948,607.50—as a "loan" on the books of Citizens Consulting, Inc. CCI, the accounting and financial management arm of ACORN and its complex web of affiliates, is housed in the same building as the national ACORN headquarters in New Orleans. It's also home to ACORN International, which Wade Rathke continues to head. ACORN brass cooked up a "restitution" plan to allow the Rathkes to pay back a measly $30,000 a year in exchange for secrecy about the deal. Dale Rathke kept his job and his $38,000 annual salary until the story leaked to donors and board members outside the Rathke circle.

A close friend and benefactor of the Rathkes, ultra-liberal philanthropist Drummond Pike, volunteered to foot the rest of the bill for the embezzled funds by buying a promissory note worth $800,000. Pike founded the radical Tides Foundation, a key ACORN donor which bills itself as committed to "positive social change"; Wade Rathke sits on the Tides Foundation board of directors. ACORN whistleblowers, disgusted with the cozy cover-up, again spilled the beans to the *New York Times*:

> Mr. Pike refused to confirm or deny that he had bought the note. "As a rule, I do not comment on my personal finances," he wrote in e-mail messages in answer to questions about the deal.
>
> But e-mail messages among Acorn's senior executives discuss how to keep Mr. Pike's identity secret, even as they acknowledge that some of the foundations and philanthropic advisers that have supported Acorn and its affiliates know that he bought the note.

"Does Drummond know the word is out?" Steven Kest, the executive director of Acorn, wrote on July 4. "If not, shouldn't someone tell him?"

In a July 12 e-mail message to Mr. Kest, Acorn's political director, Zach Pollett, wrote: "I talked to Drummond on this yesterday and had Beth Kingsley"—Acorn's lawyer—"prepare a 'keep your yaps shut' confidentiality memo to people at Acorn and CCI."[123]

Fortunately, the "keep your yaps shut" memo didn't stop the whistleblowers from going public with even more damning disclosures. In June 2008, ACORN national board members Karen Inman and Marcel Reid were appointed to a special committee assigned to investigate the Rathke debacle. They took the task seriously. Too seriously for the ACORN whitewashers' comfort. In September 2008, the two filed a petition for access to financial data related to the embezzlement. Inman and Reid, leading a group of twenty-five ACORN members who signed onto the complaint, charged that Rathke's henchmen at ACORN were destroying key documents. Rathke continued to meddle with employees and meet with staff members regarding his brother's financial shenanigans, the dissidents said.[24] Moreover, Inman and Reid discovered, the amount Rathke embezzled may have exceeded the $1 million first reported. Reid urged his colleagues to resist "the ACORN culture of quiescence to Wade Rathke and his family so that ACORN vindicates the poor and moderate income people it represents."[25]

In November 2008, the ACORN executive board responded by firing Inman and Reid and dismissing them from all ACORN duties. Those who helped cover for the Rathkes, however, kept their jobs. See no evil, hear no evil, speak no evil.

OH, WHAT A TANGLED WEB

As internal turmoil rattled ACORN's front office, Barack Obama's campaign was forced to admit in the summer of 2008 that it had filed misleading financial reports on its dealings with ACORN's get-out-the-vote arm, Citizens Services, Inc. The non-profit group is housed in the same New Orleans compound as ACORN, ACORN International, SEIU Local 100 (founded by Wade Rathke), and CCI (the bookkeeping arm that hid Dale Rathke's embezzlement).

Citizens Services was established in December 2004 to "assist persons and organizations who advance the interests of low- and moderate-income people," according to paperwork filed in Louisiana. In a 2006 ACORN publication, Citizen Services, Inc. (CSI) is described as "ACORN's campaign services entity." But its executive vice president, Jeff Robinson, insisted that it was a "separate organization entirely" from ACORN.[26]

In August 2008, the Obama campaign disclosed that it had paid more than $800,000 to CSI and misrepresented the expenditures. Federal Election Commission reports show that from February to May 2008, Obama paid $832,598.29 to CSI for the following services:

$310,441.20	25-FEB-08	STAGING, SOUND, LIGHTING
$160,689.40	27-FEB-08	STAGING, SOUND, LIGHTING
$98,451.20	29-FEB-08	TRAVEL/LODGING
$74,578.01	13-MAR-08	STAGING, SOUND, LIGHTING
$18,417.00	28-MAR-08	POLLING
$18,633.60	29-APR-08	STAGING, SOUND, LIGHTING
$63,000.00	29-APR-08	ADVANCE WORK
$105.84	02-MAY-08	LICENSE FEES
$75,000.00	17-MAY-08	ADVANCE WORK
$13,176.20	17-MAY-08	PER DIEM

The Obama campaign tried to shrug off the false campaign finance filing as a run-of-the-mill clerical error. But the campaign's explanation didn't pass the sniff test. "All of this just seems like an awful lot of money and time spent on political campaigning for an organization that purports to exist to help low-income consumers," Jim Terry, chief public advocate for the Washington, D.C.-based Consumers Rights League, told the *Pittsburgh Tribune-Review*. "ACORN has a long and sordid history of employing convoluted Enron-style accounting to illegally use taxpayer funds for their own political gain," Terry claimed. "Now it looks like ACORN is using the same type of convoluted accounting scheme for Obama's political gain."[27]

Indeed, there's much more to the story of Obama's amended campaign finance reports than Team Obama let on. CSI appears to have been a front to funnel payments to ACORN for campaign advance work. This same ACORN offshoot was the subject of a little-noticed complaint to the FEC by a Democrat who smelled something rotten going on between CSI, ACORN, and yet another left-wing tax-exempt political advocacy group, Communities Voting Together (CVT).

Former Maryland Democrat Congressman Al Wynn filed an FEC complaint in January 2008 linking several suspicious outfits used by his primary opponent, Donna Edwards, to one address in New Orleans. In a letter to the FEC, Lori Sherwood, Wynn's campaign manager, wrote, "Based on my examination of various records and documents I believe the Donna Edwards for Congress Committee has received substantial assistance by way of unreported, in-kind contributions from organizations who profess to have operated independently of the Edwards Campaign."[28]

In a 134-page complaint, Sherwood alleged that as executive director of the Arca Foundation, a social justice organization, Edwards was "responsible for administering and overseeing grants that are awarded and distributed" by the group—grants that went to some of her campaign's biggest supporters. Nearly forty Arca Foundation grant recipients contributed $75,000 to Edwards's campaign, including monies from board members and employees, Sherwood reported. Moreover, she noted that the tax-exempt political advocacy group Communities Voting Together (CVT), which distributed thousands of anti-Wynn flyers, is located at 1024 Elysian Fields in New Orleans—which also happens to be the address for Wade Rathke's SEIU Local 100, ACORN, CSI, and CCI.[29]

"Wade Rathke, President of Elysian Fields Corporation, is also the chief organizer for SEIU Local 100, founder of ACORN, and a member of the Board of Directors of Tides Center and Tides Foundation," Sherwood pointed out. Tides received $245,000 in grant money from Edwards's Arca Foundation from 2002 to 2006. More connections: "Donna Pharr is the Custodian of Record for Communities Voting Together, the Assistant Treasurer for ACORN, and Deputy Treasurer for the American Institute for Social Justice and Voting for America, Inc. Both of these organizations received a combined total of $230,000 in grants from Arca between 2003 and 2006."

Enter CSI again: "I learned that Citizens Services, Inc. qualified to do business in Maryland as a foreign corporation and gave a registered agent address of 11 East Chase St., in Baltimore," Sherwood wrote. After checking to verify the address, Sherwood discovered no record of CSI actually having an office in Baltimore. CSI had forfeited its license to do business in Maryland two months after the 2006 primary election. Yet, the Edwards campaign paid CSI $76,866.80 in three separate payments, all purportedly for door-to-door get out the vote activities. Sherwood tracked the payments to an ACORN office address in Baltimore.

She concluded:

The efforts of these well heeled groups in promoting the
Edwards Campaign raise serious questions about the involvement of corporations which have applied for and sought not for
profit status but are receiving monies from a candidate for services. At the same time these groups are actively engaged in a
coordinated effort to assist the Edwards Campaign. That assistance is not reflected in campaign finance reports which may
violate federal reporting requirements.[30]

Edwards defeated Wynn. In the fall of 2008, the Federal Election
Commission ruled that there was "no reason to believe" that the
Edwards campaign violated campaign finance rules.[31]

But there is at least one other example of suspiciously large payments to Citizens Services, Inc., that calls into question what kind
of work this purportedly non-partisan, non-profit offshoot of
ACORN is doing. In February 2009, liberal group Ohio Citizen
Action reported a $907,808 payment to Citizens Services for can-
vassing and $590,526.10 for "campaign consulting."[32] That's
some gold-plated get-out-the-vote and consulting services right
there. The scheme has all the appearances of another left-wing
slush fund for Democrat satellites exploiting non-profit status and
skirting campaign finance laws.

ACORN's own internal review of shady money transfers
among its web of affiliates underscores the concern. A June 2008
report by lawyer Elizabeth Kingsley raised red flags about the
incestuous relationship between ACORN and Project Vote—the
offshoot Barack Obama worked for and insisted was completely
separate from ACORN.[33]

Project Vote, a 501(c)(3) organization, was founded by left-
wing lawyer Sandy Newman to register voters in welfare offices
and unemployment lines with the explicit goal of turning back the
Reagan revolution. In 1992, Newman hired Obama to lead Proj-

ect Vote efforts in Illinois. The Illinois drive's motto: "It's a Power Thing." Despite his adamant denials of any association with the group (his "Fight the Smears" website claimed "Barack Obama never organized with ACORN"), Obama's political DNA is encoded with the ACORN agenda. The Obama campaign's "Vote for Change" registration drive, running in conjunction with ACORN/Project Vote, was an all-out scramble to scrape up every last unregistered voter sympathetic to Obama's big-government vision.

Kingsley's internal review found inextricable links between ACORN and Project Vote:

> Project Vote hires Acorn to do voter registration work on its behalf, and the two groups say they have registered 1.3 million voters this year.
>
> As a federally tax-exempt charity, Project Vote is subject to prohibitions on partisan political activity. But Acorn, which is a nonprofit membership corporation under Louisiana law, though subject to federal taxation, is not bound by the same restrictions.
>
> ...Ms. Kingsley found that the tight relationship between Project Vote and Acorn made it impossible to document that Project Vote's money had been used in a strictly nonpartisan manner. Until the embezzlement scandal broke last summer, Project Vote's board was made up entirely of Acorn staff members and Acorn members.
>
> Ms. Kingsley's report raised concerns not only about a lack of documentation to demonstrate that no charitable money was used for political activities but also about which organization controlled strategic decisions.
>
> She wrote that the same people appeared to be deciding which regions to focus on for increased voter engagement for

Acorn and Project Vote. Zach Pollett, for instance, was Project Vote's executive director and Acorn's political director, until July, when he relinquished the former title. Mr. Pollett continues to work as a consultant for Project Vote through another Acorn affiliate.

"As a result, we may not be able to prove that 501(c)3 resources are not being directed to specific regions based on impermissible partisan considerations," Ms. Kingsley said, referring to the section of the tax code concerning rules for charities.

Project Vote, for example, had only one independent director since it received a federal tax exemption in 1994, and he was on the board for less than two years, its tax forms show. Since then, the board has consisted of Acorn staff members and two Acorn members who pay monthly dues.[34]

Moreover, as the Consumers Rights League has documented, ACORN posted job ads for Citizens Services; Communities Voting Together has contributed $60,000 to Citizens Services, Inc. Project Vote has hired ACORN and CSI as its highest paid contractors, paying ACORN $4,649,037 in 2006 and CSI $779,016 in 2006.[35] ACORN, investigative journalist Matthew Vadum joked, "moves money around its network with a boldness and agility that Pablo Escobar would have admired."[36] With equal deftness, ACORN avoids taxes with the boldness and agility of any given tax cheat serving in the Obama administration.

TAX EVADERS 'R' US

Vadum traced more than 200 federal, state, and local tax liens to ACORN's office compound in New Orleans. The debt totaled more than $3 million, including the following since 2005:[37]

ACORN & Co.: Community Organizers and Tax Cheats

This table, based on public records, reflects some of the largest of those active tax liens and now-released tax liens pertaining to ACORN and affiliates that list 1024 Elysian Fields Avenue, New Orleans, Louisiana 70117 as their address. A tax lien is issued only after other attempts to collect the tax debt have been made and the tax debt is seriously delinquent. If the lien has been released, that means that after the debtor failed to pay the tax owing, it eithe rpaid the tax owing or made arrangements to pay satisfactory to the creditory tax agency. There may be many, many more ACORN tax liens pending that have been sent out to other ACORN addresses.

DEBTOR	AMOUNT	CREDITOR	FILING DATE	ORIGINAL RELEASE?	LIEN OR FILING #
ACORN	$547,312	IRS	3/10/08	lien	930254
ACORN Community Labor Organizing	$306, 407	IRS	3/6/08	lien	930015
Citizens Consulting Inc.	$140,994	IRS	3/14/07	release	893022
ACORN	$132,997	IRS	3/14/08	lien	930768
ACORN	$132, 109	IRS	3/7/07	release	892311
ACORN Housing Corp Inc.	$125,342	IRS	5/9/07	release	899820
Citizens Consulting Inc.	$118,758	IRS	8/1/07	release	912881
Citizens Consulting Inc.	$118,600	IRS	6/4/07	release	940211
SEIU	$50,000	IRS	8/2/05	lien	830295
ACORN	$33,978	California	6/7/06	lien	2006221370

The Internal Revenue Service explains its policy regarding imposing and releasing liens:

"[A] Notice of Federal Tax Lien may be filed only after: We assess the liability; We send you a Notice and Demand for Payment – a bill that tells you how much you own in taxes; and You neglect or refuse to fully pay the debt within 10 days after we notify you about it."

The IRS "will issue a Release of the Notice of Federal Tax Lien: Within 30 days after you satisfy the tax due (including interest and other additions) by paying the debt or by having it adjusted, or Within 30 days after we accept a bond that you submit, guaranteeing payment of the debt." (Source: http://www.irs.govt-businesses/small/article/0 _id=108339,00.html#release)

Yes, the White House has entrusted the same organization that can't bother to keep track of its taxes to gather and report accurate census data.

MUSCLE FOR THE MONEY

One of ACORN's most outspoken critics and former employees is Anita MonCrief. Fired from her Washington, D.C., strategic research/writing position in January 2008 for using a Project Vote credit card for personal expenses worth less than $2,000, she served as the primary source for the rare investigative forays by the *New York Times* into ACORN's fraudulent empire. In sworn testimony for a lawsuit filed by the Pennsylvania Republican Party against ACORN, as detailed by Ballotpedia, MonCrief (an Obama supporter) revealed how:

- ACORN's quality-control efforts were "minimal or nonexistent";
- The quality control policies of ACORN were "largely window dressing";
- ACORN knew that most new voter registration forms it had gathered were fraudulent;
- When she was employed by the organization, it was given lists of potential donors by several Democratic presidential campaigns, including that of Barack Obama;
- In November of 2007, ACORN's Project Vote development director Karyn Gillette told her that Gillette had direct contact with the Obama campaign and had obtained their donor lists. Ms. MonCrief also testified she was given a spreadsheet to use in cultivating Obama donors who had maxed out on donations to the candidate, but who could contribute to voter registration efforts. Project Vote calls the allegation "absolutely false";
- Internally, ACORN had a policy of cooperating with authorities in prosecuting those who got caught trying

to falsify registration forms, a policy referred to by staffers as "throwing them under the bus."[38]

MonCrief's testimony was backed by other former ACORN employees. "There's no quality control on purpose, no checks and balances," former California ACORN organizer Nate Toler told the *Wall Street Journal*'s John Fund. Gregory Hall, a former Acorn employee, told Fund he was instructed on his "first day in 2006 to engage in deceptive fund-raising tactics."[39]

At congressional hearings in March 2009, Republican lawyer Heather Heidelbaugh further outlined how ACORN would bully companies into providing donations through aggressive protests. The program was referred to as "Muscle for the Money":

> ACORN had official and unofficial programs called 'Muscle for the Money'. The first program, the official program, is the marketing name ACORN gives for its voter registration drives. Citizens Services Incorporated (CSI), an affiliate of ACORN, prices the cost to register a voter, drive the voter to the poll, and eventually get the voter to vote. CSI does voter identification, turnout and [get out the vote].
>
> ...ACORN/CSI markets its program to candidate or campaigns and sells their services by stating that if you use [the] program with their proven methodologies, they will get it done at a certain price...CSI worked with ACORN and Project Vote. "All the affiliate organizations worked together...Ms. Moncrief testified about a document she had access to...: "It talks about America Votes and some notes from a meeting that took place I would say. [The document states under 'Political Money Rules']...we prefer that political money go to us in the form of a vendor, which would be CSI, our for profit business, which doesn't have to report the cash because it's a business, like the phone company."

...The second unofficial 'Muscle for the Money' Program is a corporate directed program for donations. Ms. Moncrief testified: "That [program] is what I learned in the local offices. That's where—let's say the D.C. office where I was. They would be given a project to go work on, even if they didn't have interest in it. At the time, even after I was fired, I was working with ACORN, going to barbecues, doing other stuff with D.C. local. They got involved with a group called the Carlyle Group. They were paid by SEIU to harass a man named Mr. Rubenstein, and they wanted me to go out—the D.C. local did, wanted me to go out and break up a banquet dinner, protest out in front of his house. But the local—D.C. local did not have an invested interest really in messing with the Carlyle Group. It was because they were paid by SEIU to do this. And it was always referred to as 'Muscle for Money' because they would go out there, intimidate these people, protest. They did it in front of Sherwin Williams. They did it at H&R Block, where H&R Block was a target for years. And instead of, you know, reforming the way they did the rapid anticipation loans, they ended up giving money to the ACORN tax sites which paid for new computers and money to run these tax filing sites around the country."

... "The protesting was used to get companies to negotiate. The companies would pay money to get the protesting to stop. In addition to calling this activity 'Muscle for the Money,' the insiders at ACORN called it "PROTECTION."

...Ms. Moncrief testified: "Protection. We were very—not to be flippant, but we were just always very sarcastic about it in the offices. We knew what was going on. And its not that we thought it was funny, it was just one of those things that we talked about...."[40]

(A few weeks later, ACORN flexed that muscle again—by busing dozens of its radical activists to the private homes of AIG executives targeted because they accepted taxpayer-subsidized retention bonuses.)

The overwhelming evidence of ACORN's racketeering and corruption persuaded one of the organization's fiercest defenders to change course—if ever so briefly. Democrat chairman of the House Judiciary Committee John Conyers signaled his desire in April 2009 to pursue hearings on ACORN's mob tactics. Defying fellow Democrats crying 'right-wing smear job,' Conyers pushed for further investigation into Heidelbaugh and MonCrief's allegations.[41] But by early May 2009, Conyers had retreated. On the day he announced publicly that there would be no probe, Nevada Democrat officials unveiled a whopping thirty-nine felony charges against ACORN related to voter registration fraud.[42]

Fortunately, Conyers's cowardice did not quiet ACORN's critics. Nor did the attempt by the *New York Times* to stifle the growing controversy over the organization's vast, interlocking network—and the Obama campaign's involvement in it. In response to congressional testimony by Pennsylvania lawyer Heather Heidelbaugh alleging that the *Times* had killed a "game changer" story on how Team Obama had shared donor lists with Project Vote, the newspaper's ombudsman Clark Hoyt dismissed it as the "tip that didn't pan out."[43]

Hoyt airily dismissed the charges by ACORN whistleblower Anita MonCrief as "nonsense" and quoted a *Times* editor who shrugged, "You have to cut bait after a while." It was an all-too-convenient judgment that just happened to be made as Election Day loomed. (Contrast this with the editorial doggedness of the *Times*'s editors in pursuing and publishing the *Star* magazine-quality insinuations that GOP presidential candidate John McCain had carried on an affair with Washington lobbyist Vicki Iseman.[44]) Hoyt attempted to paint MonCrief as an unreliable source. But *Times* reporter Stephanie Strom had happily relied on her for months to break a series of ACORN corruption stories.

And e-mail messages from Strom show not only the *New York Times* reporter's repeated praise and gratitude for MonCrief's information, but also her concurrence with MonCrief's assessment of the vast, money-funneling ACORN enterprise.[45]

On July 10, 2008, Strom wrote to MonCrief: "I'm a little miffed with the funders, too. They have to be aware that the grants they make to c(3)s like Project Vote are being funneled to Acorn, which, whether c(4) or simply nonprofit corporation under state law, they aren't supposed to give money to."

On July 31, 2008, she wrote: "I really want to see 1024 Elysian Fields in New Orleans. It's the official 'home' of something like 50-plus Acorn related entities. The real story to all this is how these myriad entities allow them to shuffle money around so much that no one really knows what's getting spent on what—and for the charities like the housing orgs, that's a problem. Charitable money cannot be spent on political activities. It's a big no-no that can cost organizations their exemptions."

Later that same day she wrote: "You are a gold mine! =)."

On September 7, 2008, after MonCrief alerted Strom to my reporting on the ACORN/CSI/Obama campaign ties, Strom replied: "Am also onto the Obama connection, sadly. Would love the donor lists. As for helping the Repubs, they're already onto this like white on rice. SIGH."

On October 6, 2008, Strom told MonCrief about her nasty run-in with the Obama campaign: "I'm calling a halt to my efforts. I just had two unpleasant calls with the Obama campaign, wherein the spokesman was screaming and yelling and cursing me, calling me a rightwing nut and a conspiracy theorist and everything else... I'd still like to get that file from you when you have a chance to send it. One of these days, the truth is going to come out."

Critics suggested that the donor lists could have been compiled through public records. But I obtained the lists—not only of

Obama donors, but also lists of Democratic National Committee, Hillary Clinton, and John Kerry contributors. The records include small donors to the Obama campaign who are not disclosed in public campaign finance databases. It's information only a campaign could supply.

MonCrief testified under oath last fall that her then-boss, Karyn Gillette, gave her the Obama donor list and told her the campaign had furnished it. Moreover, e-mail between ACORN, Project Vote, and CSI make explicit references to working on "Obama campaign related projects." The "list of maxed out Obama donors" is explicitly mentioned in staff e-mail. Another message from ACORN/Project Vote official Nathan Henderson-James warns ACORN and affiliated staff to prepare for "conservatives...gearing up a major oppo research project on Obama." Henderson-James wrote obligatorily, "Understand I'm not suggesting that we gear up to defend a candidate's campaign." But that, of course, is exactly what the ACORN network did.[46]

A few Republican lawmakers have begun to grasp the enormity and significance of ACORN's coordinated political corruption. Minnesota GOP Representative Michele Bachmann called on Congress to block federal housing funds for the group in the wake of the Nevada felony voter fraud case.[47] Iowa GOP Representative Steve King renewed efforts to launch a congressional probe into ACORN's finances. He told the *American Spectator*: "This spider web, this myriad web of ACORN dollars and revenue streams, every bit of them should be looked at, all the corporations that they are networked with all of the boards of directors of those corporations, the inner locking connecting, the faces that are the same from board to board."[48] And on May 29, 2009, constitutional lawyer and former Bush administration official Kris Kobach entered the race for Kansas Secretary of State, citing Obama's favorite radical left-wing racket as his primary motivation. Kobach distilled the essence of the vast web of its partnerships:

"ACORN is a criminal enterprise."[49]

For its part, the Obama White House has remained tight-lipped. Like the mafia, ACORN has its own golden rule of *omerta*—the code of silence among criminals.

It's a language the Clinton mob is well-versed in, too.

CHAPTER 9

THE CLINTONS
TWO FOR THE PRICE OF ONE

Cameras clicked and reporters scribbled as the wife of Bill Clinton picked up a dainty, mint-colored gift box and grinned from ear to ear. Standing next to her was Russian Foreign Minister Sergei Lavrov. Mrs. Clinton, on behalf of her bitter rival and now boss, Barack Obama, grandiosely presented her "little gift" to Lavrov. As she untied the matching bow, Secretary of State Clinton explained that the mysterious item symbolized what she and Obama wished for U.S.–Russian relations.

Lavrov watched as Clinton pulled out a big red button on a yellow and black base with a Russian word painted on it. "We want to reset our relationship," she proudly declared. Clinton placed her hand over Lavrov's, and they jointly pressed the button for the carefully planned photo op. "We worked hard to get the right Russian word," she told Lavrov as camera bulbs continued to flash. "Do you think we got it?"

Nyet. Hillary's "little gift" turned out to be a big blunder. Lavrov politely broke the awkward news as Mrs. Clinton's smile froze. "You got it wrong," Lavrov said as he pointed to the button's base.

"This says 'Peregruzka,' which means 'overcharged.'" Forced laughter ensued as "Smart Power"—the name Mrs. Clinton humbly gave her diplomatic philosophy to restore America's standing in the world—turned into an international bad joke.[1]

Too bad the American people can't hit the reset button on Secretary of State Hillary Clinton's appointment. It's only a matter of time before her gaffe with the Russians is overshadowed by far more serious problems. Mrs. Clinton's Democrat Senate colleague (and fellow failed presidential candidate) John Kerry praised her as "extraordinarily capable and smart, an individual with the global stature and influence to help shape events."[2] Capable? Smart? Debatable at best. But there's certainly no question she has used her considerable influence—derived largely from her hubby's presidential prestige—to help shape favorable public policies for deep-pocketed donors at home and abroad.

"There is barely an oligarch, royal family, or special-interest group anywhere in the world that does not know how to get the former president's attention," journalist Christopher Hitchens joked.[3] With Mrs. Clinton in command of Foggy Bottom, the conflicts are no laughing matter. Pay-to-play is the Clinton way.

Republicans made token noises over the Clintons' ethical morass, but ultimately only two GOP Senators voted against their colleague's confirmation—Senators Jim DeMint of South Carolina and David Vitter of Louisiana. One of Mrs. Clinton's most vocal Republican defenders? Ethics crusader John McCain, who used his first Senate floor speech since the end of his presidential campaign to push for his good friend's speedy approval: "I think the message that the American people are sending us now is they want us to work together and get to work....I think we ought to let Senator Clinton, who is obviously qualified and obviously will serve, get to work immediately."[4] McCain, the Senate's loudest critic of earmarks, saw no problem elevating his dear pal to the nation's highest diplomatic post, despite her obvious penchant for influence peddling.

Never mind that Mrs. Clinton requested nearly $2.3 billion in porky federal earmarks for 2009, nearly triple the largest amount received by any other senator the previous year.[5]

Never mind that since taking office in 2001, Clinton delivered half a billion dollars in earmarks to fifty-nine corporations— roughly 64 percent of which provided funds to her campaign through donations made by employees, executives, board members, or lobbyists, according to the *Los Angeles Times*.[6]

Never mind that while she shoveled out taxpayer funds to campaign contributors, her hubby was raking in dough from foreign leaders and tycoons to the tune of at least $46 million.[7]

How could Hillary's Republican cheerleaders be so recklessly tolerant of business-as-usual at this level of government? Favor-trading at home jeopardizes Americans' wallets; favor-trading abroad puts Americans' sovereignty and security at risk. The stakes are high. Shouldn't the standards be, too?

LIAR, LIAR, PANTSUIT ON FIRE

Mrs. Clinton promised not to let her husband's financial dealings sway her decisions as Secretary of State. But those who take the Clintons at their word haven't been paying attention to the last two decades. Whitewater. Travelgate. Chinagate. Pardongate. Lewinskygate. Healthcaretaskforcegate. Is there a pair of politicians any less deserving of the benefit of the doubt than Bill and Hillary Clinton?

Seeking to burnish her foreign policy leadership credentials during the 2008 presidential campaign, Senator Clinton repeatedly peddled a harrowing anecdote about dodging sniper fire during a trip to Tuzla, Bosnia, in 1996. "I remember landing under sniper fire," she said gravely in a speech at George Washington University in March 2008. "There was supposed to be some kind of a greeting ceremony at the airport, but instead we just ran with our heads down to get into the vehicles to get to our base."[8]

Mrs. Clinton told the gripping story in her 2003 autobiography and resurrected it during 2008 campaign stops in Dubuque, Iowa; Waco, Texas; and Washington, D.C., to illustrate her bravery, fortitude, expertise, and massive foreign policy experience edge over Barack Obama. But she left a few details out.

Along with her on the dangerous mission: her then-teenage daughter Chelsea, entertainer Sinbad, and singer Sheryl Crow. And, oh yeah, there was eight-year-old Bosnian girl Emina Bikakcic, who calmly embraced the intrepid First Lady and read her a poem on the tarmac—while a huge contingent of children and parents and other onlookers surrounded them with not the least bit of concern about flying bullets.

After Sinbad,[9] the *Washington Post*,[10] the *Philadelphia Daily News*,[11] and every fact-checker on the Internet[12] and under the sun had debunked her tall tale, Senator Clinton doubled down. Asked about how perilous the trip was, Sinbad cracked: "I think the only 'red-phone' moment was: 'Do we eat here or at the next place.'"[13] A miffed Mrs. Clinton dismissed Sinbad as a mere comedian.[14] She asserted again that she and her compatriots ran for safety with "our heads down."[15] She clung to her story that she "had to be moved inside because of sniper fire."[16] And she embellished further: "There was no greeting ceremony, and we were basically told to run to our cars. Now, that is what happened."[17]

When a video of the cheery greeting ceremony surfaced in March 2008 showing no such thing, Hillary's excuses poured forth. She "misspoke." Besides, she pooh-poohed: "I say a lot of things—millions of words a day—so if I misspoke, that was just a misstatement."[18] She sniffed that her Tuzla hustle was just a "minor blip."[19] Finally, Hillary blamed her congenital dissembling on being "sleep-deprived."[20] If that is so, then Hillary has been a walking zombie for years.

This is the woman who insisted for more than a decade that she was named after the late, great mountain-climber Sir Edmund Hillary—never mind that she was born six years before he became famous for scaling Mount Everest in 1953. Her husband repeated the lie in his 2004 autobiography. Mrs. Clinton finally admitted it was untrue in 2006, when she blamed it on her mother.[21]

This is the woman who claimed to have "helped to start" the federal Children's Health Insurance Program—never mind that the program's original sponsors noted that Senator Clinton fought the initial bill and had no role in writing the legislation.[22]

This is the woman (echoed by her husband and daughter) who bragged that she was the "first" to call the disaster in Darfur "genocide"—never mind that several other senators had done so in 2004, while her first press statement referring to Darfur as "genocide" wasn't until March 2006.[23]

This is the woman who claimed to have organized "instrumental"[24] meetings in Belfast, Ireland, and baldly asserted that she "helped to bring peace to Northern Ireland"—never mind that key negotiators dismissed her as "totally invisible," "cheerleading," and "a wee bit silly."[25]

This is the chronic sufferer of Truth Deficit Disorder whom President Obama—with the advice and consent of the U.S. Senate—has entrusted to conduct good-faith negotiations on foreign affairs and put America's interests above all else.

Feeling queasy yet?

TRANSPARENCY AND
TWO FOR THE PRICE OF ONE

"I think I'm probably the most transparent person in public life," Senator Hillary Clinton asserted in 2008.[26] To borrow a trademark

Clintonian phrase, it all depends on what the meaning of "transparent" is. Her insatiable ambition is as see-through as a Britney Spears top. But her commitment to openness in government earns a big, fat "F."

It took a public disclosure lawsuit by Washington, D.C.-based Judicial Watch to force Mrs. Clinton to release thousands of pages from her schedules while serving as First Lady. The group also successfully filed suit to obtain records regarding Mrs. Clinton's secret health care task force—including internal memos detailing the creation of a government "interest group database" to collect personal information on interest group leaders, such as their home phone numbers, addresses, "biographies, analysis of credibility in the media, and known relationships with Congresspeople."[27]

For years, the Clintons refused to disclose donors to the Clinton presidential library. The *Washington Post* called the Clintons' lack of full disclosure "outrageous," noting that "presidential libraries, though built and endowed with private funds, are public property, run by the National Archives. The public has a right to know who's underwriting them."[28] "To the best of my knowledge, I didn't take money from anybody I shouldn't have," former president Clinton said in explaining why the public should simply trust his judgment instead of opening the books.[29] In 2004, a *New York Sun* reporter accessed a public touch-screen computer terminal at the facility that produced a list of donors to the $165 million compound. The *Sun* reported that in addition to the infamous $450,000 gift from pardon-seeker Marc Rich's ex-wife, donations included "gifts of $1 million or more each from the Saudi royal family and three Saudi businessmen," as well as $1 million-plus each contributions from the "governments of Dubai, Kuwait, and Qatar and the deputy prime minister of Lebanon."[30] After the *Sun*'s article appeared, the list of donors available on the library's computer terminal disappeared.[31]

For years, the Clintons refused to disclose their full income tax forms.[32] It took her rival-turned-boss Barack Obama's full IRS document disclosure to force Hillary to follow suit in April 2008.[33] The tax documents covering 2000–2007 revealed the Clintons' get-rich windfall of approximately $111 million in total income over that time period. "Their income increased by nearly 50 times in the first year after Bill Clinton left office," the *Politico* reported, "highlighting the lucrative opportunities awaiting former presidents."[34]

For years, the couple refused to disclose donors to the former president's mega-charity, the William J. Clinton Foundation (described by the *Chronicle of Philanthropy* as "one of the most successful fund-raising organizations in the United States").[35] It took Mrs. Clinton's secretary of state nomination to force this treasure trove of foreign conflicts of interests to be dislodged. But even this belated, reluctant gesture was incomplete.

To close the deal on the nomination, the Clintons released a public list of past donors to the foundation and signed a "memorandum of understanding" with the Obama transition team agreeing to disclose new donors once a year. Foreign government donations will be reviewed by State Department ethics officials. Former President Clinton agreed to step down as the public face of the Clinton Foundation and break off a separate program, the Clinton Global Initiative. Mrs. Clinton called her disclosure agreement "unprecedented" in its scope and cited government reviews concluding that "there is not an inherent conflict of interest in any of my husband's work at all."[36]

But through thick and thin, through hell and high water, through stained blue dresses and purple fits of rage, Bill and Hillary Clinton are joined at the hip. As GOP Senator Richard Lugar put it while pondering how to disentangle their "cosmic ties" and conflicted interests: "I don't know, frankly...I would just suspect that given all of the ties, all of the influence that he has, all of the relationships that he is a major player in foreign policy. Now, Mrs. Clinton is going to be the secretary of state. They are married, they are a team."[37]

Like they promised in 1992, America gets "two for the price of one" with the Clintons. No matter which of them is in office.

COSMIC TIES

The Clinton Foundation donor list did not provide precise amounts, date of the donations, or background information on the donors' employers. Non-governmental foreign sources were not and will not be disclosed.

But among the information the Clintons did disclose was the donation of "up to $5 million" to the Clinton foundation from one Gilbert Chagoury, a Lebanese businessman born in Nigeria who calls himself an "economic adviser to Benin" and a UNESCO ambassador to St. Lucia.[38] He also happens to be a scandal-tainted operative who was tight with Nigerian General Sani Abacha, a dictator who seized power in a coup in the 1990s. In 2001, Chagoury forked over $300 million to the Nigerian government to get rid of a pesky probe into charges that billions of dollars had been improperly siphoned out of Nigeria during the Abacha regime.[39] During those years, *Harper's* magazine reported, "Chagoury received oil concessions and large-scale government construction contracts, and allegedly offered Abacha help with his financial affairs."[40] And during that time, Chagoury used his wealth to insinuate himself into the Clinton White House and the Democrat party—arranging a $100,000 speaking fee for Clinton at a Caribbean event and pitching in $460,000 for a Miami-based voter registration drive backed by the Democratic National Committee.[41] For his *quid*, the foreign national Chagoury enjoyed many *quos*. The *Wall Street Journal* reported that Chagoury attended Clinton's 60th birthday bash in New York and joined the former president at a gala wedding party in France for a top Clinton aide.[42] For her part, Mrs. Clinton received thousands of dollars in donations from stateside relatives of Chagoury, including Michel Chaghouri—identified as a bundler who raised at least $100,000 for Hillary—and several other donors who maxed out with $4,600 in individual contributions using the names "Chagoury" or "Chaghouri" or "Chamchoum." (The latter is the maiden name of Gilbert Chagoury's wife.)[43]

Another wealthy donor listed as giving up to $5 million to the Clinton Foundation: billionaire Viktor Pinchuk, the son-in-law of former Ukrainian strongman Leonid Kuchma. The steel company magnate was fingered in several sweetheart deals and accused by Ukrainian reformers of crony capitalism. In 2006, he settled a lawsuit that accused him of bribing officials of a mega-iron alloy producer, skimming $41 million in profits, and wrongfully diverting other funds worth an estimated $500 million.[44] Sidling up to former President Clinton helped burnish Pinchuk's philanthropic credentials. After donating millions to Clinton's anti-poverty and AIDS programs, Pinchuk was warmly received at the inauguration of the Clinton Library in Little Rock and at Clinton's 60th birthday bash. (No word on whether Chagoury and Pinchuk ran into each other.)

More worrisome for Hillary, her husband displayed abysmal judgment in 2007—while she was running for president—when he flew to Yalta to join his pal Pinchuk. At a conference on the future of Ukraine, former President Clinton embraced a tainted symbol of the troubled corruptocracy's recent past. *Newsweek* reported:

> Clinton dazzled the audience with a powerful address about the global challenges facing Ukraine. But he also inadvertently caused a stir when he was embraced by Pinchuk's father-in-law,

Ukraine's former president Leonid Kuchma, whose authoritarian rule had been condemned by the State Department. Three
years ago, a Ukrainian government investigation linked
Kuchma's regime to the decapitation in 2000 of dissident journalist Georgy Gongadze. When Gongadze's widow, Myroslava,
saw a newspaper photo of Clinton and Kuchma at the conference, "I wanted to throw up," she told *Newsweek*. Clinton, she
says, was being used by Pinchuk "to clean up and legitimize
Kuchma's legacy." (A Clinton spokesman declined to comment
on the ex-president's encounter with Kuchma.)[45]

Gongadze's death was no obscure historical blip. The investigative Internet reporter, found mutilated in a shallow grave, was an
intrepid critic of Kuchma's corruption. His grisly murder sparked
the Orange Revolution that swept Kuchma out of power.
Kuchma's own former bodyguard released audiotapes with a
voice identified as Kuchma's conspiring to harm the journalist.
Gongadze's wife and two children won political asylum in the U.S.
and have lived here since 2001. In March 2008, three former
police officers were convicted of Gongadze's murder. And a former Interior Ministry chief of Kuchma's is still wanted for his role
in plotting the crime.[46]

    After observing the November 21, 2004, elections in Ukraine
as an election monitor, Senator Lugar (then chair of the Senate
Committee on Foreign Relations) reported that "the government
of President Kuchma allowed, or aided and abetted, wholesale
fraud and abuse" that changed the results of the election. Widespread physical intimidation of voters and "illegal use of govern-
mental administrative and legal authorities" were persistent
throughout the campaign.[47] Yet three years later, Bill Clinton lent
his name and fame to the Yalta summit, organized by Kuchma's
wealthy son-in-law and top contributor to the Clinton Foundation and attended by Kuchma himself.

In addition to all that foreign funny money, the Clinton Foundation received $10 million to $25 million from the Kingdom of Saudi Arabia and a total of at least $46 million from foreign governments, including Norway, Kuwait, Qatar, Brunei, Oman, Italy, Jamaica, and the Dutch national lottery, which pitched in $5 million to $10 million.[48] Israeli business executives, the Blackwater private security company, oil, gas, and mining interests were all represented on the list as well. The Associated Press broke down more of the donor info, incomplete as it was, which was posted on the Clinton Foundation website:[49]

- Saudi businessman Nasser Al-Rashid gave between $1 million to $5 million. So did two private entities, Friends of Saudi Arabia and the Dubai Foundation.
- Amar Singh, another donor in the $1 million to $5 million category, is an Indian politician who hosted Bill Clinton on a visit to India in 2005 and met Hillary Clinton in New York in September to discuss an India–U.S. civil nuclear agreement.
- Tulsi Tanti, a wealthy executive also from India, chairs a wind turbine company that donated up to $5 million. He unveiled plans for a $5 billion project to develop environmentally friendly power generation in India and China.
- AUSAID, the Australian government's overseas aid program, and COPRESIDA-Secretariado Tecnico, a Dominican Republic government agency formed to fight AIDS, each gave $10 million to $25 million.[50] COPRESIDA benefited from an Export-Import Bank loan at the 11th hour of the Clinton administration, according to a watchdog group, which also wondered: "Why would a cash-strapped AIDS agency accused of mismanagement[51] in a country of 9.5 million give

President Clinton one of his largest donations to do the same thing it is trying to do—collect money and redistribute for AIDS projects?"[52] AIDS patients protested that the agency had failed to build long promised treatment centers and failed to expand treatment access.

- China Overseas Real Estate Development and the U.S. Islamic World Conference gave $250,000 to $500,000 each.

GOP Senator Lugar stated the obvious at Mrs. Clinton's Senate confirmation hearing:

> The core of the problem is that foreign governments and entities may perceive the Clinton Foundation as a means to gain favor with the Secretary of State. Although neither Senator Clinton, nor President Clinton, has a personal financial stake in the Foundation, obviously its work benefits their legacy and their public service priorities. There is nothing wrong with this, and President Clinton is deservedly proud of the Clinton Foundation's good work in addressing HIV/AIDs, global poverty, climate change and other pressing problems.
>
> But the Clinton Foundation exists as a temptation for any foreign entity or government that believes it could curry favor through a donation. It also sets up potential perception problems with any action taken by the Secretary of State in relation to foreign givers or their countries. The nature of the Secretary of State post makes recusal from specific policy decisions almost impossible, since even localized U.S. foreign policy activities can ripple across countries and continents. Every new foreign donation that is accepted by the Foundation comes with the risk that it will be connected in the global media to a proximate State Department policy or decision. Foreign perceptions are incred-

ibly important to U.S. foreign policy, and mistaken impressions or suspicions can deeply effect the actions of foreign governments toward the United States. Moreover, we do not want our own government's deliberations distracted by avoidable controversies played out in the media. The bottom line is that even well-intentioned foreign donations carry risks for U.S. foreign policy.

The only certain way to eliminate this risk going forward is for the Clinton Foundation to forswear new foreign contributions when Senator Clinton becomes Secretary of State.[53]

Senator Clinton rejected that call and adamantly refused to take reasonable measures proposed by Senator Lugar to achieve true transparency, including provisions to immediately report all gifts of $50,000 or more and all such donations from foreigners at the time they are pledged, and a requirement to review all donations above $50,000 from individual and corporate foreign sources, not just foreign governments.[54]

"[F]or an administration that had committed itself to full transparency, it's a disappointing way to start," the *New York Post* sighed.[55] Indeed, the Clintons' ethical baggage, past, present, and future, is now Barack Obama's burden.

ADVENTURES IN KAZAKHSTAN

Hillary's hubby has left no international cash behind. Among his thorniest dalliances is his relationship with mining financier Frank Giustra. The Canadian tycoon flew Clinton in his private corporate jet to meet with Kazakhstan's authoritarian ruler Nursultan Nazarbayev in 2005. The *New York Times* reported that the trio enjoyed a "sumptuous midnight banquet." Clinton endorsed Nazarbayet's lip service to fair elections, despite official State Department condemnations of his repressive tactics. Giustra won lucrative agreements with the country's state-owned uranium agency. And the Clinton Foundation's coffers swelled after the deal—"turning an unknown shell company into one of the world's largest uranium producers in a transaction ultimately worth tens of millions of dollars to Mr. Giustra, analysts said"—was sealed.

After showering more than $130 million on Clinton's charity, the *Times* reported, Giustra secured "a place in Mr. Clinton's inner circle, an exclusive club of wealthy entrepreneurs in which friendship with the former president has its privileges."[56]

Secretary of State Hillary Clinton insists her husband's interests pose no inherent conflict for her. But Giustra's reach is global. How could there not be the appearance of a conflict of interest in any policy decision the State Department might make in the countries where Giustra operates or plans to operate?

Stanley Brand, a former counsel for House Democrats, told the *Washington Post* there was only one ethical exit strategy for the Clintons: "There's only one way, which is draconian, which is to void the bequest....I don't how else you remedy it."[57] But in a well-worn pattern, the Clintons rejected the simplest and cleanest solution and refused to put their country's interests above their own.

PAYING AND PLAYING AT HOME

Mrs. Clinton's dealings with donors on American soil do not inspire confidence, either. An Associated Press investigation found at least six cases where Hillary Clinton, while serving in the U.S. Senate, intervened in government issues that directly affected companies and others that later contributed to her husband's foundation through the Clinton Global Initiative.[58] The beneficiaries of Mrs. Clinton's actions included Merck & Co. and Barr Laboratories—companies in the same pharmaceutical industry she demonized in the 1990s:

Pharmaceutical company Merck & Co. is...a member of the Clinton Global Initiative, company spokeswoman Amy Rose said. Merck joined CGI in 2006, when dues were $15,000, and also was a member in 2007 and in 2008, when membership dues rose to $20,000. As part of its commitment to CGI, Merck sponsors public health initiatives around the world, Rose said. Merck joined CGI on its own initiative, she said.

Sen. Clinton wrote a November 2005 letter to Health and Human Services Secretary Mike Leavitt urging approval of the human papillomavirus vaccine. Merck applied in December 2005 for approval of its HPV vaccine, Gardasil, and the vaccine was approved for use in females ages 9 to 26. Merck is still seeking approval for use in older women, Rose said.

Rose said Merck's participation in the Clinton Global Initiative was unrelated to Sen. Clinton's letter. Merck didn't communicate with Clinton or her office about its HPV vaccine and was unaware of her letter before it was sent, Rose said.

Another letter involved an issue important to Barr Laboratories. Sens. Clinton and Patty Murray, D-Wash., wrote to Leavitt in August 2005 urging that "science, not politics" guide the agency and "that a decision be brought swiftly on Plan B's application." Leavitt's office described the Clinton letter as pertaining to Barr's application for Plan B, the emergency contraceptive also called the morning-after pill.

Barr Laboratories gave $10,001 to $25,000 to Clinton Foundation, the charity's donor list shows. Barr joined the Clinton Global Initiative in April 2007, spokeswoman Carol Cox said. Cox didn't comment on Clinton's letter.[59]

In Hillary's own backyard, upstate New York developer Robert Congel donated $100,000 to the Clinton Foundation in the fall of 2004—just a few weeks after Mrs. Clinton helped pass legislation allowing Congel to use tax-exempt bonds to fund the construction of his company's massive entertainment and shopping complex in Syracuse. Senator Clinton also paved the path for Congel—literally—by securing $5 million for the complex's roadway construction. The set-aside passed in August 2005.[60] Congel and the Clintons denied any connection between the charitable donation and legislative benefits, of course. Congel, who typically donated to Republican politicians and was a top donor for George W. Bush, explained that he had given to the Clinton Foundation out of patriotic zeal: "I have a huge interest in our country, and I thought Clinton was a great president," he told the *Times*. "I think he's a dedicated, dedicated American, and I'm a dedicated, dedicated American."[61] Dedicated, it seems obvious, to showering his affections on a president whose wife just happened to represent his best business interests in legislation coincidentally pending before the Senate.

One of Mrs. Clinton's pork projects that didn't fly: a $1 million earmark for billionaire and cable TV executive Alan Gerry's Woodstock museum. Clinton and fellow New York senator Charles Schumer heralded federal funding for the hippie shrine in the summer of 2007. Gerry and his family contributed nearly $30,000 to Senator Clinton and Schumer's Democratic Senatorial Campaign Committee within days of the earmark surviving a legislative hurdle—including maximum contributions from Gerry and his wife to Hillary Clinton and $20,000 from the Gerrys and two of their kids to the DSCC.[62] Like developer and fellow New Yorker Robert Congel, Gerry had given gobs of money to both parties. Like Congel, he denied he was seeking favors and played the civic card. The family donations—nearly half a million dollars since 1998 to both parties—were "something we think a good citizen should do."[63] But other good citizens balked at spending federal tax dollars on hippie tourism. Clinton and Schumer ran into a fiscal accountability backlash when they tried to attach the pet project to a supersized health and education spending bill.[64] Not too groovy.

THE BOTTOM OF HILLARY'S BARREL

The Clintons have always had a knack for attracting the dregs of society to their donor rolls—and an even greater talent for avoiding the kind of sustained media scrutiny that would ensue were they Republicans. Imagine the Beltway outrage that would have erupted had Hillary donor Mauricio Celis been a deep-pocketed supporter of GOP presidential candidate John McCain.

Celis is a Mexican-born con artist who was convicted of fourteen counts of falsely representing himself as an attorney. A prominent Democratic Party donor and Hillary supporter, Celis made a living defrauding clients and was ordered to pay restitution estimated at about $1.35 million to victims.[65] Before the law caught up to the fake lawyer who owned no law license in the U.S. and dubiously claimed to hold one in Mexico, Celis lived life in the fast lane—flying a private jet, driving a Ferrari, frequenting strip clubs, "handing out fat checks to Democratic candidates, hosting fundraisers and serving on the board of Catholic Charities of Corpus Christi."[66] From 2003 to 2008, he wrote checks totaling more than $110,000 to Democrat candidates and causes, including a maximum contribution to Hillary Clinton covering her primary campaign and huge chunks to the DSCC and DNC. The *Washington Post* reported that he raised $100,000 for the Democratic Senatorial Campaign in 2007, pitching in $28,500 of his own money. In May 2009, his sentence of one year in jail was reduced to ten years' probation because of the "appearance of bias" by the original sentencing judge. He was ordered to pay $1 million in restitution.

Celis's fakery was exposed in September 2007 when police arrested him in his bathrobe outside a Corpus Christi convenience store. He had tried to escape from police by flashing a county sheriff's department badge at officers on the scene. The disturbing incident was just one of several offense reports in which Celis allegedly tried to impersonate law enforcement.[67]

That's the tame stuff. In January 2008, Texas Attorney General Greg Abbott raided Celis's offices after determining that Celis was engaged in suspect cross-border activity following large cash withdrawals.[68] The attorney general's office released details of its affidavit, which concluded that Celis had "committed the felony offense of money laundering" and was "rumored to be associated with questionable criminal element (sic) possibly related to drug trafficking."[69] Celis faces three more trials on charges of money laundering, theft, and impersonating a peace officer—in addition to a possible indictment on charges of aggravated perjury and misrepresentation before a judge.[70] Several recipients have returned Celis's stained cash, but Hillary Clinton's office refused to comment.[71]

Mrs. Clinton was just as tight-lipped over the sordid case of Rehman Jinnah. A prized rainmaker for the Democrat Party, Jinnah was wanted in Pakistan on corruption charges and wanted in the U.S. on tax and bankruptcy fraud. Yet, the Democrats still took money from him[72]—$30,000 of which went into Mrs. Clinton's coffers and another $50,000 or so that went to California Sen. Barbara Boxer.[73] The feds indicted him in 2006; he pulled a Marc Rich and fled soon after, but returned to the U.S. to plead guilty to funneling illegal contributions to the two senators' campaign war chests.

The practice of bundling—rounding up many small, individual contributions to donate in one lump sum—has long been a recipe for trouble at Camp Clinton. In October 2007, the *Los Angeles Times* traced about 150 donations of between $500 and $2,000 each from dishwashers, street vendors, and other low-wage workers in New York City Chinatown. Of the contributions examined, one-third of the donors could not be found, and a $1,000 donor denied giving a contribution, according to the report.[74] The *New York Post* also had trouble tracking down mystery Hillary donors in October 2007:

A search of Chinatown donors yesterday by *The Post* found several bogus addresses and some contributions that raised eyebrows.

Shin K. Cheng is listed twice in federal records for giving $1,000 donations to Clinton's campaign on April 17.

But the address recorded on campaign reports is a clinic for sexually transmitted diseases, hemorrhoids and skin disease.

No one at the address knew of a Shin K. Cheng.

Another donation came from a Shih Kan Chang on Canal Street. But the address listed is a shop that sells knock-off watches and other pirated goods. The sales clerk there did not know the donor.

Hsiao Yen Wang, a cook in Chinatown, is listed as giving Clinton $1,000 on April 13. Contacted yesterday, she told *The Post* she had written a check.

But it was on behalf of a man named David Guo, president of the Fujian American Cuisine Council, and Wang told *The Post* that Guo had repaid her for the $1,000 contribution.

Such "straw donations" are strictly prohibited by federal law.

In addition, yesterday's search by *The Post* also turned up several $1,000 donations from Chinatown that were made by cooks, dishwashers, a cashier and a college student.[75]

The jaded *Washington Post* put it ever so mildly: "This appears to be another instance in which a Clinton campaign's zeal for campaign cash overwhelms its judgment."[76] What judgment?

Shaking down employees was the route tireless Democrat donor and Hillary fundraiser Norman Hsu took, too. The Hong Kong native raised money like a madman for Clinton and mostly Democrat recipients at every level of government, totaling more than $1.2 million in recent years. Former President Bill Clinton referred to the prodigious fund-raiser at a gala dinner as "our friend Norman Hsu."[77] And Barack Obama was the fourth largest recipient of Hsu-raised funds.[78] (See chart.)

Candidates (including candidate PACs) who received campaign donations from Norman Hsu or his associates

RECIPIENT (OFFICE, STATE)	ALL RECEIPTS	HSU ONLY	ASSOCIATES
Clinton, Hillary (Sen/Pres, NY)	$850,000	$22,600	$827,400
Cuomo, Andrew (AG, NY)	86,600	60,100	26,500
Spitzer, Eliot L (Gov, NY)	72,600	60,100	12,500
Obama, Barack (Sen/Pres, IL)	72,100	12,000	60,100
Harkin, Tom (Sen, IA)	59,800	4,600	55,200
Kennedy, Ted (Sen, MA)	49,900	9,000	40,900
Rendell, Ed (Gov, PA)	45,366	37,866	7,500
Granholm, Jennifer M (Gov, MI)	42,100	13,400	28,700
Ford, Harold E Jr (House, TN)	41,800	14,700	27,100
Biden, Joe (Sen, DE)	39,100	39,100	
Kennedy, Patrick J (House, RI)	38,500	6,200	32,300
Stabenow, Debbie (Sen, MI)	33,813	4,200	29,613
Angelides, Phil (Gov, CA)	32,600	32,600	
McCaskill, Claire (Sen, MO)	30,100	30,100	
Weiner, Anthony (Mayor, NY)	28,150	4,250	23,900
Gillibrand, Kirsten E (House, NY)	27,800	4,600	23,200
Ma, Fiona (Assembly, CA)	27,600	8,300	19,300
Richardson, Bill (Gov, NM)	23,000	23,000	
Rockefeller, Jay (Sen, WV)	23,000	4,000	19,000
Liu, John (Undeclared, NY)	22,950	4,950	18,000
Feinstein, Dianne (Sen, CA)	22,162	1,000	21,162
Landrieu, Mary L (Sen, LA)	19,300	3,000	16,300
Matsui, Doris O (House, CA)	16,850	10,100	6,750
Cantwell, Maria (Sen, WA)	15,398	4,200	11,198
Casey, Bob (Sen, PA)	14,950	4,200	10,750
Hertzberg, Bob (Mayor, CA)	12,600	7,000	5,600
Pryor, Mark (Sen, AR)	12,000	2,500	9,500
Reid, Harry (Sen, NV)	12,000	4,000	8,000
Reed, Jack (Sen, RI)	10,000	2,500	7,500
Strickland, Ted (Gov, OH)	10,000	10,000	
Quinn, Christine (Undeclared, NY)	9,900	4,950	4,950
Newsom, Gavin (Mayor, CA)	9,450	750	8,700
Duckworth, Tammy (House, IL)	8,750	8,750	
Kerry, John (Senate, MA)	8,650	4,000	4,650
Nelson, Bill (Senate, FL)	7,700	2,500	5,200
Pallone, Frank Jr (House, NJ)	7,500	7,500	
Westly, Steve (Controller, CA)	7,000	5,000	2,000
Webb, James (Senate, VA)	6,500	6,500	
Lampson, Nick (House, TX)	6,500	6,500	

Used with permission from Flip Pidot, Suitably Flip, http://www.suitablyflip.com/suitably_flip/norman_hsu/.

RECIPIENT (OFFICE, STATE)	ALL RECEIPTS	HSU ONLY	ASSOCIATES
Tester, Jon (Senate, MT)	6,250	6,250	
Brown, Jerry (AG , CA)	5,500	5,500	
Boxer, Barbara (Senate, CA)	5,000	4,000	1,000
Titus, Dina (Governor , NV)	5,000	5,000	
Honda, Mike (House, CA)	5,000	1,000	4,000
Whitehouse, Sheldon (Senate, RI)	5,000	5,000	
Thompson, Jr., William (Undeclared, NY)	4,950	4,950	
Culver, Chet & Judge, Patty (Governor, IA)	4,500	4,500	
Ferrer, Fernando (Mayor, NY)	4,500	4,500	
Loebsack, David (House, IA)	4,300	2,000	2,300
Allen, Tom (House, ME)	4,000	1,000	3,000
Vilsack, Thomas J (Governor, IA)	3,800	2,300	1,500
Murphy, Patrick J (House, PA)	3,250	1,000	2,250
Brunner, Jennifer L (Sec. of State, OH)	3,000	3,000	
Kleeb, Scott (House, NE)	3,000	3,000	
Sestak, Joe (House, PA)	2,750	1,000	1,750
Destefano, John (Governor , CT)	2,500	2,500	
Cardin, Ben (Senate, MD)	2,500	2,500	
Franken, Al (Senate, MN)	2,300	2,300	
Doyle, Jim (Governor, WI)	2,000	2,000	
Morgenthau, Robert (District Attorney , NY)	2,000	2,000	
Delgadillo, Rockard (City Attorney, CA)	2,000	1,000	1,000
Akaka, Daniel K (Senate, HI)	2,000	2,000	
Chiang, John (Controller, CA)	2,000	2,000	
Lynch, John (Governor , NH)	2,000	2,000	
Brown, Sherrod (Senate, OH)	2,000	2,000	
Pratcher, Tyson Anwar (House, TN)	1,750	1,750	
Harris, Kamala (District Attorney, CA)	1,250	1,250	
Filson, Steve N (House, CA)	1,250	1,250	
Bean, Melissa (House, IL)	1,000	1,000	
Cahill, Timothy P (Treasurer, MA)	1,000	500	500
Carter, John William (Senate, NV)	1,000	1,000	
Corzine, Jon S (Governor , NJ)	1,000	1,000	
Gallagher, Tom (Governor, FL)	1,000	1,000	
Garamendi, John (Lt. Gov, CA)	1,000	1,000	
Gerson, Alan (City Council, NY)	1,000	1,000	
Lautenberg, Frank R (Senate, NJ)	1,000	1,000	
Menendez, Robert (Senate, NJ)	1,000	1,000	
Ting, Philip (Assessor, CA)	1,000	1,000	
Udall, Mark (House, CO)	1,000	1,000	
Villaraigosa, Antonio (Mayor, CA)	1,000	1,000	
Klobuchar, Amy (Senate, MN)	1,000	1,000	
Alioto-Pier, Michela (Supervisor, CA)	500	500	

RECIPIENT (OFFICE, STATE)	ALL RECEIPTS	HSU ONLY	ASSOCIATES
Mak, Jaynry (Supervisor, CA)	500	500	
Sebelius, Kathleen & Parkinson, Mark (Governor, KS)		500	500
Sing, Lillian (Supervisor, CA)	500	500	
Dufty, Bevan (Supervisor, CA)	100	100	
Candidate Total (86)	$1,974,539	$411,866	$1,562,673

State Democratic Parties, Committees, Advocates

RECIPIENT (STATE)	ALL RECEIPTS	HSU ONLY	ASSOCIATES
DSCC	$145,533	$43,700	$101,833
DNC Services Corp	85,938	35,000	50,938
Tennessee Dem Party (TN)	58,000	58,000	
NY State Dem Cmte (NY)	50,000	50,000	
New Jersey Dem Party (NJ)	49,000	49,000	
Michigan Dem Party (MI)	35,000	35,000	
Cmte For A Dem Majority	23,000	5,000	18,000
DCCC	22,500	2,500	20,000
Rhode Island Dem Party (RI)	11,000	11,000	
Yes On 82 Preschool For All (CA)	11,000	10,000	1,000
Dem Party Of Wisconsin (WI)	10,000	10,000	
Ohioans For Fair Min. Wage (OH)	10,000	10,000	
Personal PAC Inc (IL)	10,000	10,000	
Phila Dem Campaign Cmte (PA)	10,000	10,000	
Working Families Party (NY)	10,000	10,000	
Florida Dem Party (FL)	6,000	6,000	
NH Senate Dem Caucus (NH)	6,000	5,000	1,000
Dem Exec. Cmte Of Florida (FL)	5,000	5,000	
DSCC of NY (NY)	5,000	5,000	
No on 77 (CA)	4,100	4,100	
25th Ward Regular Dem Org. (IL)	3,500	3,500	
Dem State Central Cmte of CA (CA)	3,500	1,500	2,000
Pennsylvania Dem Party	2,000	2,000	
Emily's List	1,500	1,000	500
California Dem Party	1,000	1,000	
Illinois Democratic Party	1,000	1,000	
Credit Suisse Securities	500	500	
Workforce Housing for Prop J (CA)	500	500	
Non-Candidate Total (28)	$580,571	$377,200	$203,371

ALL RECIPIENTS	ALL RECEIPTS	HSU ONLY	ASSOCIATES
Candidate Total (86)	1,974,539	411,866	1,562,673
Non-Candidate Total (28)	580,571	377,200	203,371
Total (114)	$2,555,110	$789,066	$1,766,044

In September 2007, Hsu was finally arrested after having evaded the law for fifteen years over grand theft swindling charges. Hsu pleaded no contest to those old charges and was supposed to serve jail time. Instead, he managed to remain a fugitive while raking in hundreds of thousands of dollars for Democratic candidates and officeholders—and posing openly for photographs with the likes of Hillary Clinton. The arrest took place after a bizarre train sojourn Hsu took after skipping out on a California court appearance related to a felony theft conviction. He was apprehended in Grand Junction, Colorado.

Former President Clinton, who left the White House up to his eyeballs in campaign finance scandals, retreated to Southern folksy talk when asked about the Hsu scandal. "You could have knocked me over with a straw, especially when I heard the L.A. people had been allegedly looking for him for 15 years when he was in plain view," he said.[79] Why such shock? Hillary Clinton's campaign had been warned directly by a California businessman in June 2007 that Hsu's investment operation didn't smell right.[80] No plausible deniability here.

In November 2007, Hsu was indicted by a federal grand jury and accused of cheating investors of at least $20 million by promising them "short-term, high-return investments." No Ponzi scheme lasts forever, but Hsu bullied his targets into giving him every penny they had. He pressured victims to contribute thousands of dollars to political candidates, made "direct and implied threats... leading them to believe that their failure to make" the donations would jeopardize their business relations, and conned them into illegal reimbursement schemes for donations.[81] Two months after the indictment was issued, a California judge sentenced the bagman to three years in prison for the old fraud charges. A week before Inauguration Day 2009, Hsu was back in the news (or on the Internet, anyway) to complain that press coverage of the more famous Ponzi scheme under the spotlight—the Bernie Madoff case—would prejudice his own trial. In May 2009,

Hsu was convicted in a New York federal court on four campaign finance corruption counts. At trial, jurors heard a gushing voice message from Senator Clinton in praise of Hsu's fundraising prowess:

> What am I going to do with you, Norman? You are working so hard for me that I just don't know what to say any more. I've never seen anybody who has been more loyal and more effective and really just having greater success supporting someone than you. . . . Everywhere I go, you're there. If you're not, you're sending someone to be part of my events. You know, we're going to win this campaign, Norman, because you're singlehandedly going to make that happen. . . . Get some sleep. Slow down for a few minutes. We're going to get to the end of the first quarter and then we can all take a little rest. Lots of love. Bye bye.[82]

The once-smitten Senator Clinton agreed to return $850,000 in bundled contributions gathered by Hsu—but her campaign asserted an option to re-purpose the dirty donations "by saying that it would take back the money if it clearly came from the donor's bank account."[83] The botched attempt to pay lip service to ethics while setting up a rinse-and-spin cycle for Hsu's tainted cash invited further ridicule. One Democratic presidential primary rival who spared Mrs. Clinton no mercy was Connecticut senator Chris Dodd. He took a dig at Hillary's Hsu headache in a mocking press release announcing his "campaign policy on money raised by fugitives from justice."[84]

"I understand that it is simply impossible for a presidential campaign to know everything about its donors and raisers, however once criminal activity of this sort—being a fugitive from justice—comes to the candidate's attention they certainly should not keep the money linked to those criminals," Senator Dodd stated smugly. Unfortunately for Dodd and so many of Hillary's colleagues on Capitol Hill, they were in no position themselves to be casting ethical stones.

BIRDS OF A FEATHER

"I can't say it any clearer: I will be helping Chris Dodd because he deserves the help," President Obama told the *Boston Globe*. "He just has an extraordinary record of accomplishment, and I think the people of Connecticut will come to recognize that."[1] The public endorsement of Dodd's 2010 re-election campaign was a much-needed morale boost for the Democratic senator from Connecticut. In April 2009, his approval rating had dropped to its lowest level ever.[2]

Damaged birds of a feather flock together. Obama wasn't doing the beleaguered Senator Dodd any special favors. This was business as usual. Senator Dodd, a fellow Democratic presidential rival, had endorsed Obama over Hillary Clinton after he dropped out of the race following the Iowa caucuses. Both camps courted Dodd aggressively. His endorsement came at a critical point ahead of big primaries in Texas and Ohio. Clinton had launched a full-throttle attack on Obama's flimsy foreign policy credentials. But the veteran Democrat threw his weight behind the rookie.

Declared Senator Dodd: "Barack Obama is a 21st century candidate who will express the aspirations and hopes of so many."[3]

Obama's hope-filled followers should cringe at their president's embrace of one of the most ethically compromised politicians on Capitol Hill. The Beltway swamp is teeming with Democratic corruption scandals (Pennsylvania congressman John Murtha's earmark factory and tax-subsidized airports and radars to nowhere; New York representative Charlie Rangel's rent-controlled apartment scams and tax scandals; Illinois representative Jesse Jackson's role in the Blagojevich pay-for-Senate seat debacle; California representative Maxine Waters's business ties to a minority-owned bank that received $12 million in TARP money under smelly circumstances, for starters), which are fodder for a separate encyclopedia set.[4] But Dodd's career epitomizes the most fetid aspects of Washington's culture of corruption. It's a textbook case of nepotism, self-dealing, back-scratching, corporate lobbying, government favors, entrenched incumbency, and hypocrisy.

Everything you need to know about the befouling of the Beltway swamp can be found in the rise and fall of Chris Dodd—and in Barack Obama's affirmation of his "extraordinary record of accomplishment."

THE SENATOR FROM COUNTRYWIDE

As you'll recall from chapter 6, Obama threw his close confidante Jim Johnson off the campaign vice presidential search committee when the *Wall Street Journal* exposed Johnson's multi-million-dollar sweetheart deals with reviled lender Countrywide Financial. To repeat his words again: Obama excoriated Countrywide's officials from CEO Angelo Mozilo on down as "the people who are responsible for infecting the economy and helping to create a home foreclosure crisis.... These executives crossed the line to boost their bottom line." Johnson's relationship with Countrywide cost him a plum spot on Obama's search committee.

But what about Chris Dodd?

In June 2008, Portfolio.com published an exclusive report on the other VIPs who benefited from Mozilo's special loan arrangements with political bigwigs. Among the beneficiaries: former Bush Secretary of Housing and Urban Development Alphonso Jackson, former Secretary of Health and Human Services Donna Shalala, and former U.N. ambassador and assistant Secretary of State Richard Holbrooke. Most noteworthy, two sitting Democrat senators were identified as recipients: Kent Conrad and Chris Dodd. Dodd is chairman of the Senate Banking, Housing, and Urban Affairs Committee.

Portfolio.com reported that Senator Conrad "borrowed $1.07 million in 2004 to refinance his vacation home with a balcony and wraparound porch in Bethany Beach, Delaware, a block from the ocean." Senator Dodd received two discounted loans in 2003 through Countrywide's VIP program. He borrowed $506,000 to refinance his elite townhouse in Washington, D.C., and $275,042 to refinance a home in East Haddam, Connecticut.[5] Countrywide helpfully waived fractions of points on the loans. The lower interest rates could have saved Senator Dodd a combined $75,000 during the life of the 30-year loans, Portfolio.com concluded.

While he was secretly enjoying the benefits of being a Countrywide VIP, Senator Dodd publicly lambasted "unscrupulous lenders," milked the subprime mortgage crisis, and also championed a $300 billion mortgage industry rescue bill that would, as GOP Senator Jim Bunning put it, serve as "a bailout for borrowers and investors who made bad decisions."[6] In October 2008, when Countrywide announced its decision to refinance up to $16 billion in adjustable-rate mortgages, Dodd was happy to speak to the press—offering qualified praise for the announcement as a "welcome, if late, decision."[7] He did not, however, disclose his own unscrupulous borrowing arrangements with Countrywide to the press or to the public.

As a mini-maelstrom of outrage grew over the Countrywide VIP program, the once-garrulous Dodd went into hiding. *Roll Call* reported that Dodd had known about the preferential treatment on his loans since 2003, yet continued to deny that he was treated like a VIP and refused to acknowledge wrongdoing.[8] Voters at home were paying attention. A Quinnipiac poll in July 2008 showed Dodd's approval rating drop from 60 to 51; 59 percent of Connecticut voters polled said Dodd's mortgage ties should be investigated.[9] Heat came from left, right, and center. In the *Boston Globe*, economist Richard Parker, a senior fellow at Harvard Kennedy School's Shorenstein Center, fumed:

> A chief beneficiary of the Dodd bill is Bank of America, which has just bought Countrywide. If Dodd's bill passes, taxpayers will take on much of the Bank of America's risk of further portfolio default—a move worth billions to the bank.
>
> Washington desperately needs to stanch the forced liquidation of millions of American homeowners. Yet once again, the benefits of its rescue efforts will accrue unequally—stacked heavily in favor of the wealthy and the powerful—because in American politics, as in Orwell's "1984," some are more equal than others.
>
> Especially the VIPs.[10]

Dodd's hometown newspaper pressed for transparency. He promised to release supporting documentation to back his claim that he received no special discounts. Obama must have approved. As public discontent with Dodd increased, the Obama vice presidential search team (sans Jim Johnson) leaked its potential picks. Among the front-runners: Senator Chris Dodd![11] The news prompted a biting response from Edith Prague, a longtime Democratic lawmaker in Connecticut: "I think Obama would be stupid at this point to put [Dodd] on the ticket," Prague said. "This mortgage deal. Give me a break."[12]

On July 30, 2008, as part of the bailout-palooza frenzy championed by both parties, President George W. Bush signed into law the $300 billion mortgage bailout pushed by the senator from Countrywide. In September 2008, pushing for further government intervention, Dodd published a righteous press release lambasting "reckless, careless, and sometimes unscrupulous actors in the mortgage lending industry" with an "insatiable appetite for risk."[13]

In October 2008, Justice Department officials began a probe of the Countrywide VIP program. A former loan officer for the company, Robert Feinberg, told NBC News that he had been specifically tasked to offer VIP loans: "You spoke in a manner that was different than you spoke with a regular customer," said Feinberg. "'Your loan has been specially priced by Angelo.' 'You're getting special discounts because you're in the VIP loan department.'" The bennies included interest rate discounts, fee discounts, and other perks before closing.[14] One of the favors Dodd received was something called a "float down." Feinberg explained to the *Wall Street Journal*:

> As to Mr. Dodd, Mr. Feinberg says he spoke to the Senator once or twice and mostly to his wife and that like other FOAs Mr. Dodd got "a float down," which means that even after he had a preferred rate, when the prevailing rate dropped just before the closing, his rate was reduced again. Regular borrowers would pay extra for a last-minute adjustment, but not FOAs. "They were aware of it because they were notified and when they went to the closing they would see it," Mr. Feinberg says, adding that he "always let people in the program know that

they were getting a very good deal because they were 'Friends of Angelo.'" All of this matters because Mr. Dodd was one of those encouraging [government-sponsored mortgage enterprises Fannie Mae and Freddie Mac] to plunge into "affordable housing" loans made by companies like Countrywide.[15]

Months passed. Senator Dodd continued to toil away on Capitol Hill on legislation affecting the financial services industry. In January 2009, he negotiated a deal with Citigroup Inc. to let bankruptcy judges modify home loans in an effort to prevent foreclosures and urged other lenders to do the same.[16] The supporting documentation he had promised on his Countrywide deals was still missing.

Finally, on February 2, 2009, Senator Dodd announced he would refinance his Countrywide home loans. A special report, Senator Dodd claimed, absolved him of wrongdoing. The sponsor of the "independent" report? Why, Senator Dodd, of course. In response to pressure that he disclose his financial records to the public, as he had promised to do eight months prior, Senator Dodd "released" about 100 pages of information to members of the press—who weren't allowed to copy them and could only take notes for a short period before returning them. Other reporters who requested to view the documents were refused.[17] "I regret I did not do this sooner and I apologize to the people of Connecticut for the delay," he said.[18] He stubbornly insisted that he had not benefited financially:

> I am proud of my service as a United States Senator for these past 28 years. I understand there will always be people who disagree with my positions on certain issues, but I do not want anyone to ever believe that I would trade my office for personal financial gain. To believe that is to misunderstand everything

that is important to me and everything that has motivated my work serving the people of Connecticut.[19]

FOLLOW THE MONEY

Repeatedly throughout this book, you have read the words of Barack Obama lamenting the influence of Big Business and the Washington games. "I'm not in this race to continue the special interest-driven politics of the last eight years. I'm in this race to end it," he preached.[20] How, exactly, does crusading for Senator Dodd achieve that goal?

Senator Dodd has been in the middle of every major legislative battle in 2008–2009 expanding the Big Government–Big Business alliance. He championed the bailouts of Fannie Mae and Freddie Mac, supported the $700 billion TARP banking bailout, sponsored massive injections of taxpayer funding into the mortgage industry, and crusaded for Obama's pork-filled stimulus package.

The number one recipient of campaign finance contributions from scandal-plagued financial behemoths Fannie Mae and Freddie Mac is five-term Senator Chris Dodd. Between 1998 and 2008, Dodd raked in $165,400 in donations from the federally-sponsored mortgage enterprises, including $48,500 from political action committees and $116,900 from individuals, according to OpenSecrets.org.[21]

The number five recipient of PAC money from Countrywide is Senator Chris Dodd, who received $20,000 from the company—$10,000 of which Countrywide's PAC donated in the 2008 election cycle. Two slots ahead of Dodd? Barack Obama, with $22,900 in the bank from Countrywide's PAC.

In the first three months of 2009, the Associated Press reported, more than $100,000 of the $1 million Dodd raised came from political action committees for the financial, insurance, and real estate industries, according to his latest fundraising report. Connecticut is home to a wide array of insurance companies and hedge funds (yes, those dreaded hedge funds again. Alert Michelle Obama). The finance, insurance, and real estate industries have given Dodd a grand total of $13.2 million from 1989 through 2008, according to the Center for Responsive Politics.

PAC money from American Insurance Association, Mortgage Bankers Association, Vanguard, Oppenheimer Funds, Charles Schwab, Real Estate Roundtable and Ameriprise Financial poured in.[22] From nearly 400 individual donors, Dodd took in $608,995. The deep-pocketed supporters included top executives from financial titans Fidelity, Citigroup and Citizens Financial Group. The most extraordinary and damning piece of data from Dodd's first quarter campaign disclosure forms:

A whopping five Connecticut residents gave a combined total of $4,250 to his campaign.[23]

Who else was lining Dodd's pockets? Left-leaning *Mother Jones* magazine spotlighted the den of lobbyists dashing off checks:

After his industry backers, one of Dodd's largest donor constituencies is Washington lobbyists. Ogilvy lobbyist (and one-time chief of staff to Sen. Kit Bond of Missouri) Julie Dammann, whose finance industry clients have included the private equity firm Blackstone Group, AIG, Visa, and Fannie Mae, contributed $1,000. So did lobbyists Thomas Quinn and Jeffrey Kurzweil, who are both on the payroll of Beacon Capital Partners. (In 2008, Quinn also lobbied for Bear Stearns, the National Association of Credit Unions, and State Street Corporation, among other finance sector clients.) Former Dick Gephardt aide Steve Elmendorf, whose firm has recently lobbied for Citigroup, Ernst & Young, the Managed Funds Association, and other financial clients, donated $2,400.

Dodd, who in 2007 blasted the "predatory, abusive, and irresponsible" practices of subprime lenders, also received campaign money from one of the subprime industry's chief lobbyists, Wright Andrews ($1,000). Andrews has run several cleverly named industry-backed trade groups, including the Coalition for Fair and Affordable Lending and the Responsible Mortgage Lending Coalition. Along with his wife, Lisa, once a chief in-house lobbyist for Ameriquest Mortgage, which shut down in 2007, Andrews "coordinated" the subprime industry's lobbying campaign to blunt state efforts to crack down on risky lending, according to the *Wall Street Journal*.[24]

Leading corporate moochers that sought and/or secured government bailout money had enough change to spare for Dodd, including Citigroup ($428,300), Morgan Stanley ($211,300), and Lehman Brothers ($154,300).[25] *Washington Examiner* columnist Tim Carney noted that Bank of America, which bought out Countrywide in 2008, also tossed in approximately $70,000 between 2006–2008 and stood to benefit from Dodd's subprime mortgage bailout measures. The two candidates who brought in more Bank of America cash than Dodd? Hillary Clinton and Barack Obama.[26]

And then there's American International Group, Inc.

THE SENATOR FROM AIG

In September 2008, the crony Republicans of the Bush administration announced what would be the first of four major taxpayer bailouts of international insurance corporation American International Group (AIG), stretched out over the last days of the lame duck GOP White House and the first months of Obama's Reign of Hope and Change. An initial $60 billion loan would be followed by $50 billion to buy toxic assets, $40 billion to purchase preferred shares of stock, and $30 billion siphoned off from the TARP banking bailout bill.

That should have been enough to send the public onto the streets for mass protests, but it was the issue of executive compensation that finally stirred taxpayer rage. In mid-March 2009, Capitol Hill exploded over $165 million in retention bonuses mailed out to employees. Senator Dodd initially denied playing a role in protecting those perks, but was forced to admit that at the behest of the Treasury Department, he inserted protection measures in the stimulus bill to ensure that AIG's bonuses would not be limited. [27]

Between 1993 and 2008, AIG contributed $8,526,940 to politicians, according to the Center for Responsive Politics. Senator Chris Dodd ranked second with $103,900 in donations from the insurance giant. The number one AIG recipient? Barack Obama, who collected $104,332.

A Dodd family member also benefitted from AIG-connected largesse. The senator's wife, Jackie Clegg Dodd, served as an active "outside" director of something called "IPC Holdings, Ltd." The Bermuda-based company was controlled by AIG, according to *Hartford Courant* columnist Kevin Rennie. AIG had a 20 percent stake in the company, which it sold in 2006. "Clegg was compensated for her duties to the company, which was managed by a subsidiary of AIG. In 2003, according to a proxy statement, Clegg received $12,000 per year and an additional $1,000 for each Directors' and committee meeting she attended," Rennie reported. "Clegg served on the Audit and Investment committees during her final year on the board. IPC paid millions each year to other AIG-related companies for administrative and other services."

Somehow, it slipped Dodd's mind to mention these potential conflicts of interest, too.

THE COZY IRISH COTTAGE

Throughout this book, we've seen crony Democrats from Barack Obama to the Clintons to urban czar Adolfo Carrión to special envoy Richard Holbrooke and advisor Jim Johnson benefit from real estate deals that ranged from shady to septic-tank foul. But Senator Dodd one-upped them all. On top of his Countrywide sweetheart loans, Dodd joined in on an astonishing real estate deal with a longtime pal whose criminal history stunk to high heaven. The *Hartford Courant*'s Kevin Rennie again blew the whistle:

In 1993, Dodd's close friend, New York bon vivant Edward R. Downe Jr., got a heaping helping of justice when his insider trader scheme caused him to plead guilty to violating tax and securities laws. Downe, who lived at exclusive 25 Sutton Place on the Upper East Side with his then wife, heiress Charlotte Ford, was nabbed setting up foreign accounts to make illegal insider stock trades for himself and some socialite friends. Dodd attended Downe's sentencing, where the schemer received three years' probation and 3,000 hours of community service. Downe agreed a year later to pay $11 million to the SEC.

While Downe fought the SEC in 1994 about paying the penalty, Dodd and William Kessinger of Kansas City, Mo., whom Dodd knew through Downe, purchased a house and nearly 10 acres (4 hectares in local parlance) on the island of Inishnee in the affluent Roundtree section of Connemara, in County Galway, Ireland, for $160,000. Kessinger and Downe have a history as business partners in a Missouri real estate investment company.

Dodd, who says he contributed $12,000 to the purchase price, owned one-third of the house, Kessinger two-thirds. They purchased the property with a two-year mortgage from the seller of the property that was, according to Dodd's Senate financial disclosures for both 1994 and 1995, between $100,001 and $250,000.

The Irish land registry isn't open to the public in the manner of the American system. It probably appeared unlikely that anyone would discover the curious appearance of Downe's nearly illegible signature as the witness to Kessinger's signing the official transfer document. Downe, convicted, on probation and banned for life from the securities business, described himself as "private investor" on the document and included his New York address.

When Downe agreed to pay $11 million to the SEC in 1994, he claimed he was virtually bankrupt. Six months later, he made $2,000 in contributions to Dodd, again listing his occupation as "private investor."[28]

It gets worse. In 2001, Senator Dodd helped Downe obtain one of the treasured Clinton pardons on Bill Clinton's last day in office. A year after that, as Irish real estate prices went through the roof, Dodd purchased Kessinger's share of the estate at a discount. Judicial Watch, the public interest watchdog group in Washington, D.C., filed a complaint with the U.S. Senate Select Committee on Ethics over the pay-for-play scheme. They also charged Dodd— who continues to rail against corporations for failures to disclose accurate financial information—with failing himself to properly disclose his Irish land deals on his Senate Financial Disclosure forms.

The penalty for filing false financial disclosure forms is $50,000 and up to one year in prison.

"This seems a straight-up quid pro quo. Dodd helped his apparently crooked friend and seems to have received a cut-rate real estate deal on a property in Ireland in exchange. Moreover, it appears Dodd attempted to cover up the gift by failing to disclose it on his financial disclosure forms. To put it mildly, this type of behavior clearly does not reflect well on the United States Senate," stated Judicial Watch President Tom Fitton.[29]

Yes, it reflects poorly on Dodd and on the U.S. Senate. But most of all, this sordid mess reflects poorly on the man in the White House who cast himself as the only political leader in the country capable of transforming how Washington works. When he launched his presidential bid in February 2007, Barack Obama inspired millions and rallied the world with his pledge to "build a more hopeful America." He told a cheering crowd in Springfield, Illinois, land of Lincoln, that he recognized "that there is a certain presumptuousness in this, a certain audacity to this announcement. I know that I have not spent a long time learning the ways of Washington, but I have been there long enough to know that the ways of Washington have to change."[30]

Two years later, Barack Obama declared his support for an entrenched U.S. senator knee-deep in the decrepit old politics of pay-for-play.

Two years later, at an "historic" and "unprecedented" record pace, Barack Obama presided over a heap of botched nominations, crony appointments, lobbyist paybacks, union and left-wing activist payoffs, and abandoned promises to make government more transparent and accountable to ordinary Americans.

"Washington is broken," Obama lamented on the campaign trail. Yet, under President Obama, the business of Washington is booming. The collapse of the Era of HopeNChangeyness demonstrates the first and last law of political physics: As government grows, corruption flows. Massive new federal spending plus tens of thousands of pages of new regulations plus unprecedented new powers over taxpayers and the economy = limitless new opportunities for sleaze, favor-trading, deal-cutting, and influence-peddling. The president's blind faithful may still cling to the belief that he can work miracles. But no one, not even Barack Obama, can drain a swamp by flooding it.

ACKNOWLEDGMENTS

This book would not have been possible without the invaluable assistance of gallons of caffeinated products, hot, cold, bottled and canned. Special thanks to Circle K premium coffee, Sonic Mocha Java Chillers, and 5-hour Energy, which I highly recommend to National Economic Council chief Larry "Sleepy" Summers and President Obama, who was too "overwhelmed" and tired to give British Prime Minister Gordon Brown a proper welcome in March 2009.

At least my all-nighters didn't cause international incidents.

No author is an island. Robert Stacy McCain, fellow ink-stained wretch-turned-blogger and co-author of the essential *Donkey Cons: Sex, Crime, and Corruption in the Democratic Party,* provided invaluable writerly advice and counsel (every bit of which I took, except for his valiant insistence that I drop my accurate transcription of our president's pronunciation of the word "otha"). Blogger and columnist extraordinaire Doug Powers pitched in with guest-posting at my website, michellemalkin.com, while I worked offline to meet a tight deadline. Ed Morrissey and

Allahpundit kept hotair.com hot and fresh—and both contributed to this book in untold ways with their trenchant, comprehensive coverage of Team Obama during the election cycle, transition, and flabbergasting first year in office.

Thanks also to bloggers Flip Pidot at suitablyflip.com for his excellent investigative work on Norman Hsu; Stefan Sharkansky of soundpolitics.com for his dogged reporting on the shenanigans of King County executive-turned-HUD No. 2 official Ron Sims; and Tennyson Hayes of galtslist.com for his creative genius.

Warm and humble thanks to my favorite right-wing Marks— Levin and Steyn—for their support.

Thanks to everyone at Regnery—especially Marji Ross for her years of support and publicist Patricia Jackson for her tireless work. Thanks to editor Harry Crocker for his persistent efforts to persuade me to write another book. Thanks to Christian Tappe and Mary Beth Baker for their meticulous editing. Thanks also to Amanda Larsen for enduring my pestering e-mails. Thanks to the sales staff. And thanks to Tim Carney for his input.

Several organizations left, right, and center deserve singling out for their principled and unwavering dedication to transparency, open government, and accountability. This book drew on vital research by the National Right to Work Foundation, Capital Research Center, Employment Policy Institute, and Center for Responsive Politics. Many individual whistleblowers provided invaluable information, but I'd like to give special thanks to Anita MonCrief for her enormous courage and vigilance on ACORN corruption—and to Mike Gaynor and Matthew Vadum for their foresight and insight in reporting on the story when no one else would.

Thanks to Carole and Dick, for everything and more.

And finally: A big group hug to the loves of my life—Jesse, Veronica, and J.D.—for their patience, understanding, inspiration, and good humor while Mommy worked on "book, just book." Go Malkins!

NOTES

INTRODUCTION

1. David Brooks, "The Insider's Crusade," *New York Times*, November 21, 2008; available online at: http://www.nytimes.com/2008/11/21/ opinion/21brooks.html?ref=opinion [accessed April 29, 2009].

2. Jennifer 8. Lee, untitled Twitter post, April 29, 2009; available online at: http://twitter.com/jenny8lee/status/1652326401 [accessed April 29, 2009].

3. George Stephanopoulos, "Obama Cabinet: Mix of Star Power, Brain Power, and Political Muscle," ABC News, November 24, 2008; available online at: http://blogs.abcnews.com/george/2008/11/obama-cabinet-s.html [accessed April 29, 2009].

4. George Stephanopoulos, "Grading Obama's Transition," ABC News, December 4, 2008; available online at: http://blogs.abcnews.com/ george/2008/12/grading-obamas.html [accessed April 29, 2009].

5. Peter Baker and Helene Cooper, "Issues Pressing, Obama Fills Top Posts at a Sprint," *New York Times*, December 4, 2008; available online at: http://www.nytimes.com/2008/12/05/us/politics/05obama.html?_r= 1&ref=washington [accessed April 29, 2009].

6. Al Kamen, "Just Inside 100 Days, Sebelius Completes the Cabinet," *Washington Post*, April 29, 2009; available online at: http://www. washingtonpost.com/wp-dyn/content/article/2009/04/28/ AR2009042803534.html [accessed April 29, 2009].

7. Ibid.

8. Jackie Calmes, "For a Washington Job, Be Prepared to Tell All," *New York Times*, November 12, 2008; available online at: http://www. nytimes.com/2008/11/13/us/politics/13apply.html [accessed April 29, 2009].

9. Shailagh Murray and Carol D. Leonnig, "Obama Teams Are Scrutinizing Federal Agencies," *Washington Post*, December 3, 2008; available online at: http://www.washingtonpost.com/wp-dyn/content/article/ 2008/12/02/AR2008120203489.html [accessed April 29, 2009].

10. Scott Whitlock, "George Stephanopoulos: Obama Cabinet Unparalleled in 'Brain Power,'" newsbusters.org, November 24, 2008; available online at: http://newsbusters.org/blogs/scott-whitlock/2008/11/24/ george-stephanopoulos-obama-cabinet-unparalleled-brain-power [accessed April 29, 2009].

11. William Safire, "On Language; Crony Capitalism," *New York Times* Magazine, February 1, 1998; available online at: http://www. nytimes.com/1998/02/01/magazine/on-language-crony-capitalism.html? sec=&spon=&partner=permalink&exprod=permalink [accessed April 29, 2009].

12. Barack Obama, Change.gov, Agenda Ethics page; available online at: http://change.gov/agenda/ethics_agenda/ [accessed April 29, 2009].

13. Paul Blumenthal, "White House Breaks Transparency Promise," Sunlight Foundation, January 29, 2009; available online at: http://blog. sunlightfoundation.com/2009/01/29/white-house-breaks-transparency- promise/ [accessed April 29, 2009].

14. "Barack Obama 'Public Will Have 5 Days To Look At Every Bill That Lands On My Desk,'" youtube.com, February 14, 2009; available online at: http://www.youtube.com/watch?v=o5t8GdxFYBU [accessed April 29, 2009].

15. Jim Harper, "A Flagging Obama Transparency Effort," *Cato@Liberty*, April 9, 2009; available online at: http://www.cato-at-

liberty.org/2009/04/09/a-flagging-obama-transparency-effort/ [accessed April 29, 2009].

16. Martina Stewart, "Obama responds to tea party movement," CNNPolitics.com, April 29, 2009; available online at: http://politicalticker. blogs.cnn.com/2009/04/29/obama-responds-to-tea-party-movement/

17. Change.gov, op cit.

18. Ed Morrissey, "The world has noticed the Obama hypocrisy on lobbyists," *Hot Air*, February 2, 2009; available online at: http://hotair. com/archives/2009/02/02/the-world-has-noticed-the-obama-hypocrisy-on-lobbyists/ [accessed April 29, 2009].

19. Julie Kosterlitz, "Obama Aiming To Lock Turnstile For Lobbyists," *National Journal*, March 21, 2009; available online at: http://www. nationaljournal.com/njmagazine/sl_20090321_5174.php [accessed April 29, 2009].

20. Michelle Malkin, "Results for 'bush cronyism,'" michellemalkin. com (all dates); available online at: http://michellemalkin.com/?s =bush + cronyism [accessed April 29, 2009].

21. Michelle Malkin, "Michael Brown Relieved of Duty," michelle-malkin.com, September 9, 2005; available online at: http:// michellemalkin.com/2005/09/09/michael-brown-relieved-of-duty/ [accessed April 29, 2009].

22. (Stevens's conviction was subsequently thrown out due to prose-cutorial misconduct.)

23. Sam Fullwood III, "For Obama, hipness is what it is," *Politico*, April 24, 2009; available online at: http://www.politico.com/news/ stories/0409/21522.html [accessed April 29, 2009].

24. Alex Leo, "CNN Story On Obama's 'Swagga' The Most Embar-rassing Ever? (VIDEO)," *Huffington Post*, April 29, 2009; available online at: http://www.huffingtonpost.com/2009/04/29/the-most-embarrassing-cnn_n_193095.html [accessed April 29, 2009].

CHAPTER 1: ONWS

1. Julian Sancton, "Keeping Up with History," *Vanity Fair*, March 2009; available online at: http://www.vanityfair.com/magazine/2009/03/ on-the-cover200903 [accessed April 25, 2009].

2. Maureen Orth, "Can Obama's New Team Make Government Cool Again?" *Vanity Fair*, February 2, 2009; available online at: http://www.vanityfair.com/online/politics/2009/02/can-obamas-new-team-make-government-cool-again.html [accessed April 25, 2009].

3. Julian Sancton, "Keeping Up with History," op cit.

4. Jonathan Martin, "West Wing on steroids in Obama W.H.," *Politico*, January 25, 2009; available online at: http://dyn.politico.com/printstory.cfm?uuid=0C0BFFC6-18FE-70B2-A81DFADDD12EF731 [accessed April 25, 2009].

5. Maureen Orth, "Can Obama's New Team Make Government Cool Again?" op cit.

6. R. Jeffrey Smith, Cecilia Kang, and Joe Stephens, "Old Ways Doomed New Job for Daschle," *Washington Post*, February 4, 2009; available online at: http://www.washingtonpost.com/wp-dyn/content/article/2009/02/03/AR2009020300912.html [accessed April 25, 2009].

7. "Daschle out as health nominee due to tax problems," Associated Press, February 3, 2009; available online at: http://www.thetimes-tribune.com/articles/2009/02/03/news/doc4988966f32a06429069907.txt [accessed April 25, 2009].

8. Jeff Zeleny, "Daschle Ends Bid for Post; Obama Concedes Mistake," *New York Times*, February 3, 2009; available online at: http://www.nytimes.com/2009/02/04/us/politics/04obama.html?hp [accessed April 25, 2009].

9. Alina Selyukh, "Obama Challenges Clinton For Most Nominee Dropouts," *National Journal*, February 17, 2009; available online at: http://lostintransition.nationaljournal.com/2009/02/obama-nominee-dropouts.php [accessed April 25, 2009].

10. Barbara Slavin, "Obama backs out on Iraq appointment," *Washington Times*, February 4, 2009; available online at: http://www.washingtontimes.com/news/2009/feb/04/obama-backs-out-iraq-appointment/ [accessed April 25, 2009].

11. Laura Rosen, "General Zinni gets undiplomatic treatment from Obama team," *Foreign Policy*, February 4, 2009; available online at: http://thecable.foreignpolicy.com/posts/2009/02/04/zinni_unloads [accessed April 25, 2009].

12. Eric Schmitt and Mark Landler, "General Says His Iraq Envoy Job Was Rescinded," *New York Times*, February 5, 2009; available online at: http://www.nytimes.com/2009/02/06/washington/06envoy.html [accessed April 25, 2009].

13. See, e.g., http://www.fark.com/cgi/comments.pl?IDLink=4263810 [accessed April 25, 2009].

14. Lynn Sweet, "President-elect Obama sixth press conference," *Chicago Sun-Times*, December 3, 2008; available online at: http://blogs.suntimes.com/sweet/2008/12/presidentelect_obama_sixth_pre.html [accessed April 25, 2009].

15. Jeff Zeleny, "Richardson Endorses Obama," *New York Times*, March 21, 2008; available online at: http://www.nytimes.com/2008/03/21/us/politics/21cnd-endorse.html [accessed April 25, 2009].

16. Lynn Sweet, "President-elect Obama sixth press conference," op cit.

17. David Plotz, "Energy Secretary Bill Richardson," *Slate*; available online at: http://www.slate.com/id/84864/sidebar/84866/ [accessed April 25, 2009].

18. "Richardson Admits Errors in Wen Ho Lee Case Contradicting Earlier Stance," *Democracy Now!* December 14, 2007; available online at: http://www.democracynow.org/2007/12/14/i_wish_id_been_stronger_richardson [accessed April 25, 2009].

19. Toby Smith, "One-Time Prospect Acknowledges Draft Info Wrong," *Albuquerque Journal*, November 24, 2005; available online at: http://www.abqjournal.com/news/special/410505sports11-24-05.htm [accessed April 25, 2009].

20. Michelle Malkin, "How *not* to honor a fallen hero," michellemalkin.com, May 28, 2007; available online at: http://michellemalkin.com/2007/05/28/how-not-to-honor-a-fallen-hero/ [accessed April 25, 2009].

21. "National Media Getting Wind of 'Dollar Bill' Richardson's Role in Peregrine Scandal," New Mexico Republicans, March 27, 2007; available online at: http://www.gopnm.com/index.php?option=com_content&view=article&id=281%3Anational-media-getting-wind-of-dollar-bill-richardsons-role-in-peregrine-scandal&Itemid=61 [accessed April 25, 2009].

22. James Ridgeway, "Bill Richardson: In Big Oil's Pocket?" *Mother Jones*, July 26, 2007; available online at: http://www.motherjones.com/ politics/2007/07/bill-richardson-big-oils-pocket [accessed April 25, 2009].

23. Martin Z. Braun and William Selway, "Grand Jury Probes Richardson Donor's New Mexico Financing Fee," Bloomberg News, December 15, 2008; available online at: http://www.bloomberg.com/ apps/news?pid=20601103&sid=aL0GGUluJeT8&refer=us [accessed April 25, 2009].

24. "Richardson withdrawal leaves cabinet gap," NBC News, January 6, 2009; available online at: http://www.msnbc.msn.com/id/ 28493919/ [accessed April 25, 2009].

25. Ibid.

26. James Ridgeway, "Why Did Obama's Transition Team Ignore Bill Richardson's Long History of Dubious Dealings?" *Mother Jones*, January 4, 2009; available online at: http://www.motherjones.com/mojo/ 2009/01/why-did-obamas-transition-team-ignore-bill-richardsons-long-history-dubious-dealings [accessed April 25, 2009].

27. Sen. Tom Daschle, Congressional Record, May 7, 1998, p. S4507. Cited in "Daschle On Tax Cheats: IRS Should Enforce Laws," *RealClearPolitics*, February 3, 2009; available online at: http://www. realclearpolitics.com/video/2009/02/daschle_on_tax_cheats_irs_shou. html [accessed April 25, 2009].

28. "Driving Mr. Daschle," *Wall Street Journal*, February 2, 2009; available online at: http://online.wsj.com/article/SB123353200827537439. html [accessed April 25, 2009].

29. Sheryl Gay Stolberg and Robert Pear, "Daschle Knew of Tax Issues Over Car Use Last June," *New York Times*, February 1, 2009; available online at: http://www.nytimes.com/2009/02/01/us/politics/ 01daschle.html [accessed April 25, 2009].

30. Ceci Connolly and Paul Kane, "Daschle Faces Questions From Senators on Tax Glitch," *Washington Post*, February 2, 2009; available online at: http://www.washingtonpost.com/wp-dyn/content/article/2009/ 02/01/AR2009020101960.html [accessed April 25, 2009].

31. Jonathan Weisman, "Daschle Paid $100,000 in Back Taxes During HHS Vetting," *Wall Street Journal*, January 30, 2009; available

online at: http://blogs.wsj.com/washwire/2009/01/30/daschle-paid-100000-in-back-taxes-during-hhs-vetting/ [accessed April 25, 2009].

32. Michelle Levi, "Obama Says Sorry. A Lot." CBS News *Political Hotsheet*, February 4, 2009; available online at: http://www.cbsnews.com/blogs/2009/02/04/politics/politicalhotsheet/entry4775468.shtml [accessed April 25, 2009].

33. Jonathan Weisman, "Daschle's Confirmation Bogs Down in Committee," *Wall Street Journal*, January 15, 2009; available online at: http://online.wsj.com/article/SB123199063403384785.html [accessed April 25, 2009].

34. Toby Harnden, "Tom Daschle: symbol of Barack Obama's hypocrisy," *UK Telegraph*, February 2, 2009; available online at: http://blogs.telegraph.co.uk/toby_harnden/blog/2009/02/02/tom_daschle_symbol_of_barack_obamas_hypocrisy [accessed April 25, 2009].

35. David Herbert, "Killefer Cites Tax Problems In Ending CPO Bid," *National Journal*, February 3, 2009; available online at: http://lostintransition.nationaljournal.com/2009/02/killefer-withdraws-cpo.php [accessed April 25, 2009].

36. "Obama spokesman defends ethics standards," Associated Press, February 3, 2009; available online at: http://www.breitbart.com/article.php?id=D9649J682&show_article=1 [accessed April 25, 2009].

37. "Timothy Geithner, alone and working night and day," AFP, March 8, 2009; available online at: http://www.breitbart.com/article.php?id=CNG.4b23a31c3686bc071c5b2ae66b18d1d8.601&show_article=1&catnum=-1 [accessed April 25, 2009].

38. "Treasury secretary's choice for deputy withdraws," Associated Press, March 5, 2009; available online at: http://finance.yahoo.com/news/Treasury-secretarys-choice-apf-14561901.html?.v=1 [accessed April 25, 2009].

39. Deborah Solomon, "Top Treasury Candidates Pull Out," *Wall Street Journal*, March 6, 2009; available online at: http://online.wsj.com/article/SB123629285769044959.html [accessed April 25, 2009].

40. Robert Schmidt and Rebecca Christie, "Geithner Effort to Staff Treasury Hit by Nazareth's Withdrawal," Bloomberg News, March 6, 2009; available online at: http://www.bloomberg.com/apps/news?pid=20601103&sid=aOQEGlU0qVS0&refer=us [accessed April 25, 2009].

41. George Stephanopoulos, "Staff Trouble At Treasury Department?" ABC News, March 6, 2009; available online at: http://blogs.abcnews.com/george/2009/03/staff-trouble-a.html [accessed April 25, 2009].

42. "Democratic National Cmte: Top Contributors," OpenSecrets. org (based on Federal Election Commission data released on March 2, 2009); available online at: http://www.opensecrets.org/parties/contrib. php?cmte=DNC&cycle=2008 [accessed April 25, 2009].

43. George Stephanopoulos, "Third Top Treasury Pick Withdraws From Consideration," ABC News, March 13, 2009; available online at: http://blogs.abcnews.com/george/2009/03/another-top-tre.html [accessed April 25, 2009].

44. Matthew Karnitsching and David Enrich, "A Lawyer for All Wall Street Navigates Tempestuous Times," *Wall Street Journal*, October 9, 2008; available online at: http://online.wsj.com/article/SB122351145980417529.html [accessed April 25, 2009].

45. Andrew Ross Sorkin, "A Rich Education for Summers (After Harvard)," *New York Times* DealBook, April 6, 2009; available online at: http://dealbook.blogs.nytimes.com/2009/04/06/a-rich-education-for-summers-after-harvard/ [accessed April 25, 2009].

46. Deborah Solomon, "Treasury's Top Candidate to Run TARP Drops Out," *Wall Street Journal*, March 25, 2009; available online at: http://online.wsj.com/article/SB123792884135530101.html [accessed April 25, 2009].

47. Michael R. Crittenden, "UPDATE: OTS Acting Director Polakoff Put On Leave," *Dow Jones Newswires*, March 26, 2009; available online at: http://online.wsj.com/article/BT-CO-20090326-718651.html [accessed April 25, 2009].

48. Michelle Malkin, "The strange sacking of a top Treasury official," michellemalkin.com, March 27, 2009; available online at: http://michellemalkin.com/2009/03/27/the-strange-sacking-of-a-top-treasury-official/ [accessed April 25, 2009].

49. "EPA Statement on Jon Cannon," Environmental Protection Agency, March 26, 2009; available online at: http://yosemite.epa.gov/opa/admpress.nsf/0/dc63acdf7010f7b885257584006da5f8? OpenDocument [accessed April 25, 2009].

50. "America's Clean Water Foundation Incurred Costs for EPA Assistance Agreements X82835301, X783142301, and X82672301," U.S. Environmental Protection Agency Office of Inspector General, February 20, 2007; available online at: http://www.epa.gov/oigearth/reports/2007/20070220-2007-4-00045_glance.pdf

51. Ibid.

52. Alan Guebert, "EPA wants millions back from NPPC partner," *The Prairie Star*, June 21, 2007; available online at: http://www.theprairiestar.com/articles/2007/07/16/ag_news/columnists/alan.txt [accessed April 25, 2009].

53. Lindsay Barnes, "Torpedoed: Pork politics and the undoing of an Obama nominee," *The Hook*, April 13, 2009; available online at: http://www.readthehook.com/blog/index.php/2009/04/13/torpedoed-bookkeeper-pork-led-to-cannons-exit/ [accessed April 25, 2009].

54. Ibid.

55. Eli Lake, "Foreign ties of nominee questioned," *Washington Times*, March 5, 2009; available online at: http://www.washingtontimes.com/news/2009/mar/05/foreign-ties-of-nominee-queried/ [accessed April 25, 2009]

56. Jon Chait, "Obama's Intelligence Blunder," *Washington Post*, February 28, 2009; available online at: http://www.washingtonpost.com/wp-dyn/content/article/2009/02/27/AR2009022702485.html [accessed April 25, 2009].

57. Michael Goldbfarb, "The Realist Chas Freeman," *Weekly Standard*, February 24, 2009; available online at: http://www.weeklystandard.com/weblogs/TWSFP/2009/02/the_realist_chas_freeman.asp [accessed April 25, 2009].

58. "Intelligence Failure," *National Review*, March 4, 2009; available online at: http://article.nationalreview.com/?q=NjdhZDgwMTFhMjUzNWZkYTUyMmEwNTkwMWQ5YWZmZDc= [accessed April 25, 2009].

59. "Democracy, Peace, and the War on Terror: U.S.-Arab Relations, Post-September 11," Washington Institute for Near East Policy Conference Keynote (2002); available online at: http://www.washingtoninstitute.org/templateC07.php?CID=102 [accessed April 25, 2009].

60. Gabriel Schoenfeld, "Obama's Intelligence Choice," *Wall Street Journal*, February 25, 2009; available online at: http://online.wsj.com/article/SB123552619980465801.html [accessed April 25, 2009].

61. Rich Lowry, "Chas of Arabia," National Review Online, March 6, 2009; available online at: http://article.nationalreview.com/?q=NWFjOWJjYWUyZGQzZTBhMmMzYTNmMWVlNjY1MmIyMTg= [accessed April 25, 2009].

62. Siobahn Gorman, "Intelligence Pick Derailed by Critics," *Wall Street Journal*, March 11, 2009; available online at: http://online.wsj.com/article/SB123671973608687743.html [accessed April 25, 2009].

63. "Charles Freeman's Statement in Wake of Withdrawal From Intelligence Post," *Wall Street Journal*, March 10, 2009; available online at: http://online.wsj.com/article/SB123672847973688515.html [accessed April 25, 2009].

64. Frank Gaffney, "GAFFNEY: Garbage in, garbage out," *Washington Times*, March 3, 2009; available online at: http://washingtontimes.com/news/2009/mar/03/garbage-in-garbage-out/print/ [accessed April 25, 2009].

CHAPTER 2: BITTER HALF

1. *The View*, ABC TV, June 18, 2008; video available online at: http://www.youtube.com/watch?v=59twO1fJwtQ [accessed April 20, 2009].

2. Helena Andrews, "Michelle O: Suited to be Jackie's successor," *Politico*, January 31, 2008; available online at: http://www.politico.com/news/stories/0108/8221.html [accessed April 20, 2009].

3. "Michelle Obama: A First Lady Fashionista," CBS News, *The Early Show*, November 7, 2008; available online at: http://www.cbsnews.com/stories/2008/11/07/earlyshow/main4583142.shtml [accessed April 20, 2009].

4. Michelle LaVaughn Robinson, "Princeton-Educated Blacks and the Black Community," Princeton University Thesis, 1985, pp. 2-3; available online at: http://www.politico.com/pdf/080222_MOPrincetonThesis_1-251.pdf [accessed March 23, 2009].

5. Liza Mundy, *Michelle: A Biography* (New York: Simon & Schuster, 2008).

6. Ibid., 25.

7. Imayen Ibanga, "Obama Warns GOP 'Lay Off My Wife,'" ABC News *Good Morning America*, May 19, 2008; available online at: http://abcnews.go.com/GMA/Vote2008/story?id=4881883&page=1 [accessed March 23, 2009].

8. Mikki Halpin, "Barack Obama tells Glamour: 'Debate me, not Michelle,'" *Glamour*, July 17, 2008; available online at: http://www.glamour.com/sex-love-life/blogs/glamocracy/2008/07/barack-obama-tells-glamour-deb.html [accessed March 23, 2009].

9. Katie Connolly and Evan Thomas, "The Busiest Woman in Washington," *Newsweek*, February 28, 2009; available online at: http://www.newsweek.com/id/186963 [accessed March 23, 2009].

10. All Things Considered, "White House Social Secretary Reflects On Role," January 29, 2009; available online at: http://www.npr.org/templates/story/story.php?storyId=100027497 [accessed March 23, 2009].

11. The HistoryMakers, "Desiree Rogers Biography," April 27, 2007; available online at: http://www.thehistorymakers.com/biography/biography.asp?bioindex=1685&category=Businessmakers&occupation=Corporate%20Executive&name=Desiree%20Rogers [accessed March 23, 2009].

12. White House For Sale, "Bundler: Desiree Glapion Rogers," available online at: http://www.whitehouseforsale.org/bundler.cfm?Bundler=25484 [accessed March 23, 2009].

13. Chicago Business, "Desiree Rogers," undated; available online at: http://www.chicagobusiness.com/cgi-bin/article.pl?article_id=27749&seenIt=1 [accessed March 23, 2009].

14. John D. McKinnon, "Obama Team's Finances Released," *The Wall Street Journal*, April 6, 2009; available online at: http://online.wsj.com/article/SB123897383937190973.html

15. Matthew Mosk and Alec MacGillis, "Big Donors Among Obama's Grass Roots," *Washington Post*, April 11, 2008; available online at: http://www.washingtonpost.com/wp-dyn/content/article/2008/04/10/AR2008041004045.html?hpid=topnews [accessed March 24, 2009].

16. Barack Obama, "The problem with bundling money," *Chicago Tribune*, May 21, 2007; cached version available online at: http://209.

85.173.132/search?q=cache:ziFZIpuyR1MJ:www.chicagotribune.com/
news/opinion/chi-42f3tq7may21,0,4110308.story%3Fcoll%3Dchi-
newsopinioncommentary-hed + bundling + barack + obama&hl=en&ct=
clnk&cd=1&gl=us&client=safari [accessed March 24, 2009].

17. Josh Gerstein, "GOP transparency push seen as attack on
Michelle O.," *Politico*, March 26, 2009; available online at: http://www.
politico.com/blogs/joshgerstein/0309/GOP_transparency_push_seen_as_
attack_on_Michelle_O.html [accessed March 30, 2009].

18. Liza Mundy, "When Michelle Met Barack," *Washington Post*,
October 5, 2008; available online at: http://www.washingtonpost.com/
wp-dyn/content/article/2008/09/26/AR2008092602856_pf.html
[accessed March 24, 2009].

19. Lynn Sweet, "Sweet blog column special: Valerie Jarrett steps up
role in Obama campaign. 'She's always been the other side of Barack's
brain,'" *Chicago Tribune*, September 20, 2007; available online at: http:/
/blogs.suntimes.com/sweet/2007/09/sweet_blog_column_special_vale.
html [accessed March 24, 2009].

20. M. J. Stephey & Claire Suddath, "Valerie Jarrett," *Time*, November 11, 2008; available online at: http://www.time.com/time/politics/
article/0,8599,1858012,00.html/vogue [accessed March 24, 2009].

21. Don Terry, "Insider has Obama's ear: What's she telling him?"
Chicago Tribune, July 27, 2008; available online at: http://archives.
chicagotribune.com/2008/jul/27/health/chi-072708-jarrett   [accessed
March 24, 2009].

22. Jodi Kantor, "An Old Hometown Mentor, Still at Obama's Side,"
New York Times, November 23, 2008; available online at: http://www.
nytimes.com/2008/11/24/us/politics/24jarrett.html?_r=2 [accessed March
24, 2009].

23. John King, "Source: Obama wants Valerie Jarrett to replace him
in Senate," CNNPolitics.com, November 9, 2008; available online at:
http://politicalticker.blogs.cnn.com/2008/11/09/source-obama-wants-
valerie-jarrett-to-replace-him-in-senate/ [accessed March 24, 2009].

24. Marcia Froelke Coburn, "Valerie Jarrett & Desirée Rogers,"
Chicago Magazine, August 2000; available online at: http://www.
chicagomag.com/Chicago-Magazine/August-2000/Valerie-Jarrett-
Desiree-Rogers/ [accessed March 24, 2009].

25. White House, "Senior Advisor Valerie Jarrett," available online at: http://www.whitehouse.gov/administration/staff/valerie_jarrett/ [accessed March 24, 2009].

26. Jonathan Van Meter, "Barack's Rock," *Vogue* Style.com, October 2008; available online at: http://www.style.com/vogue/feature/2008_Oct_Valerie_Jarrett/ [accessed March 24, 2009].

27. Ibid.

28. Liza Mundy, "Excerpt from 'Michelle: A Biography,'" *USA Today*, December 5, 2008; available online at: http://www.usatoday.com/life/books/excerpts/2008-12-05-Michelle-A-Biography_N.htm [accessed March 24, 2009].

29. White House, "Senior Advisor Valerie Jarrett," op cit.

30. Binyamin Appelbaum, "Grim proving ground for Obama's housing policy," *Boston Globe*, June 27, 2008; available online at: http://www.boston.com/news/nation/articles/2008/06/27/grim_proving_ground_for_obamas_housing_policy/?page=full [accessed March 24, 2009].

31. David Freddoso, *The Case Against Barack Obama: The Unlikely Rise and Unexamined Agenda of the Media's Favorite Candidate* (Washington DC: Regnery Publishing, 2008), 217–19.

32. Associated Press, "Obama plans boost for low-income housing," February 26, 2009; article formerly available online at: http://www.google.com/hostednews/ap/article/ALeqM5hJXeuFtmocS2aiejfbO4755x2s5wD96JC7FO0 [accessed March 24, 2009].

33. Fran Spielman and Andrew Herrmann, "Another Daley will push for Olympics," *Chicago Sun-Times*, April 13, 2007; available online at: http://www.suntimes.com/news/metro/340351,CST-NWS-oly13.article [accessed March 24, 2009].

34. Mike Dorning, "Employer: Michelle Obama's raise well-earned," *Chicago Tribune*, September 27, 2006; available online at: http://archives.chicagotribune.com/2006/sep/27/news/chi-0609270216sep27 [accessed March 24, 2009].

35. Steve Gilbert, "Michelle Obama Got $63K For No Show Job?" *Sweetness & Light*, April 16, 2009; available online at: http://sweetness-light.com/archive/michelle-obama-got-63k-for-job-she-had-quit [accessed April 23, 2009].

36. Ibid.

37. Mike Dorning, "Employer: Michelle Obama's raise well-earned," op cit.

38. University of Chicago Medical Center, "Michelle Obama appointed vice president for community and external affairs at the University of Chicago Hospitals," May 9, 2005; available online at: http://www.uchospitals.edu/news/2005/20050509-obama.html   [accessed March 24, 2009].

39. Rosalind Rossi, "The woman behind Obama," *Chicago Sun-Times*, January 20, 2007; available online at: http://www.suntimes.com/news/politics/obama/221458,CST-NWS-mich21.article [accessed March 24, 2009].

40. Joe Stepehens, "Obama Camp Has Many Ties to Wife's Employer," *Washington Post*, August 22, 2008; available online at: http://www.washingtonpost.com/wp-dyn/content/article/2008/08/21/AR2008082103646_pf.html [accessed March 24, 2009].

41. Lynn Sweet, "U of Chicago Hospital VP Susan Sher tapped to be White House associate counsel," *Chicago Tribune*, January 5, 2009; available online at: http://blogs.suntimes.com/sweet/2009/01/u_of_chicago_hospital_chief_su.html [accessed March 27, 2009].

42. Bruce Japsen, "University of Chicago hospital to trim 7% of budget," *Chicago Tribune*, January 10, 2009; available online at: http://archives.chicagotribune.com/2009/jan/10/business/chi-sat-uofc-restructuring-jan10 [accessed March 24, 2009].

43. University of Chicago, "Michelle Obama Resigns Position at University of Chicago Medical Center," January 9, 2009; available online at: http://news.uchicago.edu/news.php?asset_id=1520 [accessed March 24, 2009].

44. Lynn Sweet, "U of Chicago Medical Center exec and Obama pal Eric Whitaker at White House health forum," *Chicago Sun-Times*, March 5, 2009; available online at: http://blogs.suntimes.com/sweet/2009/03/u_of_chicago_medical_center_ex.html [accessed March 24, 2009].

45. Joe Stephens, "Obama Camp Has Many Ties to Wife's Employer," op cit.

46. Jason Grotto, "University of Chicago ER sends kid mauled by pit bull home," *Chicago Tribune*, February 13, 2009; available online at:

http://www.chicagotribune.com/news/local/chi-ucmedicalfeb15,0,
3035589,full.story [accessed March 24, 2009].

47. American College of Emergency Physicians, "University of Chicago Medical Center Is Failing Emergency Patients, Nations Emergency Physicians Say; Urge Congress to Hold Hearings on the State of Emergency Care," February 19, 2009; available online at: http://www. acep.org/pressroom.aspx?id=44294 [accessed March 24, 2009].

48. "Sen. Grassley Requests GAO Investigation Of Not-for-Profit Hospitals," *Medical News Today*, April 11, 2007; available online at: http://www.medicalnewstoday.com/articles/67375.php [accessed March 24, 2009].

49. Letter from Sen. Charles Grassley to James Madara, MD, August 29, 2008; available online at: http://grassley.senate.gov/private/upload/August-29-2008-CEG-to-CEO-of-University-of-Chicago-Medical-Center.pdf [accessed March 24, 2009].

50. Bruce Japsen, "U. of C. medical practices drawing critical eye," *Chicago Tribune*, September 8, 2008; available online at: http://archives. chicagotribune.com/2008/sep/08/business/chi-mon-uofc-hospital-obama-sep08 [accessed March 24, 2009].

51. Ibid.

52. Joe Stephens, "Grassley Seeks Information About Hospital With Ties to the Obamas," *Washington Post*, September 3, 2008; available online at: http://www.washingtonpost.com/wp-dyn/content/article/2008/09/02/AR2008090202681.html?nav=emailpage [accessed March 24, 2009].

53. Mike Dorning, "Employer: Michelle Obama's raise well-earned," op cit.

54. Chuck Neubauer and Tom Hamburger, "Obama donor received a state grant," *Los Angeles Times*, April 27, 2008; available online at: http://www.latimes.com/news/nationworld/nation/la-na-killerspin27apr27,0,7333598,full.story [accessed March 24, 2009].

55. Joe Stephens, "Contracts Went to a Longtime Donor," *Washington Post*, August 22, 2008; available online at: http://www. washingtonpost.com/wp-dyn/content/article/2008/08/21/AR2008082103432.html [accessed March 24, 2009].

56. David Catron, "Cronyism We Can Believe In," *American Spectator*, August 26, 2008; available online at: http://spectator.org/archives/2008/08/26/cronyism-we-can-believe-in [accessed March 25, 2009].

57. Christpher Drew and Jo Becker, "Obama Lists His Earmarks, Asking Clinton for Hers," *New York Times*, March 14, 2008; available online at: http://www.nytimes.com/2008/03/14/us/politics/14campaign.html [accessed March 25, 2009].

58. "Barack Obama interview on March 16, 2008," *Chicago Tribune*, March 16, 2008; available online at: http://redeye.chicagotribune.com/entertainment/chi-obamafullwebmar16-archive,3,591421.story [accessed March 25, 2009].

59. Michael Powell and Jodi Kantor, "After Attacks, Michelle Obama Looks for a New Introduction," *New York Times*, June 18, 2008; available online at: http://www.nytimes.com/2008/06/18/us/politics/18michelle.html [accessed March 25, 2009].

60. Jay Newton-Small, "Michelle Obama's Savvy Sacrifice," *Time*, August 25, 2008; available online at: http://www.time.com/time/politics/article/0,8599,1835686,00.html [accessed March 25, 2009].

61. Anne Kornblut, "Michelle Obama's Career Timeout," *Washington Post*, May 11, 2007; available online at: http://www.washingtonpost.com/wp-dyn/content/article/2007/05/10/AR2007051002573.html?hpid=artslot [accessed March 25, 2009].

62. Leslie Bennetts, "First Lady in Waiting," *Vanity Fair*, December 27, 2007; available online at: http://www.vanityfair.com/politics/features/2007/12/michelle_obama200712?printable=true&currentPage=all [accessed March 27, 2009].

63. Byron York, "Michelle's struggle," National Review Online, February 29, 2008; available online at: http://article.nationalreview.com/?q=MmEyN2RkNzcwYzgyZDY2MDBiY2U5MjJlZGMwNDM2ODg [accessed March 29, 2009].

64. Director Blue, "Chart: Michelle Obama's Salary," January 15, 2009; available online at: http://directorblue.blogspot.com/2009/01/chart-michelle-obamas-salary.html

65. Jay Newton-Small, "Michelle Obama's Savvy Sacrifice," op cit.

66. Philip Sherwell, "Obama called hypocrite for wife's Wal-Mart link," *UK Telegraph*, May 12, 2007; available online at: http://www.

telegraph.co.uk/news/worldnews/1551441/Obama-called-hypocrite-for-wifes-Wal-Mart-link.html [accessed March 27, 2009].

67. Tula Connell, "Wal-Mart: Poster Store for Greed," AFL-CIO Bow Blog, May 2, 2008; available online at: http://blog.aflcio.org/2008/05/02/wal-mart-poster-store-for-greed/ [accessed March 27, 2009].

68. Markus Kabel, "Obama throws weight behind Wal-Mart critics," Associated Press, November 15, 2006; Reprinted on Wakeup Walmart web site at: http://wakeupwalmart.com/news/20061115-ap.html [accessed March 27, 2009].

69. Greg Hinz, "Off message," *Chicago Business News*, December 11, 2006; available online at: http://www.chicagobusiness.com/cgi-bin/article.pl?article_id=26965 [accessed March 27, 2009].

70. Political Radar, "Michelle Obama Cuts Ties with Controversial Wal-Mart Supplier," ABC News, May 22, 2007; available online at: http://blogs.abcnews.com/politicalradar/2007/05/michelle_obama_.html [accessed March 27, 2009].

71. "Obama sets executive pay limits," CNN, February 4, 2009; available online at: http://www.cnn.com/2009/POLITICS/02/04/obama.executive.pay/ [accessed March 27, 2009].

72. Michelle Malkin, "Watch our for Barney Frank's paws," michellemalkin.com, February 4, 2009; available online at: http://michellemalkin.com/2009/02/04/watch-out-for-barney-franks-paws/ [accessed March 27, 2009].

73. Stanley Kurtz, "Michelle, Anti-American Radicals, and U of C," National Review Online's "The Corner," August 22, 2008; available online at: http://corner.nationalreview.com/post/?q=NzQxYTk4NjhkMTM0ZmI4MDQyNGQ3NjYxNWI4YWYwZDU= [accessed March 27, 2009].

74. University of Chicago News Office, "Should a child ever be called a 'super predator?'" November 4, 1997; available online at: http://www-news.uchicago.edu/releases/97/971104.juvenile.justice.shtml [accessed March 27, 2009].

75. Zombie, "Barack Obama's review of William Ayers' book," zomblog, October 18, 2008; available online at: http://www.zombietime.com/zomblog/?p=64 [accessed March 27, 2009].

76. Michelle Malkin, "Oh, these are the people in your neighborhood..." michellemalkin.com, October 19, 2008; available online at:

http://michellemalkin.com/2008/10/19/oh-these-are-the-people-in-your-neighborhood/ [accessed March 27, 2009].

77. Andrew McCarthy, "Why Won't Obama Talk About Columbia?" National Review Online, October 7, 2008; available online at: http://article.nationalreview.com/?q=NjY4YzdhMDBkZGQ3ZmU2MTUzYjdkMzc5ZjUzYmViZWM= [accessed March 27, 2009].

CHAPTER 3: VETTING THE VEEP

1. Mike McIntire and Serge F. Kovaleski, "Biden is an everyman on the campaign trail, with perks at home," *International Herald Tribune*, October 2, 2008; article previously available online at: http://www.iht.com/articles/2008/10/02/america/02finances.php [accessed March 29, 2009].

2. "Transcript: The Vice-Presidential Debate," *New York Times*, October 2, 2008; available online at: http://elections.nytimes.com/2008/president/debates/transcripts/vice-presidential-debate.html [accessed March 29, 2009].

3. Patricia Talorico, "Joe gives Delaware shout-outs: UPDATED," Delaware Online, October 2, 2008; available online at: http://www.delawareonline.com/blogs/secondhelpings/2008/10/joe-gives-delaware-shout-outs.html [accessed March 29, 2009].

4. "Radio Host Calls De Home Depots To Check Biden 'Spend A Lot Of Time' Claim," Curtis Sliwa Radio Show, October 3, 2008; available online at: http://www.breitbart.tv/?p=187833 [accessed March 29, 2009].

5. Michelle Malkin, "Biden slanders a dead man, family grieves," michellemalkin.com, September 4, 2008; available online at; http://michellemalkin.com/2008/09/04/biden-slanders-a-dead-man-family-grieves/ [accessed March 29, 2009].

6. "Delaware corporation," Economicexpert.com (undated); available online at: http://www.economicexpert.com/a/Delaware:corporation.htm [accessed March 29, 2009].

7. Ted Griffith, "MBNA gone, but what about jobs?" Delaware Online, January 1, 2006; available online at: http://www.delawareonline.com/apps/pbcs.dll/article?AID=/20060101/NEWS/601010334/1006 [accessed March 29, 2009].

8. Lowell Bergman and Patrick McGeehan, "Expired: How a Credit King Was Cut Off," *New York Times*, March 7, 2004; available online at: http://www.nytimes.com/2004/03/07/business/07mbna.html [accessed March 29, 2009].

9. Nicholas Varchaver, "Who's The King Of Delaware? Du Pont ruled the home state of corporate America for 200 years. Enter MBNA, usurper. A tale of blue blood vs. new blood," *Fortune*, May 13, 2002; available online at: http://money.cnn.com/magazines/fortune/fortune_archive/2002/05/13/322906/index.htm [accessed March 29, 2009].

10. Bergman and McGeehan, "Expired: How a Credit King Was Cut Off," op cit.

11. Byron York, "The Senator from MBNA," National Review Online, August 23, 2008; available online at: http://article.nationalreview.com/?q=ZDU4OTdhMTFhN2YwZTY3MmMzNGFhYzc3ODdhOTA0ZjQ= [accessed March 29, 2009]. Originally published in 1998 in *The American Spectator*.

12. McIntire and Kovaleski, "Biden is an everyman on the campaign trail, with perks at home," op cit.

13. Cris Barrish, "Analysis: Biden's wealth in his house," *Wilmington News Journal*, September 6, 2008, p. A1.

14. York, "The Senator from MBNA," op cit.

15. Barrish, "Analysis: Biden's wealth in his house," op cit.

16. Christopher Drew and Mike McIntire, "Obama Aides Defend Bank's Pay to Biden Son," *New York Times*, August 25, 2008; available online at: http://www.nytimes.com/2008/08/25/us/politics/25biden.html [accessed March 29, 2009].

17. Ibid.

18. Associated Press, "Obama slaps McCain on bankruptcy laws," *USA Today*, July 28, 2008; available online at: http://www.usatoday.com/news/politics/election2008/2008-07-08-obama-bankruptcy_N.htm [accessed March 29, 2009].

19. David Mildenberg, "Bank of America Credit-Card Unit Loses $373 Million," Bloomberg News, October 21, 2008; available online at: http://www.bloomberg.com/apps/news?pid=20601087&sid=aaCdPylW8B.U&refer=home [accessed March 29, 2009].

20. Eric Ruth, "Feds boost Bank of America again," *The News Journal*, January 17, 2009.

21. Peter Barnes and Joanna Ossinger, "BofA to Get $20B More From TARP, Plus Backstop on $118B," foxbusiness.com, January 16, 2009; available online at: http://www.foxbusiness.com/story/markets/industries/finance/bofa-shares-falter-reports-needs-new-tarp-money/ [accessed March 29, 2009].

22. Drew and McIntire, "Obama Aides Defend Bank's Pay to Biden Son," op cit.

23. "Remarks of Senator Barack Obama: A Change We Can Believe In," barackobama.com, November 3, 2007; available online at: http://www.barackobama.com/2007/11/03/remarks_of_senator_barack_obam_30.php [accessed March 29, 2009].

24. Jim McElhatton, "Lobby ties counter Biden's 'outsider' label," *Washington Times*, August 26, 2008; available online at: http://www.washingtontimes.com/news/2008/aug/26/lobby-ties-contradict-outsider-label-on-sen-biden/ [accessed March 29, 2009].

25. Lindsay Renick Mayer, "The Money Behind Biden," opensecrets.org, August 23, 2008; available online at: http://www.opensecrets.org/news/2008/08/the-money-behind-biden.html [accessed March 29, 2009].

26. David Brody, "Video Flashback: Biden on Lobbyists and Public Financing," CBNnews.com, August 23, 2008; available online at: http://www.cbn.com/CBNnews/432860.aspx [accessed March 29, 2009].

27. Timothy J. Burger, "Biden's Son Employed in Profession Obama Disdains: Lobbying," Bloomberg News, August 4, 2008; available online at: http://www.bloomberg.com/apps/news?pid=20601070&refer=home&sid=a6QrVqdTZKv4 [accessed March 29, 2009].

28. Emma Schwartz, "My Son, The Lobbyist: Biden's Son a Well-Paid DC Insider," ABC News, August 24, 2008; available online at: http://abcnews.go.com/Blotter/Story?id=5640118&page=2 [accessed March 29, 2009].

29. James V. Grimaldi and Kimberly Kindy, "Obama, Biden's Son Linked by Earmarks," *Washington Post*, August 27, 2008; available online at: http://www.washingtonpost.com/wp-dyn/content/article/2008/08/26/AR2008082603894.html [accessed March 29, 2009].

30. Ibid.

31. Timothy J. Burger, "Biden's Son Employed in Profession Obama Disdains: Lobbying," op cit.

32. Steven E. F. Brown, "Achaogen inks $26M plague-drug contract," *San Francisco Business Times*, March 2, 2009; available online at: http://www.bizjournals.com/sanfrancisco/stories/2009/03/02/daily37.html [accessed March 29, 2009].

33. Brody Mullins, "Biden's Son Quits Lobbying Business," *Wall Street Journal*, September 12, 2008; available online at: http://blogs.wsj.com/washwire/2008/09/12/bidens-son-quits-lobbying-business/ [accessed March 29, 2009].

34. Nicole Gaudiano, "UD gets earmarks with help of lobbyists connected to Biden," Delaware Online, March 7, 2009; available online at: http://www.delawareonline.com/article/20080608/NEWS02/103070001/1006/NEWS [accessed March 29, 2009].

35. Emma Schwartz, "Working the Campaign Trail Fattens Lobbyists' Bottom Line," *Legal Times*, October 23, 2006; available online at: http://www.obblaw.com/pdf/Schwartz10-23-06.pdf [accessed March 29, 2009].

36. Ibid.

37. Jim McElhatton, "Lobby ties counter Biden's 'outsider' label," op cit.

38. Nicole Gaudiano, "UD gets earmarks with help of lobbyists connected to Biden," Delaware Online, March 7, 2009; available online at: http://www.delawareonline.com/article/20080608/NEWS02/103070001/1006/NEWS [accessed March 29, 2009].

39. Emma Schwartz, "My Son, the Lobbyist: Biden's Son a Well-Paid DC Insider," op cit.

40. Nicole Gaudiano, "UD gets earmarks with help of lobbyists connected to Biden," op cit.

41. Barackobama.com web site. Available online at: http://answercenter.barackobama.com/cgi-bin/barackobama.cfg/php/enduser/std_adp.php?p_faqid=130&p_created=1176309944&p_sid=7EUnxFQi&p_accessibility=0&p_redirect=&p_lva=&p_sp=cF9zcmNoPTEmcF9zb3J0X2J5PSZwX2dyaWRzb3J0PSZwX3Jvd19jbnQ9MiwyJnBfcHJvZHM9JnBfY2F0cz0wJnBfcHY9JnBfY3Y9JnBfcGFn

ZT0xJnBfc2VhcmNoX3RleHQ9YnVuZGxcg**&p_li=&p_topview=1 [accessed March 30,2009].

42. David Lightman, "More on earmarks: Obama's chief of staff has some in bill," *McCaltchy Newspapers*, March 2, 2009; available online at: http://www.mcclatchydc.com/homepage/story/63125.html [accessed March 30, 2009].

43. Opensecrets.org, "Adler Planetarium & Astronomy Museum"; available online at: http://www.opensecrets.org/lobby/clientsum.php? lname=Adler+Planetarium+%26+Astronomy+Museum&year=2008 [accessed March 30, 2009].

44. Nicole Gaudiano, "UD gets earmarks with help of lobbyists connected to Biden," op cit.

45. Jim McElhatton, "'Rainmaker' Lobbyist aids Biden," *Washington Times*, August 29, 2008; available online at: http://www.washingtontimes.com/news/2008/aug/29/rainmaker-lobbyist-aids-biden/ [accessed March 30, 2009].

46. Ibid.

47. Olivia Clarke, "Choosing sides: Local lawyers help the presidential campaigns," *Chicago Daily Bulletin* (undated); available online at: http://www.chicagolawbulletin.com/chicagolawyer.cfm?sessionid= [accessed March 30, 2009].

48. Rachel Breitman, "The Legal Ties That Bind the Bidens," *The American Lawyer*, August 28, 2008; available online at: http://www.law.com/jsp/article.jsp?id=1202424110233 [accessed March 30, 2009].

49. Chris Rizo, "Palin's take on legal reform unknown; Biden said to be too cozy with trial lawyers," LegalNewsline.com, September 10, 2008; available online at: http://legalnewsline.com/news/215599-palins-take-on-legal-reform-unknown-biden-said-to-be-too-cozy-with-trial-lawyers [accessed March 30, 2009].

50. Rachel Breitman, "The Legal Ties That Bind the Bidens," op cit.

51. Kelsey Volkmann, "Biden backer SimmonsCooper gives $196,050," *St. Louis Business Journal*, September 2, 2008; available online at: http://stlouis.bizjournals.com/stlouis/stories/2008/09/29/story8.html?b=1222660800^1707116 [accessed March 30, 2009].

52. Ibid.

53. "Biden & Partners," *Wall Street Journal*, October 1, 2008; available online at: http://online.wsj.com/article/SB122282666595993003.html [accessed March 30, 2009].

54. Steve Korris, "Bidens owe SimmonsCooper $1 million in hedge fund deal," *Madison County Record*, September 26, 2008; available online at: http://www.madisonrecord.com/news/215023-bidens-owe-simmonscooper-1-million-in-hedge-fund-deal [accessed March 30, 2009].

55. "Biden & Partners," *Wall Street Journal*, op cit.

56. Steve Korris, "Bidens owe SimmonsCooper $1 million in hedge fund deal," op cit.

57. Ibid.

58. Ibid.

59. Jenny Strasburg and Thom Weidlich, "Biden's Son Sues Ex-Partner," *Washington Post*, February 21, 2007; available online at: http://www.washingtonpost.com/wp-dyn/content/article/2007/02/20/AR2007022001404.html [accessed March 30, 2009].

60. Ibid.

61. Steve Korris, "Bidens owe SimmonsCooper $1 million in hedge fund deal," op cit.

62. Ibid.

63. Chris Rizo, "Fraud claims against Biden's son, brother settled," LegalNewsline.com, January 11, 2009; available online at: http://www.legalnewsline.com/news/218448-fraud-claims-against-bidens-son-brother-settled [accessed March 30, 2009].

64. Associated Press, "Lawsuit against Biden's son, brother settled," *USA Today*, January 9, 2009; available online at: http://www.usatoday.com/news/nation/2009-01-09-bidens-son-lawsuit_N.htm [accessed March 30, 2009].

65. Dareh Gregorian, "Judge to banker, Bidens: give peace a chance," *New York Post*, February 28, 2009; available online at: http://www.nypost.com/seven/02282009/business/judge_to_banker__bidens__give_peace_a_ch_157288.htm [accessed March 30, 2009].

66. Susan Schmidt, Steve Stecklow, and John R. Emshwiller, "Stanford Had Links to a Fund Run by Bidens," *Wall Street Journal*, February 24, 2009; available online at: http://online.wsj.com/article/

SB123543815326954907.html?mod=article-outset-box [accessed March 30, 2009].

67. Jeff Montgomery, "Bidens' clients pull out of fund," Delaware Online, February 25, 2009; article previously available online at: http://www.delawareonline.com/article/20090225/NEWS02/902250319/1006/NEWS [accessed March 30, 2009].

68. http://brontecapital.blogspot.com/

69. http://www.sec.gov/news/press/2009/2009-90.htm

70. More at http://zerohedge.blogspot.com/2009/04/is-joe-biden-associated-with-hedge-fund.html. Financial blogger Tyler Durden concludes:

"I see lots of possibilities: all of them reflect very poorly on the Bidens.

- They were and remain controllers of a fund of funds which they allege misrepresented its returns and yet which they kept operational.
- They were and remain controllers of a fund of funds which houses an alleged fraud in its offices (Ponta Negra).
- They were and remain controllers of a fund of funds which employed a marketing organisation (Onyx) which was associated with distributing alleged frauds (Ponta Negra and Stanford).
- They were and remain controllers of a fund that claimed to have 28 staff many of whom are difficult to trace and where the revenue to fund those staff did not obviously exist. This suggests that either the staff were not paid, did not exist or (more sinisterly) they were paid by stealing from the small amount of funds under management. You could only steal the client money if the asset custody safeguards were not robust. There is an audit statement on the SEC files qualified as to the robustness of these protections—however there is no evidence that the lack of robustness was exploited."

71. United States District Court Northern District of Illinois Eastern Division, *United States of America vs. Stuart Levine, Joseph Cari, and Steve Loren*; available online at: http://www.ipsn.org/indictments/levine/IndictReTRSfinal.pdf [accessed March 30, 2009].

72. United States District Court Northern District of Illinois Eastern Division, *United States of America vs. Joseph Cari* (No. 05 CR 691);

available online at: http://www.capitolfax.com/PleaCariFinalSept151.
pdf [accessed March 30, 2009].

73. United States District Court Northern District of Illinois Eastern
Division, *United States of America vs. Joseph Cari and Antoin Rezko*
(No. 05 CR 691); available online at: http://www.bettergov.org/pdfs/
Rezko.Levine.Indictment.pdf [accessed March 30, 2009].

74. David McKinney, "Biden has deep ties to Rezko accomplice,"
Chicago Sun-Times, August 25, 2008; available online at: http://www.
suntimes.com/news/metro/rezko/1124666,CST-NWS-rezko25.article
[accessed March 30, 2009].

75. Chris Fusco, Dave Mckinney, Abdon Pallasch, and Steve Warm-
bir, "Feds charge 3 in kickback scheme," *Chicago Sun-Times*, August 4,
2005; available online at: http://www.ipsn.org/indictments/levine/feds_
charge_3_in_kickback_scheme.htm [accessed March 30, 2009].

76. Perry Bacon, Jr., "Joe Biden, D-Amtrak," *Washington Post*,
August 23, 2008; available online at: http://voices.washingtonpost.
com/44/2008/08/23/joe_biden_d-amtrak.html [accessed March 30,
2009].

77. Ben Pershing, "Rail-Riding Biden Is a Strong Backer Of Amtrak
in Senate," *Washington Post*, September 2, 2008; available online at:
http://www.washingtonpost.com/wp-dyn/content/article/2008/09/01/
AR2008090102391.html [accessed March 30, 2009].

78. Mike McIntire and Serge F. Kovaleski, "Biden is an everyman on
the campaign trail, with perks at home," op cit.

79. "Biden's Amtrak admission," CBS News Video, January 17, 2009;
available online at: http://www.cbsnews.com/video/watch/?id=4729932n
[accessed March 30, 2009].

80. Andrew Glass, "A Younger Biden Goes the Extra Miles for
Amtrak," *Politico*, February 12, 2007; available online at: http://dyn.
politico.com/printstory.cfm?uuid=9E164D6F-3048-5C12-
008BC7D405BE0D37 [accessed March 30, 2009].

81. "Biden: Amtrak money a boost for Del.," Delaware Online,
March 13, 2009; cached version previously available online at: http://
209.85.173.132/search?q=cache:UjL054vfn_AJ:www.delawareonline.
com/article/20090313/NATIONAL/90313045 + Biden: + Amtrak +

money + a + boost + for + Del. + news + journal&cd=1&hl=en&ct=clnk&gl=us&client=firefox-a [accessed March 30, 2009].

82. Byron York, "The RAT hiding deep inside the stimulus bill," *Washington Examiner*, February 19, 2009; available online at: http://www.washingtonexaminer.com/politics/The-RAT-hiding-deep-inside-the-stimulus-bill-39805642.html [accessed March 30, 2009].

83. Jimmy Orr, "'Nobody messes with Joe' Biden warns governors," *Christian Science Monitor*, February 25, 2009; available online at: http://features.csmonitor.com/politics/2009/02/25/nobody-messes-with-joe-biden-warns-governors/ [accessed March 30, 2009].

84. Michelle Malkin, "Audio comedy gold: Bozo the Vice President is looking out for you," michellemalkin.com, March 19, 2009; available online at: http://michellemalkin.com/2009/03/19/audio-comedy-gold-bozo-the-vice-president-is-looking-out-for-you/ [accessed March 30, 2009].

CHAPTER 4: MEET THE MESS

1. David Von Drehle, "The Year of the Youth Vote," *Time*, January 31, 2008; available online at: http://www.time.com/time/politics/article/0,8599,1708570-3,00.html [accessed April 12, 2009].

2. Ibid.

3. Sophie Gilbert, "Who Are the Wealthiest Members of the Obama Administration?" *Washingtonian*, March 19, 2009; available online at: http://www.washingtonian.com/blogarticles/people/capitalcomment/11857.html [accessed April 12, 2009].

4. Brian Faughnan, "Obama's CIA Designee Sought CIA Cuts, Threatened Director," *Red State*, January 5, 2009; available online at: http://www.redstate.com/brianfaughnan/2009/01/05/obamas-cia-designee-sought-cia-cuts-threatened-director/ [accessed April 12, 2009].

5. Leon E. Panetta, "No torture. No exceptions," *Washington Monthly*, January/February/March 2008; available online at: http://www.washingtonmonthly.com/features/2008/0801.panetta.html [accessed April 12, 2009].

6. Greg Miller and Christi Parsons, "Leon Panetta is Obama's pick for CIA director," *Los Angeles Times*, January 6, 2009; available online at:

http://articles.latimes.com/2009/jan/06/nation/na-obama-cia-panetta6 [accessed April 12, 2009].

7. Donald Lambro, "Panetta faces qualification questions," *Washington Times*, January 25, 2009; available online at: http://washingtontimes.com/news/2009/jan/25/obamas-cia-pick-faces-qualification-questions/ [accessed April 12, 2009].

8. Glenn R. Simpson, "CIA Nominee Panetta Received $700,000 in Fees," *Wall Street Journal*, February 5, 2009; available online at: http://online.wsj.com/article/SB123378062602049003.html [accessed April 12, 2009].

9. Peter D. Hart Research Associates, "2008 Survey of America's College Students," April 2008; available online at: http://www.panettainstitute.org/surveys/survey-2008.pdf [accessed April 12, 2009].

10. Glenn R. Simpson, "CIA Nominee Panetta Received $700,000 in Fees," op cit.

11. Chris Cillizza, "Locke called cabinet pick," *Washington Post*, February 24, 2009; available online at: http://www.washingtonpost.com/wp-dyn/content/article/2009/02/23/AR2009022302618.html [accessed April 12, 2009].

12. William Yardley, "Commerce Pick Carries Lengthy China Résumé," *New York Times*, February 24, 2009; available online at: http://www.nytimes.com/2009/02/25/us/politics/25locke.html [accessed April 12, 2009].

13. Tom Banse, "Obama's New Commerce Pick Has Clean Reputation," National Public Radio, February 25, 2009; available online at: http://www.npr.org/templates/story/story.php?storyId=101158637 [accessed April 12, 2009].

14. Rick Anderson, "Gary Locke: Another Obama Mispick?" *Seattle Weekly*, February 24, 2009; available online at: http://blogs.seattleweekly.com/dailyweekly/2009/02/gary_locke_another_obama_mispi.php [accessed April 12, 2009].

15. Rick Anderson, "The State's Two-Timing Consultant," *Seattle Weekly*, March 17, 2004; available online at: http://www.seattleweekly.com/2004-03-17/news/the-state-s-two-timing-consultant [accessed April 12, 2009].

16. Rick Anderson, "Clean Harbor?" *Seattle Weekly*, July 10, 2002; available online at: http://www.seattleweekly.com/2002-07-10/news/clean-harbor [accessed April 12, 2009].

17. Rick Anderson, "In-laws and outlaws," *Seattle Weekly*, April 3, 2002; available online at: http://www.seattleweekly.com/2002-04-03/news/in-laws-and-outlaws.php?page=full [accessed April 12, 2009].

18. Michelle Malkin, "The Chinagate/Buddhist temple cash skeletons in Gary Locke's closet," michellemalkin.com, February 24, 2009; available online at: http://michellemalkin.com/2009/02/24/the-chinagatebuddhist-temple-cash-skeletons-in-gary-lockes-closet/ [accessed April 12, 2009].

19. Michelle Malkin, "It's Not Racist To Question Locke's China-Linked Funds," *Seattle Times*, August 11, 1998; available online at: http://community.seattletimes.nwsource.com/archive/?date=19980811&slug=2765830 [accessed April 12, 2009].

20. Robert Gavin, "Locke returns fund-raiser's money campaign committee gives up $1,000 in contributions from John Huang," *Seattle Post-Intelligencer*, June 2, 1999.

21. Michelle Malkin, "Will Gov. Locke Ever Return His Huang-Linked Funds?" *Seattle Times*, June 1, 1999; available online at: http://community.seattletimes.nwsource.com/archive/?date=19990601&slug=2963943 [accessed April 12, 2009].

22. Michelle Malkin, "Locke's cash donations eluded public disclosure," *Seattle Times*, March 18, 1997; available online at: http://web.archive.org/web/20000821060540/www.michellemalkin.com/malk_031897.html [accessed April 12, 2009].

23. Michelle Malkin, "Locke's money trail leads to Buddhist temple's door," *Seattle Times*, September 23, 1997; available online at: http://web.archive.org/web/20000821060254/www.michellemalkin.com/malk_092397.html [accessed April 12, 2009].

24. Ibid.

25. According to the state Public Disclosure Commission, which conducted a cursory investigation of this matter after I first wrote about it in the fall of 1997, the master of the temple handed Locke an envelope containing a $5,000 cashier's check from temple member Moon Chuen Lo. Locke, however, has insisted that the one large donation he personally

accepted during his temple visits came on July 11, not the 27th, and was $5,000 cash, not a cashier's check. Then there's Lo, who told the PDC he handed a $5,000 cashier's check directly to Locke. Clearly, someone is not telling the truth. The story of how Lo's alleged $5,000 cashier's check came to be converted into five separate, sequentially-ordered cashier's checks by the Locke campaign makes absolutely no sense.

Lo told the PDC he gathered $1,000 each in cash from himself, his wife, and three friends in order to purchase a $5,000 cashier's check from Seafirst Bank to donate to Locke's campaign. Yet Seafirst, responding to a PDC subpoena, stated it has no record of the check's existence. The check somehow landed on Locke campaign consultant Dia Hujar's desk—nobody remembers who put it there—along with a list of the five donors who supposedly pooled their money together to buy the check. Hujar neither returned nor photocopied nor deposited Lo's mysterious check. Instead, she said she "may have cashed it," but she has no record of the transaction and "can't remember" where it occurred.

Using $5,000 in cash from a source that remains undocumented to this day, Hujar then purchased five $1,000 cashier's checks in the names of Lo, his wife, and three other temple members whose names were on Lo's donor list. Hujar admitted to the PDC that she did not talk to any of the named temple members to get their permission to purchase checks on their behalf. The PDC concluded that "there is no reason to believe" the donations allegedly bundled by Lo were laundered. However, there is no record of Lo having bought a $5,000 cashier's check. There is no record of the Locke campaign having received the check, despite Hujar's insistence in sworn testimony to the PDC that the campaign made "photocopies of every check that comes in." There is no evidence that Hujar either cashed or deposited the check. Bank records showed that Ms. Hujar used cash—not a check—to buy the five $1,000 cashier's checks. The source of the $5,000 cash remains undocumented to this day.

In my own interviews with two of the Buddhist monks (Moon Chuen Lo and Siu Wai Wong), conducted prior to initiation of the PDC investigation, they could not remember if they had contributed to the Locke campaign with cash or a check. Nor did they mention the bundling scheme for which no records exist.

In short, Hujar's testimony related to the check simply is not credible. The evidence is clear: the Locke campaign received $5,000 in cash from a source that still has not been documented and used it to buy checks made out in the names of Buddhist monks. The Public Disclosure Commission, whose members are appointed by the Governor, absolved Locke of any wrongdoing despite overwhelming evidence of misconduct. Copies of the bank records, cashier's checks, temple donation spreadsheets, and subpoenas are available at: http://web.archive.org/web/20000708023109/www.michellemalkin.com/locketemple.htm [accessed May 18, 2009].

26. Les Blumenthal, "Locke on the road to Cabinet confirmation after hearing," *The Olympian*, March 19, 2009; available online at: http://www.theolympian.com/southsound/story/792011.html [accessed April 12, 2009].

27. Harumi Gondo, "How Asian are Obama's Asian-American Cabinet picks?" *United Press International*, March 2, 2009; available online at: http://www.upi.com/Features/Culture_Society/2009/03/02/How_Asian_are_Obamas_Asian-American_Cabinet_picks/12359767253702/ [accessed April 12, 2009].

28. Kenneth P. Vogel, "Locke's China work complicates bid," *Politico*, February 25, 2009; available online at: http://dyn.politico.com/printstory.cfm?uuid=AEDDF46C-18FE-70B2-A81AE6E4FD5B35B1 [accessed April 12, 2009].

29. Ted Van Dyk, "President Obama: Spice up the honeymoon," Crosscut.com, March 16, 2009; available online at: http://crosscut.com/2009/03/16/politics-government/18908/ [accessed April 12, 2009].

30. Stefan Sharkansky, "Public Non-Disclosure," *Sound Politics*, August 25, 2005; available online at: http://soundpolitics.com/archives/005002.html [accessed April 12, 2009].

31. *Yousoufian v. Office of Ron Sims*, January 15, 2009; available online at: http://www.courts.wa.gov/opinions/pdf/800812.opn.pdf [accessed April 12, 2009].

32. Stefan Shaarkansky, "Sharkansky v King County," *Sound Politics*, October 25, 2005; available online at: http://www.soundpolitics.com/archives/005224.html [accessed April 12, 2009].

33. Stefan Sharkansky, "Speaking of Ron Sims," *Sound Politics*, April 24, 2009; available online at: http://soundpolitics.com/archives/012881.html [accessed April 24, 2009].

34. Barack Obama, "Memorandum For The Heads Of Executive Departments and Agencies," The White House, January 21, 2009; available online at: http://www.whitehouse.gov/the_press_office/Freedom_of_Information_Act/ [accessed April 12, 2009].

35. Cited in OG-Blog, "AP Story on Obama-Appointee Ron Sims' Horrible Open Gov't Track Record," Open-Government Blog, March 22, 2009; available online at: http://og-blogdotcom.blogspot.com/2009/03/ap-story-on-obama-appointee-ron-sims.html [accessed April 12, 2009].

36. Byron York, "Michelle Obama: 'Don't Go Into Corporate America," *The Corner*, February 29, 2008; available online at: http://corner.nationalreview.com/post/?q=OTViZjhhNGI1Y2Qx YjE0ZDc0YmMwMjJiNmUyZjQ3MmU [accessed April 12, 2009].

37. Kenneth P. Vogel, "Lawyers cash out to join administration," *Politico*, January 28, 2009; available online at: http://www.politico.com/news/stories/0109/18080.html [accessed April 12, 2009].

38. Daphne Eviatar, "Eric Holder: the $2 Million Nominee," *Washington Independent*, December 23, 2008; available online at: http://washingtonindependent.com/22858/eric-holder-the-2-million-plus-ag-nominee [accessed April 12, 2009].

39. Andrew Longstreth, "Making History With Obama," *The American Lawyer*, June 5, 2008; available online at: http://www.law.com/jsp/article.jsp?id=1202421950304 [accessed April 13, 2009].

40. Ibid.

41. U.S. Department of Justice, "Chiquita Brands International Pleads Guilty to Making Payments to a Designated Terrorist Organization And Agrees to Pay $25 Million Fine," press release #07-161, March 19, 2007; available online at: http://www.usdoj.gov/opa/pr/2007/March/07_nsd_161.html [accessed April 13, 2009].

42. Daphne Eviatar, "Left Holds Holder Concerns," *Washington Independent*, January 14, 2009; available online at: http://washingtonindependent.com/25595/left-holds-holder-concerns [accessed April 13, 2009].

43. Andrew Longstreth, "Making History With Obama," op cit.

44. Marc Falkoff, ed., *Poems from Guantánamo: The Detainees Speak* (Iowa City, Iowa: University of Iowa Press, 2007).

45. Debra Burlingame, "From Gitmo to Miranda, With Love," *Wall Street Journal*, July 30, 2008; available online at: http://online.wsj.com/article/SB121737320982594975.html?mod=opinion_main_commentaries [accessed April 13, 2009].

46. Gordon Cucullu, "Holder's conflict of interest," *New York Post*, February 26, 2009.

47. Joe Palazzolo, "Some Justice Department Lawyers Have Gitmo Conflicts," *Legal Times*, March 2, 2009; available online at: http://www.law.com/jsp/article.jsp?id=1202428688933 [accessed April 13, 2009].

48. Ibid.

49. Chris Fusco, "Holder omitted Blagojevich link from question-naire," *Chicago Sun-Times*, December 17, 2008; available online at: http://www.suntimes.com/news/metro/blagojevich/1334978,CST-NWS-holder17web.article [accessed April 13, 2009].

50. David Corn, "Why Eric Holder Represents What's Wrong with Washington," *Mother Jones*, January 14, 2009; available online at: http://www.motherjones.com/mojo/2009/01/why-eric-holder-represents-whats-wrong-washington [accessed April 13, 2009].

51. Shannon P. Duffy, "Merck to Pay $671 Million to Settle Whistle-blower Suits," *The Legal Intelligencer*, February 8, 2008; available online at: http://www.law.com/jsp/article.jsp?id=1202426501094 [accessed April 13, 2009].

52. "Merck to pay $671 million to settle fraud cases," *Los Angeles Times*, February 8, 2008; available online at: http://articles.latimes.com/2008/feb/08/business/fi-merck8 [accessed April 13, 2009].

53. Josh Meyer and Tom Hamburger, "Eric Holder pushed for controversial clemency," *Los Angeles Times*, January 9, 2009; available online at: http://articles.latimes.com/2009/jan/09/nation/na-holder9 [accessed April 13, 2009].

54. Andrew C. McCarthy, "Opposed to Holder without Apology," National Review Online, November 25, 2008; available online at: http://article.nationalreview.com/?q=

ZGVjMTJiMzk1OTNiNTMxNzAyODI1MGNhOTQ3OWIyYmU=
[accessed April 13, 2009].

55. Brian Blomquist, "Memos Add To Furor Over Rich's Pardon," *New York Post*, February 2, 2001.

56. "Senate Confirmation Hearings: Eric Holder, Day One," *New York Times*, January 16, 2009; available online at: http://www.nytimes.com/2009/01/16/us/politics/16text-holder.html?pagewanted=16 [accessed April 13, 2009].

57. Carrie Johnson, "A Split at Justice on D.C. Vote Bill," *Washington Post*, April 1, 2009; available online at: http://www.washingtonpost.com/wp-dyn/content/article/2009/03/31/AR2009033104426.html?hpid=topnews [accessed April 13, 2009].

58. Edward Whelan, "Look Who's Politicizing Justice Now," *Washington Post*, April 5, 2009; available online at: http://www.washingtonpost.com/wp-dyn/content/article/2009/04/03/AR2009040302835_pf.html [accessed April 13, 2009].

59. "A Way to Pay off the Deficit," http://laughlines.blogs.nytimes.com/2009/02/05/a-way-to-pay-off-the-deficit/

60. "Trade Nominee Ron Kirk to Pay $10,000 in Back Taxes," http://www.foxnews.com/politics/2009/03/02/trade-nominee-ron-kirk-pay-taxes/

61. Jeff Zeleny, "Kirk Agrees to Pay Back Taxes," *New York Times*, March 2, 2009; available online at: http://thecaucus.blogs.nytimes.com/2009/03/02/kirk-agrees-to-pay-back-taxes/

62. "Sen. Cornyn Introduces Trade Rep. Nominee Ron Kirk At Senate Finance Committee Confirmation Hearing," March 9, 2009; available online at: http://cornyn.senate.gov/public/index.cfm?FuseAction=ForPress.CommitteeStatements&ContentRecord_id=ed3afd19-802a-23ad-4065-d2c9b97fb4bd&Region_id=247c157b-b469-90c2-e743-36841183774b&Issue_id=

63. Brian Montopoli, "Another Obama Nominee Has Tax Issues," March 31, 2009; available online at: http://www.cbsnews.com/blogs/2009/03/31/politics/politicalhotsheet/entry4908247.shtml

64. United States Senate Committee on Finance, "Hearing to Consider the Nomination of Kathleen G. Sebelius," April 2, 2009; available online at: http://finance.senate.gov/sitepages/hearing040209.htm

65. Sen. Edward M. Kennedy, "Hilda Solis: A Profile In Courage," *Huffington Post*, December 19, 2008; available online at: http://www. huffingtonpost.com/sen-edward-m-kennedy-/post_245_b_152415.html [accessed April 13, 2009].

66. Soren Dayton, "Hilda Solis long-time SEIU ally; supported in Dem primary in 2000 against incumbent," *The Next Right*, December 19, 2008; available online at: http://www.thenextright.com/soren-dayton/hilda-solis-long-time-seiu-ally-supported-in-dem-primary-in-2000-against-incumbent [accessed April 13, 2009].

67. Philip Klein, "Labor's Girl: Hilda Solis's Long Struggle for Unions," *Capital Research Center Labor Watch*, February 2009; available online at: http://www.capitalresearch.org/pubs/pdf/v1233347080. pdf [accessed April 13, 2009].

68. Greg Sargent, "Labor Leaders Hail Obama's Pick for Labor Secretary," *TPM Election Central*, December 18, 2008; available online at: http://tpmelectioncentral.talkingpointsmemo.com/2008/12/andy_stern_on_obamas_labor_sec.php [accessed April 13, 2009].

69. Ruth Marcus, "Hearings and Evasions," *Washington Post*, January 14, 2009; available online at: http://www.washingtonpost.com/wp-dyn/content/article/2009/01/13/AR2009011302283_pf.html [accessed April 13, 2009].

70. Ibid.

71. Lisa Mascaro, "Card check issue stalls panel's vote on nominee," *Las Vegas Sun*, January 23, 2009; available online at: http://www.lasvegassun.com/news/2009/jan/23/card-check-issue-stalls-panels-vote-nominee/ [accessed April 13, 2009].

72. Hans A. von Spakovsky, "The Nominee Who Lobbied Herself," *Weekly Standard*, February 3, 2009; available online at: http://www.weeklystandard.com/Content/Public/Articles/000/000/016/101mswgc.asp [accessed April 13, 2009].

73. "Senators should ask Solis why she approved campaign spots paid for by her non-profit," *Washington Examiner*, February 5, 2009; available online at: http://www.washingtonexaminer.com/opinion/Senators-should-ask-Solis-why-she-approved-campaign-spots-paid-for-by-her-non -profit.html [accessed April 13, 2009].

74. Kevin Bogardus, "Solis affidavit moves Labor bid forward," *The Hill*, February 11, 2009; available online at: http://thehill.com/leading-the-news/solis-affidavit-credited-with-moving-labor-bid-forward-2009-02-11.html [accessed April 13, 2009].

75. Matt Kelley, "Tax snafus add up for Obama team," *USA Today*, February 5, 2009; available online at: http://www.usatoday.com/news/washington/2009-02-05-solis-husband-taxes_N.htm [accessed April 13, 2009].

76. Alina Selyukh, "A Precedent For 'Unprecedented' Bipartisanship," *National Journal*, February 11, 2009; available online at: http://lostintransition.nationaljournal.com/2009/02/precendent-for-unprecedented.php [accessed April 13, 2009].

77. Alex Altman, "Transportation Secretary: Ray LaHood," *Time*, December 24, 2008; available online at: http://www.time.com/time/nation/article/0,8599,1868036,00.html [accessed April 13, 2009].

78. Karen McDonald, "LaHood showed 18th District the money," *Peoria Journal Star*, December 6, 2008; available online at: http://www.pjstar.com/archive/x1231767262/LaHood-showed-18th-District-the-money [accessed April 13, 2009].

79. Michael A. Fletcher and Philip Rucker, "Obama to Add GOP's LaHood to Cabinet," *Washington Post*, December 18, 2008; available online at: http://www.washingtonpost.com/wp-dyn/content/article/2008/12/17/AR2008121703483.html [accessed April 13, 2009].

80. William Neikirk and Judith Graham, "Illinois congressmen push child health plan," *Chicago Tribune*, February 16, 2007; available online at: http://archives.chicagotribune.com/2007/feb/16/health/chi-0702160176feb16 [accessed April 13, 2009].

81. Craig S. O'Connell, "Mineta Unveils Bush Plan of Attack on Amtrak," *Light Rail Now!* February 2005; available online at: http://www.lightrailnow.org/features/f_amtrak_2005-02.htm [accessed April 13, 2009].

82. Carol D. Leonnig, "LaHood Sponsored Millions in Earmarks," *Washington Post*, January 14, 2009; available online at: http://www.washingtonpost.com/wp-dyn/content/story/2009/01/14/ST2009011402310.html [accessed April 13, 2009].

83. "Obama's Secretary of Earmarks," *Wall Street Journal*, December 26, 2008; available online at: http://online.wsj.com/article/ SB123025488582034591.html [accessed April 13, 2009].

84. Carol D. Leonnig, "LaHood Sponsored Millions in Earmarks," op cit.

85. John Kass, "Governor waxes poetic, but Combine rolls on," *Chicago Tribune*, December 20, 2008; available online at: http://archives. chicagotribune.com/2008/dec/20/news/chi-kass-bd-deadmeatdec21 [accessed April 13, 2009].

86. Tim Novak, Dave Mckinney and Chris Fusco, "Who is William Cellini?" *Chicago Sun-Times*, October 31, 2008; available online at: http://www.suntimes.com/news/politics/1252597,CST-NWS-profile31. article [accessed April 13, 2009].

87. Impeached former Illinois Governor Rod Blagojevich's criminal indictment; available online at: http://www.slideshare.net/LegalDocs/ findlaw-blagojevich-indictment [accessed April 13, 2009].

88. Citizens Against Government Waste, "CAGW Names Transportation Secretary Ray LaHood Porker of the Month," Porker of the Month, January 2009; available online at: http://www.cagw.org/site/ PageServer?pagename=news_porkerofthemonth_2009_Jan [accessed April 13, 2009].

89. "Obama to Nominate First Black EPA Chief," DiversityInc, December 15, 2008; available online at: http://www.diversityinc.com/ public/4968.cfm [accessed April 13, 2009].

90. Brad Heath and Blake Morrison, "EPA nominee to focus on science not politics," *USA Today*, January 15, 2009; available online at: http://www.usatoday.com/news/nation/environment/2009-01-14-epa-inside_N.htm [accessed April 13, 2009].

91. Cited in Dave Burdick, "EPA Chief Pick's Record Raises Eyebrows," *Huffington Post*, December 15, 2008; available online at: http:// m.huffpost.com/top/14288/full/%3Bjsessionid= 487E63004B9B438723FC3F70A42AA460.test [accessed April 13, 2009].

92. "EPA Report Blasts New Jersey Toxic Clean-Ups—State Failures to Enforce Law Lead to Worst Delays in the Country," Public Employees for Environmental Responsibility, June 19, 2008; available online at:

http://www.peer.org/news/news_id.php?row_id=1068 [accessed April 13, 2009].

93. Carol Ann Campbell, "Feds accept guilty pleas in Superfund kick-backs," NJ.com, July 23 2008; available online at: http://www.nj.com/news/index.ssf/2008/07/feds_accept_guilty_pleas_in_su.html [accessed April 13, 2009].

94. "N.J. Industrial Pipes Supply Company and Its Co-Owner Plead Guilty to Fraud at Two N.J. Superfund Sites," PR Newswire, March 4, 2009; available online at: http://www.redorbit.com/news/business/1649228/nj_industrial_pipes_supply_company_and_its_coowner_plead_guilty/ [accessed April 13, 2009].

95. Christine Hall, "Statement on Nomination of Lisa Jackson to EPA Administrator," Competitive Enterprise Institute, January 13, 2008; available online at: http://cei.org/node/21486 [accessed April 13, 2009].

CHAPTER 5: BACKROOM BUDDIES

1. Letter from Senator Robert Byrd to President Barack Obama, February 23, 2009; available online at: http://www.eenews.net/public/25/9865/features/documents/2009/02/25/document_gw_02.pdf [accessed March 27, 2009].

2. Tom LoBianco, "Senators ponder vetting czar Browner," *Washington Times*, January 19, 2009; available online at: http://www.washingtontimes.com/news/2009/jan/19/senators-ponder-vetting-czar-browner/ [accessed March 27, 2009].

3. Tom Hamburger and Christi Parsons, "White House czars' power stirs criticism," *Chicago Tribune*, March 5, 2009; available online at: www.chicagotribune.com/news/nationworld/chi-czars_for_thursmar05,0,885860.story [accessed March 27, 2009].

4. Byrd letter, op cit.

5. Ian Talley, "EPA Set to Move Toward Carbon-Dioxide Regulation," *Wall Street Journal*, February 23, 2009; available online at: http://online.wsj.com/article/SB123531391527642021.html [accessed March 27, 2009].

6. Tom LoBianco, "Obama climate plan could cost $2 trillion," *Washington Times*, March 18, 2009; available online at: http://

washingtontimes.com/news/2009/mar/18/obama-climate-plan-could-cost-2-trillion/ [accessed March 27, 2009].

7. "Browner is an environmental radical – and a socialist (seriously)," *Washington Examiner*, January 8, 2009; available online at: http://www.washingtonexaminer.com/opinion/Browner_is_an_environmental_radical__and_a_socialist_seriously_010809.html [accessed March 27, 2009].

8. Michelle Malkin, "The Trouble with Obama's Energy Czar," *Human Events*, December 12, 2008; available online at: http://www.humanevents.com/article.php?id=29896.

9. John Solomon, "EPA Head Browner Asked for Computer Files to Be Deleted," Associated Press, June 29, 2001.

10. Ibid.

11. Michelle Malkin, "Crooked Carol Browner: Obama's Ethically-Challenged Energy Czar," michellemalkin.com, December 12, 2008; available online at: http://michellemalkin.com/2008/12/12/crooked-carol-browner-obamas-ethically-challenged-energy-czar/.

12. Ibid.

13. "Judge Lamberth's Contempt Order Against the EPA," posted by Landmark Legal Foundation, July 24, 2003; available online at: http://www.landmarklegal.org/uploads/jl1.htm [accessed March 28, 2009].

14. John H. Cushman Jr., "E.P.A. Chief Is Accused Of Lobbying," *New York Times*, March 4, 1995; available online at: http://www.nytimes.com/1995/03/04/us/epa-chief-is-accused-of-lobbying.html [accessed March 28, 2009].

15. Kathy Shaidle, "The Rule of the Green Czar," *FrontPage Magazine*, January 16, 2009; available online at: http://www.frontpagemag.com/Articles/Read.aspx?GUID=B733BA80-D8A2-42FD-8859-C15F36C5A6A1 [accessed March 28, 2009].

16. Max Schulz, "Browner and Greener," National Review Online, December 11, 2008; available online at: http://article.nationalreview.com/print/?q=NWQyZWEzOWQ3MTRhOTYxMzZjNDlkYTg5NzdhODRmOWM= [accessed March 28, 2009].

17. Brad Haynes and T. W. Farnam, "Browner's Husband Lobbied on Energy Issues," *Wall Street Journal*, December 11, 2008; available online

at: http://online.wsj.com/article/SB122903665464999775.html [accessed March 28. 2009].

18. Charlie Savage and David Kirkpatrick, "Spousal Ties to Lobbying Test a Vow From Obama," *New York Times*, December 14, 2008; available online at: http://www.nytimes.com/2008/12/15/us/politics/15lobby.html [accessed March 28, 2009].

19. The web site for Downey's lobbying firm, Downey McGrath Group Inc., states that the firm no longer accepts energy or environment-related work before the Executive Branch or the Congress. See http://www.dmggroup.com/clients.htm [accessed March 28, 2009].

20. Josh Barbanel, "An Embattled Downey Defends His Record," *New York Times*, October 31, 1992; available online at: http://www.nytimes.com/1992/10/31/nyregion/an-embattled-downey-defends-his-record.html [accessed March 28, 2009].

21. Allison Mitchell, "For One Lawmaker, Allure of Capital Had Double-Edge," *New York Times*, November 8, 1992; available online at: http://www.nytimes.com/1992/11/08/nyregion/for-one-lawmaker-allure-of-capital-had-double-edge.html? [accessed March 28, 2009].

22. Robin Shulman, "White House Urban Affairs Chief Picked," *Washington Post*, February 20, 2009; available online at: http://www.washingtonpost.com/wp-dyn/content/article/2009/02/19/AR2009021903148.html [accessed March 28, 2009].

23. "Executive Order: Establishment of the White House Office of Urban Affairs," The White House, February 19, 2009; available online at: http://www.whitehouse.gov/the_press_office/Executive-Order-Establishment-of-the-White-House-Office-of-Urban-Affairs/ [accessed March 28, 2009].

24. Benjamin Lesser and Greg B. Smith, "Buildings sprang up as donations rained down on Bronx Borough President Adolfo Carrion," *New York Daily News*, March 1, 2009; available online at: http://www.nydailynews.com/ny_local/bronx/2009/02/28/2009-02-28_buildings_sprang_up_as_donations_rained_.html [accessed March 28, 2009].

25. Ibid.

26. Ibid.

27. Robert Gearty and Greg B. Smith, "White House urban czar Adolfo Carrion OKd architect Hugo Subotovsky's Bronx plans," *New York Daily News*, March 12, 2009; available online at: http://www. nydailynews.com/news/politics/2009/03/12/2009-03-12_white_house_ urban_czar_adolfo_carrion_ok.html [accessed March 28, 2009].

28. "Press Briefing by Press Secretary Robert Gibbs," The White House, March 11, 2009; available online at: http://www.whitehouse.gov/ the_press_office/Briefing-by-WH-Press-Secretary-Gibbs-3-11-09/ [accessed March 28, 2009].

29. Benjamin Lesser, "Obama appointee Adolfo Carrión spent big on lavish staff retreats in Bronx," *New York Daily News*, March 15, 2009; available online at: http://www.nydailynews.com/ny_local/bronx/2009/ 03/15/2009-03-15_obama_appointee_adolfo_carrin_spent_big_.html [accessed March 28, 2009].

30. Ibid.

31. Mary Clare Leury, "Journalists Living Large," *Washingtonian*, January 29, 2007; available online at: http://www.washingtonian.com/ blogarticles/Homes/openhouse/3247.html [accessed March 28, 2009].

32. Significantly, DeParle simultaneously sat on the board of directors of DaVita and served on MedPAC at the time that MedPAC recommended a change in Medicare regulations favorable to dialysis providers—a change championed by the president and CEO of DaVita Inc.

33. Andrew Zajac, "Health czar has deep ties to industry," *Chicago Tribune*, March 29, 2009; available online at: http://www. chicagotribune.com/news/nationworld/chi-deparlemar29,0,7090806. story [accessed March 29, 2009].

34. Philip Klein, "New Health Czar Challenges Obama's Ethics Reforms," *American Spectator*, March 3, 2009; available online at: http:/ /spectator.org/archives/2009/03/03/new-health-czar-challenges-oba [accecssed March 28, 2009].

35. "Press Briefing by Press Secretary Robert Gibbs," The White House, March 2, 2009; available online at: http://www.whitehouse.gov/ the_press_office/Briefing-by-White-House-Press-Secretary-Robert-Gibbs-3/2/09/ [accessed March 28, 2009].

36. Kenneth P. Vogel and Carrie Budoff Brown, "Will DeParle bring ethics conflicts?" *Politico*, March 2, 2009; available online at: http://

www.politico.com/news/stories/0309/19502.html [accessed March 28, 2009].

37. Zajac, "Health czar has deep ties to industry," op cit.

38. *Lou Dobbs Tonight* transcript, CNN.com, March 5, 2009; available online at: http://transcripts.cnn.com/TRANSCRIPTS/0903/05/ldt.01.html [accessed March 28, 2009].

39. Richard Gibbons, "How to Profit From Obama's Stimulus Bill," *Motley Fool*, February 27, 2009; available online at: http://www.fool.com/investing/value/2009/02/27/how-to-profit-from-obamas-stimulus-bill.aspx [accessed March 28, 2009].

40. Jeffrey Young, "DeParle's industry ties a non-issue," *The Hill*, March 5, 2009; available online at: http://thehill.com/business—lobby/deparles-industry-ties-a-non-issue-2009-03-05.html [accessed March 28, 2009].

41. Jonathan Cohn, "The Early Word on Nancy-Ann Min DeParle," *The New Republic*, February 3, 2009; available online at: http://blogs.tnr.com/tnr/blogs/the_treatment/archive/2009/03/02/the-word-on-daschle-s-replacement-and-i-don-t-mean-sebelius.aspx [accessed March 29, 2009].

42. Sheryl Gay Stolberg, "Obama Taps Health Aide With Links to Industry," *New York Times*, March 2, 2009; available online at: http://www.nytimes.com/2009/03/03/us/politics/03czar.html [accessed March 28, 2009].

43. Securities And Exchange Commission Amendment Complaint No. 09-CV-2518 (CM); available online at: http://www.sec.gov/litigation/complaints/2009/comp21001.pdf [accessed April 19, 2009]. See also Peter Rattman and Craig Karmin, "Rattner involved in inquiry on fees," *Wall Street Journal*, April 17, 2009. The SEC complaint does not identify Rattner by name, but according to the *Journal*, the senior Quandrangle executive referred to in the SEC complaint is Rattner.

44. Ibid.

45. Securities And Exchange Commission Amendment Complaint No. 09-CV-2518 (CM); available online at: http://www.sec.gov/litigation/complaints/2009/comp21001.pdf [accessed April 19, 2009].

46. Peter Rattman and Craig Karmin, "Rattner involved in inquiry on fees," op cit.

47. Securities And Exchange Commission Amendment Complaint No. 09-CV-2518 (CM); available online at: http://www.sec.gov/litigation/complaints/2009/comp21001.pdf [accessed April 19, 2009].

48. Ibid.

49. Heath Haussamen, "Bingaman says he wasn't involved in Rattner deal," *New Mexico Independent*, April 22, 2009; available online at: http://newmexicoindependent.com/25618/bingaman-says-he-wasn%E2%80%99t-involved-in-rattner-deal [accessed April 23, 2009].

50. Louise Story, "Quadrangle Facing Questions Over Pension Funds," *New York Times*, April 21, 2009; available online at: http://www.nytimes.com/2009/04/22/business/22quadrangle.html [accessed April 23, 2009].

51. Heath Haussamen, "Bingaman says he wasn't involved in Rattner deal," op cit.

52. Ed Morrissey, "Kundra's record?" *Hot Air*, March 16, 2009; available online at: http://hotair.com/archives/2009/03/16/kundras-record/ [accessed April 4, 2009].

53. Michael J. Sniffen, "Obama's computer chief once shoplifted 4 shirts," Associated Press, March 18, 2009; article previously available online at: http://www.google.com/hostednews/ap/article/ALeqM5jDaDxxs5nOL4AAGUyMQLOKlaXNWwD970LN784 [accessed April 4, 2009].

54. Ed Morrissey, "Kundra's record?" op cit.

55. Ed Morrissey, "Kundra back on job, White House dodging; Update: WH finally responds! Update: Missing evidence?" *Hot Air*, March 19, 2009; available online at: http://hotair.com/archives/2009/03/19/kundra-back-on-job-white-house-dodging/ [accessed April 4, 2009].

56. White House Press Office, "President Obama Names Vivek Kundra Chief Information Officer," whitehouse.gov, March 5, 2009; available online at: http://www.whitehouse.gov/the_press_office/President-Obama-Names-Vivek-Kundra-Chief-Information-Officer/ [accessed March 5, 2009].

57. K. C. Jones, "Two Charged With Bribery After FBI Raids D.C. CTO Office," *Information Week*, March 12, 2009; available online at: http://www.informationweek.com/news/government/technology/showArticle.jhtml?articleID=215900061 [accessed April 4, 2009].

58. Jonetta Rose Barras, "No surprise here," *Washington Examiner*, March 15, 2009; available online at: http://www.washingtonexaminer. com/opinion/columns/JonettaRoseBarras/No-surprise-here-41291297. html [accessed April 4, 2009].

59. Eric Krangel, "Time For America's CIO Vivek Kundra To Resign," *Silicon Alley Insider*, March 17, 2009; available online at: http:/ /www.businessinsider.com/americas-cio-vivek-kundra-must-go-2009-3 [accessed April 4, 2009].

60. Office of the Chief Technology Officer, Testimony of Vivek Kundra, Chief Technology Officer, before the Committee on Workforce Development and Government Operations, December 12, 2007.

CHAPTER 6: MONEY MEN

1. The speech is available on Obama's official campaign YouTube Channel: http://www.youtube.com/watch?v=FlZ-_Sstt5I.

2. The Rezko story is recounted thoroughly in David Freddoso, *The Case Against Barack Obama* (Washington, DC: Regnery Publishing, Inc., 2008). See Chapter 11, "Pinstripe Patronage: Obama Takes Care of His Friends," 211–34.

3. Joe Stephens, "Obama Got Discount on Home Loan," *Washington Post*, July 2, 2008; available online at: http://www.washingtonpost.com/ wp-dyn/content/article/2008/07/01/AR2008070103008_pf.html [accessed April 28, 2009].

4. Michael Kinsley, "The Conspiracy Of Trivia," *Time*, March 10, 1997; available online at: http://www.cnn.com/ALLPOLITICS/1997/03/ 10/time/kinsley.html [accessed April 28, 2009].

5. Kenneth P. Vogel, "No mortgage pinch for Obama, team," *Politico*, March 7, 2009; available online at: http://dyn.politico.com/printstory. cfm?uuid=E23E7CB1-18FE-70B2-A88A46FCD2E96E04 [accessed April 28, 2009].

6. Glenn R. Simpson and James R. Hagerty, "Countrywide Friends Got Good Loans," *Wall Street Journal*, June 7, 2008; available online at: http://online.wsj.com/article/SB121279970984353933.html [accessed April 28, 2009].

7. Karen Tumulty, "McCain Plays the Race Card," *Time*, September 18, 2008; available online at: http://swampland.blogs.time.com/2008/09/18/mccain_plays_the_race_card/ [accessed April 28, 2009].

8. "Senator Barack Obama Takes First Step Toward Presidential Bid," foxnews.com, January 16, 2007; available online at: http://www.foxnews.com/story/0,2933,243918,00.html [accessed April 28, 2009].

9. "Barack Obama's Feb. 5 Speech," *New York Times*, February 5, 2008; available online at: http://www.nytimes.com/2008/02/05/us/politics/05text-obama.html [accessed April 28, 2009].

10. Sam Graham-Felsen, "In Major Speech, Obama Calls for Modernizing Our Regulation of Financial Markets," my.barackobama.com, March 27, 2008; available online at: http://my.barackobama.com/page/community/post/samgrahamfelsen/gGBNsq [accessed April 28, 2009].

11. Sam Graham-Felsen, "Change that Works for You: Obama Vows to Protect Consumers," my.barackobama.com, June 11, 2008; available online at: http://my.barackobama.com/page/community/post/samgrahamfelsen/gG5jcy [accessed April 28, 2009].

12. Carla Marinucci, "Obama calls AIG bonuses 'outrageous,'" *San Francisco Chronicle*, March 18, 2009; available online at: http://www.sfgate.com/cgi-bin/article.cgi?f=/c/a/2009/03/18/MNUT16IU25.DTL&type=politics&tsp=1 [accessed April 28, 2009].

13. Brody Mullins and T. W. Farnam, "Critics Got Donations From Insurer," *Wall Street Journal*, March 19, 2009; available online at: http://online.wsj.com/article/SB123742426774379307.html [accessed April 28, 2009].

14. Michael Luo and Christopher Drew, "Big Donors, Too, Have Seats at Obama Fund-Raising Table," *New York Times*, August 5, 2008; available online at: http://www.nytimes.com/2008/08/06/us/politics/06bundlers.html [accessed April 28, 2009].

15. "Presidential Candidates: Selected Industry Totals, 2008 Cycle," opensecrets.org, Federal Election Commission data released electronically on Monday, March 2, 2009; available online at: http://www.opensecrets.org/pres08/select.php?ind=F27 [accessed April 28, 2009].

16. "Joe Wurzelbacher on Obama's Tax Increases," youtube.com, October 14, 2008; available online at: http://www.youtube.com/watch? v=DbWWHFLYHm0 [accessed April 28, 2009].

17. Athena Jones, "Obama: McCain Fighting For 'Joe The Hedge Fund Manager,'" Hot Line On Call, October 22, 2008; available online at: http://hotlineoncall.nationaljournal.com/archives/2008/10/obama_ mccain_fi.php [accessed April 28, 2009].

18. Louise Story, "A Rich Education for Summers (After Harvard)," *New York Times*, April 5, 2009; available online at: http://www.nytimes. com/2009/04/06/business/06summers.html [accessed April 28, 2009].

19. John D. Mckinnon and T. W. Farnam, "Hedge Fund Paid Summers $5.2 Million in Past Year," *Wall Street Journal*, April 5, 2009; available online at: http://online.wsj.com/article/SB123879462053487927. html [accessed April 28, 2009].

20. Lawrence Summers, "The $700bn bail-out and the budget," *Financial Times*, September 28, 2008; available online at: http://www.ft. com/cms/s/0/290ca9f6-8d8b-11dd-83d5-0000779fd18c.html [accessed April 28, 2009].

21. Andrew Wheat, "The Fall of the Peso and the Mexican 'Miracle,'" *Multinational Monitor*; available online at: http:// multinationalmonitor.org/hyper/issues/1995/04/mm0495_06.html [accessed April 28, 2009].

22. Article available at: http://multinationalmonitor.org/hyper/ issues/1995/04/mm0495_06.html

23. David E. Sanger, "Mexico Repays Bailout by U.S. Ahead of Time," *New York Times*, January 16, 1997; available online at: http:// www.nytimes.com/1997/01/16/business/mexico-repays-bailout-by-us- ahead-of-time.html [accessed April 28, 2009].

24. Ibid.

25. Edward Luce, "Obama promises bipartisan action on deficits," *Financial Times*, February 24, 2009; available online at: http://www.ft. com/cms/s/0/7b52319c-0205-11de-8199-000077b07658.html [accessed April 28, 2009].

26. "DC: Obama Meets With Members Of Credit Card Industry At White House," Getty Images, April 23, 2009; available online at: http://

www.gettyimages.com/Search/Search.aspx?EventId=86168542 [accessed April 28, 2009].

27. Robert Scheer, "Summers: Living Large and in Charge," *The Nation*, April 8, 2009; available online at: http://www.thenation.com/doc/20090420/scheer [accessed April 28, 2009].

28. Sharona Coutts and Jake Bernstein, "Former Clinton Official Says Democrats, Obama Advisers Share Blame for Market Meltdown," *Propublica*, October 9, 2008; available online at: http://www.propublica.org/feature/former-clinton-official-says-democrats-obama-advisers-share-blame-for-marke [accessed April 28, 2009].

29. Robert Scheer, "Summers: Living Large and in Charge," op cit.

30. Dan Froomkin, "Millions of Reasons to Doubt Summers," *Washington Post*, April 6, 2009; available online at: http://voices.washingtonpost.com/white-house-watch/financial-crisis/millions-of-reasons-to-doubt-s_pf.html [accessed April 28, 2009].

31. "A Closer Look At Treasury Sec. Geithner," Associated Press, March 28, 2009; available online at: http://www.cbsnews.com/stories/2009/03/28/politics/main4899728.shtml [accessed April 28, 2009].

32. Andrew Ross Sorkin, "Where Was Geithner in Turmoil?" *New York Times* Dealbook Column, November 24, 2008; available online at: http://www.nytimes.com/2008/11/25/business/25sorkin.html?_r=1&dbk [accessed April 28, 2009].

33. Karen Tumulty and Massimo Calabresi, "Three Men And a Bailout," *Time*, September 25, 2008; available online at: http://www.time.com/time/magazine/article/0,9171,1844554-1,00.html [accessed April 28, 2009].

34. Yalman Onaran & Michael McKee, "In Geithner We Trust?" Bloomberg News, March 3, 2009; available online at: http://www.businessmirror.com.ph/home/bloomberg-specials/6927-in-geithner-we-trust-.html [accessed April 28, 2009].

35. Jonathan Weisman, "Geithner's Tax History Muddles Confirmation," *Wall Street Journal*, January 14, 2009; available online at: http://online.wsj.com/article/SB123187503629378119.html [accessed April 28, 2009].

36. "Reid: Senate Must Confirm Geithner as Soon as Possible," democrats.senate.gov, January 21, 2009; available online at: http://

democrats.senate.gov/newsroom/record.cfm?id=307068 [accessed April 28, 2009].

37. "Obama announces economic team," MarketWatch, November 24, 2008; available online at: http://www.marketwatch.com/news/story/story.aspx?guid={27fb89d7-f5ad-4437-add5-2d6b7af8f461} [accessed April 28, 2009].

38. "Ford Foundation Links Parents of Obama and Treasury Secretary Nominee," *Chronicle of Philanthropy*, December 3, 2008; available online at: http://philanthropy.com/news/government/index.php?id=6453 [accessed April 28, 2009].

39. Ryan Donmoyer, "'Joe the Plumber,' Obama Tax-Plan Critic, Owes Taxes," Bloomberg News, October 16, 2008; available online at: http://www.bloomberg.com/apps/news?pid=20601087&sid=aC4j3T5.s_eQ&refer=home [accessed April 28, 2009].

40. Byron York, "Geithner Accepted IMF Reimbursement for Taxes He Didn't Pay," National Review Online, January 14, 2009; available online at: http://article.nationalreview.com/?q=YzJjOGQyODY2ZjhhMWY4Y2U3YmVkMjhlMWQ2MWZiNTA= [accessed April 28, 2009].

41. John D. McKinnon and Bob Davis, "IMF Informed Geithner on Taxes," *Wall Street Journal*, January 15, 2009; available online at: http://online.wsj.com/article/SB123194884833281695.html [accessed April 28, 2009].

42. Peter Hartcher, "Obama's economic saviour savaged as Keating lets rip," *Sydney Morning Herald*, March 7, 2009; available online at: http://www.smh.com.au/opinion/obamas-economic-saviour-savaged-as-keating-lets-rip-20090306-8rk7.html?page=-1 [accessed April 28, 2009].

43. Jeff Gerth, "How Citigroup Unraveled Under Geithner's Watch," *Propublica*, January 14, 2009; available online at: http://www.propublica.org/article/how-citigroup-unraveled-under-geithners-watch [accessed April 28, 2009].

44. "Hearing on Confirmation of Mr. Timothy F. Geithner to be Secretary of the U.S. Department of Treasury," Senate Finance Committee, January 21, 2009; available online at: http://finance.senate.gov/sitepages/leg/LEG%202009/012209%20TFG%20Questions.pdf [accessed April 28, 2009].

45. Hans Bader, "Geithner Seeks More Power to Ruin Our Economy," openmarket.org, March 26, 2009; available online at: http://www.openmarket.org/2009/03/26/geithner-seeks-more-power-to-ruin-our-economy/ [accessed April 28, 2009]. See also: James Piereson, "Too Big to Fail?" *The Corner*, March 23, 2009; available online at: http://corner.nationalreview.com/post/?q=MjdkYTc 0MDJkMTQxZTEwZDQyOTNiOTVlYWQ4ZDkzNDM= [accessed April 28, 2009].

46. Andrew Ross Sorkin, "Where Was Geithner In Turmoil?" op cit.

47. "To Catch a (Tax) Thief," *New York Post*, March 5, 2009; available online at: http://www.nypost.com/seven/03052009/postopinion/editorials/to_catch_a__tax__thief_158103.htm [accessed April 28, 2009].

48. Ryan Grim, "Administration Officials Met With Laughter At Bailout Briefing," *Huffington Post*, February 10, 2009; available online at: http://www.huffingtonpost.com/2009/02/10/administration-officials_n_165551.html [accessed April 28, 2009].

49. Michelle Malkin, "Geithner can't get taxes straight, can't get dates straight..." michellemalkin.com, March 20, 2009; available online at: http://michellemalkin.com/2009/03/20/geithner-cant-get-taxes-straight-cant-get-dates-straight/ [accessed April 28, 2009].

50. Ralph Z. Hallow, "Gingrich urges GOP to fight Geithner," *Washington Times*, January 20, 2009; available online at: http://www.washingtontimes.com/news/2009/jan/20/gingrich-urges-gop-to-oppose-geithner/ [accessed April 28, 2009].

51. Ibid.

52. David Gaffen, "Will You Please, Be Quiet, Please?" *Wall Street Journal*, March 25, 2009; available online at: http://blogs.wsj.com/marketbeat/2009/03/25/will-you-please-be-quiet-please/ [accessed April 28, 2009].

53. Frank James, "Geithner misses lifeline, sinks dollar," *Swamp Politics*, March 25, 2009; available online at: http://www.swamppolitics.com/news/politics/blog/2009/03/geithner_was_having_a_good_wee.html [accessed April 28, 2009].

54. David Gaffen, "The Geithner Bond Selloff," *Wall Street Journal*, January 22, 2009; available online at: http://blogs.wsj.com/marketbeat/2009/01/22/the-geithner-bond-selloff/ [accessed April 28, 2009].

55. David Gaffen, "Will You Please, Be Quiet, Please?" op cit.

56. Gary Weiss, "The Reeducation of Tim Geithner," *Portfolio*, May 2009; available online at: http://www.portfolio.com/executives/ 2009/04/22/Treasury-Chief-Tim-Geithner-Profile [accessed April 28, 2009].

57. David Cho, "At Geithner's Treasury, Key Decisions on Hold," *Washington Post*, May 18, 2009; available online at: http://www. washingtonpost.com/wp-dyn/content/article/2009/05/17/ AR2009051702268.html [accessed May 25, 2009].

58. Deborah Solomon, Jonathan Weisman, and Laura Meckler, "At Treasury, Big White House Role," *Wall Street Journal*, May 1, 2009; available online at: http://online.wsj.com/article/SB124113406528875137.html [accessed May 25, 2009].

59. David Cho and Neil Irwin, "Familiar Trio at Heart of Citi Bailout," *Washington Post*, November 25, 2008; available online at: http://www.washingtonpost.com/wp-dyn/content/article/2008/11/24/ AR2008112401118.html [accessed April 28, 2009].

60. "Citi's Taxpayer Parachute," *Wall Street Journal*, November 25, 2008; available online at: http://online.wsj.com/article/SB122757194671054783. html [accessed April 28, 2009].

61. Eliza Krigman, "The Citi-Obama Administration Connection," *National Journal*, March 3, 2009; available online at: http:// undertheinfluence.nationaljournal.com/2009/03/the-citiobama- administration-c.php [accessed April 28, 2009].

62. Christopher Weaver, "The Obama Team's Disclosure Documents," *Propublica*, April 8, 2009; available online at: http://www. propublica.org/special/the-obama-teams-disclosure-documents-407 [accessed April 28, 2009].

63. "Low-Flying Plane Strikes Fear In Some New Yorkers," *NY1 News*, April 28, 2009; available online at: http://www.ny1.com/content/ top_stories/98059/low-flying-plane-strikes-fear-in-some-new-yorkers/ Default.aspx [accessed April 28, 2009].

64. John D. McKinnon, "Obama Team's Finances Released," *Wall Street Journal*, April 6, 2009; available online at: http://online.wsj. com/article/SB123897383937190973.html [accessed April 28, 2009].

65. Matthew M. Johnson, "GOP Senators Raise Questions About Nominee to be Top Army Lawyer," CQ Today Online – Defense, April 28, 2009.

66. Austan Goolsbee, "'Irresponsible' Mortgages Have Opened Doors to Many of the Excluded," *New York Times*, March 29, 2007; available online at: http://www.nytimes.com/2007/03/29/business/29scene.html [accessed April 28, 2009].

67. Brian C. Mooney, "For Obama, a chance to push big changes," *The Boston Globe*, November 30, 2008; available online at: http://www. boston.com/news/nation/articles/2008/11/30/for_obama_a_chance_to_ push_big_changes/.

68. Bob Secter and Andrew Zajac, "Rahm Emanuel's profitable stint at mortgage giant," *Chicago Tribune*, March 26, 2009; available online at: http://www.chicagotribune.com/news/politics/obama/chi-rahm-emanuel-profit-26-mar26,0,5682373.story [accessed April 30, 2009].

69. Bob Secter and Andrew Zajac, "Rahm Emanuel's profitable stint at mortgage giant," *Chicago Tribune*, March 26, 2009; available online at: http://www.chicagotribune.com/news/politics/obama/chi-rahm-emanuel-profit-26-mar26,0,5682373.story?page=1.

70. Lynn Sweet, "Emanuel's cash clash: Emanuel's trust is supposed to be blind, not stupid," *Chicago Sun-Times*, August 14, 2003; available online at: http://www.highbeam.com/doc/1P2-1498109.html [accessed April 30, 2009].

71. Sophie Gilbert, "Who Are the Wealthiest Members of the Obama Administration?" *Washingtonian*, March 19, 2009; available online at: http://www.washingtonian.com/blogarticles/people/capitalcomment/ 11857.html [accessed April 28, 2009].

72. Lindsay Renick Mayer, "Obama's Pick for Chief of Staff Tops Recipients of Wall Street Money," OpenSecrets.org, November 5, 2008; available online at: http://www.opensecrets.org/news/2008/11/obamas-pick-for-chief-of-staff.html [accessed April 30, 2009].

73. Timothy P. Carney, "Goldman Sachs Will Be Sitting Pretty With Emanuel in the Obama White House," *Washington Examiner*, November 21, 2008; available online at: http://www.washingtonexaminer.com/

opinion/columns/TimothyCarney/Goldman_Sach_Will_Be_Sitting_
Pretty_With_Emanuel_in_the_Obama_White_House_112108.html
[accessed April 30, 2009].

74. Andrew Zajac, "Questions raised about Rahm Emanuel's housing arrangement in D.C.," *Chicago Tribune*, February 24, 2009; available online at: http://www.chicagotribune.com/news/politics/
chi-emanuel_feb24,0,6696332.story [accessed April 30, 2009].

75. Toby Harnden, "Barack Obama to appoint Louis Susman American ambassador in London," *UK Telegraph*, May 21, 2009; available
online at: http://www.telegraph.co.uk/news/worldnews/northamerica/
usa/5359230/Barack-Obama-to-appoint-Louis-Susman-American-
ambassador-in-London.html [accessed May 25, 2009].

76. Tim Shipman, "Louis Susman: Obama's choice as London envoy,"
UK Telegraph, February 21, 2009; available online at: http://www.
telegraph.co.uk/news/worldnews/northamerica/usa/barackobama/
4742696/Louis-Susman-Obamas-choice-as-London-envoy.html [accessed
April 28, 2009].

77. "Obama admits some ambassador picks political," Associated
Press, January 9, 2009; available online at: http://www.usatoday.com/
news/washington/2009-01-09-obama-ambassadors_N.htm [accessed
April 28, 2009].

78. Christopher Doering, "Senate committee approves Gensler to
head CFTC," Reuters, March 16, 2009; available online at: http://www.
reuters.com/article/politicsNews/idUSTRE52G0BI20090317 [accessed
April 28, 2009].

79. Sophie Gilbert, "Who Are the Wealthiest Members of the Obama
Administration?" *Washingtonian*, March 19, 2009; available online at:
http://www.washingtonian.com/blogarticles/people/capitalcomment/
11857.html [accessed April 28, 2009].

80. Dave Rochelson, "President-elect Obama names key regulatory
appointments," change.gov, January 27, 2009; available online at: http:/
/change.gov/newsroom/entry/president-elect_obama_names_key_
regulatory_appointments/ [accessed April 28, 2009].

81. Ken Dilanian and Matt Kelley, "Fundraisers linked to corruption
cases," *USA Today*, October 16, 2008; available online at: http://www.

usatoday.com/news/politics/election2008/2008-10-15-fundraisers-corruption_N.htm [accessed April 30, 2008].

82. Ibid.

83. Jim McElhatton, "Treasury nominee to keep corporate pay," *Washington Times*, May 12, 2009; available online at: http://www.washingtontimes.com/news/2009/may/12/treasury-nominee-can-keep-corporate-buyout/ [accessed May 25, 2009].

84. Fredreka Schouten, "Geithner names ex-lobbyist as Treasury chief of staff," *USA Today*, January 27, 2009; available online at: http://www.usatoday.com/news/washington/2009-01-27-lobbyist_N.htm [accessed April 28, 2009].

85. Paul Blumenthal, "The Revolving Door Spins in CEO Pay Protector," Sunlight Foundation, March 20, 2009; available online at: http://blog.sunlightfoundation.com/2009/03/20/the-revolving-door-spins-in-ceo-pay-protector/ [accessed April 28, 2009].

86. Timothy P. Carney, "For a Geithner intimate, the color of money is green energy," *Washington Examiner*, February 5, 2009; available online at: http://www.washingtonexaminer.com/politics/For-a-Geithner-intimate-the-color-of-money-is-green-energy39145742.html [accessed April 28, 2009].

87. U.S. Senator Russ Feingold, "Feingold and Obama Introduce The Lobbying And Ethics Reform Act," feingold.senate.gov, January 8, 2007; available online at: http://feingold.senate.gov/releases/07/01/20070108.html [accessed April 28, 2009].

88. Phil Mattingly, "AIG Chief Goes Off Script, Says Employees Will Return Some of Bonus Money," CQ Politics, March 18, 2009; available online at: http://www.cqpolitics.com/wmspage.cfm?docID=news-000003077969&cpage=2 [accessed April 28, 2009].

89. U.S. Senator Russ Feingold, "Feingold and Obama Introduce The Lobbying And Ethics Reform Act," op cit.

CHAPTER 7: SEIU

1. "Obama speaks to SEIU (9/17/2007) Part 5 of 5," youtube.com; available online at: http://www.youtube.com/watch?v=BznUPlwbQ7Q [accessed April 6, 2009].

2. "Anna Burger," seiu.org; available online at: http://www.seiu.org/a/ourunion/anna-burger.php [accessed April 6, 2009].

3. Marc Ambinder, "At SEIU, Obama 'Rocked The House,'" *The Atlantic*, September 17, 2007; available online at: http://marcambinder.theatlantic.com/archives/2007/09/highly_caffeinated_and_unusual.php [accessed April 6, 2009].

4. Associated Press, "Obama Wins Backing of 1.9-Million Member SEIU," foxnews.com, February 15, 2009; available online at: http://www.foxnews.com/politics/elections/2008/02/15/obama-wins-backing-of-19-million-member-seiu/ [accessed April 6, 2009].

5. Fred Lucas, "SEIU PAC Spent $27 Million Supporting Obama's Election, FEC Filing Says," CNSNews.com, December 18, 2008; available online at: http://www.cnsnews.com/public/content/article.aspx?RsrcID=40959 [accessed April 6, 2009].

6. Ibid.

7. "Docking Paychecks for Politics," *Wall Street Journal*, July 28, 2008; available online at: http://online.wsj.com/article/SB121720084081888385.html?mod=opinion_main_review_and_outlooks [accessed April 6, 2009].

8. Michelle Malkin, "Big Labor's Investment in Obama Pays Off," CNSNews.com, May 13, 2009; available online at: http://www.cnsnews.com/Public/Content/Article.aspx?rsrcid=48043.

9. Mickey Kaus, "Labor Payoff of the Day," *Slate*, January 30, 2009; available online at: http://www.slate.com/blogs/blogs/kausfiles/archive/2009/01/30/labor-payoff-of-the-day.aspx [accessed April 6, 2009].

10. David Stout, "With a Swipe at Bush, Obama Acts to Bolster Labor," *New York Times*, January 30, 2009; available online at: http://www.nytimes.com/2009/01/31/us/politics/31obama.html?_r=1 [accessed April 6, 2009].

11. Carter Wood, "President Obama and Organized Labor V, Executive Orders Authorship," shopfloor.org, January 31, 2009; available online at: http://www.shopfloor.org/2009/01/31/president-obama-and-organized-labor-v-executive-orders-authorship/ [accessed April 6, 2009].

12. Evan Halper, "SEIU may be linked to ultimatum on withholding stimulus funds," *Los Angeles Times*, May 11, 2009; available online at:

http://www.latimes.com/features/health/la-me-cal-healthcare11-2009may11,0,6166232.story [accessed May 25, 2009].

13. "Feds okay pay cuts for healthcare workers," *Capitol Weekly*, May 21, 2009; available online at: http://www.capitolweekly.net/article.php?_c=xzshu7zy3a9ck9&xid=xzsf2zufvrp2a9&done=.xzshu7zy3arck9 [accessed May 25, 2009].

14. Paul Pringle, "Union paid millions to companies with family ties," *Los Angeles Times*, September 26, 2008; available online at: http://articles.latimes.com/2008/sep/26/local/me-union26 [accessed April 6, 2009].

15. Federal Election Commission, "FEC To Collect $775,000 Civil Penalty From America Coming Together," fec.gov, August 29, 2007; available online at: http://www.fec.gov/press/press2007/20070829act.shtml [accessed April 6, 2009].

16. Chris Cillizza, "Patrick Gaspard to be Obama's Political Director," *Washington Post*, November 21, 2008; available online at: http://voices.washingtonpost.com/44/2008/11/21/patrick_gaspard_to_be_obamas_p.html [accessed April 6, 2009].

17. Greg Sargent, "Labor Leaders Hail Obama's Pick For Labor Secretary," TPM Election Central, December 18, 2008; available online at: http://tpmelectioncentral.talkingpointsmemo.com/2008/12/andy_stern_on_obamas_labor_sec.php [accessed April 6, 2009].

18. Michael A. Fletcher, "Solis Senate Session Postponed in Wake of Husband's Tax Lien Revelations," *Washington Post*, February 5, 2009; available online at: http://voices.washingtonpost.com/44/2009/02/05/solis_senate_session_canceled.html?hpid=topnews [accessed April 6, 2009].

19. Sam Stein, "Labor To Open Fire Over Solis Confirmation," *Huffington Post*, February 6, 2009; available online at: http://www.huffingtonpost.com/2009/02/06/labor-to-open-fire-over-s_n_164522.html [accessed April 6, 2009].

20. Greg Saregent, "Andy Stern's Email Blasting GOP For Holding Up Solis," *The Plum Line*; available online at: http://theplumline.whorunsgov.com/andy-sterns-email-blasting-gop-for-holding-up-solis/ [accessed April 6, 2009].

21. "Tell the Senate: Confirm Hilda Solis as Secretary of Labor," seiu. org; available online at: http://action.seiu.org/page/s/confirmsolis [accessed April 6, 2009].

22. "Andy Stern: Confirm Hilda Solis Now," youtube.com, February 6, 2009; available online at: http://www.youtube.com/watch?v= jTAvjeJ19Ak [accessed April 6, 2009].

23. Michael Whitney, "Congratulations, Secretary of Labor Hilda Solis!" SEIU Blog, February 24, 2009; available online at: http://www. seiu.org/2009/02/congratulations-secretary-of-labor-hilda-solis.php [accessed April 6, 2009].

24. Twitter post by "SEIU_AndyStern," February 18, 2009; available online at: http://twitter.com/SEIU_AndyStern/status/1225219095 [accessed April 6, 2009].

25. Greg Sargent, "Obama And Michelle Ask Progressive Groups For Help Driving White House Agenda," *The Plum Line*, February 19, 2009; available online at: http://theplumline.whorunsgov.com/labor/obama-and-michelle-ask-progressive-groups-for-help-driving-white-house-agenda/ [accessed April 6, 2009].

26. "Obama Names Outside Economic Advisory Board," npr.org, February 6, 2009; available online at: http://www.npr.org/templates/ story/story.php?storyId=100335758 [accessed April 6, 2009].

27. Mike Link, "Anna Burger Named to President's Economic Recovery Advisory Board," SEIU Blog, February 6, 2009; available online at: http://www.seiu.org/2009/02/anna-burger-named-to-presidents-economic-recovery-advisory-board.php [accessed April 6, 2009].

28. Ivan Osorio, "A Blagojevich-SEIU connection?" openmarket. org, December 9, 2008; available online at: http://www.openmarket.org/ 2008/12/09/a-blagojevich-seiu-connection/ [accessed April 6, 2009].

29. Nick Cote, "SEIU Bosses Gave Gov. Blagojevich More Than $1. 7 Million Already, Not Including Possible Payout for Senate Seat," Freedom@Work, December 9, 2008; available online at: http://www.nrtw. org/en/blog/seiu-blagovichs-back-pocket-years-12092108 [accessed April 6, 2009].

30. Kris Maher and David Kesmodel, "Order Highlights Close Ties With SEIU," *Wall Street Journal,* December 15, 2008; available online

at: http://online.wsj.com/article/SB122938118338308549.html [accessed April 6, 2009].

31. David Catron, "Pay-to-Play Politics, the SEIU and Obamacare," *American Thinker*, January 6, 2009; available online at: http://www. americanthinker.com/2009/01/paytoplay_politics_the_seiu_an.html [accessed April 6, 2009].

32. Clare Ansberry, "Blagojevich and Union Have Longstanding Ties," *Wall Street Journal*, December 13, 2008; available online at: http://online. wsj.com/article/SB122912760515203213.html [accessed April 6, 2009].

33. Steve Greenhouse, "Union Is Caught Up in Illinois Bribe Case," *New York Times*, December 11, 2008; available online at: http://www. nytimes.com/2008/12/12/us/politics/12union.html [accessed April 6, 2009].

34. Lynn Sweet, "Obama memo about Obama staff contacts with Blagojevich," *Chicago Sun-Times*, December 23, 2008; available online at: http://blogs.suntimes.com/sweet/2008/12/obama_memo_about_ obama_staff_c.html [accessed April 6, 2008].

35. Lynn Sweet, "Obama's Greg Craig, Robert Gibbs briefing on Blagojevich internal report. Transcript," *Chicago Sun-Times*, December 23, 2008; available online at: http://blogs.suntimes.com/sweet/2008/12/ obamas_greg_craig_robert_gibbs.html [accessed April 6, 2009].

36. Kris Maher, "Service Union Chief Met With Blagojevich," *Wall Street Journal*, January 7, 2009; available online at: http://online.wsj. com/article/SB123129925187060043.html [accessed April 6, 2009].

37. Dan Mihalopoulos, "Top labor leader cooperating in Blagojevich probe," *Chicago Tribune*, February 11, 2009; available online at: http:/ /newsblogs.chicagotribune.com/clout_st/2009/02/top-labor-leader-cooperating-in-blagojevich-probe.html [accessed April 6, 2009].

38. The Oval, "SEIU head Andy Stern predicts quick action on health care, card-check," *USA Today*, February 15, 2009; available online at: http://content.usatoday.com/communities/theoval/post/2009/02/ 63330979/1 [accessed April 6, 2009].

39. Josh Kalven, "PI @ DNC: Andy Stern Addresses The Illinois Delegation," Progress Illinois, August 31, 2008; available online at: http:// www.progressillinois.com/2008/08/31/pi-dnc-andy-stern-speech [accessed April 7, 2009].

40. Paul Pringle, "Union, charity paid thousands to firms owned by official's relatives," *Los Angeles Times*, August 9, 2008; available online at: http://www.latimes.com/news/local/la-me-union9-2008aug09,0,7839120, full.story [accessed April 7, 2009].

41. Ibid.

42. Ibid.

43. Paul Pringle, "L.A. labor leader used charity's employees for politics, workers say," *Los Angeles Times*, October 20, 2008; available online at: http://www.latimes.com/news/local/la-me-union20-2008oct20, 0,3238753.story [accessed April 7, 2009].

44. Paul Pringle, "U.S. investigates L.A.-based union's election," *Los Angeles Times*, August 16, 2008; available online at: http://www.latimes. com/news/local/la-me-union17-2008aug17,0,5401444.story [accessed April 7, 2009].

45. Paul Pringle, "Tyrone Freeman steps aside as head of SEIU chapter," *Los Angeles Times*, August 21, 2008; available online at: http:// www.latimes.com/news/local/la-me-union21-2008aug21,0,1600346. story [accessed April 7, 2009].

46. Ibid.

47. "SEIU Trustee Files Charges Against Local 6434 President," PR Newswire, September 17, 2008; available online at: http://www.reuters. com/article/pressRelease/idUS255776+17-Sep-2008+PRN20080917 [accessed April 7, 2009].

48. "Tyrone Freeman Permanently Banned from Holding SEIU Membership or Office," SEIU press release, November 26, 2008; available online at: http://www.seiu.org/2008/11/tyrone-freeman-permanently-banned-from-holding-seiu-membership-or-office.php [accessed April 7, 2009].

49. "Tyrone Freeman steps down," S.M.A.R.T.—SEIU Member Activists for Reform Today; available online at: http://www.reformseiu. org/2008/08/tyrone-freeman-steps-down.html [accessed April 7, 2009].

50. "Tyrone Freeman," SMWW Sports Agency; available online at: http://www.smwwagency.com/agents/564/ [accessed April 7, 2009].

51. Paul Pringle, "SEIU leader loses post over scandal," *Los Angeles Times*, October 15, 2008; available online at: http://www.latimes.com/ news/local/la-me-union15-2008oct15,0,6253417.story [accessed April 7, 2009].

52. Ibid.

53. Steve Early and Cal Winslow, "Tyronegate & Trusteeship: Can SEIU Members Exorcise the Purple Shades Of Jackie Presser?" *Talking Union*, September 4, 2008; available online at: http://talkingunion. wordpress.com/2008/09/04/tyronegate-trusteeship-can-seiu-members-exorcise-the-purple-shades-of-jackie-presser/ [accessed April 7, 2009].

54. Paul Pringle, "Top SEIU official in California quits three posts," *Los Angeles Times*, March 10, 2009; available online at: http://www. latimes.com/news/local/la-me-seiu11-2009mar11,0,4841460.story [accessed April 7, 2009].

55. SEIU Local 721 Press Release, "Annelle Grajeda to Assume New Role to Assist Public Sector SEIU Members," seiu721.org, March 10, 2009; available online at: http://www.seiu721.org/Annelle_Grajeda_to_ Assume_New_Role_to_Assist_Public_Sector_SEIU_Members.aspx [accessed April 7, 2009].

56. Paul Pringle, "Union paid millions to companies with family ties," op cit.

57. Paul Pringle, "Finances of charity run by SEIU official scrutinized," *Los Angeles Times*, March 11, 2009; available online at: http:// www.latimes.com/news/local/la-me-union11-2009mar11,0,4166785,full. story [accessed April 7, 2009].

58. "SEIU 1021 clears union official James Bryant of alleged wrongdoing," SanFranciscoSentinel.com, March 18, 2009; available online at: http://www.sanfranciscosentinel.com/?p=20432 [accessed April 7, 2009].

59. Paul Pringle, "Midwestern SEIU official resigns," *Los Angeles Times*, February 11, 2009; available online at: http://www.latimes.com/ news/local/la-na-union12-2009feb12,0,2653505.story [accessed April 7, 2009].

60. Ibid.

61. Patrick Mcgreevy, "Ex-Councilman Gets 5 Years' Probation," *Los Angeles Times*, June 6, 2006; available online at: http://articles.latimes. com/2006/jun/06/local/me-ludlow6 [accessed April 7, 2009].

62. "Recent Criminal Enforcement Actions," U.S. Department of Labor, Office of Labor-Management Standards (last updated January 4,

2008); available online at: http://www.dol.gov/esa/olms/regs/compliance/
enforce_2007.htm [accessed April 7, 2009].

63. "Former labor union president pleads guilty to embezzling funds
given to council candidate," U.S. Department of Justice Press Release
No. 05-156 (November 13, 2006); available online at: http://www.usdoj.
gov/usao/cac/pressroom/pr2006/156.html [accessed April 7, 2009].

64. Lenny T. Mendonca, "Shaking up the labor movement: An interview with the head of the Service Employees International Union," *McK-
insey Quarterly*, 2006 Number 1; available online at: http://www.people.
hbs.edu/ffrei/MSOMaterials/Verizon/ServiceUnion.pdf [accessed April 7,
2009].

65. "Andy Stern's Pensions," *Wall Street Journal*, July 16, 2008; available online at: http://online.wsj.com/article/SB121616792365556301.
html?mod=opinion_main_review_and_outlooks [accessed April 7, 2009].

66. "SEIU misinformation campaign against Wackenhut Services, Inc.
(WSI)," Wackenhut Services Inc.; available online at: http://www.wsihq.
com/SEIU.asp [accessed April 7, 2009].

67. Reverend C. J. Hawking, "Student Occupation, Highway Sit-
Down, and Hunger Strike at University of Miami Janitors' Strike," *Labor
Notes*; available online at: http://labornotes.org/node/223 [accessed April
7, 2009]. See also: "Award Winning Actor and Activist Ed Asner; SEIU
President Andy Stern to Meet with Striking Janitors as National Focus on
Shalala Intensifies," PR Newswire, April 21, 2006; available online at:
http://www.prnewswire.com/cgi-bin/stories.pl?ACCT=104&STORY=/
www/story/04-21-2006/0004344595&EDATE= [accessed April 7, 2009].

68. "When Voting Isn't Private," Center for Union Facts (2007), 35.

69. "The hunger strikers' families need your help!" *Picketline*,
April 18, 2006; available online at: http://picketline.blogspot.com/
2006/04/hunger-strikers-families-need-your.html [accessed April 7,
2009].

70. Paul Donahue letter to the editor of the *Miami Herald*, April 27,
2006; available online at: http://www.wsihq.com/PR20060427.asp
[accessed April 7, 2009].

71. "In largest single-day filing ever in California healthcare, care-
givers flock to new union and show SEIU the door," National Union of

Healthcare workers, February 2, 2009; available online at: http://www.
nuhw.org/media/2009/2/2/in-largest-single-day-filing-ever-in-california-
healthcare-c.html [accessed April 7, 2009].

72. Juan Gonzalez, "Service Employees International Union president
goes to the extreme," *New York Daily News*, March 25, 2009; available
online at: http://www.nydailynews.com/money/2009/03/25/2009-03-25_
service_employees_international_union_pr.html [accessed April 9, 2009].

73. "SEIU Union Must Abandon 'Card Check' Union Organizing
Drives in Pacific Northwest After Finding of Rampant Abuse of Employees' R," National Right to Work Legal Defense Foundation Inc., April
24, 2007; available online at: http://www.nrtw.org/en/press/2007/04/seiu-
union-must-abandon-card-check-union-organizing-drives-pacific-
northwest-after-fin [accessed April 7, 2009].

74. "Karen Mayhew—Taking the Lead Against 'Card Check' Coercion," National Right to Work Legal Defense Foundation Inc.; available
online at: http://www.nrtw.org/profiles/mayhew/index.htm [accessed
April 7, 2009].

75. Conn Caroll, "Morning Bell: Workers Deserve Better Than a Big
Labor Lackey," *The Foundry*, January 9, 2009; available online at: http:/
/blog.heritage.org/2009/01/09/morning-bell-workers-deserve-better-than-
a-big-labor-lackey/ [accessed April 7, 2009].

76. Todd Beeton, "SEIU Convention: Anna Burger on the Employee
Free Choice Act," MyDD, June 3, 2008; available online at: http://www.
mydd.com/story/2008/6/3/123839/5749 [accessed April 7, 2009].

CHAPTER 8: OBAMACORN

1. Bertha Lewis, "We Are Willing To Go To Any Means Necessary,"
Huffington Post, February 20, 2009; available online at: http://www.
huffingtonpost.com/bertha-lewis/we-are-willing-to-go-to-a_b_168742.
html [accessed April 22, 2009].

2. Derek Valcourt, "ACORN Trains Citizens To Protest Home Foreclosures," WJZ.com, February 19, 2009; available online at: http://wjz.
com/local/acorn.foreclosure.2.939119.html [accessed April 22, 2009].

3. Sam Graham-Felsen, "ACORN Political Action Committee Endorses
Obama," mybarackobama.com, February 21, 2008; available online at:

http://my.barackobama.com/page/community/post/samgrahamfelsen/
gGC7zm [accessed April 22, 2009].

4. "Obama caught saying ACORN and friends will shape his presidential agenda," YouTube.com, October 11, 2008; available online at:
http://www.youtube.com/watch?v=8vJcVgJhNaU&e [accessed April 22,
2009].

5. Michelle Malkin, "Document drop: The truth about ACORN's
foreclosure poster child," michellemalkin.com, February 23, 2009; available online at: http://michellemalkin.com/2009/02/23/document-drop-
the-truth-about-acorns-foreclosure-poster-child/ [accessed April 22,
2009].

6. Ibid.

7. David Montgomery, "The Foreclosees Protest An American Dream
Turned Nightmare," *Washington Post*, October 2, 2008; available online
at: http://www.washingtonpost.com/wp-dyn/content/article/2008/10/01/
AR2008100103112_pf.html [accessed April 22, 2009].

8. Edward Ericson Jr., "Victim Mentality," *Baltimore City Paper*, July
30, 2008; available online at: http://www.citypaper.com/digest.asp?id=
16077 [accessed April 22, 2009].

9. "Perpetrator or victim?" Northern Virginia Housing Bubble Fall-
out, February 11, 2009; available online at: http://novabubblefallout.
blogspot.com/2009/02/perpetrator-or-victim-propaganda-or.html
[accessed April 22, 2009].

10. Edward Ericson Jr., "Victim Mentality,"

11. John Fund, *Stealing Elections: How Voter Fraud Threatens Our
Democracy* (San Francisco: Encounter Books, 2004).

12. "Barack Obama Never Organized with ACORN," fightthes-
mears.com; available online at: http://fightthesmears.com/articles/20/
acornrumor [accessed April 22, 2009].

13. Stanley Kurtz, "Obama Acorn Cover-up?," *The Corner*, October
8, 2008; available online at: http://corner.nationalreview.com/post/?q=
MTNiN2YwMmQ4Njc2MzE4ZDUxYWVlYTA1NzZlMmY3YmM=
[accessed April 22, 2009].

14. Sam Graham-Felsen, "ACORN Political Action Committee
Endorses Obama," mybarackobama.com, February 21, 2008; available

online at: http://my.barackobama.com/page/community/post/samgra hamfelsen/gGC7zm [accessed April 22, 2009].

15. Michelle Malkin, "The left-wing mortgage counseling racket," michellemalkin.com, April 3, 2008; available online at: http:// michellemalkin.com/2008/04/03/the-left-wing-mortgage-counseling-racket/ [accessed April 22, 2009].

16. "ACORNS's hypocritical house of cards," Consumer Rights League; available online at: http://www.consumersrightsleague.org/ UploadedFiles/ACORN_AHC_Report.pdf [accessed April 22, 2009].

17. Ibid.

18. Christina Corbin, "ACORN to Play Role in 2010 Census," foxnews.com, March 18, 2009; available online at: http://www.foxnews. com/politics/2009/03/17/lawmakers-concerned-role-acorn-census/ [accessed April 22, 2009].

19. Judicial Watch Obtains Obama Commerce Department Documents Detailing ACORN Partnership for 2010 Census, JudicialWatch. org, May 28, 2009; available online at: http://www.judicialwatch.org/ news/2009/may/judicial-watch-obtains-obama-commerce-department-documents-detailing-acorn-partnership [accessed May 31, 2009].

20. Wade Rathke full biography; available online at: http:// waderathke.com/index.php?id=76 [accessed April 22, 2009].

21. Richard Danielson, "Vote drives defended, despite fake names," *St. Petersburg Times*, October 14, 2008; available online at: http://www. tampabay.com/news/politics/elections/article852295.ece [accessed April 22, 2009].

22. Stephanie Strom, "Funds Misappropriated at 2 Nonprofit Groups," *New York Times*, July 9, 2008; available online at: http://www.nytimes. com/2008/07/09/us/09embezzle.html [accessed April 22, 2009].

23. Stephanie Strom, "Head of Foundation Bailed Out Nonprofit Group After Its Funds Were Embezzled," *New York Times*, August 17, 2008; available online at: http://www.nytimes.com/2008/08/17/us/ 17acorn.html [accessed April 22, 2009].

24. Stephanie Strom, "Lawsuit Adds to Turmoil for Community Group," *New York Times*, September 10, 2008; available online at: http:/ /www.nytimes.com/2008/09/10/us/10acorn.html [accessed April 22, 2009].

25. "ACORN can't escape Wade Rathke," *The Union News*, October 15, 2008; available online at: http://theunionnews.blogspot.com/2008/10/acorn-cant-escape-wade-rathke.html [accessed April 22, 2009].

26. David M. Brown, "Obama to amend report on $800,000 in spending," *Pittsburgh Tribune-Review*, August 22, 2008; available online at: http://www.pittsburghlive.com/x/pittsburghtrib/news/election/s_584284.html [accessed April 22, 2008].

27. Ibid.

28. Kevin Agnese, "Wynn files FEC complaint against Edwards," Politicker.com, January 29, 2008; available online at: http://www.politicker.com/maryland/9087/wynn-files-fec-complaint-against-edwards [accessed April 22, 2009].

29. Lori Sherwood complaint to Federal Election Commission, January 29, 2008; available online at: http://www.mydd.com/images/admin/edwards.complain_6_.pdf [accessed April 22, 2009].

30. Ibid.

31. See http://eqs.nictusa.com/eqsdocs/29044222943.pdf [accessed May 25, 2009].

32. Paul Ryder, "Should we go to the ballot? Some considerations," Ohio Citizen Action, February 17, 2009; available online at: http://www.ohiocitizen.org/about/training/ballotconsiderations.html [accessed April 22, 2009].

33. "Barack Obama Never Organized with ACORN," fightthesmears.com, op cit.

34. Stephanie Strom, "Acorn Report Raises Issues of Legality," *New York Times*, October 22, 2008; available online at: http://www.nytimes.com/2008/10/22/us/22acorn.html [accessed April 22, 2009].

35. David M. Brown, "Obama to amend report on $800,000 in spending," op cit.

36. Matthew Vadum. "Cracking ACORN," National Review Online, November 3, 2008; available online at: http://article.nationalreview.com/?q=MDY2ZWFjNTk4ZDdiZmFjYmY5YjQwMzhmMjM1YmNmO-TA= [accessed April 22, 2009].

37. Ibid.

38. "Anita MonCrief," Ballotpedia; available online at: http://ballotpedia.org/wiki/index.php/Anita_MonCrief [accessed April 22, 2009].

39. John Fund, "An Acorn Whistleblower Testifies in Court," *Wall Street Journal*, October 30, 2008; available online at: http://online.wsj.com/article/SB122533169940482893.html [accessed April 22, 2009].

40. "Testimony of Heather S. Heidelbaugh, Esquire," House Judiciary Committee; available online at: http://judiciary.house.gov/hearings/pdf/Heidelbaugh090319.pdf [accessed April 22, 2009].

41. S. A. Miller, "Conyers weighing probe of ACORN," *Washington Times*, April 1, 2009; available online at: http://www.washingtontimes.com/news/2009/apr/01/conyers-weighing-probe-of-acorn/ [accessed April 22, 2009].

42. "ACORN Charged In Vegas Fraud Case," KVVU, May 4, 2009; available online at: http://www.fox5vegas.com/news/19365409/detail.html [accessed May 25, 2009].

43. Clark Hoyt, "The Tip That Didn't Pan Out," *New York Times*, May 16, 2009; available online at: http://www.nytimes.com/2009/05/17/opinion/17pubed.html?_r=3 [accessed June 1, 2009].

44. Howard Kurtz, "Lobbyist Settles Libel Suit Over N.Y. Times Story Linking Her to McCain," *Washington Post*, February 20, 2009; available online at: http://www.washingtonpost.com/wp-dyn/content/article/2009/02/19/AR2009021903112.html [accessed June 1, 2009].

45. All e-mails available at: michellemalkin.com, "The Truth about ObamACORN," May 29, 2009; available online at: http://michellemalkin.com/2009/05/29/document-drop-the-truth-about-obamacorn/ [accessed June 1, 2009].

46. Ibid.

47. "Bachmann Calls on Congress to Block Funds to ACORN," FoxNews.com, May 14, 2009; available online at: http://www.foxnews.com/politics/2009/05/14/bachmann-calls-congress-block-funds-acorn/ [accessed May 31, 2009].

48. Matthew Vadum, "Lawmaker Demands Probe of ACORN's Finances," AmericanSpectator.org, May 28, 2009; available online at:

http://spectator.org/blog/2009/05/28/lawmaker-demands-probe-of-acor [accessed May 31, 2009].

49. Duane Schrag, "ACORN prompts Kobach to run," *Saline Journal*, May 29, 2009; available online at: http://www.saline.com/news/story/kobach-5-28-2009 [accessed May 30, 2009].

CHAPTER 9: THE CLINTONS

1. "Clinton Goofs on Russian Translation, Tells Diplomat She Wants to 'Overcharge' Ties," foxnews.com, March 6, 2009; available online at: http://www.foxnews.com/politics/first100days/2009/03/06/clinton-goofs-russian-translation-tells-diplomat-wants-overcharge-ties/ [accessed April 15, 2009].

2. John Kerry, "Kerry Statement on Secretary of State Confirmation Hearing," Sen. John Kerry's Online Office, January 13, 2009; available online at: http://kerry.senate.gov/cfm/record.cfm?id=306579 [accessed April 15, 2009].

3. Christopher Hitchens, "More Than a Good Feeling," *Slate*, January 12, 2009; available online at: http://www.slate.com/id/2208425/ [accessed April 15, 2009].

4. "Hillary Clinton sworn in as secretary of state," CNNPolitics.com, January 22, 2009; available online at: http://www.cnn.com/2009/POLITICS/01/21/clinton.confirmation/index.html [accessed April 15, 2009].

5. Manu Raju and Kevin Bogardus, "Clinton: $2.3B in earmarks," *The Hill*, April 28, 2008; available online at: http://thehill.com/leading-the-news/clinton-2.3b-in-earmarks-2008-04-28.html [accessed April 15, 2009].

6. Tom Hamburger and Dan Morain, "Clinton rolls a sizable pork barrel—The senator embraces 'earmarks' as a way to help N.Y. She's received campaign funds from project beneficiaries," *Los Angeles Times*, December 10, 2007; available online at: http://articles.latimes.com/2007/dec/10/nation/na-earmarks10 [accessed April 15, 2009].

7. Beth Fouhy and Sharon Theimer, "Saudis, Indians Among Clinton Foundation Donors," Associated Press, December 18, 2008; available

online at: http://abcnews.go.com/Politics/wireStory?id=6487689 [accessed April 15, 2009].

8. Mark Halperin, "Obama Camp Memo on Clinton Saying She 'Misspoke,'" *The Page*; available online at: http://thepage.time.com/ obama-camp-memo-on-clinton-saying-she-misspoke/ [accessed April 15, 2009].

9. Mary Ann Akers, "Sinbad Unloads on Hillary Clinton," *The Sleuth*, March 11, 2008; available online at: http://blog.washingtonpost. com/sleuth/2008/03/sinbad_unloads_on_hillary_clin.html [accessed April 15, 2009].

10. Michael Dobbs, "Hillary's Balkan Adventures, Part II," *The Fact Checker*, March 21, 2008; available online at: http://blog. washingtonpost.com/fact-checker/2008/03/hillarys_balkan_adventures_ par.html [accessed April 15, 2009].

11. PA Primary Team, "Hillary's Bosnia 'misstatement,'" philly.com, March 25, 2008; available online at: http://www.philly.com/philly/hp/ news_update/20080325_Hillarys_Bosnia_misstatement.html [accessed April 15, 2009].

12. See http://www.google.com/search?q=hillary + tuzla

13. Mary Ann Akers, "Sinbad Unloads on Hillary Clinton," op cit.

14. Ed Morrissey, "Sinbad's a comedian, Hillary's a clown," Hot Air, March 21, 2008; available online at: http://hotair.com/archives/2008/03/ 21/sinbads-a-comedian-hillarys-a-clown/ [accessed April 15, 2009].

15. Patrick Healy and Katharine Q. Seelye, "Clinton Says She 'Misspoke' About Dodging Sniper Fire," *New York Times*, March 25, 2008; available online at: http://www.nytimes.com/2008/03/25/us/politics/ 25clinton.html [accessed April 15, 2009].

16. Ibid

17. Mark Halperin, "Obama Camp Memo on Clinton Saying She 'Misspoke,'" op cit.

18. "Clinton 'misspoke' over Bosnia sniper claims," Associated Press, March 25, 2008; available online at: http://www.msnbc.msn.com/id/ 23789011/ [accessed April 15, 2009].

19. Jill Lawrence and Eugene Kiely, "Clinton says she 'misspoke' about sniper fire, calls misstatement a 'minor blip,'" *USA Today*, March

25, 2008; available online at: http://blogs.usatoday.com/onpolitics/2008/03/clinton-says-sh.html [accessed April 15, 2009].

20. Michael Dobbs, "Clinton Appears Weary Of Taking 'Sniper Fire,'" *Washington Post*, March 26, 2008; available online at: http://www.washingtonpost.com/wp-dyn/content/article/2008/03/25/AR2008032502446.html?hpid=sec-politics [accessed April 15, 2009].

21. Danny Hakim, "Hillary, Not as in the Mount Everest Guy," *New York Times*, October 17, 2006; available online at: http://www.nytimes.com/2006/10/17/nyregion/17hillary.html [accessed April 15, 2009].

22. Susan Milligan, "Clinton role in health program disputed," *Boston Globe*, March 14, 2008; available online at: http://www.boston.com/news/nation/articles/2008/03/14/clinton_role_in_health_program_disputed/ [accessed April 15, 2009].

23. Political Radar, "Bill and Chelsea Clinton Might Want to Fact-Check Their Speeches," abcnews.com, January 24, 2008; available online at: http://blogs.abcnews.com/politicalradar/2008/01/bill-and-chelse.html [accessed April 15, 2009].

24. Tony Harnden, "Hillary Clinton: I was 'instrumental' in Northern Ireland peace process," *UK Telegraph*, March 16, 2008; available online at: http://www.telegraph.co.uk/news/worldnews/1581606/Hillary-Clinton-I-was-instrumental-in-Northern-Ireland-peace-process.html [accessed April 15, 2009].

25. Ibid

26. Libby Copeland, "What Makes Hillary Tick? Her Schedule Doesn't Say," *Washington Post*, March 20, 2008; available online at: http://www.washingtonpost.com/wp-dyn/content/story/2008/03/19/ST2008031902656.html [accessed April 15, 2009].

27. "Judicial Watch Releases Records Regarding Hillary's Health Care Reform Plan," *Judicial Watch*, January 17, 2008; available online at: http://www.judicialwatch.org/judicial-watch-releases-records-re-hillary-s-health-care-reform-plan-0 [accessed April 15, 2009].

28. "Mr. Clinton's Library Lesson," *Washington Post*, November 18, 2004; available online at: http://www.washingtonpost.com/ac2/wp-dyn/A58805-2004Nov17?language=printer [accessed April 15, 2009].

29. Ian Wilheim, "Campaigning for Charity: an Interview With Bill Clinton," *Chronicle of Philanthropy*, September 18, 2008; available online at: http://philanthropy.com/free/articles/v20/i23/23002001.htm [accessed April 15, 2009].

30. Josh Gerstein, "Saudis, Arabs Funneled Millions to President Clinton's Library," *New York Sun*, November 22, 2004; available online at: http://www.nysun.com/national/saudis-arabs-funneled-millions-to-president/5137/ [accessed April 15, 2009].

31. John Solomon and Jeffrey H. Birnbaum, "Clinton Library Got Funds From Abroad," *Washington Post*, December 15, 2007; available online at: http://www.washingtonpost.com/wp-dyn/content/article/2007/12/14/AR2007121402124_pf.html [accessed April 15, 2009].

32. Adam Hanft, "Why Won't Hillary Clinton Release Her Tax Returns?" *Huffington Post*, February 13, 2008; available online at: http://www.huffingtonpost.com/adam-hanft/why-wont-hillary-clinton_b_86471.html [accessed April 15, 2009].

33. Kenneth P. Vogel, "Tax returns show Clintons got rich quick," *Politico*, April 4, 2008; available online at: http://www.politico.com/news/stories/0408/9393.html [accessed April 15, 2009].

34. Ibid.

35. Ian Wilheim, "Clinton Foundation Donors Under Renewed Scrutiny," *Chronicle of Philanthropy*, November 18, 2008; available online at: http://philanthropy.com/news/updates/6310/clinton-foundation-donors-under-renewed-scrutiny [accessed April 15, 2009].

36. "Senate Confirmation Hearing: Hillary Clinton," *New York Times*, January 13, 2009; available online at: http://www.nytimes.com/2009/01/13/us/politics/13text-clinton.html [accessed April 15, 2009].

37. Mary Bruce, "Questions Linger Over Bill Clinton's International Work, Lugar Says," abcnews.com, November 30, 2008; available online at: http://www.abcnews.go.com/ThisWeek/story?id=6361640&page=1 [accessed April 15, 2009].

38. Gilbert Chagoury web site; available online at: http://www.gilbertchagoury.com/background.html [accessed April 15, 2009].

39. Ibid

40. Ken Silverstein, "Clinton Foundation Donors and Hillary's Confirmation," *Harper's*, January 21, 2009; available online at: http://harpers.org/archive/2009/01/hbc-90004256 [accessed April 15, 2009].

41. John R. Emshwiller, "Bill Clinton's Complicated World," *Wall Street Journal*, December 20, 2008; available online at: http://online.wsj.com/article/SB122973023139522863.html [accessed April 15, 2009].

42. Ibid.

43. Ibid.

44. Lander Thomas Jr., "Can the New Rich Buy Respect? One Ukrainian Oligarch Is Trying," *New York Times*, August 7, 2008; available online at: http://www.nytimes.com/2008/08/08/business/worldbusiness/08oligarch.html [accessed April 15, 2009].

45. Michael Isikoff and Mark Hosenball, "Here an F.O.B., There an F.O.B.," *Newsweek*, February 4, 2008; available online at: http://www.newsweek.com/id/105650 [accessed April 15, 2009].

46. "3 Guilty in Death Leading to Ukraine's Orange Revolution," Associated Press, March 16, 2008; available online at: http://www.nytimes.com/2008/03/16/world/europe/16Ukraine.html [accessed April 15, 2009].

47. Archives of Ukraine, House International Relations Committee Hearing; Ukraine Elections: Fraud And Abuse Run Rampant, December 7, 2004; available online at: http://www.archives.gov.ua/Sections/Ukraineomni/rlugar.htm [accessed April 15, 2009].

48. Beth Fouhy and Sharon Theimer, "Saudis, Indians among Clinton foundation donors," Associated Press; available online at: http://www.politicalbase.com/news/saudis-indians-among-clinton-foundation-donors/154219/ [accessed April 15, 2009].

49. Clinton Foundation web site; available online at: http://www.clintonfoundation.org/contributors/index.html [accessed April 15, 2009].

50. Beth Fouhy and Sharon Theimer, "Saudis, Indians among Clinton foundation donors," op cit.

51. Richard Stern, Eugene Schiff, and Laura Porras, "Dominican PLWA call for Massive Scaling Up of Treatment Access and End to Illegal but Widespread Discrimination," *Agua Buena*, June 2006; available

online at: http://www.aguabuena.org/ingles/articules/dominicana200606.
html [accessed April 15, 2009].

52. "Hillary Clinton's Pay for Play Problem," obamanoms.com, January 8, 2009; available online at: http://obamanoms.com/?p=54 [accessed April 15, 2009].

53. Richard Lugar, "Senator Richard G. Lugar Opening Statement for Confirmation Hearing of Senator Hillary Clinton to be Secretary of State," U.S. Senate Committee on Foreign Relations, January 13, 2009; available online at: http://foreign.senate.gov/testimony/2009/LugarStatement090113a.pdf [accessed April 15, 2009].

54. "The Senate's Advice," *Washington Post*, January 14, 2009; available online at: http://www.washingtonpost.com/wp-dyn/content/article/2009/01/13/AR2009011302567.html [accessed April 15, 2009].

55. "What Hillary won't promise," *New York Post*, January 14, 2009; available online at: http://www.nypost.com/seven/01142009/postopinion/editorials/what_hillary_wont_promise_150034.htm [accessed April 15, 2009].

56. Jo Becker and Don Van Natta Jr., "After Mining Deal, Financier Donated to Clinton," *New York Times*, January 31, 2008; available online at: http://www.nytimes.com/2008/01/31/us/politics/31donor.html [accessed April 15, 2009].

57. Matthew Mosk and Joe Stephens, "A Complex Knot of Conflicts," *Washington Post*, November 22, 2008; available online at: http://www.washingtonpost.com/wp-dyn/content/article/2008/11/21/AR2008112103538_2.html [accessed April 15, 2009].

58. Michelle Malkin, "Hillary's pay-for-play troubles, continued," michellemalkin.com, January 13, 2009; available online at: http://michellemalkin.com/2009/01/13/hillarys-pay-for-play-troubles-continued/ [accessed April 15, 2009].

59. Ibid.

60. Charlie Savage, "A Donor's Gift Soon Followed Clinton's Help," *New York Times*, January 3, 2009; available online at: http://www.nytimes.com/2009/01/04/washington/04clinton.html [accessed April 15, 2009].

61. Ibid.

62. Ken Dilanian, "Timing of gifts stirs 'earmark' debate," *USA Today*, October 17, 2008; available online at: http://www.usatoday.com/news/washington/2007-10-16-earmarks_N.htm [accessed April 15, 2009].

63. Ibid.

64. "Hippie Museum Funding Proposed by Hillary Clinton Shot Down in Senate," Associated Press, October 19, 2007; available online at: http://www.foxnews.com/story/0,2933,303376,00.html [accessed April 15, 2009].

65. "Democratic donor jailed for impersonating a lawyer," Associated Press, March 28, 2009; available online at: http://sg.news.yahoo.com/ap/20090327/twl-donor-scandal-trial-1be00ca.html [accessed April 15, 2009].

66. "Clash is one for the law books," mysanantonio.com, October 5, 2007; available online at: http://www.mysanantonio.com/news/MYSA100607_08A_lawyer_350d4df_html887.html [accessed April 15, 2009].

67. Rudy Trevino, "Police Reports Reveal More About Celis," kiiitv.com, October 18, 2007; available online at: http://www.kiiitv.com/news/local/10653896.html [accessed April 15, 2009].

68. Dan Kelley and Denise Malan, "State raids office of Celis," *Caller-Times*, January 5, 2008; available online at: http://www.caller.com/news/2008/jan/05/state-raids-office-of-celis/ [accessed April 15, 2009].

69. Ibid.

70. "Mauricio Celis Could Face New Charges," KRIS-TV, May 20, 2009; available online at: http://www.kristv.com/Global/story.asp?S=10398589&nav=menu192_2 [accessed May 25, 2009].

71. April Castro, "Texas Donor Under Investigation," *Washington Post*, November 6, 2007; available online at: http://www.washingtonpost.com/wp-dyn/content/article/2007/11/06/AR2007110601067_2.html [accessed April 15, 2009].

72. Chuck Neubauer and Robin Fields, "Clinton, Boxer donor to plead guilty," *Los Angeles Times*, February 21, 2008; available online at: http://articles.latimes.com/2008/feb/21/nation/na-jinnah21 [accessed April 15, 2009].

73. Christine Field, "Pro-Clinton 'Dirty Cash' Man Flees," *New York Post*, March 4, 2007; available online at: http://www.nypost.com/seven/03042007/news/nationalnews/pro_clinton_dirty_cash_man_flees_nationalnews_christine_field.htm [accessed April 15, 2009].

74. Peter Nicholas and Tom Hamburger, "Clinton campaign taps into an unlikely treasure-trove," *Los Angeles Times*, October 19, 2007; available online at: http://www.latimes.com/news/politics/la-na-donors19oct19,0,4231217.story?coll=la-home-center [accessed April 15, 2009].

75. Charles Hurt, "Hill's Cash Eyed As Chinese-Laundered," *New York Post*, October 20, 2007; available online at: http://www.nypost.com/seven/10202007/news/nationalnews/hills_cash_eyed_as_chinese_lau.htm [accessed April 15, 2009].

76. "Dishwashers for Clinton," *Washington Post*, October 22, 2007; available online at: http://www.washingtonpost.com/wp-dyn/content/article/2007/10/21/AR2007102101069.html [accessed April 15, 2009].

77. Tom Hamburger, Dan Morain and Robin Fields, "Candidates' reliance on 'bundlers' let Hsu thrive," *Los Angeles Times*, September 14, 2007; available online at: http://articles.latimes.com/2007/sep/14/nation/na-hsu14 [accessed April 15, 2009].

78. "Dem fundraiser Norman Hsu indicted," *USA Today*, December 4, 2007; available online at: http://www.usatoday.com/news/politics/2007-12-04-hsu_N.htm [accessed April 15, 2009].

79. Geoff Earle, "Bill had no clue on Hsu," *New York Post*, September 3, 2007; available online at: http://www.nypost.com/seven/09032007/news/nationalnews/bill_had_no_clue_on_hsu.htm [accessed April 15, 2009].

80. James Gordon Meek and Michael Mcauliff, "Team Clinton can't explain ignoring warnings on Hsu," *New York Daily News*, September 12, 2007; available online at: http://www.nydailynews.com/news/us_world/2007/09/12/2007-09-12_team_clinton_cant_explain_ignoring_warni.html [accessed April 15, 2009].

81. "U.S. v. Norman Hsu," FindLaw, November 27, 2007; available online at: http://news.findlaw.com/usatoday/docs/hsu/ushsu112707ind.html [accessed April 15, 2009].

82. Thomas Zambito, "Jury hears Secretary of State Hillary Clinton's call to swindler Norman Hsu," *New York Daily News*, May 13, 2009; available online at: http://www.nydailynews.com/news/politics/2009/05/13/2009-05-13_jury_hears_hillary_clintons_call_to_swindler.html [accessed May 25, 2009].

83. Patrick Healy, "Clinton Sees Fear Realized in Trouble With Donor," *New York Times*, September 12, 2007; available online at: http://www.nytimes.com/2007/09/12/us/politics/12clinton.html [accessed April 15, 2009].

84. Christina Bellatoni, "Dodd slams Clinton," *Washington Times*, September 6, 2007; available online at: http://video1.washingtontimes.com/bellantoni/2007/09/dodd_slams_clinton.html [accessed April 15, 2009].

EPILOGUE

1. Christopher Keating, "President Obama Will Help Sen. Chris Dodd in 2010 Race," *Hartford Courant*, April 17, 2009; available online at: http://blogs.courant.com/capitol_watch/2009/04/president-obama-will-help-sen.html [accessed: April 30, 2009].

2. "Dodd Falls Way Behind As Approval Drops To Lowest Ever, Quinnipiac University Poll Finds; Voters Are Angry At AIG Bonuses And Blame Dodd," April 2, 2009; available online at: http://www.quinnipiac.edu/x1284.xml?ReleaseID=1283&What=&strArea [accessed: April 30, 2009].

3. Michael Powell and John Sullivan, "Dodd Endorses Obama for President," *New York Times*, February 26, 2008; available online at: http://www.nytimes.com/2008/02/26/us/politics/26cnd-campaign.html [accessed April 30, 2009].

4. For a good overview through 2006, see Lynn Vincent and Robert Stacy McCain, *Donkey Cons: Sex, Crime and Corruption in the Democratic Party* (Nelson Current: 2006).

5. Daniel Golden, "Countrywide's Many 'Friends,'" Portfolio.com, June 12, 2008; available online at: http://www.portfolio.com/news-markets/top-5/2008/06/12/Countrywide-Loan-Scandal [accessed: April 30, 2009].

6. Michelle Malkin, "Another Massive Mortgage Boondoggle," michellemalkin.com, April 2, 2008; available online at: http://

michellemalkin.com/2008/04/02/another-massive-mortgage-boondoggle-and-one-lone-dissenting-vote/ [accessed: April 30, 2009].

7. David Mildenberg and Sebastian Boyd, "Countrywide to Refinance Up to $16 Billion of Loans (Update7)," October 23, 2008, Bloomberg News; available online at: http://www.bloomberg.com/apps/news?pid=20601087&refer=worldwide&sid=agNUe.4oR6mc [accessed: April 30, 2009].

8. Jennifer Yachnin, "Dodd Knew He Was Countrywide VIP Since 2003," *Roll Call*, June 17, 2008; available online at: http://www.rollcall.com/news/25999-1.html [accessed April 30, 2009].

9. "Connecticut Voters Are Down, But Still Like Gov. Rell, Quinnipiac University Poll Finds; Mortgage Scandal Takes Small Toll On Sen. Dodd," Quinnipiac University press release, July 1, 2008; available online at: http://www.quinnipiac.edu/x1296.xml?ReleaseID=1189 [accessed April 30, 2009].

10. Michelle Malkin, "Stop the Dodd/Countrywide bailout boondoggle," michellemalkin.com, July 7, 2008; available online at: http://michellemalkin.com/2008/07/07/stop-the-doddcountrywide-bailout-boondoggle/

11. Ted Barrett, "Obama VP team discusses 20 possible picks," CNNPolitics.com; available online at: http://www.cnn.com/2008/POLITICS/06/10/obama.vp/index.html

12. Christopher Keating, "Edith Prague Opposes Chris Dodd as Obama VP," Courant.com, July 11, 2008; available online at: http://blogs.courant.com/capitol_watch/2008/07/edith-prague-says-obama-should.html

13. "Opening Statement: Turmoil in U.S. Credit Markets," Office of Sen. Christopher Dodd, September 23, 2008; available online at: http://dodd.senate.gov/?q=node/4572 [accessed April 30, 2009].

14. Lisa Myers & Amna Nawaz, "Feds probe Countrywide's 'VIP' program," NBC News, October 30, 2008; available online at: http://deepbackground.msnbc.msn.com/archive/2008/10/30/1613877.aspx [accessed April 30, 2009].

15. "Dodd and Countrywide," *Wall Street Journal*, October 10, 2008; available online at: http://online.wsj.com/article/SB122360116724221681.html [accessed April 30, 2009].

16. "Citi agrees to let judges alter mortgages," Associated Press, January 8, 2009; available online at: http://www.msnbc.msn.com/id/28562890/ [accessed April 30, 2009].

17. Christopher Weaver, "Show Us the Documents, Sen. Dodd," *ProPublica*, February 9, 2009; available online at: http://www.propublica.org/article/show-us-the-documents-sen-dodd [accessed April 30, 2009].

18. Jesse A. Hamilton, "Dodd Releases Countrywide Mortgage Documents," Courant.com, February 2, 2009; available online at: http://blogs.courant.com/on_background/2009/02/dodd-releases-countrywide-mort.html

19. Chris Dodd, U.S. Senator from Connecticut, "Dodd makes public all of the documents related to his 2003 mortgages," February 2, 2009; available online at: http://blogs.courant.com/on_background/Dodd's%20Full%20Statement%20on%20Mortgages.doc.

20. Nicholas Riccardi and Johanna Neuman, "Obama criticizes McCain for lobbyist-run campaign," *Los Angeles Times*, May 20, 2008; available online at: http://articles.latimes.com/2008/may/20/nation/na-campaign20

21. Lindsay Renick Mayer, "Update: Fannie Mae and Freddie Mac Invest in Lawmakers," Open Secrets, September 11, 2008; available online at: http://www.opensecrets.org/news/2008/09/update-fannie-mae-and-freddie.html [accessed April 30, 2009].

22. Andrew Miga, "Dodd taps Wall Street money for re-election," Associated Press, April 20, 2009; available online at: http://www.google.com/hostednews/ap/article/ALeqM5ixvoSkF4yknffeFgV_hCeE5mT1OQD97MBTP00 [accessed April 30, 2009].

23. Peter Urban, "Only 5 state residents donated to Dodd," *Connecticut Post*, April 16, 2009; available online at: http://www.connpost.com/ci_12158273 [accessed April 30, 2009].

24. Jonathan Stein and Daniel Schulman, "Chris Dodd's Personal Bailout," *Mother Jones*, April 2009; available online at: http://www.motherjones.com/politics/2009/04/chris-dodds-personal-bailout [accessed April 30, 2009].

25. Lindsay Renick Mayer, "Power Players: Struggling Financial Firms Are Banking on Dodd," opensecrets.org, January 27, 2009; avail-

able online at: http://www.opensecrets.org/news/2009/01/power-players-struggling-finan.html [accessed April 30, 2009].

26. Timothy P. Carney, "Bank of America PAC money behind Dodd's Countrywide loan," Examiner.com, June 19, 2008; available online at: http://www.examiner.com/a-1449448~Bank_of_America_PAC_money_behind_Dodd_s_Countrywide_loan.html [accessed April 30, 2009].

27. "BREAKING: I was responsible for bonus loophole, says Dodd," CNN.com, March 18, 2009; available online at: http://politicalticker. blogs.cnn.com/2009/03/18/breaking-i-was-responsible-for-bonus-loophole-says-dodd/ [accessed April 30, 2009].

28. Kevin Rennie, "Dodd's 'Cottage': A Cozy Purchase," *Hartford Courant*, February 22, 2009; available online at: http://www.courant. com/news/opinion/editorials/hc-rennie0222.artfeb22,0,3796755.column [accessed April 30, 2009].

29. "Judicial Watch Files Senate Ethics Complaint against Senator Christopher Dodd," *Judicial Watch*, April 27, 2009; available online at: http://www.judicialwatch.org/news/2009/apr/judicial-watch-files-senate-ethics-complaint-against-senator-christopher-dodd [accessed April 30, 2009].

30. "Obama launches presidential bid," BBC News, February 10, 2007; available online at: http://news.bbc.co.uk/2/hi/americas/6349081. stm [accessed April 30, 2009].

INDEX